GREENBERG'S® GUIDE TO LIONEL® TRAINS

1945-1969   Volume II

BEHIND THE SCENES

By Bruce C. Greenberg

Edited by Dallas J. Mallerich III and Marcy Damon

Greenberg Publishing Company, Inc.
Sykesville, Maryland

LIONEL® IS THE REGISTERED TRADEMARK OF LIONEL TRAINS, INC., MT. CLEMENS, MICHIGAN.

Copyright © 1991
by Greenberg Publishing Company, Inc.

Greenberg Publishing Company, Inc.
7566 Main Street
Sykesville, MD 21784
(301) 795-7447

Second Edition
First Printing

Manufactured in the United States of America

Greenberg Publishing Company, Inc. offers the world's largest selection of Lionel, American Flyer, LGB, Marx, Ives, and other toy train publications as well as a selection of books on model and prototype railroading, dollhouse building, and collectible toys. For a complete listing of Greenberg publications, please call or write at the above address and request a current catalogue.

Greenberg Shows, Inc. sponsors *Greenberg's Great Train, Dollhouse and Toy Shows,* the world's largest of its kind. The shows feature extravagant operating train layouts, and a display of magnificent dollhouses. The shows also present a huge marketplace of model and toy trains, for HO, N, and Z Scales; Lionel O, and Standard Gauges; and S and 1 Gauges; plus layout accessories and railroadiana. It also offers a large selection of dollhouse miniatures and building materials, and collectible toys. Shows are scheduled along the East Coast each year from Massachusetts to Florida. For a list of our current shows please call or write at the above address and request our current "show schedule."

Greenberg Auctions, a division of Greenberg Shows, Inc., offers nationally advertised auctions of toy trains and toys. Please contact our auction manager at (301) 795-7447 for further information.

ISBN 0-89778-188-0 (Hardback)
ISBN 0-89778-187-2 (Softback)

Library of Congress Cataloguing-in-Publication Data

Greenberg, Bruce C.
    Greenberg's guide to Lionel trains, 1945-1969.

        Vol. 2: 2nd ed.
        Vol. 2 edited by Dallas J. Mallerich III and Marcy Damon.
        Contents: v. 1. Motive power and rolling stock —
v. 2. Behind-the-Scenes.
        1. Railroads — Models. 2. Lionel Corporation.
    I. LaVoie, Roland, 1943-   II. Burgio, Wendy J.
    III. Mallerich, Dallas J.   IV. Title   V. Title: Guide
    to Lionel trains, 1945-1969.
    TF197.G667   1989   625.1'9   89-17118
    ISBN 0-89778-188-0   ISBN 0-89778-187-2 (pbk.)

Cover Photographs: (Top) The 1948 paper box for the 45N gateman accessory. T. Rollo Collection. (Middle) In 1956 the United States Navy developed its first and only midget submarine, the X-1. Although the facts are unconfirmed, it was enough like Lionel's "fantasy" 3830 submarine to allow one to suppose that it may have been Lionel's prototype. The submarine shown is a reproduction of the Lionel unit made by MTSI. T. Ryan Collection, R. Stem comment. (Bottom) The Russian-made version of the automatic gateman. R. Clement Collection.

TABLE OF CONTENTS

Freight Cars

Special Topics

A Special Tour

INTRODUCTION

Bruce C. Greenberg

Haven't you always wanted to know what goes on "Behind the Scenes" at Lionel? How new products were developed? What the origins of the automatic gateman accessory were? Why Lionel sold trains in different kinds of boxes over the years? Let a unique group of Lionel insiders give answers to your "what, where, how, and why."

This book provides an insightful look at a number of facets of Lionel. It considers the beginnings of the production process with the creation of prototypes and mock-ups and follows these through their development into final production. And, with production, invariably comes errors. Such examples of misproduction are extensively reported and illustrated in this volume. Specific types of productions and their special features — from trucks to locomotives to passenger cars to accessories — are also examined.

In addition, Volume II evaluates the sales and service aspects of Lionel. Clearly Lionel was a remarkably successful sales organization and this book examines the strategies that made this possible. Overall, this book gives the reader a unique understanding of the special place that was Lionel.

The following notes link the articles to the larger themes of the book.

Both **Lee Price's** and **Al Francescetti's** recollections offer a glimpse into Lionel corporate culture and how this related to its long-term market success. Lee Price comments on the prestige and respect accorded to Lionel employees. He also explains why several important Lionel products were either remade or discontinued. His insider explanations are at variance with views widely held in the collector community.

James Sattler contributed extensively to this volume. His article, "Prototypes, Samples, Mock-Ups, and Errors," outlines Lionel's development process, from the first mock-up to the finished product, and describes the various types of models that evolved during this process. His second article, "The 3665 Minuteman Missile Launching Car," also traces the process by studying one model's development in great detail. His third article on the 2456 and 6456 hopper cars explores the connection between Lionel's two-tier marketing program, its numbering system, and the production process. Lionel's marketing needs resulted in some very peculiar products! And Sattler's final article, "New Haven Automobile Cars," examines the 6468-25 boxcars as they were illustrated in Lionel catalogues from 1956 through 1958 and compares the illustrations to known manufactured examples.

Robert Swanson analyzes the first postwar set, the 463W from 1945, in two articles that explain how Lionel cleverly utilized the limited resources at hand to meet the enormous demand for Lionel trains. His third article, "Order Out of Chaos," is a systematic study of Lionel's 9-1/4" boxcars. The 1945-1946 truck and coupler is discussed in his fourth article for this volume.

Ronald Griesbeck shows how Lionel responded to both consumer needs and cost considerations in the development of the Berkshire locomotive. This article identifies subtle but significant differences between models.

Pat Scholes tracks the progression of Lionel's popular twenty-wheel steam turbine from when it was first introduced in 1946 until it was discontinued in 1955 and then follows it to 1985 when Lionel produced its most spectacular version of the locomotive. Since the turbine was one of Lionel's longest running locomotives, its development reflects Lionel's major manufacturing changes, including the replacement of the smoke bulb by a resistance coil, the change from two-part wheels to one-part wheels, and the changes in tender design.

"The Postwar 1666 Locomotives" is the title of **Warren Blackmar's** article in which he points out their similarities and differences. Lionel's changes reduced production cost without sacrificing quality. One change, from a die-cast front truck to a stamped-steel truck, actually improved durability.

Thomas Rollo's analysis of the Madison car, coupled with **Lee Price's** article, explains why this car was dropped from production despite its continuing market appeal. His study of Lionel boxes provides insight into how Lionel organized its production and the changing relationship of packaging and marketing. The box article is very useful in determining whether a Lionel item is packed in its correct box. His third article, "From Persian Gods to Smoking Locomotives," is a detailed examination of Lionel's all-important miniature lamps or light bulbs.

Ralph Hutchinson has contributed two articles on the development of two types of Lionel cars: the first on the 2400-series passenger cars and the second on the 6362-series flatcars. The passenger car article explains how Lionel — by offering different decorating schemes — effectively used and reused its tooling. The flatcar article also shows Lionel's creative marketing and clever die modifications.

Norman Anderson's article clarifies the differences between a reefer and an insulated plug-door boxcar, thereby helping to end the confusion in terminology among collectors. His article also reports on the new body styles created by Fundimensions which add to the diversity of Lionel trains.

One of the most popular accessories ever made by Lionel, the automatic refrigerated milk car, is the subject of **David Fleming's** article. Drawings and a detailed chart reveal the changes made to this fascinating accessory over the postwar years.

Gordon Wilson describes the great variety of Lionel space and military action trains and their loads, from helicopters to missiles to exploding boxcars. The Lionel space and military trains were Lionel's marketing response to a decline in the market for traditional toys and an attempt to reposition its train line as a then contemporary toy. Unfortunately, this strategy did not work. Nonetheless, the military and space trains are highly prized by collectors today.

Joseph Kotil's analysis of the development of the Lionel metal truck shows the ingenuity of Lionel engineers in reducing the cost of the single most important rolling stock component without sacrificing reliability. It also shows how an insightful engineer can reconstruct the production process without direct factory knowledge.

Linda Greenberg's and **Roland LaVoie's** story of the automatic gateman, "Half a Century of Entertainment," suggests the primacy of the toy concept in Lionel marketing. Clearly this "giant of the rails" does not fit a 1/48 layout but nevertheless, its novelty features have delighted several generations of Lionel enthusiasts. **Roland LaVoie** also chronicles one company's role in the publishing industry's expanding production of books on model railroading in "The History of Greenberg Publishing Company."

We would also like to thank certain other individuals for their important contributions to this book. In particular, **Paul Ambrose** lent his considerable expertise by reviewing the majority of chapters. He added significant information and greatly expanded the text and charts in the chapters on Lionel boxes, space trains, and passenger cars. His prompt and thorough reviews are very much appreciated.

Neil Fagan carefully checked the entire book and helped with stylistic consistency. **Michael J. Denuty** and **Jerry Williams** assisted with the book review.

In-house at Greenberg, **Dallas Mallerich** edited the text, organized the material, and designed the layout for the book. **Marcy Damon** also edited the material, fine-tuned the layout, and completed the detail work that goes into getting a book ready for publication. **Donna Price** was the tireless proofreader and, along with **Maureen Crum,** completed the paste-up work. **Rick Andrews** and **Jan Smith** compiled the index; **Samuel Baum** designed the cover; and Greenberg photographers, **Bill Wantz** and **Brad Schwab,** reproduced photographs and line art.

We hope this volume, by providing a rich background history and unique insight into the workings of Lionel, will enhance the reader's enjoyment of Lionel trains.

BREAKING THE MOLD

REMEMBRANCES OF LEE PRICE, LIONEL SALES AND SERVICE REPRESENTATIVE — as told to Bruce C. Greenberg

L ee Price started with Lionel in 1947 as an office boy "gofer." Once his efforts and abilities were recognized, he became a sales and service representative for the Chicago district office. Working with office management, he designed and set up special displays for exhibits and industry shows. In 1953 he regretfully left Lionel at the request of his father in order to assist with the family business. However, he has continued to be a devoted Lionel enthusiast to this day.

BG: *Lionel used Bakelite extensively in the late 1940s. Could you tell us about its use?*

LP: Lionel used a compression-molded phenolic whose tradename is Bakelite for a number of items, including transformer cases, the 164 log loader base, the 97 coal loader base, the 156 station platform and roof, 022 switch controllers, switch bases, motor covers and operating bins, and, of course, the Madison-type heavyweight Pullmans. *[Lionel used Bakelite on about 50 percent of the brush and motor covers, primarily on the better motors.]*

BG: *What were the advantages of Bakelite compared with the use of stamped steel?*

LP: Bakelite permitted the manufacturing of complex shapes with fine surface detail with only one mold. An item could be manufactured from Bakelite at a lower cost than items produced from stamped-steel components, which required assembly. Bakelite dies were much more flexible than dies for stamping finely detailed metal parts. Prior to Bakelite, items with compound curved surfaces with detailed features were made from stamped brass. Furthermore, brass "findings," such as those used in the jewelry trade and in contemporary super-detailed imported brass trains, were not suitable for toy train use because of their lack of durability.

BG: *The Madison cars are probably Lionel's best known Bakelite product other than the transformer cases and 022 switches. There has been considerable speculation as to why Lionel discontinued the production of the Madison-type Pullman. One tale is that the dies for the Madison cars were accidentally lost when Lionel included them in a shipment of scrap metal for the Korean War effort.*

LP: From my inquiries with Lionel factory staff in the late 1940s and early 1950s, I learned that Lionel had substantial production problems with the Bakelite used for Madison cars. Molds using Bakelite had several notable features.

Lionel used a phenolic resin called Bakelite to produce several different items. For example, the base of the 164 log loader (above) is made of this granular, compression-molded material.

First, the molds required that the car have very thick walls for strength and to retain detail. Hence, substantial quantities of plastic were required for each car. Second, the car bodies and other items sometimes required special chemical treatment after molding, if the item was to be painted. Bakelite tends to reject paint because of its oily surface. Third, the plastic bodies were subject to breakage in assembly (epoxy and other "super glues" were not available in the 1940s and 1950s). Small fractures readily occurred during assembly, because of Bakelite's brittle structure. Bakelite was called a "one bounce" plastic — one bounce and pick up the pieces. There were related problems from the car's design, which required six or eight machine-inserted screws. If the screw-inserting machine was not properly adjusted, the screws would either strip or crack the mounting post. Assembling the metal vestibule also caused some handling losses.

BG: *Do you have an estimate of the number of cars that were lost through production problems in assembly and painting*

LIONEL "O" GAUG

No. 2116 WS

Magnificent Giant of the Rails Puffs Realistic
SMOKE — — Whistles

No. 2117 WS

No. 2116WS LIONEL "O" PASSENGER TRAIN—WITH SMOKE
Featuring built-in remote control whistle

Powered by the same magnificent locomotive described above, this set consists of the following: No. 703 Locomotive with SMOKE—No. 2703W Whistle Tender—4 No. 2625 Pullman Cars (each 14¼" long)—8 sections OC Curved Track—7 sections OS Straight Track—RCS Track Set—UTC Lockon—No. 926-5 Instruction Booklet—No. 167 Controller.

No. 2117WS LIONEL "O" GAUGE FREIGHT TRAIN—WITH SMOKE
Also featuring the built-in remote control whistle

Powered by one of the finest scale detailed locomotives made by Lionel—a 6-wheel worm drive. The whistle tender has two trucks of six wheels each, and every car features electro magnetic remote control, real railroad knuckle couplers, solid steel wheels, and die cast trucks.

This freight outfit consists of: No. 703 Locomotive with SMOKE—No. 2703W Whistle Tender—No. 2856 Hopper Car—No. 3854 Operating Merchandise Car—No. 2855 Oil Car—No. 2857 Caboose—8 sections OC Curved Track—7 sections OS Straight Track—RCS Track Set—UTC Lockon—No. 926-5 Instruction Booklet—No. 167 Controller.

A Supply of Smoke Pellets
Included with Each WS Train Outfit.

There certainly was no shortage of demand for the semi-scale Hudson and matching cars shown in the 1946 advance catalogue. But, sadly, the dies for these beautiful trains were permanently scarred while they were in storage during the war.

or the number of extra bodies needed to cover production losses.

LP: Ten to fifteen percent.

BG: *Why didn't Lionel convert the Madison car dies to styrene?*

LP: Apparently, the Madison car molds were not convertible because of mold design. A relatively new plastic, A.B.S., which would have been compatible with these molds, was only developed a few years ago by Hooker Chemicals of Talawanda, New York. Hooker is the corporate successor to Union Carbide, which originally supplied Bakelite resins.

BG: *Did Lionel convert some of its metal die-casting molds to plastic?*

LP: Yes. Eventually, Lionel succeeded in converting a few simple Bakelite molds as technology improved. Lionel did convert a number of other molds, including the formerly die-cast 1130 Scout-series locomotive.

BG: *What were some of the advantages of conversion?*

LP: One of the advantages of styrene was that scrap material could be recycled *[while Bakelite could not be reground].* Leftover *[styrene]* plastic in the preheat hopper, as well as cut-off sprues and other scrap from damaged but unpainted items could be recycled. The use of recycled plastic accounts for colors found on whistle motor and sound boxes under tender bodies, the 2411 flatcar, and some other formerly die-cast items.

BG: *Williams Reproductions reproduced the Madison-type Pullmans. Did they have similar problems with Bakelite?*

LP: I recently talked with "Butch" Christianson, who is the supplier of the beautiful Williams Madison-type cars. He stated that production losses of ten to fifteen percent were common. Losses were so great that discontinuing production was considered if more usable bodies could not be produced. Furthermore, Williams also had assembly and paint problems with Bakelite. Fortunately, another plastic — A.B.S. —

was now available. A.B.S. plastics were beginning to be used by the auto manufacturers. A.B.S had previously been used successfully in the manufacture of plumbing pipe and fittings. Mr. Christianson successfully used A.B.S plastic for the Madison cars by changing the "gate" or mold-filling process to a quicker and far less wasteful injection process. There would no longer be the abrasive mold and die wear and the inevitable detail loss found with Bakelite. *[See Tom Rollo's article on page 84 for more information about die wear on the original Madison cars.]* Furthermore, A.B.S. plastic is very tough. It can even be assembled with glues, and it can be roughly handled without breaking. Bakelite usually breaks when dropped. Parting lines, sprues, and flash can be trimmed without the danger of chipping exposed surface detail. When a gray base color is used, painting results are predictable, and a great looking model can be produced.

BG: *Do you know why the semi-scale 703 Hudson, the 2856 hopper, and 2857 were not produced in 1946. Was it a case of insufficient demand?*

LP: No! Lionel planned to update the 1941 models of the 700, 2956, and 2957. The 1946 catalogue listings produced hundreds of dealers and consumer phone calls and even checks with open amounts for the sales departments. There was no order shortage! However, the Lionel sales offices returned the checks with their thanks and expressed the hope that the trains would soon be at the local dealers' stores. As everybody knows, the semi-scale train never rolled off the assembly line ... sadly, it never would again until the 1980s. During the war, the die-casting molds for the full scale and semi-scale 700 series (as the group of items were referred to in house) were improperly stored and became badly oxidized. These dies were made from highly polished metal and had very close tolerances. Once the oxidation attacked the inner surfaces of these molds, there

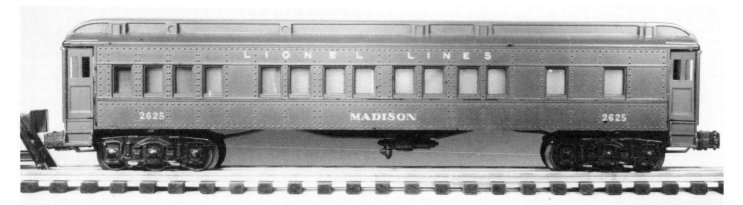

It is widely believed that Lionel accidentally included dies for the Madison cars in a shipment of scrap metal for the Korean War effort. However, Lionel encountered so many molding, handling, and assembly problems with these cars that they were almost certainly glad to see them gone. Whether or not they were "accidentally" dispatched, we may never know.

was no way to buff out the damage and still retain the very fine detail. The pitted and scaled areas would show up on almost every surface, be it flat, concave, convex, or recessed detail. It was impossible to produce items that met "Built by Lionel" standards of excellence. My boss, Jack Caffery, said, "J. L. C. took one look at the sample castings that had been assembled on prewar frames and almost cried." Lionel's crowning achievement, the 700 Hudson, would not be made again if it could not meet the same Lionel quality standard established before the war. Reportedly, Cowen watched the destruction of the damaged and unrepairable dies that made those poor body castings. This story may be simply fiction! But in some respects, it is plausible. By the time this event took place (if, in fact, it did happen), J. L. C. was very ad-

vanced in years and was a very autocratic leader. I am reporting it as it was told to the Chicago staff.

Later, I heard the story dozens of times in another context. In the late 1940s, many dealers and Service Stations had customers returning 700 and 763 locomotives for repair because of cracked boilers and cabs. These dealers and Service Stations needed replacement parts to repair their customers' prized (and very expensive locomotives). These parts were not available, since Lionel chose not to rerun those poor quality castings. The story of the dies and Cowen's personal grief was told in response to dealer and Service Station complaints about the lack of parts.

BG: *Thank you for sharing your insights with us.*

Lee Price helped to maintain this Lionel display layout at the Union Pacific exhibit during Chicago's Railroad Fair in 1947. Sitting at the head of the amusement park F unit is none other than Lionel President Lawrence Cohen (1). Other employees enjoying the ride are Arthur Raphael (2), National Sales Director; Lee Price (3); Annette Borris (4), Merchandise Mart secretary; Reg Parnel (5), Merchandise Mart salesman; and Jack Caffrey (6), Merchandise Mart office manager. Reprinted courtesy of *Classic Toy Trains.*

LIFE WITH LIONEL IN THE 1950s

A SERVICE STATION WORKER'S VIEWPOINT — *as told by Al Franceschetti*

The following is an edited transcript of Bruce Greenberg's interview with Al Franceschetti on August 3, 1987. Mr. Franceschetti worked in the Lionel Service Department for several years; one of his jobs was also to set up display layouts for the major New York department stores. This interview reveals many interesting insights into Lionel's sales and repair practices during its most successful years.

BG: *How did you become connected with Lionel, Mr. Franceschetti?*

AF: Back in 1952, after I graduated from college, I found great difficulty in getting a job in my major field. There just weren't any available, so I did a few and sundry things along the way. During the fall of 1952, I wandered over to R. H. Macy & Company, asked them if they had any Christmas positions available, and spoke to an interviewer. I don't remember exactly how we got on the subject, but Macy's made the determination that I was handy with toy trains. They said that they were going to have a twelve-train operating layout in six windows facing 34th Street, and they needed someone to maintain it.

So, I got a job with Macy's. It was paid out of a window display fund and from 8 o'clock in the morning until we shut down around 10 o'clock at night, seven days a week, I maintained the twelve trains. We had a backup for each one, so that we could keep them running continuously. We would take a locomotive off, put the backup on, and go ahead and lubricate it and do whatever was necessary. I remember that after several weeks of running practically continuously, the locomotive wheel bearings were wearing out, even with lubrication, and since Lionel owned the trains and Macy's didn't, I was instructed to go down to Lionel at their 26th Street showroom to get whatever parts I needed.

I went down there and I spoke with Irving Shull, who was in charge of the repair department. Irving asked me if I'd like a job there in addition to working for Macy's, and I said that I would. So I started working for Lionel in the fall

Edited by Roland E. LaVoie.

of 1952, evenings after leaving Macy's. The walk over to Lionel was short, perhaps a quarter to a half a mile walk. I would work there until the evening's repairs were finished and then I'd go home, get between four and six hours of sleep, and start all over again. Of course, we didn't work Sunday at Lionel, but we did work Saturday night. I did this rather grueling routine until right after New Year's. The trains were completely dismantled and shipped back to Lionel. Lionel was satisfied with my work and I went to work there full time.

During the summers, the amount of repairs Lionel would get weren't sufficient to keep a full staff on, so a lot of the repair people were laid off. They actually went on unemployment during the summer, and then they'd be rehired by Lionel in the fall. But I went on and did other things. I was self-employed during the summers when I wasn't working for Lionel, and I also did repairing for an authorized Lionel Service Station in New Rochelle. This may seem like a little bit of this, that, and the other, but basically that's how I got started at Lionel. I stayed with Lionel off and on until April of 1957, when I took a job in Washington, DC as an oceanographer.

BG: *Is that what you were trained for in college?*

AF: No, my degree was a BS in Zoology because I had hoped to become a medical doctor, but the colleges and universities were so filled up and medical school applicants were in such great numbers that I would have had to be on a waiting list for fifteen years. I could have been accepted in a European medical school, but I chose not to pursue that course at that point, so we went on to other things. But basically that was what my degree was in, Zoology, not engineering or anything of that sort.

BG: *What are your recollections of that twelve-train layout? What did it look like?*

AF: The trackwork was basically done in ovals with no switches. The layout had a little bit of scenery, some action items, crossing gates, semaphores, things like that. There were twelve very simple layouts with a little bit of scenery and each one of the trains represented a different item from

Bruce Greenberg (*left*) and Al Franceschetti (*right*) discuss the career of Mr. Franceschetti at Lionel.

the catalogue. We had freight trains, passenger trains, we had the Alco diesels, we had the steam engines of the period, but nothing super fancy such as the turbines or Berkshires.

BG: *When you first met Irving Shull and saw the Lionel showroom, what were your initial impressions?*

AF: Well, I'd gone to the Lionel showroom as a child many times — once a year at least — to look at the trains. They had a museum in the back where the service department was and that was one of the places that I went, and then later on they had a more modern museum at the entrance-way. The Lionel showroom was not new to me; I'd been there many many times prior to my employment. I think what I found to be somewhat thrilling was to be a part of the action finally, instead of being outside looking in.

BG: *Was the New York showroom the center of the sales organization?*

AF: It was definitely the center of the sales operation. The salesmen had their offices there in small rooms surrounding the main showroom where the big layout was, and Cowen had his office there also. At the opposite end of the showroom from the main entrance, through a small doorway, was the service department, a large area with a big long counter, test tracks, and a lot of their special items such as the extra long prototype 381 that had been hand-built in Italy. Several things of that sort were there. There was another dividing wall between the service counter and the actual area where the repairing was done. The building stretched from 26th Street right across to 27th Street and the repair department faced 27th Street. The workbenches were lined up right underneath big windows that looked out upon 27th Street, so it was a very light and airy service department.

BG: *How many people would be working there in peak season?*

AF: During the peak season I would say Lionel had around ten mechanics fixing trains. Irving was there at his desk, which was not in a private office, but rather out in the open. If you needed a part, you just went back and got what you needed from the parts room and nobody questioned anything. You didn't have to turn in the old part to get a new part or anything like that. Then you ran a log on the repairs that you did. You would record what was involved and that sort of thing. I understand from Irving that the NYC repair facility was more or less a money-loser for Lionel. It was really operated for good will and public relations.

BG: *Was there another repair facility at the factory?*

AF: The factory had a repair facility also, but that was run in an entirely different way. The factory's repair facility was totally unionized, while our NYC showroom was not. At the

A Scout locomotive and tender like the one Mr. Franceschetti worked on. H. Holden Collection.

factory, the parts department was closed to everyone, and if you needed a part, you had to turn in the old part and the worksheet number under which the repair was being done. It was run in a very businesslike fashion, whereas the NYC showroom was not run in a businesslike fashion at all. This led to one interesting complication. Every time the people at the NYC showroom would start agitating for a pay raise, Irving would threaten them with running the facility the way they did in New Jersey, very strictly, and everyone would shut up and get back to work. We would hear nothing more about getting a pay raise. The reason was that a lot of the people were doing repairs in the local neighborhoods where they lived and they were getting the parts from Lionel without charge. That was a benefit that they preferred to keep, rather than higher wages and being unionized.

BG: *Interesting choice! Do you recall any pieces where Lionel obviously had production problems and the defective items started to appear in larger numbers than other items?*

AF: Yes, I remember the Lionel Scout with its plastic motor. That was one item that started coming back by the barrelful. Lionel tried to resolve the problem by coming up with a new type of all-metal motor; I believe it was a 1034-type motor, but I don't recall if that is the correct number or not. *[Mr. Franceschetti was only off by one digit; he was referring to the 2034-type motor first made in 1951. — Ed.]* Something like that, all metal, was a good solution. Any Scout locomotive that had a malfunctioning motor and was under the warranty, and even some that were no longer under the warranty, would have the plastic motor removed and a brand new metal motor put in by the factory, or at least by the New York showroom. And this was done at no charge.

BG: *I believe the Service Manual says something to the effect that it is better to replace the motor than to try to repair it.*

AF: I don't recall having read that in the Service Manual but having gone into the motors recently to try to keep them as original as possible, I can almost appreciate that. They can be finicky.

BG: *I remember when I rediscovered trains, one of the first things I acquired was a Scout locomotive. I had to take the case apart, and I discovered that I needed about four hands and eight or ten extra fingers to get it all back together.*

AF: Well, I believe the biggest problem with disassembling a Scout motor is the fact that you have to pull the drive

wheels off the axles first, and without a wheel-puller you could do more damage than good with them, so most people, not having the proper wheel-pullers, were stymied right at the very beginning.

BG: *Yes. You obviously had a natural affinity for mechanics, and Lionel recognized it. Did they have any kind of training program when you were brought in?*

AF: No training program whatsoever. You sat down at the bench, and if you didn't know how to do something you asked the fellow alongside of you. He would show you how to make the repair, and that was how it all came down. In addition to repairing, I also handled displays at department stores. I remember going as far as Philadelphia to set up a display. We went out to Long Island also and I used to maintain the rather large Lionel layout at F. A. O. Schwarz up near Central Park in New York City when they had problems. And every once in a while, there'd be a train display put on by various charitable organizations which wanted a Lionel representative to make sure that the layout kept working, and I would go out on those cases too. Also, whenever Josh would bring in a special repair or a special request for someone close to him, such as the repair of an old Standard Gauge locomotive, they would always give those to me. And one time he wanted a 700EW scale Hudson, and, of course, this was back in the 1950s and they weren't available any longer, but I was given the job to make one. So I spent a number of days in the parts department pulling bins and whatnot, and I came up with every single part that I needed to assemble a complete 700EW from parts. I remember one time Josh brought in a Lionel No. 10, I believe, that belonged to a neighbor of his. The loco had disintegrated drive wheels and it was given to me to overhaul. I started looking around for replacement drive wheels because Lionel couldn't come up with any, so I was told to go down to Madison Hardware, where the owners had all the parts. So I went down to Madison and talked to them about the No. 10; I told them it was a repair for Josh Cowen. They said, "No problem," and they handed me all the parts that I needed. It was after that that I made regular trips down to Madison Hardware for parts to fix Lionel trains for Lionel. *[This story would appear to validate that Lionel's relationship with Madison Hardware was unique. No hard evidence has ever turned up that Lionel made special train or train part runs for Madison Hardware, but there has always been ample circumstantial evidence to support that thesis — Ed.]*

BG: *Where did Madison get the wheels?*

AF: Right after the Second World War, Lionel ran a production run of black oxide, black-tired drive wheels for its steam engines. Evidently, most of them were grabbed up by Service Stations and people of that sort, and the supply disappeared rather quickly. So by the time the 1950s came along, Lionel had no more of these wheels and the demand had gone down to the point where, I believe, they didn't feel it was cost effective to make another production run, especially since you could always go down to Madison and buy the parts you wanted. Madison had stockpiled a big supply of genuine Lionel parts.

BG: *Did Mr. Cowen come out from his office and wander around the repair department on occasion?*

AF: I don't recall ever seeing him in the repair department. He used to wander around the showroom on occasion. One time we did have a Christmas party. I was considered a temporary employee because I was not on full-time because of seniority. The ones that were on full-time, including the summer, were people who had been there for twenty years at least and so I was not considered a full-time employee, just temporary. But we had a small Christmas party in the showroom and Josh gave me a bonus and said something to the effect that this was the first time he'd ever had the pleasure of giving a Christmas bonus to a temporary employee, which I appreciated to the point that I'll never forget it.

BG: *That is certainly very nice. What was the interaction between the employees in the service department like? Was it very relaxed, was it conducive to information sharing, or was there a lot of pressure to perform?*

AF: No, I would say that we really weren't under pressure. The pressure, if it was there, was very subtle and accepted all in a friendly way. If we had a lot of work to do, we would just stay later at night, and there were times that we would work until two o'clock in the morning. There was never really what I would call pressure. Occasionally some of the Service Stations in the New York area which did not have repair facilities of their own would bring large boxes full of repairs in, and then we would have to drop everything that we were doing and turn to their repairs. This really gave us a problem with keeping up with our own repairs; but as a general rule, the atmosphere was fairly relaxed.

One repair really gave us problems when we were rushed. On the early horizontal armature F-3 motors, the motor trucks would wear out, the bearings would wear out — the axle bushings, actually. The worm wheels would lose their teeth. With these motors, there was another problem because the motors were in effect riveted together. Over a period of time and usage, the peened-over separators that held everything together would loosen a bit and then the motors would not ground properly and fail to operate correctly as a result. We would have to disassemble these motors, drill out the spacers and tap the 4-40 screws, and put them together with new screws.

Generally, during the Christmas rush, which would be a period of two to three weeks, we did not, if at all possible, repair items. Instead, we exchanged them. For example, if a

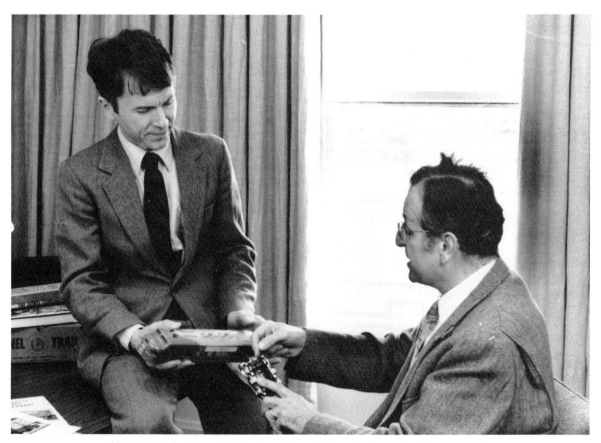

Al Franceschetti explaining how the axle bushings on the F-3s wore out.

A close-up view of a horizontal motor in an F-3 diesel.

person came in with a worn-out motor truck, we didn't sit down and repair the motor truck. Instead, we exchanged it. We had a big box full of rebuilt motor trucks or rebuilt motors, and we would just swap everything. The defective items would go into another big box, and this is what kept the service department busy during the summer when things were slow. We would spend our time rebuilding motors, motor trucks, and things of that sort. Even the bushings on 736 and 671 frames would wear out, and we wouldn't even bother rebushing those. Instead, we would just change frames. *[This is a highly significant detail for collectors, since the repair swap process described by Mr. Franceschetti could account for a significant number of F-3 variations as reported over the years — Ed.]*

BG: *That's very interesting. It's a very logical way of dealing with a problem of workload and lack of workload.*

AF: Sure. You could turn a worn-out F-3 around in about five to ten minutes flat that way.

BG: *Even given the quality of the construction of the F-3, these pieces must have experienced remarkably heavy wear.*

AF: That plus, amazingly, lack of lubrication. Some of these more sophisticated motor trucks require disassembly to lubricate properly, and this was beyond the capability of a lot of people. So a lot of the wear was due to a lack of lubrication rather than unusually heavy wear.

BG: *I think it would have taken a great deal to wear out a 736 axle bearing. That takes an awful lot of wear.*

AF: There was another problem, too. Lionel always gave the customer a little tube of their grease to use as a lubricant, but the problem with the grease was that it never got to where it was supposed to be. Oil would get into bushings and bearings, but the grease just made a big lump on the outside and never did penetrate where it was supposed to do any good.

BG: *There was no way to force it in because the fitting was too tight.*

AF: That's correct. The wheels were so close up against the frame sides that there was no way to get grease into the wheel bearings without applying oil with a very fine needle-like oiler.

BG: *Did you have any contact with the sales people?*

AF: I believe one time, there was something going on at the factory and all the sales people were at the factory. Lionel needed somebody to stay out in the showroom, and I got the job. I was told to come in with a tie and a suit the next day, so I spent the day out in the showroom talking to people. Actually, I did speak to several of the salesmen, but they spent very little time in the showroom. They were out on the road most of the time, traveling all over the country. So I rarely saw a salesman. They had offices at the showroom, but I just didn't see them.

BG: *Going back to the Macy's train layout, the factory would provide these layouts without charge to the major retailers and send a man to help set it up and come by once a week or once every few weeks to help him out.*

AF: Regarding the department store layouts in the toy departments, if the store did not have the expertise in-house to construct the layout, it would request assistance from Lionel. The store would supply all their own merchandise, their own trains, and all Lionel did was supply one or two people from their repair department to actually put up the layout. After that, it was the store's responsibility. In the case of R. H. Macy, it was such a large affair that Lionel took that on for advertising, and I don't recall whether the layouts were built by Macy's or built by Lionel, but all the equipment was furnished by Lionel. At the conclusion of the holiday season, the equipment went back to Lionel and was disposed of, because most of it was too worn out to do much else with. Macy's furnished the people to maintain the layout and paid for them.

BG: *Cooperative advertising.*

AF: More or less, yes. Of course, we're talking about a period now in the early 1950s, quite a while ago, because I was connected with Lionel from the fall of 1952 until the spring of 1957.

BG: *Did you ever visit the factory?*

AF: I never went to the factory. I often wanted to go; but for some reason I never had the time or just never made it, and of course now it's gone. My entire experience was with the New York City showroom.

BG: *When you were working in the service department, did you see some Standard Gauge equipment periodically?*

AF: Very, very little. Any time people came in off the street with Standard Gauge repairs, they were referred to Madison Hardware by Lionel. The only Standard Gauge equipment I got were items that were brought in by Joshua Lionel Cowen himself. They no longer had the equipment to handle it and they just didn't want to be bothered, really.

BG: *In other words, they didn't feel under any obligation for maintaining it.*

AF: That's correct.

BG: *How many items were in the museums there?*

AF: Offhand, there were approximately six shelves from floor to ceiling and the length was perhaps 30 to 40 feet. The items were fairly spaced out so that nothing was really crowded and there might have been 40 or 50 items in the back and perhaps 30 or 40 items in the front. The items that were in the back were the specialty items, the hand-built prototypes, very, very old things, whereas the items that were up in the front were all Golden Era. *[Mr. Franceschetti is probably referring to items produced in the 1920s and 1930s — Ed.]* And I think the Golden Era was more attractive to people of that period because it was bright, had a lot of trim on it, whereas the older stuff was kind of drab in comparison.

BG: *Oh yes, that increase in color came about in the 1920s. It was unusual for a factory to have that in the 1950s and people paid to see it by that time.*

AF: A lot of people came down to look at the older items that were on display, and one of Irving Shull's jobs was as curator of the museum. It was his job to pick up items for the museum. I suppose he had a special kitty for that purpose, but I remember from time to time people would come with Standard Gauge sets to sell to him and if Irving was interested, he would buy the items, cash on the spot, and if he wasn't interested, he knew that I was a collector and would offer them to me.

BG: *I had no idea your collection went back that far.*

AF: Oh yes, I've been collecting ever since the 1940s. Being on a very limited budget, I don't have that great a collection.

BG: *I had no idea you had the collecting interest at that time.*

AF: Well, I've liked trains ever since I got my first 384 Standard Gauge loco when I was two and one half years old (which I still have, I might add) with the three freight cars. I remember people coming in with a suitcase full of items, such as a brown 10E with brown passenger cars, all in absolutely mint condition, and walking out with $2.00 in their pocket for that whole set. I was spoiled, since I saw how low prices were being paid for trains back then.

BG: *Without a collector's market, they had very little value. They were obsolete hardware.*

AF: As a matter of fact, I had a wartime cardboard Lionel train set. I forget the name of it or the number that was used on it, but it was a punch-out type of train set and I didn't know what to do with it. I gave it to Irving Shull, just gave it to him. And I understand that's worth some money now. *[Mr. Franceschetti is referring to the No. 50 Paper Train of 1943, which is worth several hundred dollars at this writing. It has also been reproduced by the Greenberg Publishing Company — Ed.]*

BG: *Was there any talk about what Gilbert was doing? Any interest?*

AF: I think any time Gilbert was mentioned it was always done in a derogatory fashion, as if they were absolutely of no consequence to Lionel and what Lionel was doing. They just never thought of Gilbert even being in contention.

BG: *That would make sense.*

AF: Once in a while we would wander over to the Gilbert Hall of Science which was diagonally across from the 26th Street showroom and walk around there, but it was rather difficult to get to see very much at the Gilbert Hall of Science. They never had too much in operation.

BG: *A much smaller display.*

AF: Much smaller, yes. I believe I read somewhere that most of the trains were upstairs and people off the street were not allowed up there. Only potential customers or salesmen were allowed up there. What they had on display was not very representative of what they had to offer.

BG: *It's interesting that they didn't seek the opportunity to make a competitive display. As I recall my experience with trains in the 1950s, my problems were balky reversing switches or my milk car jamming. I didn't know how to fix either of them, so I'd go to the service station, and it was very, very expensive to have either fixed. Were these repairs among the most common you faced?*

AF: Yeah, normally the biggest problem with E-units was that one of the little pins on the end of the drum that the E-unit contacts rotated on would break off and then the drum would get cocked at an angle inside between the side frames and, of course, cease to function at that point. We replaced many, many drums. We did not replace fingers unless the ends were burned off. What we would do was use some very, very fine emery cloth to shine up the ends of the E-unit fingers and rebend them so they were all even and made proper contact. We'd then just replace the drum. Sometimes we'd get one that the customer thought he'd make work better by oiling and then we'd have to wash all the oil out. Sometimes the sticky plunger was very quickly repaired with a little bit of graphite. We could do an E-unit overhaul in about five minutes.

Concerning the sticky milk car doors, generally a little bit of graphite down in the moving parts on those was all that it required to get those out very fast. A bigger problem was milk cans that would jam in the chute sideways inside the car, and, of course, that required a bit of disassembly, and a little bit of realignment so that the cans couldn't be put in backwards or upside down.

BG: *Were there any tests by the engineering department to learn from the service department what were the problems?*

AF: Not from the New York City showroom because they had their own service department. I suppose if they felt that input was needed they would just go to their own service area right at the factory. What they would occasionally do with something new, such as the cop and hobo car, was to send a hand-built prototype to the New York City showroom for evaluation and, there again, I was the one who always got those things for evaluation. I would play with these prototypes for a couple of days, just putting the repairs aside. I would make minor adjustments here and there and make a list of recommendations that I felt would make the car operate better, something of that sort, and give them back to Irv and he'd send them back to the factory. And on occasion I designed and built several prototype items which were forwarded to the factory and evaluated for production.

I don't recall any of my prototypes ever being accepted for production, but the reasons for not doing so were very understandable. I remember one particular item. I built a very compact test panel and test operation which would test everything Lionel built from about the teens on up to the modern stuff, and put it in a small slope-front panel with one piece of track on top. It was that small. I then took pictures of it and made schematics which were all sent to the factory, and the factory thought it was terrific. Supposedly, they would design and build these test panels to send to the Service Stations. But the reason they didn't accept the idea for production was that they felt that the unit was so compact that it was not impressive enough. Customers expected to see an enormous test panel even if most of the functions could be incorporated with one switch. They wanted to see acres of switches to make it look impressive, whereas I had reduced mine to one selector switch which chose the functions and a couple of toggle switches, and that was it.

BG: *That's a very interesting comment, because even in the 1950s, electricity was a mystery to most people. In fact, look at the world today. People have only the vaguest idea of what electricity is about and how to control it other than their use of a switch. Part of the appeal of trains was the magic of electricity.*

AF: A lot of trains were sold on the basis of learning all about electricity and I believe it really did work in the early days for people. I think today electricity is regarded as unsophisticated. Electronics has replaced the basic science of electricity to a point now where it's regarded as old-fashioned.

BG: *People who don't understand electricity don't understand electronics either. To understand electricity and electronics allows you to go beyond what a person can directly experience and understand. Some people don't have that inclination. Or you go beyond something that's other than it appears to be. People have no way of dealing with it unless it's in the form of a train.*

AF: I remember a game that my father and I used to play in my early years. I think we started playing this game when I was about six years old, and it was troubleshooting — the scientific approach to troubleshooting. And it's amazing how somebody can learn at a very early age a proper methodical approach to solving a problem. What my father would do was to sabotage something on my trains, perhaps short out a piece of track in such a way that it wasn't readily obvious. I would go to play with my trains around Christmas time and there was a dead short. And then I had to find out what was wrong. Of course, we would start with taking the cars and the locomotive off the track one by one, and then we would start isolating the track out into sections until we finally located the actual area where the problem was, and then it was a simple matter to find the problem. And he used to do this about once a week and the object of course was to see how fast I could find the problem. I would say that probably my interest in science may have started as a result of these games that we used to play when I was six or seven years old.

BG: *That certainly is good training. What other things do you think we should tell people about concerning the showroom at 26th Street?*

AF: Well, perhaps some of the anecdotes. Things would sometimes be slow and everybody would leave early. The few of us who were left back in the service department to finish up would have a little fun by doing such things as taking a No. 41 or No. 51 switcher, which are notoriously slow, and installing gang car worm wheels and gang car armatures on them. This took a little bit of machine work. We would then have races on the main layout there and see whose kitbash was fastest, little games of that sort.

And I remember one time that we pulled a real stunt on one of the old-time servicemen who was a little high on himself. He felt that if he couldn't fix an item, it was beyond the capability of anyone to repair. So we were going to take him down a notch or two, we younger ones. I came up with this scheme of replacing the armature on a gang car with a different armature that had a slightly different pitch to the worm on the armature. But it was something that would not readily be apparent to anyone looking at it, and, of course, it chewed up the worm wheel. And this fellow replaced the worm wheel three times! Each time the worm wheel got chewed up. Finally, he had a fit of disgust — he just couldn't understand it, and we all got a big laugh and told him what we'd done. He was so angry with us that he didn't talk to any of us for two weeks. We deflated his ego!

But little games like this tended to keep a person interested and sharp and on his toes, too. I think the greatest fun was modifying equipment and racing it on the big layout. What minor machining we did was done on the drill press with files, kind of crude, but when you had nothing else, it worked. They did have an airbrush, a little diaphragm compressor and airbrushing equipment which they would occasionally use to paint up a prototype with special colors. There was one fellow, the assistant manager, Tony Xifo, who used to do all the painting and things like that. I built an O Gauge trolley car and didn't know how I was going to go about getting it painted, because I was living in an apartment house. This was before the days of the aerosol can. I happened to mention it to Tony, who said to bring it in so that he could paint it. We stayed until 2 o'clock one morning, and he gave me a beautiful custom paint job on my trolley car.

BG: *Do you still have the trolley car?*

AF: I still have the trolley car.

BG: *Oh, good. You were there during the greatest years in Lionel history and then things went downhill. Did you sense it in the service department in 1956 or 1957?*

AF: No, to me it seemed like everything was still going full-blown when I left in April of 1957. We were not seeing a slowdown at all. From my recollection, I was not aware that anything was slowing down. Is it possible that things didn't start slowing down until 1958?

BG: *No, there was a fall-off as early as 1954.*

AF: Well, there was a problem, I remember overhearing, from discount houses. A lot of the small Lionel dealers were very, very upset because of what discount houses were doing to their business.

BG: *Oh yes, for good reason. [This refers to Lionel's attempts to enforce the Fair Trade laws among their major distributors while discounters were free to set their own lower prices — Ed.]*

AF: In fact, I picked up some very good items in my collection from small shops which had decided to give up the sale of Lionel and made their stock available at very, very low prices. As a matter of fact, I got my 1957 773 Hudson with a metal tender, a brand new seal on the box, for $35 from a small shop up in Rye, New York.

BG: *So people in the showroom knew about these problems.*

AF: I would say probably the salesmen in the showroom were more aware of it, but we in the repair department didn't see it. The repairs were still coming in.

BG: *Cowen was born in 1877. By 1955, he was 78 years old. How spry was he, to your recollection?*

AF: I never looked at him as being that old of a person. He seemed to be fairly mobile. As a matter of fact, I would say that he was very spry. Right up until 1957, when I last saw him, he did not seem to me to be an old man. I wasn't aware of the fact that he was that old. *[Joshua Lionel Cowen died in 1965 at the age of 88 — Ed.]*

BG: *Okay, that's interesting. He aged slowly, and he retained his vigor.*

AF: He had a little white hair, of course; I think he was bald, quite bald. He moved effortlessly.

BG: *Was there a sense of the man's brilliance and capability with mechanical and electrical concepts?*

AF: Actually, I never really spoke to the man except the one time when he handed me the bonus check at the Christmas party. I had seen him speak to salesmen from time to time when I was walking through the showroom. He could get very angry if a salesman gave him a bad time. I remember at one point a salesman didn't want to do something the way Cowen wanted him to do it and they got into a big argument. The salesman wouldn't back down. I think the man was 64 years old and one year from retiring, and he was fired on the spot. I remember him going back crying because he had lost his entire Lionel retirement because of being fired. All he would have gotten at that point was Social Security and he begged for his job back, but to the best of my knowledge he was not rehired. So the point here is that if Josh had made up his mind that something needed to be done a certain way, then you did not want to argue with him.

BG: *There's a style of entrepreneurship like that, where you keep course regardless, whether there's a locomotive coming the other way or not. And very often you keep going until the locomotive goes away. Sometimes you can get out of the way, but not always.*

AF: And yet he never interfered with the operation of the repair department, maintenance department, or anything like that. All his heavy interaction, at least in the New York City showroom, was with the salespeople. Of course, when he

Al is holding a Lionel 381, one of Lionel's finest Standard Gauge locomotives. This engine is a very credible model of the Chicago, Milwaukee, St. Paul Olympian locomotive. Although the model is powered by only one motor, it will pull three very large passenger cars.

went to New Jersey he was involved with production, but I didn't get to see that. *[See Ron Hollander's* All Aboard! *for some great anecdotes concerning Joshua Lionel Cowen's behavior in the New York showroom. According to Hollander, Cowen would often pretend to be an interested spectator, remarking about the novelty of the showroom items, to get customers interested — Ed.]*

BG: *Did he keep regular office hours? Was he there every day?*

AF: Pretty much so, unless he was in New Jersey or something like that. He was there pretty regularly, because that's where his main office was.

BG: *His home was nearby.*

AF: It was one of those apartments, I believe, uptown. I'm not sure exactly where he lived. *[According to Hollander, Cowen lived in a large apartment at 270 Park Avenue with his second wife, Lillian. By 1957 he was spending half his time in Palm Beach, Florida — Ed.]*

BG: *What about his son? Do you have an impression of his son?*

AF: To the best of my knowledge, I may have seen him once, but really I had no impression at all, none whatsoever. It is my understanding that his son did work on Wall Street, and he was much more interested in stocks and brokerage than he was in running factories. *[This is true, but Lawrence Cowen did exhibit a great deal of interest in marketing strategies. — Ed.]*

BG: *What about Mr. Shull, do you have any impressions of him?*

AF: Irving Shull had been with Lionel many, many years. He had worked his way up to where he was manager of the repair facility and had other functions as well. I guess he was one of the staff people because when they would have staff meetings he would go on to Lionel's office and was involved in the staff meetings. He operated the repair facility the way he wanted to. As near as I could tell, he had very little interference, if any at all, even to hiring who he wanted to, when he wanted to, and how he wanted to. I believe he even controlled the pay raises; and if he felt it was necessary to work overtime, he just had everybody working overtime and paid the monies with no question.

As far as the construction of the layouts, I believe that the factory had a facility for building layouts and they would ship them to various places that needed a layout, but the New York City showroom was not really involved with any of the stuff. Therefore I was not aware of what the factory was doing, but I would say Lionel's operation was very similar to what Gilbert was doing. They were building their layouts in New Haven and shipping them, and I imagine Lionel was building theirs out in New Jersey and shipping them.

I believe that there was one layout connected with a Fresh Air Fund. The purpose of that fund was to collect money to send disadvantaged children to summer camp. I sat with that layout for a week in Grand Central Station in New York City. The layout was built at the factory. When it was set up by factory people, I came in with my suit and tie, and sat with it, since there was no maintenance to be done. For one week, with all brand new equipment, it all operated except for derailments. I was to answer questions about the trains and things like that. After it was all over, the layout went back to New Jersey, and I went back to the New York City showroom.

But I wasn't even involved with putting the factory-built layouts up. The types of layouts that I actually put up or helped to put up were department store layouts where the department store furnished all the equipment. Then all we would do was to come up with a suitable layout and screw the track down, if you will, and do the wiring. First we put down this green grass paper. We may have called it grass paper, but it really was splinters of wood glued down to this heavy-based paper which we would staple to plywood. Then, while you were crawling across this stuff, you would get some of these splinters into the palm of your hand and into your knees, and then you'd get green paint on your pant knees. We really didn't care to work with the stuff that much, but it was all that was available at the time. It was rather nice looking for a short period of time.

I do remember one very interesting anecdote, though. We were called to put up a layout for R. H. Macy. They were not going to have a layout in the window at this particular time, but they wanted to have a rather large layout up in the toy department. We were called in to put the layout together using Macy's equipment. The interesting part was that the electrician's union had such a strong hold on the employees of R. H. Macy that we were not permitted to do the wiring. Now this was all low voltage wiring. So they gave us a union electrician who came by. He said, "Okay, I don't know the first thing about this, you'll have to tell me what to do." So what we would do, taking turns, was to lay down under the table next to the electrician, telling him how to wire the layout. We'd say things like "Okay, now you fish this wire up through that hole and you attach it to that point, and then you run it down to this end and you attach it to there," item by item. And of course he was making about five times more money than we were for doing nothing, really, in effect. In fact, he thought it was all a big joke. So there's one of those little side stories you get involved in. But that was only in New York City itself.

I also remember several incidents that happened while I was working at Lionel. One day Louis Hertz wandered into the back to the repair department. He came up to me and said, "I understand you're looking for a tender for a 392." And I said, "How did you find out?" He said, "Irving Shull told me. I have a nice tender for you and six-wheel trucks, a big tender, spare, in fact I brought it with me. That will be $15." And at first I was aghast at paying $15 for a tender for a locomotive that I only paid $2 for, but since he had gone through the trouble of wrapping it and bringing it down and everything, I went ahead and paid him the $15." But I thought that was a horrible price to pay for a tender. That gives you an idea of how prices have changed.

BG: *I think that was a high price for the time.*

AF: Louis Hertz's prices were not cheap, but he gave you good stuff. And another time John Marron wandered down. He was a long-time TCA member. As a matter of fact, he was a founding member, who joined in 1954. He said, "I understand you're a train collector. I found this out from Harvey Roe." Harvey was also a founding member who joined in '54. "And we'd like you to join TCA." So they signed me up in 1955 and I was member number 77. And that's how that happened. It all happened while I was working at Lionel.

BG: *If you read the earliest TCA quarterlies, there was a tension between the collecting of trains and their dollar value. There was a notion that collecting is something that shouldn't be measured by dollars, that the goal of collecting should not be based on increasing one's net worth, but rather the joy and love of the toy. Conflicting with that idea was the perception that people were charging outrageous prices for things, and there was continual complaining about these price increments and what is seen as price gouging.*

AF: Back when I started, collecting was purely an avocation, not a business interest. The value of toy trains really had not started to be recognized at that point. That's the reason items were still available fairly inexpensively. We did not have investors, in other words, getting into the fray. Trains were plentiful, and, although a few people were making some money out of it, the amounts of money being made were modest by today's standards. So at that point, I didn't notice the investors making inroads into hurting the hobby until later on. Where we had some problems was with the restored items versus the collectors of original equipment. There were people who felt that an item should be left in its original state even if it was nothing but a pile of rust. My feeling was that an item should be restored to the condition that it was in when it left the factory, and it never left the factory a pile of rust. So I was always at odds with the purists on that score.

BG: *Mr. Hertz's position was the purist position. However, within the hobby of automobiles, for example, restoration is mandatory. It is not only acceptable, but one wouldn't want a car unless it was restored.*

AF: But oftentimes many prize-winning old automobiles today are overrestored. They are made into much more than they were when they left the factory. They're too perfect. With trains, one of the things that we used to joke about was the paint job. If it had runs in it and had thin areas then it was original. And if it was beautifully done, evenly, with no runs, then it must be a restoration.

BG: *I think that's a reasonable interpretation. Now, of course, restorers have gotten smarter.*

AF: They learned how to do shoddy work.

BG: *Train collecting is an interesting sort of passion. You said you've pursued this hobby for forty years?*

AF: Actually, I remember that during one summer when I was home from college, I believe it was in 1950, I worked for a Lionel authorized service station on 25 Park Row in downtown Manhattan. The fellow's name was Frank Agello, and he's long since departed this world. That's when I first really got started on repairing modern trains. Prior to this I was fairly adept at the older stuff, but I didn't know about replacing knuckle coupler springs and rivets and things of that sort. This was all new to me. I got my early training as a repairman for this authorized service station. I spent three months at it and when it was all over, I went back to school, and then it was about two and one half years later that I went to work for Macy's and Lionel. But prior to that, even prior to working for Frank Agello, I'd done some repairs for friends and neighbors at home.

Generally money was not plentiful in those days. Therefore, if it was something that could be repaired with ingenuity and not the replacement of a part, we could handle it, but if it required the replacement of a part, then we were in trouble, because I remember back in the late 1930s, you could buy a brand new armature for your Lionel Bild-A-Locomotive for $1.75. Back in the late 1930s, $1.75 represented an awful lot of weeks of allowance.

The general problem that would happen with these armatures was that the pinion gear on the end of the armature would wear out, because the little teeth on there take a terrible beating. Rather than replace the pinion gear, you would just replace the entire armature. This is how the repair was done back then. Also, when the early two-position reversing unit would become defective, Lionel did not attempt to repair them. It's only modern craftsmen that will repair a defective one rather than replace the unit. Remember, these units were very inexpensive in the locomotive originally.

Lionel replaced the early two-position E-units with the later three-position E-units; at least I can speak for the case of my own locomotive. They drilled a hole in the cab in the back and installed a toggle switch instead of using the little lever that went through a slot in the roof. They would remove that lever and wire the toggle switch in place of the lever so that you could turn the E-unit off and on. Actually, this was a lot more convenient than having to lift the locomotive up off the track to reach the small lever that would disengage the early two-position reverse unit. In addition, the three-position unit had a neutral position, and you could have the train sit at the station with the headlight on waiting to be loaded up with passengers and all, rather realistically. So, we all looked at this replacement of the early reversing unit with the later one as a real boon. Today, things are a little different. People would like to see everything converted back to the way it was originally, even the old two-position reversing units.

BG: *Al, you've given us a great deal of interesting information. Thank you for sharing your recollections of Lionel.*

PROTOTYPES, SAMPLES, MOCK-UPS, AND ERRORS

SEEKING A BETTER UNDERSTANDING — *James M. Sattler*

It is vitally important to define and understand terms in order for collectors and dealers to distinguish the various categories of Lionel collectibles which differed in some significant way from those that were mass-produced in regular production runs. Many collectors and dealers indiscriminately use, fail to use, or misuse terms such as "prototype" and "factory error."

In the fifth edition of *Greenberg's Guide to Lionel Trains, 1945-1969* (then only a single volume), we separated the factory errors and prototypes from the main text. Since then, considerable study has been made of such items and numerous previously unreported examples have come to light. In this edition we have substantially revised and expanded our previous definitions and listings of such items.

In an effort to attempt to bring clarity and order to these areas, we have defined each of these terms and have added a number of other definitional categories.

PROTOTYPES

A prototype is the epitome of the rarest of the Lionel collectibles. A prototype is a one-of-a-kind item, or one of an extremely small number of items, made by the manufacturer prior to the time when all of the necessary tools, dies, or equipment were available to commence mass-production. Prototypes were made in order to allow the manufacturer to:

- Provide a three-dimensional representation of what a proposed item would look like.
- Test market reaction to the proposed item.
- Study the feasibility and potential problems of mass producing the proposed model.

Prototypes were made for the purpose of assisting in making production and marketing decisions. Some prototypes were used for making catalogue illustrations.

Because of the nature of a prototype, a prototype will have one or more of the following characteristics which will readily distinguish it from any similar mass-produced item:

- Numbers, lettering, or logos will be handpainted, hand-applied, or will appear as hand-cut decals rather than as the normal methods of application found on similar mass-produced items. Almost without exception, mass-production methods of lettering and numbering were not used on prototypes.

- In many cases, prototypes were made either with a blocked-out number such as "0000" or "0000000" or with no number at all. Some prototypes were made using num-

The prototype of the 44 U. S. Army locomotive. Note that the prototype does not have the three side cylinders found on the mass-produced version.

DEFINITIONS

In addition to the already great interest in mass-produced Lionel items, there is a special interest in more unusual and esoteric items that differ from the main body of Lionel collectibles. Although there has been much confusion, and even debate, over the differentiation of these items, Jim Sattler's definitions, arranged here alphabetically, help both the neophyte and the advanced collector.

A more detailed explanation of each definition, along with the description of one or more examples, for each term can be found in the text. If you still find this complex area confusing, come back to this chart for comparison and study the photographs — it will soon fall into place.

Prototype: A one-of-a-kind item, or one of an extremely small number of items, made by the manufacturer prior to the time when all of the necessary tools, dies, or equipment were available to commence mass-production. Prototypes were made in order to allow the manufacturer to:

- Provide a three-dimensional representation of how a proposed item would look.

- Test market reaction to the proposed item.

- Study the feasibility and potential problems of mass producing the new proposed models.

Factory Mock-Up: A one-of-a-kind item, or one of an extremely small number of items, made by the manufacturer before all of the necessary tools, dies and equipment were available to mass-produce such an item or items. Factory mock-ups often share some of the same characteristics as prototypes, except that the decision to proceed with production has already been made, probably from the approval of a prior prototype. Factory mock-ups usually bear a small paper tag that reads: "This is a factory mock-up not a production item."

Salesman's Samples: One of an extremely small number of items made by the manufacturer before mass-production began for demonstration or use by salesmen.

Paint or Color Sample: A one-of-a-kind item, or one of an extremely small number of items, made after all of the necessary tools, dies, or equipment were available to mass-produce such an item and made either before or after mass-production began. A paint or color sample will have one or more characteristics that distinguish it from any prototype or similar mass-produced item:

- Numbers, lettering, or logos will be applied by customary mass-production methods.

- Except for the colors of numbers, lettering, logos, and/or the color scheme (paint), it will be identical to mass-produced items.

Post-Factory or Chemically-Altered Cars: Because of the high prices that legitimate paint or color samples command, some unscrupulous elements of the train collecting hobby have altered the appearance of individual cars by using a chemical process to change the color of paint or lettering. The presence of fraudulent pieces makes it necessary for collectors to proceed cautiously when buying or selling unusual items.

Corporate Public Relations: Lionel made up special cars for public relations purposes.

Personal Favors: From time to time, the factory has created special products for special people. Some of these items were produced in response to special requests, others as a special gesture to friends and associates of the firm.

Factory Variation: One of a substantial number of a series of items, which varies in some way from other similar items produced in factory runs. A factory variation varies or departs in some determinable way from other simlar mass-produced items. Factory variations appear as one of two general types:

- Major variation — such as easily and readily determinable differences in colors or lettering. Example: the dark yellow versus the light yellow 6456 stock car.
- Minor variation — such as a change in the plastic body mold color. Example: the various 6464-475 Boston & Maine boxcars.

Any factory variation is the result of an *intentional change* in the production process.

Factory Error: A one-of-a-kind item, or one of an extremely small number of items, made by the manufacturer after all of the necessary tools, dies, and equipment were made or available to mass-produce such an item or items and made after mass-production began. A factory error varies or departs in some significant way from the mass-produced examples of the item because of an *unintentional mistake* in the production process.

Three unusual Lionel items. This chapter will assist the reader in identifying and differentiating these items. *Top Shelf:* 212T United States Marine Corps dummy A unit. This came with uncatalogued set X646. The A unit is referred to in *Greenberg's Lionel Service Manual, Volume I: II-63.* We classify this as a factory variation since it appears to be an intentionally mass-produced item, although made in small numbers. *Middle Shelf:* United States Navy Alco prototype. Decaled letters and numbers were applied to a heat-stamped 1055 shell. This was likely prepared to make a production or marketing decision. *Bottom Shelf:* 233 chassis with a plastic shell made from marbleized plastic. This was probably made in preparation for use as a paint or color sample. M. Sokol Collection.

The colorful 2350 electric illustrated above was probably made by Lionel to show at the New York Toy Fair to determine the demand for such a model. Because it was made before the decision to produce the item had been made, we call this a prototype. Lionel used a drawing of this prototype on an envelope *(right)* sent to Lionel dealers for marketing purposes.

Top Shelf: 0000 Burlington / Way of the Zephyrs and 0000 Great Northern. *Second Shelf:* 0000 (XP476) D & R G W / Cookie Box and 0000 N Y M X (XP534) mechanical refrigerator car. *Third Shelf:* 0000 Pillsbury Flour using operating boxcar body and 0000000 (XP527) Duluth South Shore and Atlantic. *Bottom Shelf:* Timken Roller Freight. H. Holden Collection.

bers found on real-world examples of the items being modeled. A few prototypes have been found which used the Lionel production run number which was often applied in the form of hand-cut decals.

- Most prototypes were not wired or otherwise assembled for operation.

- Many prototypes were modified or assembled from other previously mass-produced items.

- Different sides of the item may be decorated differently.

Many prototypes reflect designs that were later mass-produced. For example:

- 0000 Pennsylvania GE EP-5 rectifier electric (produced as number 2352).

- 6464-725 New Haven boxcar made with a gray plastic, orange-painted, never heat-stamped body with black hand-cut decals identical to the regular production, mass-produced lettering and numbering.

- 3376 Bronx Zoo car made from orange plastic 6646 body painted blue with white hand-cut decals, a square opening was hand cut in the roof on one end to allow the giraffe's head and neck to pass through car roof, with die-cast metal giraffe's head and neck attached to car floor with a threaded metal rod inserted in center of giraffe's head and neck and attached to the car's floor with nut on bottom

A Grand Trunk Western GP-9 prototype that was never put into production.

side of floor, and with all other body characteristics of a regular production 6646 stock car body, frame, and trucks.

- Unnumbered and unlettered tan plastic body painted green, one of the first test shots out of a modified 6646 body mold with simulated hatch doors molded in roof and roof opening on one end to allow giraffe's head and neck to pass through the car roof, with die-cast metal giraffe's head and neck attached to car floor with a nut on bottom side of floor holding threaded metal rod inserted in center of giraffe's head and neck. This prototype was produced as the green 3376 Bronx Zoo car.

- Unnumbered, unlettered, and unpainted black plastic 68 executive inspection car with clear plastic windows and unchromed bumpers.

Six boxcars with decaled lettering and two cabooses with heat-stamped lettering. *Top Shelf*: 0000 Hotpoint in red and 0000 Hotpoint in yellow. *Second Shelf*: 3494550 Monon and 6464525 M St L. *Third Shelf*: 0000 B M and 63521 Pacific Fruit Express. *Bottom Shelf*: 6516 Santa Fe caboose and 6017 Boston and Maine Caboose. H. Holden Collection.

Some prototype designs were never put into production, including:

- 0000 Southern Pacific Fairbanks-Morse diesel made for and displayed at the 1954 Toy Fair.
- 2401 (a real-life prototype number) Jersey Central Fairbanks-Morse diesel in olive drab and yellow.
- 0000 Grand Trunk Western GP-9.

The following descriptive listings for prototypes are broken into three sections: unnumbered prototypes, prototypes with "0000" or "0000000" markings, and numbered prototypes.

UNNUMBERED PROTOTYPES LISTING

	Gd	VG	Ex	LN

NO LETTERING: 6464-type boxcar; Type IIB bright blue unpainted plastic body, 1953-type black unpainted plastic door. **NRS**

NO LETTERING: Bronx Zoo car, green-painted tan body mold, with die-cast metal giraffe's head and neck attached to

	Gd	VG	Ex	LN

car floor with a threaded metal rod inserted in center of giraffe's head and neck and attached to the car's floor with a nut on bottom side of floor. This prototype was produced as the green 3376 Bronx Zoo car. J. Sattler Collection. **NRS**

NO LETTERING: 68 executive inspection car; unpainted black plastic with clear plastic windows and non-chromed bumpers. J. Sattler Collection. **NRS**

"0000" AND "0000000" PROTOTYPES LISTING

Items in this section are arranged alphabetically by road name, whether they have "0000" or "0000000" markings.

0000 BURLINGTON: Type III blue plastic body painted red, 1956-type gray plastic door painted red, white decals. H. Holden Collection. **NRS**

0000 (XP476) D & R G W COOKIE BOX: Type IIB blue plastic body painted shiny gloss white, 1956-type blue plastic door painted shiny gloss white, black and red decal lettering, body screws and two tabs painted white. H. Holden Collection. **NRS**

Top Shelf: 0000 M ST L / The Peoria Gateway and 0000 N Y C (XP670). *Second Shelf:* 64640000 (XP572) Tidewater Southern and 0000000 (XP540) Norfolk Southern. *Third Shelf:* 0000000 (XP521) Wabash and NP000 Northern Pacific stock car. *Bottom Shelf:* 0000000 (XP571) Louisville & Nashville / The Old Reliable and 00000000 (XP709) L & N / Dixie Line. H. Holden Collection.

	Gd	VG	Ex	LN

0000000 (XP527) DULUTH, SOUTH SHORE AND ATLANTIC: Type IIB gray plastic painted red and black, 1956-type blue plastic door painted red, white decal lettering, marked "XP476" on underframe. H. Holden Collection. **NRS**

0000 GREAT NORTHERN: Type IV gray plastic body painted green, 1956-type gray plastic door painted green, white and red decal lettering. H. Holden Collection. **NRS**

0000 HOTPOINT: Boxcar; Type IIB body, unpainted white 1956 doors, white-painted body, dark blue "Hotpoint" at upper left of door, smaller "LOOK FOR THAT / HOTPOINT DIFFERENCE" and "LIVE BETTER ELECTRICALLY" circular logo to right of door; "BLT 7-59 / BY LIONEL" to lower left of door, bar-end trucks. Note differences between this prototype and the two other Hotpoint prototypes we list from the former Eddins Collection. T. Klaassen Collection. **NRS**

0000 HOTPOINT: Type IIB gray plastic body painted red and white, 1956-type yellow plastic door painted red, primarily white lettering, different designs on each side.

(A) "LOOK FOR THAT / HOT POINT DIFFERENCE" on upper right side. **NRS**

Lionel also used the short boxcar body for a Pillsbury Flour prototype boxcar.

	Gd	VG	Ex	LN

(B) "LOOK FOR THAT / HOT POINT DIFFERENCE" on upper left side. **NRS**

0000 HOTPOINT: Type III white plastic body painted yellow and black, 1956-type red plastic door painted yellow, black decal lettering, different designs on each side. **NRS**

0000000 (XP571) LOUISVILLE & NASHVILLE: Type IIB gray plastic body painted red, 1956-type yellow plastic door painted red, white decal, underframe marked "XP570". H. Holden Collection. **NRS**

A prototype of the 202 Union Pacific Alco. Note the open portholes and number boards, the "202" decal, and the use of a die-cast frame. The mass-produced "202" had closed portholes, heat-stamped lettering, and a sheet metal frame.

The Lionel 1957 accessory catalogue on page 7 illustrated a locomotive that resembles the factory prototype piece. Note the punched-out portholes and truck details. However, the front skirt was extended on the catalogue illustration example as it was on the mass-produced piece.

	Gd	VG	Ex	LN

0000000 (XP709) LOUISVILLE & NASHVILLE: Type III gray plastic body painted blue, 1953-type red plastic door painted blue, yellow decal lettering. H. Holden Collection. **NRS**

0000 M & ST L: Type I clear plastic body painted green, 1953-type black plastic door painted green, yellow decal lettering. H. Holden Collection. **NRS**

0000 (XP670) N Y C: Type I black plastic body painted chocolate brown with double automobile doors, gray plastic doors painted chocolate brown, white decals. H. Holden Collection. **NRS**

0000 (XP534) N Y C (N Y M X): Type I reefer, white plastic body painted yellow with black stripe, red plastic roof painted aluminum, red plastic door with yellow paint and black stripe, white and black decal. H. Holden Collection. **NRS**

0000000 (XP540) NORFOLK SOUTHERN: Type IIB blue plastic body painted light brown, 1956-type blue plastic door painted light brown, white decal lettering. H. Holden Collection. **NRS**

0000 PILLSBURY FLOUR: Operating boxcar; formerly E. Smith Collection. **NRS**

0000 PILLSBURY FLOUR: Short boxcar; formerly E. Smith Collection. **NRS**

0000 SPOKANE PORTLAND & SEATTLE: Boxcar, decaled numbers and letters, dated 2-57, mounted on AAR trucks. **NRS**

0000000 (XP521) WABASH: Type IIB gray plastic body painted tuscan, 1956-type gray plastic door painted tuscan, white decal lettering. H. Holden Collection. **NRS**

NUMBERED PROTOTYPES LISTING

202 UNION PACIFIC: Unpainted orange plastic cab, embossed "2023-3" on the underside. This was the type of cab used on the earlier Lionel Alcos such as the 2023, 2031, 2032 and 2033 between 1950 and 1954. This cab has a single horn and slotted metal brackets at both ends which retain the swivel fastening tabs from the older Alco frames. The cab has black heat-stamped lettering "BUILT BY / LIONEL" and "UNION PACIFIC" on each side. Beneath the cab windows on each side is a black "202" decal. The cab has three open portholes on each side and openings for the number boards. Note that the later

This is a view of the prototype 202 frame from the inside. Note all the characteristics of the earlier Alco frames: die-cast construction, slots for cab fastening at ends, and battery hole plug for frame intended as a dummy unit. The frame's underside shows the original roller pickups and the screw-attached black identification plate of the earlier frames.

	Gd	VG	Ex	LN

Alco cabs do not have open portholes and letterboards; nor do they have a front hood which extends over the frame. The later cabs are fastened to the stamped-steel frames by a tab at the front and a small screw at the rear.

The frame is a die-cast frame from a 2032 Erie Alco. It is painted black with a yellow stripe along the edge. The unit does not have a motor, E-unit, front coupler, headlight, or horn. It was likely only intended for a shelf display or for photographic purposes. The production 202 came with the later sheet metal frame.

It appears that Lionel used the heat-stamping dies from the 2023 for the side lettering on this prototype 202. The numbers were, however, decals.

In the case of a newly-discovered unusual piece, great care is required to determine if a piece was factory-produced. The current owner of this piece (see accompanying photo) purchased it from a non-collector who had a large accumulation of Lionel trains in original boxes. This piece came without a box. This unit's source supports the hypothesis that it is a factory piece. The combination of the earlier cab and frame assemblies renumbered with a 1957 catalogue number would likely be the most logical way to produce prototypes for the Toy Fair and advance catalogues. The fact that this unit did not have internal parts required for operation also supports its likely use as a prototype. The lack of wheel wear and the overall excellent condition lend support to this piece's creation as a display or photographic piece. A. Weaver Collection. **NRS**

224 UNITED STATES NAVY: Alco A unit; decaled letters and numbers on blue plastic shell. **NRS**

These photos link Lionel factory prototypes to the real world prototypes. Lionel's military/space equipment of the late 1950s and early 1960s was greeted with derision by many model railroaders as representing fantasy, not model railroading. However, a closer look indicates that many of Lionel's unusual rolling stock had real world prototypes. Illustrated above is the real world prototype for the 3665 Minuteman car. The car was built by the American Car and Foundry in Berwick, Pennsylvania. Illustrated at left is possibly the prototype for Lionel's 3330 and 6830 flatcar with submarine. J. Malcovsky photographs.

	Gd	VG	Ex	LN

1011: 25-watt transformer. Wooden casing and large 1033-type handle also made of wood, as shown on page 4 of the 1948 consumer catalogue. The 1949 catalogue shows this transformer with a short handle made of metal, as it was produced. M. Sabatelle Collection. **NRS**

3376 BRONX ZOO: Giraffe car.
(A) 6646 body, made from orange plastic painted blue, with white hand-cut decals, roof hand cut on one end to allow giraffe's head and neck to pass through car roof, with die-cast metal giraffe's head and neck attached to car floor with a nut on bottom side of floor holding threaded metal rod inserted in center of giraffe's head and neck, and with all other body characteristics of a regular production 6646 stock car body, frame, and trucks. J. Sattler Collection. **NRS**

(B) Unpainted tan plastic shell dated "1960" in crayon, black giraffe and track trip. Classification of this piece is difficult. It could be a prototype made before the decision to produce the piece was made or a mock-up after the production decision was made. **NRS**

	Gd	VG	Ex	LN

3386 BRONX ZOO: Bongo and Bobo stock car, "World's Only Performing Giraffes", illustrated on page 39 in *LIONEL: A Collector's Guide and History, Volume IV.* P. Catalano Collection. — — 1300 —

3419 HELICOPTER LAUNCHING CAR: Light gray body, no lettering, white marble plastic 2" winder, clear plastic tail stand, Type A helicopter, early AAR trucks, disc couplers. J. Sattler Collection. **NRS**

3434 POULTRY DISPATCH: Decaled numbers, body was painted blue rather than tuscan red. M. Pfahl Collection. **NRS**

3494-550 MONON: Operating car. Blue plastic body and orange plastic doors painted maroon with decal lettering. **NRS**

3509 LIONEL: Satellite car. Lionel modified a blue 3419 helicopter launching car that was heat-stamped "3419" (but not lettered "LIONEL") by overspraying the car and its number with blue paint which closely matched the original unpainted blue plastic. Lionel's model maker then applied a water-re-

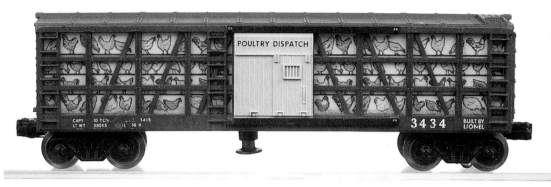

This is the decaled 3434 poultry dispatch car. M. Pfahl Collection.

	Gd	VG	Ex	LN

lease decal with the number "3509" over the old number on both sides. The car has a remote-controlled launching mechanism which is the same as that of the 3419, except that the winding spool has an extension on its neck which is necessary for the satellite. The glued-on extension is slightly smaller in diameter than the base of the neck when compared with the production 3419 and 3519, whose winding spool necks have the same diameter over their entire length. The antenna pedestal is 1/2" shorter than on the production 3519 and has no cast-in panel or rivet detail. A blue car is shown in the 1961 consumer catalogue, but the actual production green car was not shown until 1962. B. Stekoll Collection and comments. **NRS**

3512 LADDER CO.: Firefighting car; black plastic body with gray plastic lamp shell and silver ladder. Metal hand crank is 1/2" wider on each side than regular production model. **NRS**

3619 HELICOPTER RECONNAISSANCE CAR: This car has decaled lettering and utilizes a 3665 body and frame. J. DuVall Collection. **NRS**

3665 U. S. AIR FORCE MINUTEMAN CAR: Red plastic body with three open portholes on one side and two open portholes on other side and with holes for door guides (but no door guides) painted flat white with dark blue plastic roof sections (not raised in middle) painted flat dark blue; unblackened sheet metal frame with non-raising, but operating, missile launching mechanism attached to frame with two screws with nuts on underside of frame; "U. S. AIR FORCE",

"MINUTEMAN", "STRATEGIC AIR COMMAND", "AUTHORIZED PERSONNEL ONLY", and "BUILT BY LIONEL" in dark blue hand-cut decals on both sides; "N3665" under- and over-scored in red hand-cut decals; red and blue Air Force insignia with white star in hand-cut decals; Timken trucks and disc-operating couplers. J. Sattler Collection. (**Note:** For more information on the 3665 prototypes, see the next chapter which begins on page 46. **NRS**

6024-0000 NABISCO SHREDDED WHEAT: Boxcar; prototype. Decaled letters and numbers on one side only, dated 6-57. **NRS**

6076 LEHIGH VALLEY: Short hopper; unpainted shell with Colgate-Palmolive decaled letters and numbers, circa 1964; arch bar trucks with dummy couplers. Formerly E. Smith Collection. **NRS**

6346-56 ALCOA: Decal number "6346-1" at upper left (this is a Lehigh Valley number); all data lines also decals; Alcoa logo is same pressure-sensitive sticker as regular production. Two examples known to exist. This matches the car appearing in the 1956 accessory catalogue. G. Halverson and J. B. Nuzum Collections. — — 1000 —

6464-0000 (XP572) TIDEWATER SOUTHERN: Type IIB blue plastic body painted brown, 1956 blue plastic door painted brown, yellow decal lettering. H. Holden Collection. **NRS**

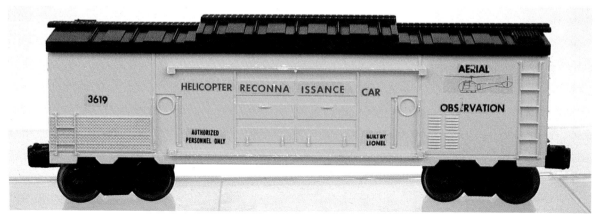

This is the 3619 helicopter reconnaissance car with decaled lettering. It utilizes a 3665 body and frame. J. DuVall Collection.

A very colorful salesman's sample. Before Lionel created the Girls' Set (1587S) as a targeted marketing to girls, it also considered manufacturing a Boys' Set (see 2018 steam locomotive on page 30) in an unusual color scheme. A very limited number of sets were made up and exhibited. Eventually these were given to several Lionel salesmen, who in turn sold them to their clients at modest prices. R. Ford Collection.

	Gd	VG	Ex	LN

6464-50 MINNEAPOLIS & ST LOUIS: Boxcar; Type I light green body, 1953-type doors, green-painted body, gold lettering, black plastic doors painted green, has "BUILT 5-53" on left side of door, unlike production pieces which have no built dates. T. Klaassen Collection. **NRS**

FACTORY MOCK-UPS

A factory mock-up is a one-of-a-kind item, or one of an extremely small number of items, made by the manufacturer before all of the necessary tools, dies, and equipment were available to mass-produce such item or items. This mock-up provides a visual sample of an item already determined for mass-production and was intended to be substantially identical to examples of the item intended for mass-production. Factory mock-ups often share some of the same characteristics as prototypes **except that the decision to produce them has already been made,** probably from the approval of a prior prototype.

Factory mock-ups usually bear a small paper tag which reads: **"This is a factory mock-up not a production item."**

	Gd	VG	Ex	LN

2460 LIONEL LINES: Crane car; cast-aluminum unpainted boom, possible factory mock-up or prototype. L. Krempel Collection. **NRS**

3619 HELICOPTER RECONNAISSANCE CAR: White unpainted plastic body with dark blue unpainted plastic roof sections raised in middle; full helicopter launching mechanism, "3619", "AUTHORIZED PERSONNEL ONLY", "BUILT BY LIONEL", and "AERIAL OBSERVATION" heat stamped on both sides in dark blue; outline of helicopter and "HELICOPTER ... CAR" faintly heat stamped in red on one side of car; outline of helicopter and "HELICOPTER RECONNAISSANCE" faintly heat stamped in red on other side of car; all portholes filled in; Timken trucks and disc-operating couplers. J. Sattler Collection. **NRS**

6464-1 WESTERN PACIFIC: Boxcar; combination of Types I and III body features. No groove on inside of roof at center, as in Type III body; has full rivets but lighter bracing and casting. Possible prototype body mold. T. Klaassen, D. Fergusson, and J. Sattler Collections. **NRS**

SALESMAN'S SAMPLES

A salesman's sample is one of an extremely small number of items made by the manufacturer before mass-produc-

The best known Lionel salesman's sample is the clear cab 2333 Santa Fe diesel. The plastic body, now yellowed with age, permitted the interior mechanism details to be shown. Photograph courtesy of Frank Hare, Iron Horse Productions.

	Gd	VG	Ex	LN

tion began for demonstration or use by salesmen. Examples are listed below.

726: 2-8-4 Berkshire steam locomotive with the number "726" applied as a decal on cab (rather than rubber-stamped or heat-stamped) and with a red (rather than black) plastic brushplate assembly (Part No. 2020M-30). According to T. Klaassen, a small number of these engines were produced as pre-production samples for use by salesmen at toy shows. However, the red brushplates may also be due to a temporary materials shortage Lionel faced in 1947; other evidence of use of red brushplates is found on the 2332 GG-1 and 671 Pennsylvania turbine from that period. The decal on this example shows that mass-production had not yet begun because Lionel rubber-stamped items used for mass-production examples. T. Klaassen Collection. — — — **1000**

2018 LIONEL LINES: 2-6-4 steam locomotive from the Boys' Set; medium blue, white numbers heat stamped on cab side, headlight, smoke unit, three-position reverse; medium blue 1130T tender, bar-end trucks, magnetic tab coupler. A set containing this locomotive and four cars was sold by Greenberg Auctions in November 1988. See also X6014, 6427, 6456, 6462. Price for set: — — — **23,000**

2055 LIONEL LINES: 4-6-4 steam locomotive; medium blue, white numbers heat-stamped on cab sides, headlight, smoke unit, three-position reverse; medium blue 6026T tender, white "LIONEL LINES" heat-stamped on tender sides, bar-end trucks, magnetic tab couplers. **NRS**

2332 PENNSYLVANIA: Pennsylvania GG1 with red brushplate. **NRS**

2333 SANTA FE: F-3 with clear cab; these locomotives were shown by Lionel salesmen to dealers. **NRS**

X6014 BABY RUTH: From Boys' Set, boxcar, brown-painted red Type I body, white lettering. See also 2018 for details. **NRS**

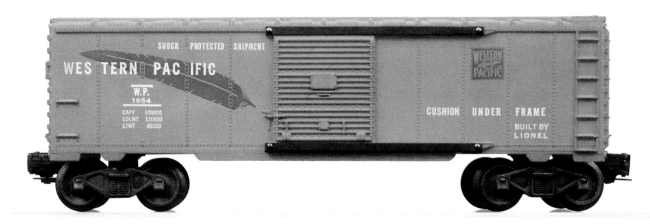

The 6464 orange Western Pacific boxcar was probably made as a salesman's sample with "1954" on the sides rather than "6464-100". Four or five are known to exist and all have Type I bodies. A car marked "1953" is illustrated on a one-page insert in the 1954 Lionel advance catalogue.

This is likely a salesman's sample of the 2332 GG1 with red brushplate assembly.

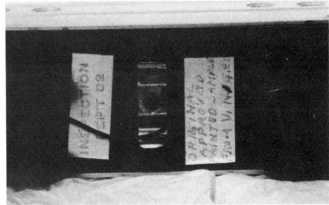

A car with a paint sample approval sticker and a close-up of the sticker.

	Gd	VG	Ex	LN

6427 LIONEL LINES: From Boys' Set, N5C caboose, light greenish-blue body, red lettering, "64273" on side. See also 2018 for details. **NRS**

6456 NORFOLK AND WESTERN: From Boys' Set, hopper, medium blue-painted black Type III body, bar-end trucks, magnetic couplers; the N & W lettering is similar to that used on the 3456 operating hopper, except it is lettered "LIONEL 56" rather than "LIONEL 3456". See also 2018 for details. **NRS**

6462 NEW YORK CENTRAL: From Boys' Set, gondola, gray-painted black Type IIa body, bar-end trucks, one magnetic coupler, one magnetic tab coupler. See also 2018 for details. **NRS**

6464 WESTERN PACIFIC: Boxcar; orange with small blue feather with the number "1954" rather than the regular mass-production number "6464-100". **NRS**

PAINT OR COLOR SAMPLES

A paint or color sample is a one-of-a-kind item or one of an extremely small number of items made after all of the necessary tools, dies, or equipment were available to mass-produce such an item and made either before or after mass-production began. This allowed decision makers to see what such an item would look like and to allow them to make production and marketing decisions concerning the colors of numbers, lettering, or logos or the entire color scheme of the item that would be mass-produced.

A paint or color sample will have one or more of the following characteristics which will distinguish it from any prototype and from any similar mass-produced item:

- Numbers, lettering, or logos will be applied by customary mass-production methods of application.
- Except for the colors of numbers, lettering, logos, and/or color scheme, it will be identical to mass-produced items.

PAINT OR COLOR SAMPLE LISTINGS

- 3454 PRR automatic merchandise car with red numbers and lettering rather than blue numbers and lettering. We have classified this car as a paint sample but it could also be a limited production variation or factory error depending on the factory's intent.
- 6464-1 silver Western Pacific boxcar with red numbers and lettering rather than blue numbers and lettering. This could be a limited-production variation.
- 6464-175 silver Rock Island boxcar with black numbers and lettering rather than blue numbers and lettering. This could be a limited-production variation.
- 6464-525 Minneapolis & St. Louis boxcar with yellow numbers, lettering, and logo rather than white numbers, lettering, and logo. The yellow markings could possibly be a result of a chemical alteration.
- 6464-525 Minneapolis & St. Louis boxcar with purple-painted gray body and silver numbers, lettering, and logo rather than a red body and white numbers, lettering, and logo.

If a paint or color sample was selected for regular mass-production, any surviving examples of such a paint or color sample, by our definition, will be indistinguishable from regular mass-produced examples and therefore should command no greater value than a regular mass-produced example.

If, however, a paint or color sample was not selected for regular mass-production, it will be easily and readily distinguishable from regular mass-produced examples of the same item and will command a significantly greater value than any regular mass-produced example because of its obvious difference, and its rarity or scarcity.

On page 10 of the 1950 Lionel catalogue, the 622 diesel switcher was illustrated with New York Central markings. The engine was actually made with "A. T. & S. F" markings (see listing under 622 Santa Fe). The engine above may be the painted lettering sample for the catalogue illustration. N. Brueckl Collection.

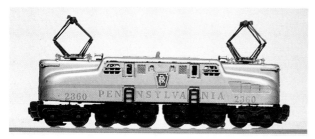

Lionel experimented with paint schemes for its 2360 GG1. The silver version paint sample *(shown above)* was never put into production. S. Robinson Collection.

	Gd	VG	Ex	LN

All paint or color samples are rare or scarce depending upon the actual number made.

60 LIONELVILLE: Trolley.
(A) With dark red lettering. D. Brill and J. Ranker Collections. **NRS**

(B) With green lettering. J. Sattler Collection. **NRS**

(C) Two-piece bumper, black lettering, people on strips in door, front and back windows, "PERRY ST. — EAST" in one end window on top and "NEAL ST — LOCAL" in other top end window. T. Klaassen Collection. **NRS**

229 MINNEAPOLIS & ST. LOUIS: Alco A unit only, olive drab body. G. Wilson Collection. **NRS**

622 SANTA FE: NW-2 switcher, not catalogued as Santa Fe but as "NEW YORK CENTRAL" (or "LIONEL"); never manufactured. **NRS**

1061: Steam locomotive, 0-4-0, drive rods, operating headlight with lens, no tires, "1061" decal over blackened heat-stamped "1060", no reverse unit, plastic side motor with rolled steel pickups, unlettered slope-back tender with arch bar trucks and fixed coupler, tender was originally lettered "LIONEL LINES",

	Gd	VG	Ex	LN

but this was blackened out; came in set with unlettered mold 6511-2 blue flatcar with orange girder, unlettered red-painted black plastic SP-type caboose with black-tabbed frame and no end rails, also has one AAR truck with no coupler and one arch bar truck with fixed coupler; 1025 transformer, four pieces of straight track and lockon. The train was mounted on a display board with screws to keep the train in place. This display board is 43-1/4" x 3-5/8" x 1-1/4". The advance catalogue set, 11415, came in a corrugated box lettered "MADE BY/THE LIONEL CORPORATION/NEW YORK N. Y." The box dimensions are 43-1/4" x 3-5/8" x 5". **NRS**

2037-500: Steam locomotive, pink, 2-6-4. 6026 square-type tender, only a few known to exist. Formerly H. Degano Collection. **— — — 1500**

2522 PRESIDENT HARRISON: Vista Dome passenger car.
(A) Top gold strip marked "GRILLE" in black serif lettering at both ends of cars. T. Klaassen Collection. **NRS**

(B) Top gold strip marked "PARLOR" in black serif lettering at both ends of car and number "2345" is present in door window in large serif numbers. T. Klaassen Collection. **NRS**

2625 IRVINGTON: Pullman passenger car. Window inserts with silhouetted people, but "LIONEL LINES" painted over in matching tuscan, yellow decal "PENNSYLVANIA" road markings above roof, yellow decal numbers over tuscan-painted, heat-stamped numbers. We would like reader comments as to whether these cars were converted outside the factory or actual factory production as part of a special set. Some readers believe that these cars were custom painted for Madison Hardware in the 1950s. J. J. Frank, Jr. Collection. **NRS**

(3349) TURBO MISSILE LAUNCHING CAR: Flatcar. "3349 LIONEL 3349" appears on the side of the car, as it did in catalogue illustrations. S. Robinson Collection. **NRS**

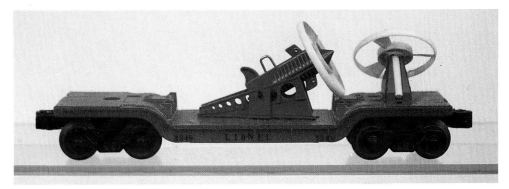

3349 was produced without its catalogue number on its side. However, at least one piece (*shown above*), and probably several more, were made stamped "3349 LIONEL 3349". S. Robinson Collection.

	Gd	VG	Ex	LN

3360 BURRO: Crane with brown cab. L. Bohn and J. Sattler observations. **NRS**

3444 ERIE: Gondola. Cop chases hobo, vibrator motor, unpainted red plastic body with white lettering, but clear unpainted plastic crates. Piker Collection. **NRS**

3454 P R R MERCHANDISE CAR: Similar to regular production car, but red numbers and lettering rather than blue. J. Sattler Collection. **NRS**

3459 LIONEL LINES: Operating dump car. Yellow-painted body with black heat-stamped lettering, rare, as illustrated on the cover of *Science Illustrated* magazine, December 1948 issue. E. Dougherty Collection. **NRS**

3469 LIONEL LINES: Operating coal dump car; black body with gold heat-stamped lettering instead of usual white. M. Sabatelle Collection. **NRS**

3927 LIONEL LINES: Track cleaning car. Unpainted dark green plastic body, white rubber-stamped lettering. The plastic pellets used in the injection-molding machines are available in different colors. Lionel was consistent in using

Two unusual series boxcars. The upper car, Western Pacific 6464-1, has red lettering; the lower car, Rock Island 6464-175, has black lettering. Both cars usually have blue lettering. H. Holden Collection.

	Gd	VG	Ex	LN

the same color pellets for its production runs. This unusual car was likely produced by the factory before its major production run, to compare alternative color schemes. A. Otten Collection. **NRS**

6014 PILLSBURY: Boxcar, not manufactured. E. Smith Collection. **NRS**

X6014 BABY RUTH P R R: Boxcar. Orange, Type I body, blue lettering, "Baby Ruth" in solid letters, bar-end trucks with tab couplers, extra hole in activator plate, round-head rivet, trucks attached with clips. J. Mayer Collection. **NRS**

6050 LIONEL SAVINGS BANK: Boxcar, coin slot, white body, red lettering, green bank and windows, letters and logos all decals, AAR trucks, two disc couplers, large "BUILT BY LIONEL". B. Hudzik Collection. **NRS**

6076 LEHIGH VALLEY: Hopper. No number, gold with gold lettering, black body, white-lettered "CAPY 100000 LD LMT 128300 CU FT 1860", no "BLT" date, no "NEW" number, AAR trucks. R. Schreiner Collection. **NRS**

6356-1 N Y C: Stock car. Gold-painted body, silver-painted roof, unpainted black doors. J. Algozzini Collection. **NRS**

6427-60 VIRGINIAN: (B)N5C caboose, with white lettering. J. Sattler Collection. **NRS**

6436-500 LEHIGH VALLEY: Quad hopper. Burgundy-painted, white heat-stamped lettering, "NEW 3-55", metal spreader bar; Lionel pre-production paint sample. H. Degano Collection. **— — 1000 —**

6346-56 ALCOA: Covered hopper; dark red deep heat-stamped lettering and numbering instead of blue. G. Halverson Collection. **— — 1000 —**

6440/6440/6441: Passenger cars painted silver with medium green-painted window and door inserts (same color green as regular production 6440-6441 car bodies) and with heat-stamped blue letters and numbers (same color combination as the regular production silver 3459 operating dump car and the regular production X3454 operating merchandise car). J. Sattler Collection. **NRS**

6445 FORT KNOX GOLD RESERVE: Boxcar, bank, gold-painted plastic with silver bullion. **NRS**

6463 ROCKET FUEL: Blue tank car with two domes and white lettering. W. Eddins Collection. **NRS**

An unusual boxcar and an unusual engine. The 6464-225 Southern Pacific boxcar usually has a yellow-outlined arrow on the right side. The car above has a solid yellow arrow. Some 2360 GG1s were specially painted in black for Bill Vagell, a long-time Lionel dealer. H. Holden Collection.

	Gd	VG	Ex	LN

6464-1 WESTERN PACIFIC: Boxcar.
(A) Clear plastic body painted silver with very heavy blue heat-stamped lettering on one side only; body is Type I, but has roof ribbing on inside which differs from usual Type III or IV ribbing. The body mold has features of a Type I exterior and a Type III or IV roof interior and may have been an experimental body mold that Lionel was considering. Some authorities believe that the earliest Type I cars were made with ribbed roofs. R. M. Caplan and J. Sattler Collections. **NRS**

(B) Silver boxcar, similar to regular production but red numbers and lettering rather than blue. This could be a limited-production variation. J. Sattler Collection. **NRS**

(C) Orange body and door, white lettering. **NRS**

(D) Dark orange body and doors, silver lettering; rare. R. M. Caplan Collection. — — 1600 —

6464-50 MINNEAPOLIS & ST PAUL: Boxcar. Flat green with gold lettering, white plastic body. **NRS**

6464-100 WESTERN PACIFIC: Boxcar. Type I body, flat orange body and door paint, blue feather, numbered "1954" instead of usual 6464-100, four examples known.

— — 2000 —

6464-175 ROCK ISLAND: Boxcar, similar to regular production item, but black numbers and lettering rather than blue. This could be a limited-production variation. J. Sattler Collection. **NRS**

6464-375 CENTRAL OF GEORGIA: Boxcar, painted gray and silver, all decal lettering, lettering matches Advance Catalogue production which is different from production.

NRS

6464-500 TIMKEN: Boxcar.
(A) All decal lettering in shades of black; "6464- 000". **NRS**

(B) Yellow body paint; red heat-stamped lettering.

— — 1200 —

6464-525 MINNEAPOLIS & ST LOUIS: Boxcar.
(A) Similar to regular production item, but numbers, lettering,

A paint sample for the 6830 flatcar with non-operating submarine; this car provides some interesting analysis. It utilized the body mold that was developed for the 6805 atomic energy disposal car; note the die modification at the flatcar ends into which Super O track rails were fitted. Also, this example was painted blue over a red body mold. The production run used an unpainted blue flatcar (usually mold 6511-2) that had stake holes along the sides into which were fitted two shaped pieces of thick gauge wire, needed to hold the submarine onto the car. B. Myles Collection.

	Gd	VG	Ex	LN

and logo in bright bold yellow rather than white. The yellow markings could possibly be a result of chemical alteration, but they give no appearance of any post-factory alteration. J. Sattler Collection. **NRS**

(B) Purple-painted gray body; silver numbers, lettering, and logo. Regular production item has red body with white markings. J. Sattler Collection. **NRS**

6464-725 NEW HAVEN: Boxcar. Copyright circle with "C" in middle located within left inside crook of "N" in "NH" logo. Authenticity not confirmed. M. Pfahl Collection. **NRS**

6517-75 ERIE: Bay window caboose, orange-painted plastic, one of three known Lionel preproduction color samples; car base rubber- stamped "6517-75" and "LIONEL" in silver. Formerly H. Degano Collection. **NRS**

6530 FIREFIGHTING INSTRUCTION CAR: Boxcar, black plastic body. — — 750 —

6812 TRACK MAINTENANCE CAR: Flatcar with all-gold superstructure. J. Algozzini Collection. **NRS**

6830 LIONEL: Flatcar with non-operating submarine; blue-painted 6805 body mold. **NRS**

POST-FACTORY OR CHEMICALLY-ALTERED CARS

Because of the high prices that legitimate paint or color samples command, certain unscrupulous (or worse) elements of the train collecting hobby have in the past few years attempted to "create" paint or color samples by various techniques to sell at high prices. The observations of Charles Weber, a chemist and long-time train collector, follow:

Recently, certain postwar equipment has been offered for sale at train meets in some very unusual colors. It is the opinion of some knowledgeable collectors that these cars have been subjected to a chemical process which altered the body color and/or the color of the lettering. These cars are not legitimate Lionel paint or color samples.

Chemically-altered cars are nothing but fakes and should be understood and treated as such. In the view of some authorities these cars have no collectable value, yet others feel that they have modest to moderate value as conversation pieces.

Some known examples of the following cars are known to have been affected by chemical processes. Several more

The 6464-825 Alaska Railroad boxcar with white lettering and markings is a controversial car. Some collectors believe it to be original, others believe it to be chemically altered. H. Holden Collection.

Lionel made up special cars *(above)* for public relations purposes. *Top Shelf:* 6445 Fort Knox Gold Reserve mint car with wooden base stamped "JALICO / A JUNIOR ACHIVEMENT CO..." and Corn Products Company boxcar with bank slot. *Second Shelf:* Gray Parker Kalon General American and black Parker Kalon General American. *Third Shelf:* Clemco Aero Products and Hathaway-Denver. *Bottom Shelf:* M. Steinthal & Co. H. Holden Collection.

may exist, so the collector is advised to exercise great care in the purchase of any car which is significantly different from regular mass-produced examples. Some legitimate color samples and cars with different colors of lettering exist as well, so the introduction of these chemically-altered cars has caused confusion in the marketplace.

Examples of the following cars which were normally produced with painted yellow or orange bodies have been chemically treated to change the yellow- or orange-painted surfaces to white or off-white without disturbing the normal shade or color of the original black lettering:

- 2454 Baby Ruth boxcar
- 3562-50 A T & S F operating barrel car (painted variation only)
- 3656 Lionel Lines operating cattle car
- 6356-1 N Y C stock car
- 6454 A T & S F boxcar
- 6454 N Y C boxcar
- 6464-725 New Haven boxcar
- 6656 Lionel Lines stock car

There is also the 3454 P R R automatic merchandise car that is usually silver, but may be chemically-treated to turn gold.

Cars which were normally produced with yellow heat-stamped lettering have had the original yellow lettering chemically altered to white or off-white:

- 3356 Santa Fe Railway Express operating horse car with green body and white lettering (note, however, that a car with this color combination appears in the 1959 Lionel consumer catalogue and it is not certain that all examples of such cars have been chemically altered).
- 6464-825 Alaska boxcar with white lettering and/or white stripe just below the roof. There is a substantial dispute as to whether some or all of the cars with white markings were chemically changed from yellow. Two authorities, Dr. Charles Weber and Joe Algozzini, state: "None of the Alaska boxcars with some or all-white markings have been proven to be frauds." However, Dr. Weber reports that a person known to have sold chemically-altered cars did sell Alaska boxcars with some or all-white markings. One Alaska boxcar with all-white markings, formerly from the W. Eddin's Collection, has been recently examined by Bruce Greenberg using high-powered magnification. No traces of yellow pigment were visible. In some cases of chemically-altered cars, such examination may reveal specks of yellow pigment amidst the white pigments. However, this test is not conclusive. The chemical analy-

During the late 1950s or early 1960s, Lionel sponsored a local Junior Achievement Company of high school students who had some role in the manufacturing of these banks which were based on either the 3435 aquarium car or the 6445 Ft. Knox car. The car bodies were mounted on a base and sold as savings banks. The photo below shows the name of the Junior Achievement Company as "JALICO". (JA= Junior Achievement, LI= Lionel, and CO= Company). The Junior Achievement cars are gold painted; the regular 6445 Fort Knox cars are silver painted. Another car of this type is owned by Joe Algozzini and is marked "JANELCO". R. P. Kimball and S. Kimball comments.

	Gd	VG	Ex	LN

sis of samples of the white markings provides a conclusive test.

The Alaska boxcar appears in the 1959 Lionel catalogue on page 23 with a white Eskimo and yellow lettering. It appears again in the 1960 Lionel catalogue on page 8 with white lettering at the bottom of the car.

The 6356 stock car (this also applies to the 6656) has been found with either a white body or white lettering on normal orange or yellow body:

6356-1 N Y C: Stock car. White-painted body (reported as ivory, but probable color fade), unpainted black doors. J. Algozzini Collection. **NRS**

CORPORATE PUBLIC RELATIONS

On several occasions Lionel made up special cars for public relations purposes. These cars were used either to pro-

	Gd	VG	Ex	LN

mote Lionel and/or its affiliates in the business world or to create good will in the community.

4810 SOUTHERN PACIFIC: FM Trainmaster, black body, red stripe. L. Shempp Collection. **NRS**

6445 FORT KNOX GOLD RESERVE: Mint Car.
(A) Gold-painted body with unpainted, clear windows, no heat-stamped lettering. Production for Junior Achievement with "JALICO / A JUNIOR ACHIEVEMENT CO. / SPONSORED BY / LIONEL CORP" stamped in dark blue on blue blotter paper on the underneath. H. Holden and J. Algozzini Collections. **NRS**

(B) Similar to (A), but with "JANELCO / A JUNIOR ACHIEVEMENT CO / SPONSORED BY / LIONEL CORP" stamped on the underneath. J. Algozzini Collection. **NRS**

CORN PRODUCTS COMPANY: Boxcar; 8-1/2" long; unpainted Type III red plastic body with double doors that do not open. Circular white and orange CP (Corn Products) decal on left, rectangular gray and white decal on right, early AAR trucks with disc couplers. One version is rubber stamped

Lionel produced the 6572 R E A car with a dark green body, subdued gold lettering, and an aluminum cover which slid back and forth. However, this pre-production example *(above)* has a medium green body, very bright gold lettering, and a piece of aluminum foil rather than the sliding plate. S. Robinson Collection.

	Gd	VG	Ex	LN

"JACPOT / A JUNIOR ACHIEVEMENT CORP" on the underside, another version is not stamped. J. Algozzini and H. Holden Collections. **NRS**

PROMOTIONAL CARS

The following cars were produced to advertise Lionel's subsidiaries — not to make a manufacturing decision.

PARKER KALON: Type IIB black or gray plastic body, 1956-type unpainted orange plastic door, decal lettering, "PARKER-KALON / GENERAL / AMERICAN" on left of door and "GENUINE PK SELF TAPPING SCREWS" on right of door, early AAR trucks, disc couplers. Reportedly shown at 1964 Toy Fair. These represent a limited production run. J. Algozzini and H. Holden Collections. **NRS**

PARKER KALON: Type IIB, unpainted gray plastic body, 1956-type unpainted black plastic door, decal lettering "PARKER- KALON / GENERAL / AMERICAN" on left of door, early AAR trucks, disc couplers.   —   —   **700**   —

CLEMCO AERO PRODUCTS INC: Type IV gray plastic body painted red, 1956-type gray plastic door painted red, paper label loosely fastened on car. Reportedly shown at 1964 Toy Fair. **NRS**

HATHAWAY DENVER: Type IV gray plastic body painted red, then blue, 1956-type gray plastic door painted red then blue, paper label loosely fastened on car, "6464(F)" does not appear on the car. Reportedly shown at 1964 Toy Fair. **NRS**

M. STEINTHAL & Co: Type IV opaque plastic body painted red, then white, 1956-type opaque plastic door painted white, paper label loosely fastened on car. Reportedly shown at 1964 Toy Fair. **NRS**

PERSONAL FAVORS

From time to time, the factory has created special products for special people. William Vagell, who died in 1987, was a long-time Lionel dealer. Reportedly Lionel specially painted a number of 2360 solid stripe GG-1s for Mr. Vagell. See the following entry:

2360: GG-1 electric, black body with one large gold stripe, decal lettering, rough surface on body casting shows through paint, repainted and lettered by Lionel for William Vagell. **NRS**

Other personal favors include the 6464-500 Timken boxcars made by MPC for Glen Uhl in 1970:

6464-500 TIMKEN: Boxcar, marked "BLT 1-71 BY LIONEL MPC":
(A) Green body paint; white heat-stamped lettering.   —   —   **750**   —
(B) Same as (N), but gold heat-stamped lettering.   —   —   **750**   —
(C) Same as (N), except red lettering.   —   —   **850**   —

Observations

Roger Bartelt has made a number of observations which can be applied to any unusual item. His observations are in the form of questions which should be considered when any such items are being considered for purchase:

- Does the item make sense?

- Is there any discernible, rational reason why the particular set of components should have been combined to make this particular item?

- Are all of the materials used contemporary with, or prior to, the indicated date such item was made?

- Are all of the components in the item from the manufacturer in question? It would be highly unlikely that Lionel would make a prototype using some other manufacturer's parts.

- Is there any evidence other than the item itself which indicates that the item is a genuine prototype such as, but not limited to, letters, factory engineering tags, or archives tags?

Due precisely to the fact that such items have commanded prices many times higher than similar items mass-produced in regular production runs, many examples of such items have appeared in the train-collecting markets during the last several years and are highly suspect. Great caution must be exercised when considering the purchase of one of these high-priced items.

Knowledge of the honesty, integrity, and reliability of the seller of any such item, coupled with insisting upon a written money-back guarantee if the item later proves to be a fake, are two steps in the right direction. Even these steps are not entirely satisfactory, however, because of the great difficulty in proving what is and what is not a fake and because of the diversity of opinion even among experienced collectors as to the authenticity of such items.

A full and unconditional money-back guarantee from the seller for return of the item is a good idea, but it is doubtful that many sellers (especially if they entertained any doubt about the authenticity of the item themselves) would be willing to give guarantees. These items are in such demand that other buyers might forego any guarantee. What it all comes down to in many cases is "you pay your money, and you take your chances."

	Gd	VG	Ex	LN

Rare and very desirable specials made for N & W are the 6446-25 hoppers:

6446-25 N & W: Quad hopper, not catalogued.

	Gd	VG	Ex	LN
(A) Gold with white lettering.	—	—	1000	—
(B) Pink with black lettering.	—	—	1000	—
(C) Light blue plastic painted light blue, white lettering.	—	—	1000	—
(D) Same as (G), but with covers and center brace holes.	—	—	1000	—
(E) Silver with white lettering.	—	—	1000	—

J. Algozzini reports that Lionel made a 6572 Railway Express car for Madison Hardware in 1964, a GG1 for La Rue Shempp, and special cars for Joe Ranker, Ed Rosenthal, Bill Eddins, and Elliott Smith.

FACTORY VARIATIONS

It is important to distinguish a **factory variation** from a **factory error**.

A "factory variation" is the result of an intended change in the production process. The mental state of the factory personnel is a critical part of the definition. Since we will probably never know what the mental state of the factory personnel in fact was, the distinction between a factory variation and a factory error in most cases will be nothing more than a sound and logical assumption.

Most factory variations made by Lionel occurred because of an intentional decision to make it easier or less expensive to manufacture its products.

In almost all instances, where a variation exists, the chronological sequence will be from a more complete or complicated item to a less complete or "stripped-down" version or one which is easier or less expensive to manufacture. Sometimes a variation exists because of a need to correct a defect in or make a change to an earlier version.

By way of example, most early postwar rolling stock had metal steps which were formed by cutting away material from the sheet metal frame and bending the remaining "steps" into shape.

When the decision was made to eliminate the steps, a considerable savings both in material and labor was realized without sacrificing realism to any great degree. Thereby, a "variation" was created by virtue of the intentional decision to make the item in a way which was different from the earlier version.

Some variations involve only very small deviations from a previous item. The change from staple-end trucks to bar-end trucks created a collectable "variation." The elimination of parts, such as brakewheels, also created a "variation." One major difference, for example, between a Lionel 2452 gondola and Lionel 2452X Pennsylvania gondola is the absence of a brakewheel on the "X" version.

The use of an "X" by Lionel, either on the item itself, or the box in which it was packed, meant a change or a "variation" from the normal or regular production run of the item.

On postwar tenders, the "X" will often appear, and it usually indicates the absence of such minor parts as handrails.

It is sometimes difficult to determine whether an item is a "factory variation" or a "factory error." Two examples will illustrate. A limited number of early production 2332 Pennsylvania GG1s were painted black. The Pennsylvania Railroad, however, painted their GG1s a dark green (called Brunswick green), which could appear to be black in a different light. Soon after Lionel's production commenced, Lionel changed the color of its GG1s from black to Brunswick green.

Was this change because painting the GG1s black rather than green was unintended? If unintended, Lionel created a factory error. Or was the change to black from Brunswick green an intended change in the production process thereby creating a "factory variation?"

In the late 1950s Lionel produced the 53 Denver & Rio Grande snowplow. Most examples have the "a" in Grande upside down and backwards. We may safely assume that Lionel did not intend to print an upside down and backwards "a". However, there are no factory personnel available to verify this assumption. Without having this mistake pointed out, most people will not notice it. Lionel did not notice the mistake until late in the production process and corrected it by creating a new and different heat-stamped die with the "a" in its correct position.

The corrected "a" variation is much more difficult to find than the incorrect "a" variation. Thus, by not discovering the mistake earlier, all of the first version (which appears to constitute the vast majority of 53 snowplows) are factory errors, while the small portion with the correct "a" are factory variations, because they came about as a result of an intended change in the production process. The application of our definition of factory variation and factory error may lead to some unusual conclusions!

Factory variations are highly collectable and add great interest and complexity to the train-collecting hobby.

Some collectors are willing to pay the much higher prices generally asked for Lionel items such as prototypes, factory mock-ups, salesman's samples, as well as many factory variations which differ in some significant way from those which were mass-produced in regular production runs. These collectors are involved in what is the riskiest specialty of all.

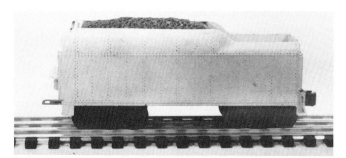

An unmarked Girls' Train tender. Authenticating this piece is very difficult.

FACTORY VARIATION LISTINGS

There will be no listing of factory variations in this portion of the book because all of the factory variations are listed in listings of the regular production items. Unless there is no known factory variation of a particular item, it would require a reproduction of the entire Volume I to list all known factory variations in this chapter.

FACTORY ERRORS

A factory error is a one-of-a-kind item, or one of an extremely small number of items, made by the manufacturer after all of the necessary tools, dies, and equipment were made or available to mass-produce such item or items and made after mass-production began which varies or departs in some significant way from the mass-produced examples of the item because of an unintended mistake in the production process.

Examples of factory errors are:

- 59 MINUTEMAN SWITCHER with lettering only on one side.

Which of the two 53 Rio Grandes has the upside down and backwards "a"? Now note the close-up of the upside down and backwards "a".

- 59 MINUTEMAN SWITCHER with lettering on both sides, but star emblem missing.
- 59 MINUTEMAN SWITCHER with no lettering and no emblem on either side.
- 645 UNION PACIFIC NW-2 SWITCHER with no lettering or numbering on one side.
- 3454 P R R AUTOMATIC MERCHANDISE CAR with numbers and lettering only on one side.

A factory error is the result of an unintended mistake which either escaped detection in the quality-control process or which was rejected by the factory for sale, but was later recovered and used. While factory errors are much more difficult to find than correct regular mass-produced items, their value should not approach anything near the value of an item which was intended to be made such as a prototype, salesman's sample, or paint or color sample. Some factory errors, when originally found, were only shells without frames and trucks. Dealers and collectors have frequently mounted these shells on frames and trucks. One type of factory error is caused by the failure to letter one side. These cars often escaped detection and were sold with trucks in normal trade. Cars that are not lettered on either side are probably plastic shells that were rejected prior to marking.

FACTORY ERROR LISTINGS

Steam Locomotives

	Gd	VG	Ex	LN

1062 LIONEL LINES: Steam locomotive; no lettering or numbering on either engine or tender. It could also be a 1061. J. Algozzini Collection. **NRS**

1656 LIONEL LINES: 0-4-0 steam switcher with 6403 slope-back tender; tender mis-stamped "6043B" on bottom. I. D. Smith observation. **NRS**

2037-500 LIONEL LINES: 2-6-4 steam engine, "Girls' Train" variant; no numbers or letters on either engine or tender. Formerly Louis Napoliello Collection, now J. Algozzini Collection. **NRS**

Diesels, Electrics, and Other Powered Units

53 RIO GRANDE: Snowplow, one yellow guardrail installed in reverse so that it is flush against the snowplow's body. B. J. Collins Collection. **NRS**

55 TIE-JECTOR: No lettering on either side, probable factory error. P. Catalano observation.

— — 325 —

58 GREAT NORTHERN: Rotary snowplow, unpainted green cab sides, no logo. R. Pauli Collection. **NRS**

59 MINUTEMAN SWITCHER
(A) Lettering only on one side. J. Algozzini Collection. **NRS**

(B) Lettering is present, but star emblem is missing. J. Algozzini Collection. **NRS**

(C) "U. S. AIR FORCE" on both sides, but one blank cab side and number "59" and only small part of insignia on other.

The unlettered 231 Rock Island Alco A unit.

One of the most commonly found Lionel factory errors is the 645 diesel without lettering on one side.

	Gd	VG	Ex	LN

Further examples of factory errors requested. J. Algozzini Collection. **NRS**

(D) No lettering or emblems on either side, unpainted white plastic cab. J. Algozzini Collection. **NRS**

231 ROCK ISLAND: Alco A unit.

(A) No lettering or numbering on either side. Formerly W. Eddins Collection. **NRS**

(B) Black-painted body, but without lettering and white upper stripe. Motor type not known. — — **150** —

232 NEW HAVEN: Alco A unit; on one side, black in the "H" of the "NH" logo carries upward to form a narrow stripe on the bottom of the white "N". G. Halverson Collection. **NRS**

520 BOX CAB ELECTRIC: Restamped on one side to form double letter image. S. Blotner Collection. **NRS**

611 JERSEY CENTRAL: NW-2 switcher; no lettering or numbering on either side. J. Algozzini Collection. **NRS**

613 UNION PACIFIC: NW-2 switcher; no lettering or numbering on either side. J. Algozzini Collection. **NRS**

622 SANTA FE: Diesel, not catalogued as Santa Fe. Small "GM" decal on lower front side of motor hood, weight cast in cab frame, but no "622". J. Kovach observation.

— — **275** —

635 UNION PACIFIC: NW-2 switcher.

(A) No lettering on one side. E. Kraemer observation. **NRS**

(B) No number on front. E. Kraemer observation. **NRS**

645 UNION PACIFIC: NW-2 switcher; lettered only on one side. J. Algozzini, J. Breslin, and R. Mertes Collections. This is one of the most common factory errors. **NRS**

2028 PENNSYLVANIA: GP-7 diesel; double-stamped on one side. J. Algozzini Collection. **NRS**

2041 ROCK ISLAND: Alco AA units, 1969, no lettering or white striping.

There are two possibilities concerning the production of these unmarked shells, which seem to be rather commonplace. One is that since this locomotive was a 1969 product, Lionel's last year, many of these shells were never finished and were left over when the factory changed hands. If that is the case, it is highly likely that these were acquired by a dealer and sold off.

The other hypothesis involves the heavy plastic stress marking on the noses of these shells. It is possible that these shells were rejected and later acquired by a dealer. In either case, these shells are often found mounted on Alco chassis with added trim pieces. They are among the more commonly avail-

able factory error shells. The regularly marked cab shells may actually be harder to find than these unmarked shells. H. Degano and R. LaVoie Collections. **NRS**

2322 VIRGINIAN: Fairbanks-Morse Trainmaster.

(A) No number or decal on either side. J. Algozzini Collection.

NRS

(B) Blue body painted yellow (with unpainted blue stripe), but decal number and logo on cab sides are under windows rather than on both ends. — — **575** —

2331 VIRGINIAN: Fairbanks-Morse diesel; lettered only on one side. R. Lord Collection. **NRS**

2338 MILWAUKEE: GP-7 road switcher. Black plastic shell painted with dull orange band, but "BUILT BY / LIONEL" missing from orange stripe and Milwaukee logo on cab is white on black background. W. Heid Collection. **NRS**

2339 WABASH: GP-9 diesel; no lettering or decals on either side. J. Algozzini Collection. **NRS**

2343C SANTA FE: F-3 dummy B unit, silver body with red, yellow, and black trim. Screen roof vents, but without Indian Head emblem on either side. P. Pesanka Collection. **NRS**

2346 BOSTON AND MAINE: GP-9 diesel; white unpainted plastic; GP-9 fan shroud known to be original. A. Arpino Collection. **NRS**

2348 MINNEAPOLIS & ST LOUIS: GP-9 diesel.

(A) Painted red body with blue roof and white stripe, but has black-painted 2329 rectifier metal chassis. C. Rohlfing Collection. **NRS**

(B) No lettering or decals on either side. J. Algozzini Collection. **NRS**

2355 WESTERN PACIFIC: F-3 AA units, 1953, no lettering on one side. E. Kraemer observation. **NRS**

The 2758 P R R automobile boxcar is double-stamped on the right side.

Two very distinctive varitions of the 3494-275 State of Maine operating car were made. The more common is *(shown on the left)* with "BAR" under- and overscored amd the catalogue number "3494275" on its side. The rarer version *(shown on the right)* has no underscoring of "BAR" and no catalogue number. *The two photographs show each side of the very same car!* D. Herman Collection.

	Gd	VG	Ex	LN

2356C SOUTHERN: B unit, no yellow striping or lettering on one side, only gray stripe. L. Moore Collection. **NRS**

2359 BOSTON AND MAINE: GP-9 diesel; black unpainted plastic GP-9 fan shroud known to be original with this example. J. Algozzini Collection. **NRS**

2379 RIO GRANDE: F-3 AB units, 1957-58, no silver stripe on B unit. E. Kraemer observation. **NRS**

Accessories

3656 STOCKYARD CORRAL: Nameplate present, but no chains or holes for chains; appears to be a hybrid of older and newer type. This piece could be classified as a variation if it was an intended factory product, or a factory error if not intended, or simply an intended transition item. Cummings Collection. **NRS**

Boxcars

X1004 BABY RUTH: Boxcar; orange with blue lettering and outlined "BABY RUTH"; Scout trucks and couplers, double-stamped on one side only. **NRS**

X2758 PENNSYLVANIA: Boxcar; brown metal body with white lettering double-stamped on one side only. J. Algozzini Collection. **NRS**

3454 AUTOMATIC MERCHANDISE CAR
(A) Same as (B) in main listing, but heat-stamped only on one side. J. Sattler Collection. — — 200 —

(B) No heat-stamped lettering on either side. M. Sabatelle Collection. — — 200 —

3464 N Y C: Operating boxcar; tan body with black metal doors, lettered on one side only. J. Algozzini Collection. **NRS**

3494-275 STATE OF MAINE: Operating boxcar.
(A) Printed on only one side. **NRS**

(B) "B. A. R." is neither underscored nor overscored; "3494275" is omitted. Collectable variation.

— — 150 —

3494-550 MONON: Operating boxcar; Type IIB maroon plastic body with white-painted stripe, unpainted maroon plastic door, no lettering either side. This is one of the more common factory errors. J. Algozzini Collection. **NRS**

3545 TELEVISION CAR: Heat-stamped lettering on one side only. J. Algozzini Collection. **NRS**

3619 HELICOPTER RECONNAISSANCE CAR: No red lettering on one side only. J. Algozzini Collection. **NRS**

3656 LIONEL LINES: Operating cattle car; double-stamped in white on one side; normal stamping on other. M. Sabatelle Collection. **NRS**

3665 MINUTEMAN: Operating car. Red number and red stripes in the insignia are missing, and rocket is all red. Reported example was purchased from Sears in 1964 in a box labeled "3665 / MINUTEMAN MISSILE CAR". B. Horton Collection. **NRS**

6014: Short boxcar.
(A) White plastic body, no lettering on either side. **NRS**

(B) Type I red plastic body, no lettering on either side. This could also be intended as a factory product for a low-end set or simply an unpainted shell that left the factory and was later mounted on a frame. — — 10 —

X6014 BABY RUTH: Boxcar; red, white lettering double-stamped on one side only. J. Algozzini Collection. **NRS**

6050 LIBBY'S TOMATO JUICE: Boxcar.
(A) Green stems on vegetable image, medium blue triangle, car labeled "PROD. / SAMPLE / 9-27-65 / 6050-175". J. Sattler Collection. **NRS**

(B) Green stems missing from vegetable image, deep blue diamond, early AAR trucks, disc couplers.

— — 100 —

6050 LIONEL SAVINGS BANK: Heat-stamped letters and logo, without "6050" and "BLT BY LIONEL". J. Sattler Collection. — — 18 —

6111 LIONEL: Flatcar with pipes, cream; lettered only on one side. G. Halverson Collection. **NRS**

6356 NEW YORK CENTRAL: Stock car; double-stamped on one side, entire car repainted to hide double stamp and erroneously double-stamped again! Unusual error. M. Sabatelle Collection. **NRS**

6428 UNITED STATES MAIL: Boxcar. Flat red paint, but no lettering on one side. Common.

— — 75 —

6434 POULTRY DISPATCH CAR: Lettered only on one side. F. J. Cordone Collection. **NRS**

6454 SANTA FE: Orange boxcar with brown doors on blue plastic shell; no lettering either side. Could also be factory

An unlettered 6014-type boxcar.

Gd VG Ex LN

error of 2454 Pennsylvania boxcar, but truck and frame details are not known. M. Sabatelle Collection. **NRS**

6454 PENNSYLVANIA: 1952, boxcar, Type 7 frame without steps, bar-end trucks, plastic doors, black plastic body painted red-brown color inside and out instead of usual tuscan color. The color of the car resembles a claret wine color; no evidence of fading or cleaning changing the color. Since the red-brown color was usually reserved for the Southern Pacific 6454, this car could qualify as a factory error. Reader comments invited. The tuscan shade usually does not have such a pronounced reddish-purple cast to it. See Robert Swanson's article on these cars in this edition. R. LaVoie and "Triple T" Collections. **NRS**

6464-1 WESTERN PACIFIC: Boxcar; heat-stamped only on one side. M. Sabatelle Collection. **NRS**

6464-100 WESTERN PACIFIC: Boxcar; Type IIA clear plastic body painted orange, orange-painted doors, all-white lettering, numbers missing on one side. J. Algozzini Collection. **NRS**

6464-150 MISSOURI PACIFIC: Boxcar.
(A) No white lettering on top or on bottom of sides, blue stripes on one side of car. T. Klaassen Collection. **NRS**

(B) Type IIB gray plastic body painted royal blue to create striping, 1956 yellow door with gray-painted stripe, no lettering on either side. J. Algozzini Collection. **NRS**

6464-375 CENTRAL OF GEORGIA: Boxcar.
(A) Entire car is maroon plastic Type IV body, no lettering, unpainted 1953-type pink-tinged doors. The most interesting part of this car is the unusual doors. J. Algozzini Collection. **NRS**

(B) Regular 1956 Type IIB boxcar without decals. Decals could not be removed without damaging the silver on the oval. These cars are occasionally offered for sale. J. Algozzini Collection. — — **150** —

(C) Type IIB duller maroon plastic body, silver-painted roof and oval, gray unpainted 1956 door, no heat-stamped lettering either side. J. Algozzini Collection. **NRS**

Gd VG Ex LN

(D) Same as (C), but doors are 1956 unpainted maroon; no lettering or decal on either side. J. Algozzini Collection. **NRS**

(E) Same as (C), but no doors. C. Weber Collection. **NRS**

6464-400 B & O TIMESAVER SERVICE: Boxcar; Type IV dark blue body mold, 1956-type B & O door, no white lettering or numbering, blue lettering on one side only. J. Algozzini Collection. **NRS**

6464-425 NEW HAVEN: Boxcar.
(A) Lettered only on one side. E. Kraemer and J. Algozzini Collections. **NRS**

(B) Type IIB black plastic body, 1956 unpainted orange plastic doors, no lettering either side. J. Algozzini Collection. **NRS**

6464-450 GREAT NORTHERN: Boxcar.
(A) Type IIB dark olive plastic painted dark olive, orange-painted band through middle of car side to include door, no yellow striping, heat-stamped lettering or decals on either side. J. Algozzini Collection. **NRS**

(B) Type IV body and door painted light olive, orange, and light yellow. Red decal only; no built date.

— — **90** —

6464-475 BOSTON AND MAINE: Boxcar.
(A) Type IV unpainted medium blue body, black 1956 unpainted door, no black lettering or numbers on one side only; white lettering is present. J. Algozzini Collection. **NRS**

(B) Type IIB unpainted medium blue plastic body, black 1956 unpainted door, "BLT 2-57 / BY LIONEL" missing from one side only. J. Algozzini Collection. **NRS**

The 6014 Baby Ruth boxcar with double-stamped lettering.

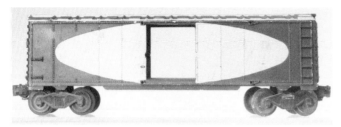

This the 6464-375 Central of Georgia without lettering. C. Weber Collection.

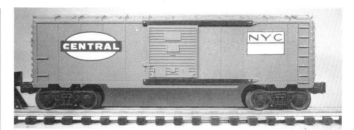

A 6464-900 New York Central boxcar without its numbers.

	Gd	VG	Ex	LN

6464-500 TIMKEN: Boxcar.
(A) Type IIB bright yellow plastic body, white-painted band through middle of car, red plastic door painted brown, no heat-stamped lettering or decal on either side. J. Algozzini Collection. **NRS**

(B) Type IIB bright yellow plastic body, white-painted band through middle of car, yellow 1956 door with white stripe, B & O Timesaver decal both sides. J. Algozzini Collection. **NRS**

6464-515 KATY: Boxcar, from Girls' Set. Overstamped with "6464-150" lettering. **NRS**

6464-650 RIO GRANDE: Boxcar.
(A) Type IIB yellow plastic body, silver-painted band, roof, and door, black stripe missing on left half of one side only. J. Algozzini Collection. **NRS**

(B) Type IIB yellow plastic body, silver-painted band and roof (but not door), 1956 gray unpainted doors, no heat-stamped lettering or striping either side. J. Algozzini Collection. **NRS**

6464-700 SANTA FE: Boxcar; Type IV gray plastic body painted red, 1956 gray plastic doors painted red, double-stamped on one side only. J. Algozzini Collection. **NRS**

6464-825 ALASKA: Boxcar; Type III gray body painted dark blue with yellow stripe, 1956 black plastic door, no lettering either side. J. Algozzini Collection. **NRS**

6464-900 NEW YORK CENTRAL: Boxcar.
(A) Type IV gray plastic body and 1956 gray plastic doors painted dark jade green, only two lines of lettering on one side. J. Algozzini Collection. **NRS**

(B) Type IV gray plastic body and 1956 gray plastic doors painted jade green, has usual white oval on left side outlined in black with "CENTRAL" in white letters on black band which passes through the oval, but is missing the usual red "NEW YORK" and "SYSTEMS", also has usual white rectangle on right side outlined in black with black "N Y C", but is missing the usual red "6464-900", and is missing all of the usual white informational data lettering on both sides. J. Sattler Collection. **NRS**

(C) Type IV gray plastic body painted forest green, unpainted green plastic door, no lettering either side. J. Algozzini Collection. **NRS**

6472 REFRIGERATOR CAR: Non-operating; triple-stamped in black, white, and blue correct; lettering on one side and triple-stamped with "3472 AUTOMATIC REFRIGERATED MILK CAR" on other side in black, white, and blue lettering. M. Sabatelle Collection. **NRS**

Cabooses

C & O: Work caboose; heat-stamped letters and numbers on one side only. J. Foss, Jr. Collection. **NRS**

6119 D. L. & W.: Work caboose; white lettering missing from red cab on one side. This is 1969 production and is even more common than the "645" lettered on one side. J. Algozzini comment. D. Anderson Collection. **NRS**

6517 LIONEL LINES: Bay window caboose.
(A) Missing all bay markings and radio wave on side. **NRS**

(B) Missing Lionel logo and "RADIO EQUIPPED". Lettering appears slightly higher than usual. G. and L. Savage Collection. **NRS**

6814 LIONEL: Rescue caboose; "LIONEL" missing from one side of frame. J. Sorensen Collection. **NRS**

Cranes and Searchlights

6822 LIONEL: "Night Crew" searchlight car; 6822 superstructure and searchlight mounted on a red 6828 flatcar body with white lettering, mold 6511-2. This could be classified as a variation or factory error, depending on the circumstances of its manufacture and the number existing. D. Pickard Collection. **NRS**

Flatcars

3361-55 LIONEL: Log dump car; heavy "LIONEL LINES" 7/32" lettering, 3361-55 to right of car, stamped upside down on both sides. J. ALgozzini Collection. **NRS**

6511 LIONEL: Flatcar with pipes; "LIONEL" and number in white missing from one side only. J. Algozzini Collection. **NRS**

6519 ALLIS-CHALMERS: Flatcar with condenser; orange base, no lettering either side. J. Algozzini Collection. **NRS**

6640 U S M C LAUNCHER: Olive drab car and superstructure, black firing ramp, white rocket with blue tip, but no lettering on flatcar. R. Shanfeld Collection.
— — 225 —

6809 LIONEL FLATCAR WITH U S M C TRUCKS: Red plastic flatcar with letters, hospital van with Navy insignia one one side. — — 125 —

6816 FLAT WITH ALLIS-CHALMERS BULLDOZER
(A) Same as listing (A), but dark orange bulldozer with "HD 16 DIESEL" missing on both sides. J. Algozzini Collection. **NRS**

	Gd	VG	Ex	LN

(B) Same as listing (A), but "HD 16 DIESEL" missing on one side of bulldozer. J. Algozzini Collection. **NRS**

Gondolas

6462 N Y C: Gondola.

(A) Pink-painted body, no lettering. J. Algozzini Collection. **NRS**

(B) Maroon body, two brakewheels, no lines over "N Y C", lines under "6462", lettering on one side only. J. Algozzini Collection. **NRS**

(C) Black body, double-stamped on one side. M. Sabatelle Collection. **NRS**

(D) Red-painted body, no lines over "N Y C", lines under "6462", no brakewheels, lettered on one side only. J. Algozzini Collection. **NRS**

(E) Black body, stamped one side only. L. Moore Collection. **NRS**

Hoppers and Dump Cars

3459 LIONEL LINES: Operating coal dump car; same as regular issue, except heat-stamped 5459 piece from Electronic Set installed on dump car body instead of usual 3459. H. Lotstein Collection. **NRS**

6436 LEHIGH VALLEY: Hopper car.

(A) Rust-painted 1963-type body, no lettering on either side. J. Algozzini Collection. **NRS**

(B) Pink-painted 1957-type body, no lettering on either side. J. Algozzini Collection. **NRS**

6436-110 LEHIGH VALLEY: 50-ton quad hopper; red-painted gray plastic with white lettering, spreader bar, no cover, AAR trucks, no lettering on one side. J. Algozzini Collection. **NRS**

6476 LEHIGH VALLEY: Short hopper; "NEW 1-48", "BUILT 1-48", Type VI pale red plastic body, white lettering, lettered on one side only. J. Algozzini Collection. **NRS**

6536 M ST L: Covered hopper; no lettering on one side. E. Kraemer Collection. **NRS**

6736 DETROIT & MACKINAC: Covered hopper; face of figure on Mackinac Mac logo is obliterated by white blotch caused by die flaw. A common variation.

— — **40** —

Passenger Cars

	Gd	VG	Ex	LN

1866 WESTERN & ATLANTIC: General-style passenger car; red plastic chassis with lights, clear plastic window inserts, heavily heat-stamped. Additional heat-stamping on upper left side where a hinge would be on the rear door. Different type of centering spring used on couplers. **NRS**

1875W WESTERN & ATLANTIC: Passenger car with whistle; heat-stamped and windows outlined with tuscan on one side only; other side is solid yellow. C. Rohlfing Collection. **NRS**

2422 CHATHAM: Passenger car; heat-stamped lettering on one side only. J. Algozzini Collection. **NRS**

2440 PULLMAN: Passenger car; green metal body with green roof and yellow trim: heat-stamped on one side only. M. Sabatelle Collection. **NRS**

2531 SILVER DAWN: Passenger car; hex-head rivets holding plates, but "SILVER DAWN" on one plate and "SILVER RANGE" on other. J. Breslin Collection. **NRS**

2543 WILLIAM PENN: Passenger car; with correct 2543 window inserts, but Canadian Pacific striping and "Blair Manor" nameplate. Came in unusually-marked box; original "2543" number is overstamped and "2553" printed; then "2553" is overstamped again and "2543" rubber stamped on box ends! Very unusual and confusing hybrid car. Classification of this car is difficult without more detailed knowledge of its history. It could be an error or variation. J. Bratspis Collection.

— — **150** —

2562 REGAL PASS: Passenger car.

(A) "REGAL PASS" off-centered to right on one side only. J. Algozzini Collection. **NRS**

(B) "SANTA FE" off-centered to right on one side only. J. Algozzini Collection. **NRS**

Tank and Vat Cars

6315 GULF: Single-dome tank car; burnt orange and black tank, "BLT 1-56", lettering on one side only. J. Algozzini Collection. **NRS**

6465 SUNOCO: Tank car; same as (I) in main listings, but Sunoco herald is double-stamped. G. Halverson Collection. **NRS**

6465 CITIES SERVICE: Two-dome tank car; silk-screened lettering and numbering on one side only; no evidence of lettering on blank side. A. Stucchio Collection. **NRS**

6465 LIONEL: Two-dome tank car; orange plastic tank with black ends, no lettering either side. J. Algozzini Collection. **NRS**

EVOLUTION OF A NEW MODEL

THE 3665 MINUTEMAN MISSILE LAUNCHING CAR — *James M. Sattler*

The study of two pre-production 3665 minuteman missile-launching cars as depicted in the 1961 Lionel advance and consumer catalogues provides an excellent opportunity to understand how Lionel developed new models from old or existing ones and to consider some of the terms defined in the previous chapter. As we apply the defined terms to surviving pre-production models and the catalogue illustrations, we gain new insights. We also learn that more than a single prototype was often involved in the development of a new model.

In the 1960 advance catalogue, Lionel introduced a new model numbered "6530" and called the "NEW FIRE PREVENTION TRAINING CAR". Regular production models of the 6530 used a one-piece unpainted red plastic body with an integral molded roof. The one-piece body was made from the same mold that had been used in making the 3530 electro mobile power car which was introduced in 1956 and catalogued through 1958.

Note the similarity of the catalogue numbers assigned by Lionel to these two cars. The 6530 car had unpainted white plastic doors which were held in place with metal door guides attached to the body with metal rivets. All graphics were applied to the sides in white. The sheet metal frame was chemically blackened and had a 3/4" "dimple" stamped in it.

STEPS IN THE PROTOTYPE MODEL-MAKING PROCESS:

1. The first version of the prototype model of the 3665 car was made using an undecorated 6530 red plastic body which had the integral molded roof carefully cut off and two plastic strips (1/4" wide and about 9" long) were glued to the tops of the body sides, leaving 1/8" gaps at each inside end (see **Figure 1**).

2. Four left-hand doors from a 6530 car were then glued in place in the door openings of the body without using the metal door guides. (Look at the inside of the sliding doors of a 6530 car and you will see that they are marked "LH" and "RH" and that the "LH" doors have two small protrusions which keep the doors from opening too far. The "RH" doors do not have the protrusions.)

3. The entire modified body assembly was then painted flat white and hand-cut decals which had been made for the new 3665 U. S. Air Force "MINUTEMAN" model were applied to both sides of the body. Note that on the first 3665 prototype model, the word "MINUTEMAN" was placed just below the edge of the fixed roof sections and cannot easily be seen with the roof sections in their fixed, open positions. It is apparent from the first 3665 prototype model

FIGURE 1: A comparison of a decorated production model 6530 fire prevention training car *(left)* with the first prototype of the 3665 minuteman car *(right)*. The 3665 was made from an undecorated 6530. Note the three portholes on the 3665 prototype. J. Sattler Collection.

that all of the lettering that would subsequently appear on the production models had already been decided upon, but the location of the lettering would change. As will be seen on production models, "MINUTEMAN" was split into two sections: "MINUT" and "EMAN" was placed on the upper panels of the two doors. The prototype body retained the two open porthole windows on one side of its body and the three open porthole windows on the other side, as well as the holes for the metal door guide rivets.

4. Next, a red plastic roof from a 6448 exploding target range car was carefully cut in half lengthwise to make two roof sections. One of the roof sections has the molded hole which was designed for the pin that holds the roof in place on the 6448 cars. Lionel introduced both the 3665 and the 6448 cars in 1961 and it appears that work on the development of both cars was going on at the same time.

5. Both of the new roof sections then had plastic "hinges" glued to them which fit in the 1/8" gaps in the glued-on strips to hold the two roof sections in the "open" position so that the missile-firing mechanism and the missile could be seen. The roof sections on the prototype do not have the "raised center" sections that appear on the later prototype, on the models depicted in the 1961 advance and consumer catalogues, and on all production versions of the 3665.

6. The frame used on the first 3665 prototype model was made from the same stamping as that used on the 6530 production model with the 3/4" "dimple" except that the prototype's frame was not chemically blackened.

7. The first 3665 prototype model used a non-operating missile-launching platform modified from a 6650 IRBM missile-launching car which had been introduced in 1959. In order to attach the launching platform to the frame, two extra holes were made in the frame to allow two screws to pass through the frame to hold the missile-launching mechanism in place. Two nuts are attached to the two screws on the underside of the modified frame.*

8. The newly-modified roof sections on the first 3665 prototype model were not intended or designed to close. At some point in the development process, probably when the first operating missile-launching mechanism was made and available, it became apparent that a new roof design was necessary for the 3665 to accommodate the fins of the missile inside the car when the missile-launching mechanism was in the closed position. Then, the decision was made to design and use "raised center" roof sections on the new 3665 cars. As was generally the case, and probably for budget considerations, Lionel used the same new "raised roof" sections in the following year on the then-new 3619 reconnaissance copter car.

Lionel now had a new prototype of the new 3665 model which could be used to make marketing feasibility and production decisions.

All production models of the 3665 have the missile facing the end of the car which has the screw hole for the body-mounting screw. The end is also the same one where the brakewheel is attached.

FIGURE 2: The cover of the Lionel 1961 advance catalogue shows then-Lionel President John Medaris holding a later prototype of the 3665. Actually, the model in his hands does not appear to be a photograph of a real model, but rather a colored rendering or depiction of a model. The photograph of Medaris is in black and white while the depiction of the 3665 model is colored red, white, and blue. The model on the cover also is not lettered "AUTHORIZED/PERSONNEL ONLY" or "BUILT BY/LIONEL", both of which appear on the first 3665 prototype model and on all of the production models of the 3665.

1961 ADVANCE CATALOGUE

A later "prototype" model of the 3665 car was shown on the cover of the Lionel 1961 advance catalogue (see **Figure 2**). After Lionel had proceeded far enough in the decision-making process to decide to show the new 3665 model on its catalogue cover, a later 3665 prototype model was put together in the Lionel model shops prior to beginning mass production. We also call this later version a prototype because:

(a) its construction indicates that Lionel apparently had not yet made all of the tools, dies, and equipment necessary to make the "raised center" roof sections that were later used on the production models. Note that the roof sections shown on the catalogue cover are

FIGURE 3: From page 22 of the 1961 advance catalogue.

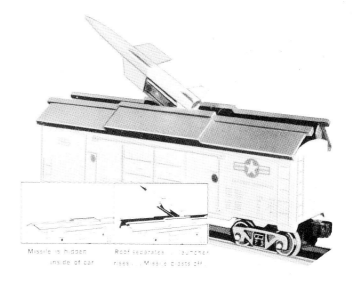

FIGURE 4: From page 23 of the 1961 advance catalogue.

smooth and do not have any of the ribs which are always found on the production models; and

(b) its construction indicates that Lionel apparently had not yet made all of the tools, dies, and equipment necessary to make the closed or filled-in porthole windows that are always found on the production models.

Also note the difference between the first prototype model (**Figure 1**) and the depiction of the later prototype model (**Figure 2**) which showed the missile-launching mechanism facing in the opposite direction. Since the 6530 body from which both of these prototype models were made could only be installed one way on the frame (because there are two slots on one end for two "fingers" of the frame to pass through and a screw hole on the opposite end for the body-mounting screw), and since the frame which would allow the missile-firing mechanism to be mounted facing the end of the car on which the two slots are made, the model depicted on the cover had to be of a later prototype model. Further note that "MINUTEMAN" does not yet appear on the upper panels of the doors on the later prototype model.

We have concluded that the model depicted on the cover of the 1961 advance catalogue was made *after* the prototype shown in **Figure 1** because the model on the catalogue cover still shows three open porthole windows but also has the new

"raised center" smooth top roof sections. We also have concluded that the model shown on the catalogue cover was made relatively early in the development process, and before production began, because the roof sections still do not yet have the "ribs" which appear on later "mock-ups" and on all production models of the 3665.

Page 22

The 1961 advance catalogue shows several other depictions of the 3665 car. On page 22 is a drawing showing a model similar to that on the cover, but it shows the opposite side of the car body which only has two open porthole windows (see **Figure 3**). As depicted, the model also does not yet have "MINUTEMAN" on the upper panels of the doors or "AUTHORIZED/PERSONNEL ONLY" and "BUILT BY/LIONEL" which appear both on the first version of the 3665 prototype model and on all production models of the 3665. The model depicted on page 22 also has the smooth top "raised center" roof sections without "ribs."

Page 23

There is another drawing of the car on page 23 of the 1961 advance catalogue (see **Figure 4**). Note that this sketch must have been based upon a prototype model made from an unmodified 6530 body mold because it still shows the open porthole windows and the holes for the metal door guide rivets. This depiction also shows the side of the car which has only two open porthole windows and shows the missile-firing mechanism facing towards the left of that side of the car. While it is not possible to tell with certainty from the catalogue illustrations, it does appear that the model upon which the catalogue depictions are based had doors glued in place and still had the rivet holes for the missing door guides. The page 23 version also has the smooth top "raised center" roof sections without "ribs." It also appears that all of the depictions in the 1961 catalogue so far described were based upon the same later version of the 3665 prototype model.

FIGURE 5: From pages 34-35 of the 1961 advance catalogue.

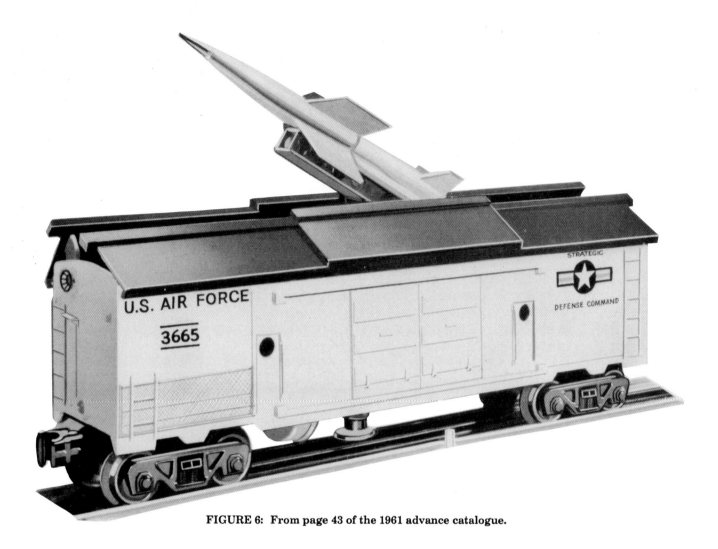

FIGURE 6: From page 43 of the 1961 advance catalogue.

Pages 34 and 35

At the center of pages 34 and 35 of the 1961 advance catalogue is still another depiction of a 3665 prototype model (see **Figure 5**). Note that this one shows the side of the car with three open porthole windows, with the missile pointing to the left of that side of the car. This indicates either that another 3665 prototype model was made with the missile facing in the opposite direction from the earlier models or that the missile direction was changed from that shown on the cover and on pages 22 and 23. Note again the absence of "MINUTEMAN" on the upper door panel sections, "AUTHORIZED/PERSONNEL", and "BUILT BY/LIONEL".

Page 43

A larger depiction of a 3665 prototype model appears on page 43 of the 1961 advance catalogue (see **Figure 6**) and shows the side of the car with only two open porthole windows, with the missile pointing to the left of that side of the car. Note that the screw which holds the body to the frame is visible at the end of the car toward which the missile is facing.

The page 43 version does not have the lettering "MINUTEMAN" on the upper door panel sections and "AUTHO-

RIZED/PERSONNEL ONLY" and "BUILT BY/LIONEL". The prototype model, upon which this depiction was based, was probably an operating version because the "plunger" and the bellows mechanism to raise the missile-launching mechanism through the open roof sections are present. It seems likely that the illustrated model on page 43 was the same one used for the depiction on the catalogue cover because the plunger mechanism is also visible, but is not on any other catalogue depictions. In both the page 43 and cover depictions, it appears that the rivet holes for the door guide rivets are missing, but the models still retain the open porthole windows.

1961 CONSUMER CATALOGUE

By the time Lionel did the artwork for its 1961 consumer catalogue, the "raised center" ribbed roof sections had been designed and produced. Note that in the drawing of the prototype from page 51 (see **Figure 7**), the door guide rivet holes are gone, but the two open porthole windows are still present. "AUTHORIZED/PERSONNEL ONLY" appears to the left of the doors under "3665", but "BUILT BY/LIONEL" is missing from the right of the doors. The screw hole for the

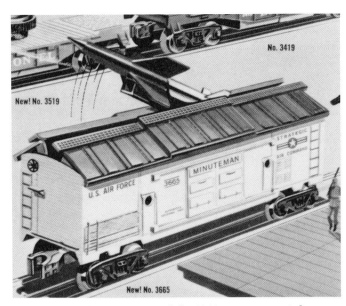

FIGURE 7: From page 51 of the 1961 consumer catalogue.

FIGURE 8: Another surviving prototype with "filled-in" porthole windows.

body-mounting screw is not shown on the brakewheel end of the car. This depiction suggests that the production models on which the porthole windows are closed had not yet been produced.

The depiction of the 3665 model in the 1961 consumer catalogue must, by our definitions, be a further version of a prototype 3665 model because all of the tools, dies, and equipment necessary to produce the closed-porthole production bodies are not yet indicated — and the missile-launching mechanism is facing to the left of the side of the car with two open porthole windows. Note also that "MINUTEMAN" has been placed on each of the upper door panel sections.

Several other illustrations of the 3665 model appear in the 1961 consumer catalogue. Some of these depictions are interesting in connection with the development and evolution of the prototype models. On page 2 an illustration shows what might be the opposite side of the same model depicted on page 51, with the missile facing to the right on the side of the car which has three open porthole windows. The

page 2 version shows the "raised center" ribbed roof sections, but does not show "BUILT BY/LIONEL" to the right of the doors.

On page 28 is another drawing of the 3665, but this time the missile-firing mechanism is facing in the wrong direction, considering that the side of the car shown has three open porthole windows! Also "AUTHORIZED/PERSONNEL ONLY" and "BUILT BY/LIONEL" are missing.

On page 32 of the catalogue, a 3665 is shown in the "gift pack" box. The illustrated car appears to be complete insofar as the lettering is concerned, but it still shows two open porthole windows.

The last other depiction of the 3665 is shown in the center of pages 40 and 41. In this version, "AUTHORIZED/PERSONNEL ONLY" is missing and the side of the car with three open porthole windows is shown with the missile-firing mechanism facing the brakewheel end of the car. As explained earlier, because of the manner in which the slots are molded in the regular production 3665 cars, this depiction must be a pre-production prototype or mock-up because it would be an impossibility for a production model of the 3665 to have the brakewheel to the left of the side of the car which had three porthole windows. But to make matters even more confusing, the ladder and brakewheel are shown on the wrong side of the end of the car!

All of these differences suggest that there probably were a series of several different prototype models or mock-ups which were used for the catalogue depictions.

LIONEL'S UNSUNG SET 463W OF 1945

THE REAL BEGINNING OF THE POSTWAR ERA — *Robert Swanson*

In Ron Hollander's book *All Aboard!* there are two tantalizing pictures of a Lionel train set that has been largely ignored by the collecting public. If you have the book, look for a moment at page 183. There you will find two publicity shots of the first postwar Lionel train set being delivered just in time for Christmas 1945. Lionel's war contracts had ended on August 7, 1945, and the firm was feverishly as-

sembling a train set in time for that year's Christmas sales. Mr. Hollander's pictures show that set — a steam engine pulling four scale-detailed cars. This is Lionel's set 463W, and it is time to bring it out of historical obscurity to give it the attention it deserves!

After all, if the sales of collector guides and other specialized books about train collecting are any indication, there is

Only the Beginning—The LIONEL Line for Christmas

463W NEW LIONEL "0" GAUGE FOUR CAR FREIGHT SET
It includes Lionel's famous remote control whistle, new remote control electro magnetic couplers, and electrically operated directional control of locomotive. The cars are equipped with new Lionel 1946 die cast trucks, solid steel wheels, and new perfected real railroad knuckle couplers.
Length of train set ____ 55½ inches.
Set includes the following:
1-No. 224 scale detailed, die cast, 262 steam type locomotive
1-No. 2224 coal tender with patented built-in railroad whistle
1-No. 2458 Automobile car
1-No. 2452 New Scale Proportioned Gondola Car

1-No. 2555 Oil car
1-No. 2457 Caboose
8-Sections of OC Curved track
3-Sections of OS Straight track
1-RCS Remote Control track set
1-No 167 Whistling controller
1-UTC Lockon
Price $33.50

REPRODUCTION
GREENBERG PUBLISHING COMPANY
605 Gaither Road   Sykesville, Md. 21784
301-442-1730

See Lionel Accessories also on the following pages

TYPE "Z" TRANSFORMER—250 WATTS
The famous Lionel "Trainmaster" *central control* station. Will operate any two trains, plus a number of accessories. Six to twenty-five volts. Price $16.00

NO. 153 AUTOMATIC BLOCK CONTROL
Controls locomotives automatically so that two trains may run at same time, on same oval of track, without accident. Contactor included. Price $3.50

NO. 152 AUTOMATIC CROSSING GATE
As train approaches, red warning light is illuminated and gate is lowered. When train has passed, light is extinguished and gate opens. Gate is 10½ inches long. Contactor included. Price $3.00

NO. 314 SCALE MODEL GIRDER BRIDGE
Die cast with sharp details. Distinct plate stiffeners, floor beam brackets and flanges. Can be slipped under track of any gauge without raising it above normal level. Single span 10 inches long. Price $2.75

NO. 308 SCALE MODEL SIGNS
Five of the most common signs found on real railroad rights-of-way. Made of steel, enameled white, with black lettering. Price $2.50

NO. 45N GATEMAN
When train nears, door opens and gateman rushes out swinging lantern. When train has passed, gateman returns to shack and door closes. Action is automatic. Lantern is illuminated by reflecting a beam of light from a concealed lamp. Complete with contactor. $4.50

Sensational Surprises on the way for 1946

FIGURE 1: The 1945 catalogue showed set 463W in fine detail. However, the actual components differed in several notable ways from the listings.

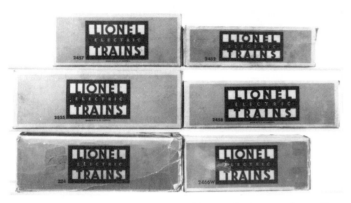

FIGURE 2: Each piece in the 463W came in its own box. Two different types of boxes are known, the New York version and the Chicago version. Shown above is the New York version with component catalogue numbers correctly printed on each box.

more interest in postwar Lionel trains than in all other eras of all other electric train manufacturers combined! Yet, for all that attention, many collectors associate the beginning of this popular era of electric trains with the introduction of smoke, the Pennsylvania S-2 turbine, and the Berkshire locomotive as shown in the 1946 catalogue. Most of us remember (and/or have heard many times) that oft-told story of the 1946 paper shortage which limited production of the 1946 Lionel catalogue and Lionel's clever response to the shortage by having *Liberty* magazine print the entire catalogue as an advertising insert. But that was not the real beginning of the postwar era at all. Production and sales of postwar Lionel trains began in the fall of 1945, a full year before the well-known *Liberty* magazine escapade.

Lionel's planning for postwar production did not begin in 1945. Internal memos dated as early as December 1942 and January 1943 were reprinted in the January 1983 issue of

FIGURE 3: Given both the shortages of paper and the limited time available for production in 1945, the Lionel 1945 catalogue is a remarkable publication.

the *Train Collector's Quarterly*. These memos show clearly that early in the war Lionel's executives were actively developing their postwar train designs and marketing strategies. With this small insight into Lionel's wartime train-planning activities, it is not too surprising to find that Lionel was able to produce and distribute one train set, the 463W, in time for Christmas 1945. The set consisted primarily of prewar rolling stock mounted on the all-new die-cast trucks with knuckle couplers. It contained the old reliable 224 die-cast steam locomotive with a 2466W whistle tender, a 2458 all-metal double-door automobile car marked with its prewar number (2758), a 2555 single-dome tank car marked with the old 2755 number, a 2452 Pennsylvania black plastic gondola (the only all-new car), and a 2457 sheet metal Pennsylvania N5 illuminated caboose. Since individual items similar to these 1945 items, right down to the catalogue descriptions and numbers, were also produced in 1946 and 1947 (and some cars in 1948), the uniqueness and even the very existence of the 1945 set is largely unknown.

The limited awareness of the 1945 set in the train collecting community can usually be attributed to the scarcity of the four-page two-color 1945 Lionel catalogue. This catalogue itself is one of the rarest pieces of postwar "paper," but excellent reproductions were printed in 1969 by Les Gordon and in 1975 by Bruce Greenberg. My own awareness of the 1945 set came about during a visit to Mr. Gordon's Indianapolis train store in 1974. I was looking at some old Lionel catalogues to complete my postwar collection when Les showed me his reprint of the 1945 catalogue. When I saw the 463W set pictured on pages 2 and 3, I was totally shocked because I had purchased this set five years earlier! I finally understood why I had not found this set in any regular postwar catalogue; it had never occurred to me that there was any 1945 production. I also began to see that this set had unique features making it different from prewar or any subsequent postwar production.

This 1945 catalogue, like many Lionel catalogues, contains several inaccuracies and errors when it is compared to the items actually produced. For example, the tender is listed as a number 2224; however, it was marked and boxed as a 2466W tender. The caboose is correctly listed as number 2457, but the catalogue pictures it as the later 2472 caboose without illumination, window frames and inserts, steps, or end windows in the cupola. The unlighted 2472 was not produced until 1946. Other discrepancies relating to the numbering of the tank and automobile cars will be discussed later.

The primary features which make the rolling stock in the 1945 set unique and identifiable are the trucks and couplers. The three-year interruption in electric train production during World War II created a tremendous demand for electric trains. The money to spend on them was there, thanks to a booming wartime economy. This pent-up demand made 1945 the ideal time to introduce a new coupler system incompatible with all the prewar couplers. (Lionel would compromise a little later by introducing coupler adapters.) Knuckle couplers and die-cast trucks were a major part of Lionel's strategy to manufacture more realistic toy trains. Improved realism would certainly benefit Lionel's sales over

FIGURE 4: The 1945 trucks all used a flying shoe design. The shoe made contact with the special uncoupling track rails to activate the coupler. Unfortunately the flying shoe design was not durable.

FIGURE 5: The earliest 1945 trucks, Type IA, featured whirly wheels and thick axles.

the long run, and the general demand for electric trains in late 1945 would minimize any temporary sales resistance caused by the incompatibility with previous coupler designs. So far, so good.

The only trouble with all this great timing was that Lionel was simply unprepared to finalize the design and manufacture it on such short notice — there simply had not been time during the war years to perfect and optimize the truck and coupler design. The result was the introduction of an unproven and imperfect truck and coupler assembly, which had many production and operational problems. The Lionel

FIGURE 6: Three different versions of the 224 locomotive. On the top shelf is the prewar version with long drawbars linking locomotive and tender. The tender has prewar trucks with stamped-steel side frames and a box coupler. On the second shelf is a 224 that came with the 1945 set. The locomotive and tender are coupled much more closely by a locomotive drawbar that fits into a slot in the tender floor. Note the black handrails along the boiler. On the bottom shelf is a 1946 model 224 with a rounded cab floor that projects beyond the cab side walls and clearly distinguishes this model. B. Greenberg photograph.

FIGURE 7: The 1945 224 came with a locomotive draw-bar with a very small hooked end. This end fitted into a slot in the tender. It is difficult to disconnect the draw-bar from the tender.

strategy apparently was to implement engineering and man-ufacturing "fixes" to these problems as quickly as they were discovered. The result was the production of at least eight different "flying shoe" truck and coupler variations during late 1945 and early 1946. Stated another way, Lionel appar-ently "fixed" the design of the early flying shoe truck about every three **weeks**, on the average!

These factory "fixes" were not the only repairs required, either. The owners of these early flying shoe trucks evi-dently experienced so many problems with them that they

brought them back to Service Stations for repair in droves. To help the Service Stations resolve the myriad of repair problems, Lionel issued a series of seven "Authorized Service Station T.C. Truck Bulletins." These bulletins cover such subjects as couplers opening unexpectedly, burned-out coils, short-circuiting rollers, broken or loose coupler heads, bro-ken fiber strips, and cars jumping the track at switches. The latest of these bulletins is dated April 1946. Ultimately, the flying shoe design was viewed by Lionel as so fragile that no amount of tinkering could save it from a well-deserved retire-ment. By mid-1946 a completely new design (Type 3 in the truck and coupler article) was introduced. In 1948 the mag-netic track-activated coupler solved the pickup shoe problem for good.

These early truck and coupler variations provide one im-portant means of identifying items produced for the 1945 set. However, since trucks can be and often are changed, it is helpful to identify other unique features as well. To help the reader discern both the obvious and subtle uniqueness of the 1945 items, the photographs accompanying this article show, from top to bottom, prewar production, 1945 production, and 1946 to 1947 production.

The obvious place to start is with the 224 locomotive. There are two features unique to the 1945 versions of this lo-comotive. First, the wire handrails are chemically blackened (or "blued"), rather than bright stainless steel, which is typi-cal of both prewar and postwar production. Evidently stain-less steel, which was in critical demand for military applications during the war, was not yet available for con-sumer products. Second, the drawbar is blackened steel with a very short vertical section at the end; this section with little "ears" is placed directly into an oval slot in the ten-

FIGURE 8: The 224 set consisted of a locomotive, tender, and four freight cars. On the center shelf is the X2758 boxcar and the 2755 tank car from the 1945 set. Note the close coupling of the cars. The top shelf shows the prewar versions of the boxcar and tank car while the bottom shelf shows the early 1946 X2458 boxcar and the 2555 Sunoco tank car (still close coupling). R. Swanson Collection.

der frame. (The 1945 224 is also the only postwar version of this locomotive with a squared-off cab end, like the prewar products.) The result of this arrangement is a much closer coupling of the engine and tender when compared with the prewar design, a change very consistent with Lionel's policy of producing "scale-like" realism in their popularly-priced toy trains. The other result of the 1945 drawbar arrangement, however, is negative. It is very difficult to couple the engine and tender together without removing both from the track and replacing them on the track as a coupled unit — no easy procedure for a six or seven-year-old boy, not to mention an older adult with "maturing" eyesight! The 1946 fix for this problem was the return of the tender drawbar, now redesigned with the engine drawbar to maintain close spacing between engine and tender. The close-coupling illusion was actually improved in 1946 by the addition of a rounded cab floor, bringing the locomotive even closer to the tender.

The 1945 version of the 2466W tender is unique to 1945 in that it has no drawbar of any kind, neither attached to the frame nor the truck pivot point. In fact, collectors unfamiliar with this tender often assume something is missing and add a drawbar. Instead of a drawbar, this tender has an oval hole in the metal frame approximately 3/8" x 3/16" to accept the drawbar directly from the engine. It also has blackened handrails made from wire similar in appearance to that used on the engine. The body is molded from the same injection-molded plastic used on the prewar 2666W tender. This leads us to the theory that the 1945 production was mostly the assembly of prewar parts which were then equipped with the new trucks and couplers. The fact that the 1945 2466W tender bodies are stamped "LIONEL LINES" in prewar white lettering, rather than the postwar silver, lends credence to this theory. Finally, the 1945 2466W tender is equipped with either Type 1A trucks (whirly wheels) or Type 1B trucks (dished wheels). Based upon many observations, I believe that production of the Type 1C truck (thick axle, regular wheels) did not begin until the early 1946 items were being assembled. By that time, virtually all of the Types 1A and 1B trucks had been used for the 1945 sets.

Production of the 2458 automobile car also represents the assembly of prewar parts with new trucks and couplers. The bodies for these cars were evidently painted and marked before the war, because cars with Type 1A or 1B trucks always carry the prewar number, 2758. (Perhaps, too, there was not time to change the heat stamp for 1945.) When these cars are found in their original boxes, the box number always agrees with the catalogue number — 2458. The only variations for the 2458 (marked 2758) automobile car relate to the trucks and couplers; several sub-variations of both Type 1A and Type 1B have been observed.

The 2555 tank car produced for the 1945 set presents a variation on the theme of assembling prewar parts. All of the parts except, of course, the trucks are from the prewar 2755 tank car, including the decals. However, the paint and the placement of the decals (number to the right, Sunoco decal to the left) are similar to the rare silver variation of the prewar 2755. Most prewar 2755 tank cars were gray. Surprisingly, the wire handrails on the 1945 version of the 2555 tank car were stainless steel in 1945, not black like the handrails on the engine and tender. Perhaps the handrails were cut and bent before the war — another use of leftover parts.

FIGURE 9: In 1945 Lionel used different letter styles on its 2755 tank car. The decal on the top car has taller lettering on the second line compared to the decal on the lower car.

Curiously, the cotter pins which attach the handrails to the tank are black, just like the cotter pins on the engine and tender! The 2555 tank car also provides something for the variation collector besides the usual Type 1A and 1B truck and coupler variations. There are at least two distinctly different 2755 number decals used on the 1945 tank cars (see **Figure 9**). One decal has noticeably taller characters on the second line than the other. The decal with taller letters is also notched on both sides of the bottom line of printing, while the other is completely rectangular. Since both decals have been observed on cars with Types 1A and 1B trucks, it appears that the decals were used concurrently rather than consecutively.

The number discrepancies on both the tank car and the automobile car were corrected in early 1946. The accompanying photograph (bottom row) shows both cars with correct numbers, but with Type 2 trucks, indicating early 1946 production. The production of Type 3A trucks began in mid or late 1946.

The 2452 Pennsylvania gondola is the only all-new car contained in the 1945 set. It has an injection-molded plastic body, completely different from the prewar 2812X tinplate gondola it replaced. The only similarity between the 2812X and the 1945 version of the 2452 is that they were both supplied with four of the hollow two-piece barrels numbered

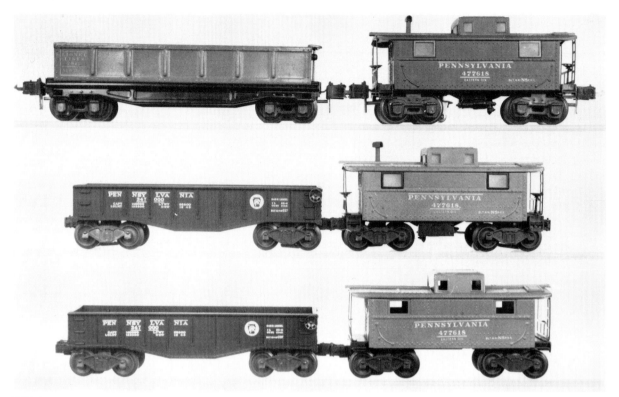

FIGURE 10: The center shelf shows a 2452 gondola and a 2457 caboose from the 1945 set, while the top shelf shows prewar equipment and the bottom shelf shows 1946 equipment. The prewar 2757 caboose was continued in 1945 with a new color, new trucks, and a new number, 2457. The prewar 2812 gondola was dropped and replaced with the 2452 gondola. The bottom shelf shows the unlighted 2472 caboose first made in 1946.

"0209". In 1946 and later years, the 2452 gondola and its successors were equipped with solid one-piece wooden barrels or no barrels at all. The more plentiful 2452X gondola

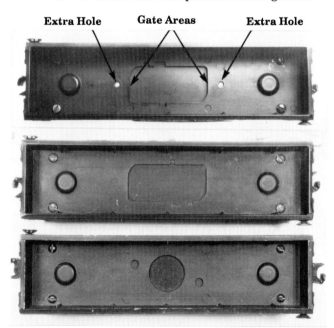

FIGURE 11: The 1945 and 1946 gondolas had an irregular rectangular hole in the car floor for mounting the electronic set receiver. In addition, some 1945 gondolas had extra holes flanking the rectangular opening which were probably intended for the electronic set wiring. In 1947 Lionel modified the die to make a round hole.

manufactured in 1946 and 1947, for O27 sets, had neither barrels nor brakewheels.

Besides being the only "new" car in the 1945 set, the 2452 gondola yields more variations than any other item manufactured in 1945 (it has a "new" date and "built" date of 12-45). The usual 1A and 1B truck variations can be found, along with different screws used to attach the body to the metal frame. Some screws are 6-32 machine screws which require the holes in the frame to be tapped. Other cars are found with thread-forming (or self-tapping) screws which do not require a separate tapping operation.

Another variation of the 2452 has to do with the finish of the large odd-shaped hole in the center of the plastic body. This large hole is shaped to match the profile of the electronic receiver unit — a clear indication that in 1945 Lionel was already preparing for the introduction of the 4109WS electronic set. (Inter-office memos from Lionel show that the application of electronics was discussed as early as December 1942.) What is not as obvious is that this large center hole also contains the "gates," or ports, where the plastic was forced into the mold. These gates are about 3/4" wide and 1/32" high (about half the thickness of the car floor). When the body was removed from the mold, the runners had to be broken off and the marked areas finished. In very early 1945 production, the runners were evidently removed by hand, and the areas were finished with either a knife or a file. The hole edges in the gate areas appear very rough and uneven. Very soon into the production run, Lionel probably produced a special tool to trim off the runner, because in most cars the marked areas are very even and uniform (as shown on the top car in **Figure 11**). Close examination shows evidence of a shearing-type fracture, suggesting a special punch and die tool to trim the hole precisely.

The final variation is probably the most noticeable of all. Some of the early gondola bodies have two extra holes molded into the body floor (see **Figure 11**). These holes go through the exact center of the two locating posts on the bottom of the car body, which project through the matching holes in the metal car frame. These holes were probably intended for wiring from a top-mounted electronic receiver to the trucks below. When Lionel realized that the receiver could be mounted below the floor instead of on top, the holes were no longer needed. The pins in the mold which caused these holes to be formed were simply removed, eliminating the holes. The large irregular hole could not be removed as quickly, even though its original purpose was gone, because (as just mentioned) the large hole was involved with the entrance ports or gates. It was not until 1947 that this area of the mold was reworked.

The 2457 caboose was another prewar carry-over, but it was painted a new color — red. The prewar 2757 semi-detailed caboose was a very good model of the Pennsylvania N5 caboose, accurate in many details, including its dull brown or tuscan color. However, Joshua Lionel Cowen knew that mothers bought lots of trains for their sons and that bright colors sold better than did dark ones. After all, every mother knew that freight trains ended with the "little red caboose," an idea that was reinforced by the children's literature of the time. Apparently, in 1945 the engineering department was persuaded to concede this point of realism for the sake of sales. The prewar Pennsylvania Railroad markings were used on the postwar 1945 caboose. Since the Lionel number did not appear on the car body, there was no numbering error, as was the case with the automobile and tank cars. The correct postwar number, 2457, was rubber stamped in silver on the underside of the frame.

Types 1A and 1B trucks are the only confirmed variations among 1945 cabooses. However, it is not unusual to find a 2457 caboose with a Type 1A truck with whirly wheels on one end and a Type 1B truck with dished wheels on the other. This mix is rarely found on the other cars in the set. The mix can probably be explained by the fact that the caboose required one TCL-1 truck with a center-rail roller pickup for the light, while the other truck was a TC-1 without the roller. This meant two different supply bins for trucks on the caboose assembly line. Obviously, for some period of time the two bins had different vintages of trucks as whirly wheels were phased out and dished wheels were introduced.

The bottom row of **Figure 10** shows late production of the 2452X gondola and the 2472 caboose. These cars are equipped with Type 3 trucks which space the cars about 1/4" further apart than the Type 1 trucks on the 1945 cars in the middle row. The close spacing, which was very realistic, operated reasonably well on the 31" diameter O Gauge curved track. However, when the flying shoe design (Types 1 and 2) was applied to cars in O27 sets, the spacing was a little too close for comfort, since this track has a 27" diameter. When backing around O27 curves, two cars with these early couplers will sometimes touch and even derail. This problem

FIGURE 12: The set carton for the 1945 set is very hard to find. Bob Swanson searched for several years before locating this carton.

was not apparent in 1945, since set 463W always included O Gauge track.

Figure 10 also shows, on the third shelf, the 2472 caboose as shown in the 1945 catalogue, but not produced until 1946 for O27 sets. The caboose pictured has Type 3A trucks, indicating late 1946 production. However, the earliest 2472 cabooses were equipped with Type 1C trucks (thick axles, regular wheels) or Type 2 trucks (regular axles and wheels). These early 2472 cabooses were probably included in the O27 sets numbered 1405, 1409, and 1411, as shown in the spring 1946 dealer catalogue, a seven-page catalogue which preceded the 1946 advance catalogue.

The boxes used with set 463W also provide some insight into 1945 Lionel production. Although I have a number of engine and car boxes for 1945 items, I just recently acquired a 463W set box. Richard Stull of Lorain, Ohio had provided a first-hand description of this set box; I knew what to look for. The part number on the set box is 463W-2. The tan corrugated box measures 14-1/4" long, 12-3/4" wide, and 7" high. It has an orange, blue, and white label pasted onto one of the 14-1/4" sides; the label reads "463W, 'O' Gauge Track, Freight Train Outfit With Built-In Whistle". The use of this label parallels late prewar practice. The box maker's seal shows that the box was made by the Gair-Bogota Corrugated and Fiber Box Corporation of Bogota, New Jersey. If any collector has information about another set box for the 463W set, I would like to hear about it.

Individual boxes for the 463W set components are not as hard to find as the set box itself. There are a number of interesting variations in the component boxes, as shown in the **table** on page 58. Some component boxes were apparently left over from prewar production. These boxes were overstamped in typical Lionel fashion to reflect the correct number of the item packaged inside. One set of rolling stock boxes from a 463W set found in the Chicago area came with the engine, tender, tank car, and caboose boxes all overstamped. The cars in this set all had Type 1A trucks with whirly wheels, indicating early production. Since the new 2452 gondola had significantly different dimensions from the prewar 2812, it is not surprising that the gondola had a new box. However, the 2458 automobile car was so much a leftover that it still carried its prewar number, 2758, on its metal sides. Why was it not in a prewar 2758 box or a 2758 box overstamped with "2458"? With all the 2758 bodies left over, why were there not any 2758 boxes left? Perhaps there

SET 463W COMPONENT BOXES

ITEM	"CHICAGO" BOXES	"NEW YORK" BOXES
Engine	224 over 1664; 11-1/2" x 3-7/8" x 3-1/4"	224: 11-5/8" x 3-7/8" x 3-1/2"
Tender	2466W over 0-2666W; 10-1/2" x 4" x 3-1/16"	2466W; 9-1/8" x 3-11/16" x 2-15/16"
Automobile Car	2458; 11-3/16" x 3-1/4" x 2-7/16"	2458; 11-3/16" x 3-1/4" x 2-7/16"
Tank Car	2555 over 2755; 11-3/4" x 4" x 3"	2555; 11-3/4" x 4" x 2-15/16"
Gondola	2452; 9-7/16" x 2-13/16" x 2-7/16"	2452; 9-7/16" x 2-13/16" x 2-7/16"
Caboose	2457 over 2757; 9-1/8" x 3-11/16" x 2-7/16"	2457; 9-1/8" x 3-11/16" x 2-7/16"

were, and I just have not seen one yet. We await the report of a 2758 automobile car box overstamped with "2458" and containing an automobile car marked "2758", but equipped with Type 1 postwar trucks.

The second set of rolling stock boxes exhibits no overstamping at all. The boxes were all printed with postwar numbers, even those for the cars marked with the prewar numbers. The cars in this second set were all equipped with Type 1B trucks (dished wheels). An example of this set was purchased from the original owner, who received it for Christmas 1945 in Islip, Long Island, New York.

I believe that these two sets may represent the extremes of the 1945 production of the 463W set. The Chicago set with overstamped boxes, Type 1A trucks, whirly wheels, and a 2452 gondola with extra holes in the body probably typifies the earliest 1945 production. On the other hand, the "New York" set with properly marked boxes, Type 1B trucks, dished wheels, and a more refined 2452 gondola probably represents the end of 1945 production of the 463W set. However, this is a somewhat risky generalization because most 463W sets probably contain a mixture of both types of wheels, not a homogeneous grouping as do these two sets.

There may be a plausible explanation for early 1945 production being found in Chicago or even further west, while the later production is concentrated more along the East Coast. It is a simple matter of time and transportation. In 1945 Lionel trains were shipped, fittingly enough, by real trains. That meant time — days or even weeks, depending upon how far the sets had to be shipped. Electric trains destined for the Midwest and beyond probably had to leave the Lionel factory by early November to reach stores in time for Christmas 1945. On the other hand, a truck full of electric trains could have left the Lionel factory in Irvington, New Jersey as late as December 20, 1945 and reached Macy's or any other New York City store on the same day, with several shopping days still remaining. Sounds like a reasonable theory, doesn't it?

But Jim Sattler of Honolulu, Hawaii relates the following story. Several years ago, he purchased a 1945 set from the original owner who received the set for Christmas in 1945. (Sounds familiar, I said.) But this set was received in Hawaii, and, in fact, the original set box is stamped "The Hawaiian Electric Company, Ltd.", an approved Lionel Service Station and the main Lionel dealer in Hawaii at the time. If my plausible explanation (about early production being shipped west) had any validity, this "Honolulu" set should have been about the first set off the line. (How much further west can you go than Hawaii? I do not think Lionel was sending electric trains to Japan in 1945.) Well, Jim reports that his "Honolulu" set is identical to my "New York" set, all Type 1B trucks with dished wheels. So much for my plausible explanation. Any other ideas?

While I am doing this report on 1945 Lionel production, I should include one last subject: instruction manuals and sheets. My "New York" set came with an instruction manual "...copyrighted 1940, Form No. 926-5, Reprinted 1941". The original owner had only this one train set, so I conclude that this was the instruction manual included with this particular 1945 463W set. Other reports have confirmed this conclusion. Has anyone seen a "Form 926-5, Reprinted 1942" manual included with a 1945 set? Or an instruction manual actually dated 1945? If so, I would like to hear from you.

There is one instruction sheet dated in 1945 — 11-45, to be exact. It is "Form No. RCS-8-140X-290M11-45 TT", titled "Instructions For Operating Lionel Electro-Magnetic Couplers". If the 1945 set contained a prewar instruction manual, the need for this sheet explaining the operation of the new knuckle couplers is obvious. What is not so obvious is why Lionel had at least three separate printings of this one instruction sheet, all dated 11-45! The only difference between the three sheets that I have detected is minor lateral shifts in the second line of print under Figures 1 and 2 on the front page. The words and figures are all the same. While I am on the subject of figures, let me point out that

Figure 2 in the instruction sheet dated 11-45 contains very detailed line drawings of 9-1/4" boxcars (e.g., 2454 postwar molded plastic boxcars). I do not believe that these boxcars were available to the public in 1945, but their development was clearly well under way. The earliest 2454 boxcars came with Type 2 trucks (regular wheels and axles) and were probably produced starting in spring 1946. But ... the 9-1/4" boxcars are another story; in fact they are a lengthy story told elsewhere in this edition.

The discussion of the 1945 items in this article is based upon direct observations of eight 463W sets by the author and on first-hand reports from about a half dozen experienced collectors from around the country who own 1945 items and/or complete 463W sets. The 1945 rolling stock features and variations discussed are all supported by independent observations of at least three identical examples. Single examples of other items containing some 1945 features have been reported; however, since these variations could have been "created" by combining components from two or more readily available prewar and postwar items, I feel that more examples must be documented to provide some confidence that the items represent true factory variations. It is likely that some of these unusual variations reflect Service Station repairs of the fragile "flying shoe" trucks and early postwar plastic parts.

Adequate and reliable data concerning factory variations during 1945 production have been very slow to surface. Do any readers have evidence that Lionel produced items, boxes, or even complete sets besides those discussed in this article? If so, please let me know so I can improve the accuracy and completeness of this article in future publications. I am sure that there is more evidence and information available that will ultimately come to light concerning this very interesting period of Lionel train production.

ACKNOWLEDGMENTS

The author would like to acknowledge the tremendous encouragement and factual information provided by Bruce Balsley. When Bruce had only a "Chicago" set and I had only a "New York" set, we had many hard discussions about who had the "real" 1945 set. In the end, we realized that both sets were authentic 463W sets from 1945, and that there were combinations and variations of sets in between. I would also like to thank Cantey Johnson for his insight into the mold design for the 2452 gondola and Rich Stull for sharing his information about set and component boxes. Discussions and written material from Jim Sattler were also appreciated and very helpful. Continuing thanks are also extended to Ed Prendeville and Bob Morgan, whose vast inventory at the Train Collectors' Warehouse has yielded some important clues to understanding Lionel's early postwar production.

And a special note of thanks to Barbara Houtsma for typing and proofreading this manuscript. She converted my "scratch" into something that the publisher and editor could read!

POSTSCRIPTS

ON SET 463W — *Robert Swanson*

Several new pieces of information concerning 1945 production have turned up since the article on set 463W was originally published. First, prewar 2758 automobile car boxes that have been overstamped with the 2458 postwar number have been found. The one that I purchased at York in April 1987 contained a 2758 automobile car with Type 1B trucks. Several other overstamped 2758 boxes have been reported by other collectors.

Next, concerning instruction sheets printed in 1945 (or at least printed with 1945 date codes), the list is much more extensive than I first realized. Besides the uncoupling track sheet RCS-8-140X-290M dated 11-45 that was reported in the article, several additional sheets have been found. These are listed in the accompanying table.

Except for the lubrication notice, these instruction sheets are printed in dark blue ink on light blue paper (various shades). They are either single or double sheets measuring 6-1/4" x 9-1/2". The lubrication notice is smaller, 4-1/2" x 6", and printed in red ink on a light gray paper.

One last and very unusual 1945 paper item has been discovered by Ron Toomajian of Fresno, California. In the bottom of his 463W-2 set box, Ron found a 4" x 4-1/2" red tag with a red braided string through two holes. The tag featured pictures of the new "Real R.R. Knuckle Couplers ... Die Cast Trucks ... Solid Steel Wheels". The reason for this tag became apparent when Ron noticed that the instruction sheet packed with the uncoupling track was marked RCS-8-JODEX-2-41 and pictured the prewar box couplers. This must have been one of the first 1945 sets that Lionel shipped. Incidentally, the automobile car in this set came in an overstamped 2758 box. The tender and cars had a mixture of Types 1A (whirly wheel) and 1B (dished wheel) trucks. [*See article on 1945 trucks for photographs of these wheels on page 184.*]

Finally, two new major variations in 1945 rolling stock have been verified by at least six different collectors in various parts of the country: the **brown** 2457 caboose and the **gray** 2755 tank car.

Initially, I was reluctant to accept the authenticity of these variations, since they could be easily "manufactured" by installing postwar knuckle coupler trucks on prewar cabooses and tank cars. However, after obtaining specific information about truck and coupler details, I now believe that many (if not all) cited examples represent true factory variations. The bodies of these cars are painted the same as prewar bodies and probably represent the use of leftover prewar parts.

The frames of most brown 2457 cabooses are unusual in that they are not rubber stamped with the car number in silver. (Only two out of ten brown 2457 cabooses had the number on the frame.) All ten brown 2457 cabooses observed had Type 1A or 1B knuckle coupler trucks; some had one Type 1A truck and one Type 1B truck. The brown cabooses all had two couplers like all the red 2457 cabooses made in 1945 that I have observed.

Most of the brown 2457 cabooses that I have observed are significantly different from the prewar 2757 in one obvious detail: the white lettering on both sides is offset about 1/4" to the left. The word "PENNSYLVANIA" starts under the left window, instead of being centered between the windows. Were these prewar bodies rejected by inspectors for not meeting 1942 quality standards, but then deemed acceptable in the rush to get trains assembled and shipped before Christmas 1945? Has anyone else ever seen a brown 2457 or 2757 on which the lettering is off-center? Much to my amazement, I recently observed a picture on page 14 in the 1946 advance catalogue that shows a brown Pennsylvania N5C caboose with die-cast trucks and knuckle couplers. And the "PENNSYLVANIA" lettering starts under the left window, just as it does on two brown cabooses in my collection.

The gray 2755 tank car has been even more difficult to authenticate than the brown 2457 caboose. The construction details of the single-dome tank cars make it very easy to swap frames, trucks, and tank bodies. However, the number of gray 2755 tank cars which I have observed (about eight) with precisely correct 1945 frames and trucks suggest that these cars are legitimate factory variations. Finally, in the fall of 1989 I found the proof that I had been waiting for. Two TCA members reported that they had completely intact 1945 sets (463W) which contained gray 2755 tanks cars, rather than silver cars.

Now all that remains is to find a single 463W set which contains **both** a gray 2755 tank car and a brown 2457 caboose. Anybody out there with a 1945 set like that?

Obviously, there are still many questions regarding Lionel's earliest postwar production, but we have come a long way toward uncovering the complete history. If you have further details regarding set 463W or its components, please write to us with this information.

1945 Instruction Sheets

Form Number	Date	Item Description
RCS-8-140X-290M	11-45	RCS uncoupling track
Z-80-20M	9-45	Z transformer
167-29-15M	10-45	167 whistle controller
022-60-25M	9-45	O Gauge switches
45N-2-15M	10-45	45N gateman
152-40-15M	10-45	152 crossing gate
153-30-15M	10-45	153 block signal
153C-18-?	12-45	153C contactor
154-20-15M	10-45	154 highway signal
926-3-IODEX	11-45	lubrication notice

LOOKING AT THE LIONEL BERKSHIRES

Ron Griesbeck

The 726(B) Lionel Lines Berkshire from 1947-1949 with vertically-mounted E unit with lever penetrating the boiler top.

If your enthusiasm for things Lionel is most evident in the pursuit of postwar steam locomotives, you know the frustration of pursuing the elusive and expensive 773 Hudsons. These magnificent locomotives seem to stay beyond the reach of most collectors. The 746 Norfolk and Western locomotives are rapidly approaching the same status. Owners of either or both of these pieces are truly to be envied. However, one of Lionel's most desirable and stately postwar steamers is still (relatively speaking) a bargain within the reach of many collectors due to the sheer volume of units produced: the Lionel 726/736 2-8-4 Berkshire steamer.

Sales of the Berkshire spanned the entire postwar to Fundimensions period, cresting with the golden years of the Lionel Corporation and foundering with its decline. In spite of the overshadowing 773 of 1950 and 1964-1966, and the brief but flashy 746 of 1957-1960, the Berkshire retained its dignity and popularity. It reigned prestigiously not for just a few years, but for more than two decades over the metal-bodied realm of steam, that multitude of rod-spinners. More-

over, its O Gauge rank was never compromised by demotion to O27 status, unlike its "poorer" cousins, the Hudsons and the turbines.

A big locomotive of 2-8-4 wheel arrangement, the Lionel Berkshire is handsome, powerful, and of excellent quality in all of its variations. Since little has been revealed concerning the scarcity of some of these variants, most models sell at comparatively low prices. The 726 Korean War model of 1952, for example, is possibly just as scarce as the coveted Norfolk and Western 726 "J" class, but it sells for less than a third of the price!

The Berkshire family embodies most of Lionel's postwar to Fundimensions steam locomotive innovations, since its production ran continuously from 1946 to 1966, and was catalogued in 1968 to deplete previously made inventory. This long twenty-one-year run put a considerable number into circulation, so they are not too difficult to acquire (that is, if any old "Berk" will do).

However, assembling a collection in decent condition is somewhat challenging! Such a collection can vary in number, depending upon how finely the collector wishes to split variation hairs. I will deal with nine examples which I feel are representative of all the types manufactured: 1946

Photographs by the author.

FIGURE 1: 1946-1949 and 1952 *(left)* and 1950-1951 *(right)*.

FIGURE 2: 1952 *(left)* and 1953-1966 *(right)*.

(726); 1947 (726); 1948-1949 (726); 1950-1951 (736); 1952 (726); 1952 (726RR); 1953-1954 (736); 1955-1956 (736); and 1957-1966 (736). I have combined 1957-1960 with 1961-1966, as only a tender variation occurred during that period.

The following discussion and accompanying photographs will show varieties which were apparently created deliberately by engineering or styling modifications. Much of the material has been covered by other books and articles. My goal is to add my findings to the known data and to condense the total picture to a reference catalogue which new collectors might find valuable.

In an effort to avoid repetition and overlap, I have arranged the photographs and text categorically rather than chronologically. A complete charted variations chronology is included on page 70 for convenient reference.

CAB NUMBERS

Although the Berkshire began life as model 726 and evolved eventually into 736, the evolutionary process was complicated by shortages of magnetic Magnetraction materials during the Korean Conflict. The silver "726" number rubber stamped in the "fat and fancy" style appeared on the first-year models of 1946 and continued through 1949 (**Figure 1**, left). The year 1950 saw the introduction of Magnetraction, and the number "736" heralded the innovation (**Figure 1**, right). The new number, however, was carried only through 1951. Enter the "Korean Connection."

Because of the Korean War, magnetic materials became scarce, and Lionel responded in 1952 by omitting the Magnetraction feature and reverting to the "726" number in two variations: the old 1946-1949 type of numbers and a new style, thin and condensed "726" numbers with small capital letters, "RR", below (**Figure 2**, left), to indicate that the locomotive was a "rerun."

As peacetime returned, so did Magnetraction, and the "736" numbering for 1953 came in a new heat-stamped white version (**Figure 2**, right). This final numbering, thinner and cleaner, would continue unchanged to the termination of production in 1966.

The photographs in **Figures 1** and **2** also exhibit an interesting and somewhat random quirk in cab window arrangement. A three-window type, with the rear horizontal frame omitted, turned up somewhat sporadically throughout the years of production. I doubt that the window struts were removed or broken by their owners, as has been suggested, since all are symmetrically opposite and on the same year models. The "broken-window" theory sounds too much like a conspiracy to be credible!

The four-window type appears to have run irregularly during 1946-1949, 1952, and 1961-1966. The three-window variety filled the gaps: 1950-1951 and 1952 (RR version). The irregularities suggest that combinations of features may be rather abundant.

BOILER DETAILS

Two front boiler assemblies are isolated (**Figure 3**) to compare the head lamp housing of 1946-1952 (left) with the 1953-1966 version (right). A small brace cast into the plate below the housing (arrow, right) gave more rigidity to the housing and may have been Lionel's response to complaints about bent or broken headlights.

A view from a different angle reveals further internal modifications to the boiler fronts (**Figure 4**). The assemblies are seen from the bottom side with the smokebox door open. In 1946 through 1949 the assembly was attached by two lugs (left). In 1950 the lower lug (A) vanished along with a notch (C) and a small hole (B) in the head lamp plate. The new top lug (D) was beefed up in width (right). The bulb clip (E) appeared in 1947, when smoke lamps were phased out in favor of a new resistance-coil smoke unit. Both boiler fronts fit all

FIGURE 3: 1945-1952 *(left)* and 1953-1966 *(right)*.

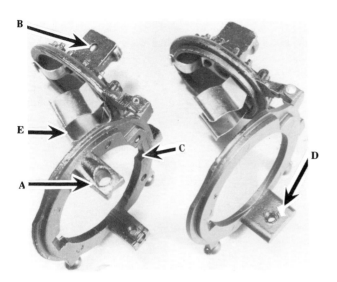

FIGURE 4: The 1946-1949 assembly *(left)* and 1950-1966 *(right)*.

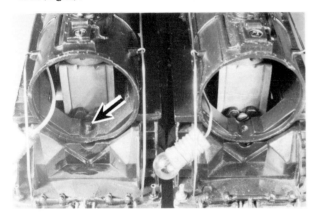

FIGURE 5: 1946-1949 *(left)* and 1950-1966 *(right)*.

FIGURE 6: 1946-1947 *(left)* and 1948-1966 *(right)*.

FIGURE 7: 1946-1954 *(left)* and 1955-1966 *(right)*.

FIGURE 8: 1946 *(left)* and 1947-1966 *(right)*.

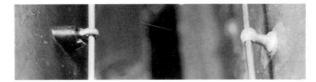

FIGURE 9: 1946 *(left)* and 1947-1966 *(right)*.

Berkshire boilers, unlike the similar conversion of the turbines, where the 1946 boiler front will not fit later models.

Locomotives from which the boiler front examples were taken (**Figure 5**, left) show the frame-to-boiler screw (arrow) extending beyond its hole. It loosely retained the lower lug of 1946-1949 fronts, as the lug hole was over-sized and un-

tapped. As the lower lug was omitted, the screw furnished was shorter (right).

The pair of pilots (**Figure 6**) compare the 1946-1947 model without coupler (left) to the more detailed redesign of 1948-1966 (right). (A similar detailed redesign occurred on the smaller 675 and 2025 locomotives.) A somewhat scale-sized drop coupler is sculpted with its attending lift gear. The brake hose is shackled by a chain. Note the deeper depressions between thinner vertical bars of the pilot.

On the corners of two pilot beams (**Figure 7**) are the two types of flagstaffs. The hexagonal base of 1946-1954 (left) is contrasted to the round base of 1955-1956 (right). These flagstaffs are found in aluminum or painted black somewhat randomly. Some locomotives turn up with no evidence of ever having flagstaffs installed in their empty holes.

FIGURE 10: 1946 *(left)*, 1947-1949 *(center)*, and 1950-1966 *(right)*.

On the top of the boiler castings (**Figure 8**), the 1946 sand dome (left) appears small and round. In 1947 (right) it was lengthened aft to nearly double its former dimensions, and a rectangular hatch finished its appearance.

Above the newer sand dome is evidence of the new E-unit, with its lever protruding through a transverse slot.

The prewar influence is apparent with a nicely turned stanchion guiding the handrail on the initial model of 1946 (**Figure 9**, left). Four of these stanchions were fastened with small brass nuts on each side of the boiler. For 1947 (right), inexpensive cotter pins were inserted through projections cast into the boiler, the method all further models would adopt.

The three inverted boiler castings reveal their simulated reverse gear details (**Figure 10**, boxed area). The easily broken 1946 open-type casting (left) was strengthened in 1947 (center) and ran through 1949. It was further simplified in 1950 (right) and ran unchanged for the balance of production.

The 1950-1966 boiler received a flat projection (arrow) indicating adaptation of the Berkshire boiler shell to other Lionel locomotives. This projection had no purpose whatsoever on the Berkshire models. New steamers, such as the 2046 Hudson, used the same boiler. It was attached to their frames by the use of a long Phillips screw which attached to this projection.

FRAME AND DRIVE

The pilot-cylinder casting was riveted to the frame on the first 1946 Berkshire. A unique frame assembly with drop-out wheels, axles, and gears, it was a serviceman's delight. A long cast plate (**Figure 11**, left), with collector arms attached, retained the entire drive train and wheels in their channels.

The first and fourth axles were geared and driven by a long, longitudinal worm shaft. Despite the impressive construction, the 1946 Berkshire was slow, gear noise was horrendous, and traction proved disappointing.

A new frame emerged in 1947. Simulated spring suspension and lower boiler contours were added to the frame casting, filling in the previously open area between boiler and frame (**Figure 12**). Axles now passed through holes across the new frame, and wheels were pressed on in conventional fashion.

Center-rail collector assemblies are of three types (**Figure 11**). In 1946 the cast four-screw plate described above held the collector arms. From 1947 through 1956 a smaller two-screw stamping was utilized (center). The same arms and wide rollers were attached. A total redesign appeared in 1957 (right). Smaller and with narrow rollers, the assembly was attached with a single large-headed screw; this arrangement ran through 1966.

FIGURE 11: 1946 *(left)*, 1947-1956 *(center)*, and 1957-1966 *(right)*.

FIGURE 12: 1946 *(top)* and 1947-1966 *(bottom)*.

FIGURE 13: 1950-1951/1953-1966 *(left)* and 1952 726/726RR *(right)*.

An extraordinary performance improvement in 1950 — Magnetraction — employed a cylindrical magnet (**Figure 13**, left, A) mounted in a cavity between the third and fourth driver axles. Magnetic flux was conducted along iron side plates (B) which flanked the frame. In 1952 the war postponed the feature, resulting in the omission of magnet and

FIGURE 14: 1946 *(left)* and 1947-1966 *(right)*.

plates (**Figure 12**, right). They returned in 1953 to run through 1966.

Pilot truck guide plates (**Figure 14**) were attached by two screws in 1946 (left). In 1947 the plate was staked to the pilot underside (right) and provided with a hole for access to the frame-boiler screw. This became the standard practice through 1966. The other pair of holes added to the cylinder casting had no purpose on the Berkshire. Again, interchangeability with other steamers necessitated the alteration.

DRIVERS AND RODS

Driving wheels of 1946 through 1949 models of the Berkshire were the attractive "Baldwin Disc" type, as lettered on the counterweights (**Figure 15**, left). These wheels were also used on other steamers of the period, such as the 224, 675, and 2025. Nickeled tires were pressed onto the cast wheels in prototype fashion. However, with Magnetraction in 1950 came the traditional spoked wheel of sintered iron (right). In reality, locomotive wheels evolved from spoked

FIGURE 16: 1947-1966 locomotive.

FIGURE 15: 1946-1949 *(left)* and 1950-1966 *(right)*.

type to disc type; Lionel's Berkshire demonstrated reverse chronology in this regard.

Eccentric cranks were given a tiny notch in 1947 (**Figure 16**, arrow). This notch appeared on all models to follow. In addition, the connecting rods of 1946 were embossed with a small bump on the simulated coupling (**Figure 17**, arrow). In 1947 and thereafter, this surface was flat. The rods themselves were nickel plated from 1946 through 1952. Brighter cadmium plating was employed thereafter.

PILOT AND TRAILING TRUCKS

In 1946 the pilot truck wheels had a hollowed area surrounding their inner raised centers (**Figure 18**, left). Two square spokes radiated at 180 degrees across this hollow area. Conventional wheels followed in 1947 through 1966 (right). Original equipment pilot trucks on the Berkshire and many other Lionel steamers are good indicators of a locomotive's "mileage." Any derailment would result in a shower of sparks from beneath the pilot truck as it dragged across the power rail, causing a short circuit. A glance back

FIGURE 17: 1946 locomotive.

FIGURE 18: 1946 *(left)* and 1947-1966 *(right)*.

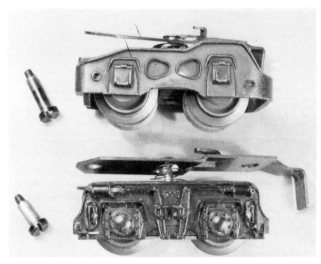

FIGURE 19: 1946-1954 *(top)* and 1955-1966 *(bottom)*.

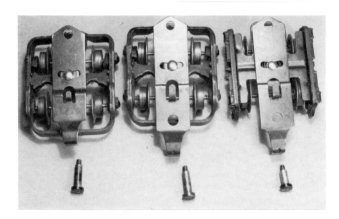

FIGURE 20: 1946-1949 *(left)*, 1950-54 *(center)*, and 1955-1956 *(right)*.

FIGURE 21: 1946 *(top)*, 1947-1948 *(center)*, and 1949-1966 *(bottom)*.

at **Figure 14** will show the progressive wear of the soft iron axle housing.

The four-wheeled rear truck of 1946 was framed in one piece of cast metal, as shown in **Figure 19** (top). It wrapped completely around the wheels, sides, front, and rear. The as-

sembly was installed with a long shank screw and was used through 1954. A cheaper rear truck (**Figure 19**, bottom) with a stamped-metal bolster and black plastic side frames appeared in 1955. Well-detailed but light in weight, it ran through 1966. A shorter screw was provided to fasten it to the frame.

FIGURE 22: 1946 "LIONEL ATOMIC PRECISION MOTOR" *(left)*, 1947-1948 "LIONEL PRECISION MOTOR" *(center)*, and 1949-1966 "LIONEL" *(right)*.

A top view of three rear truck assemblies (**Figure 20**) shows various combinations of truck and draft gear used. The 1946-1949 drawbar (left) was short and coupled the tender prototypically close to the locomotive cab. Lengthening the drawbar by 1/4" in 1950 (center) allowed clearance for the new tender design of that year. In 1955 the new plastic-sided truck mentioned earlier was equipped with the same longer drawbar (right).

FIGURE 23: 1946 *(top)*, 1947-1948 *(center)*, and 1949-1966 *(bottom)*.

ELECTRICAL SYSTEMS

In **Figure 21** the motor and reversing systems are shown in profile. A 1946 horizontally-mounted 726M-1 motor (top) shows its tubular brush holders and jack plug, while the leverless E-unit lies prone and is equipped with a return spring. The slanted 671M-1 motor installation (identical to the one employed in the 671 PRR turbine) debuted in 1947 with a smaller casing. This chassis also came with the new vertically-mounted E-unit with lever and gravity return which would appear on all future models of the Berkshire. A ballast weight of lead alloy bolted between the E-unit and the motor was an attempt to enhance traction on 1947 through 1949 locomotives.

In 1949 the motor brushes were integrated with the back plate on the new 681-100 motors (bottom). The absence of tubular projections is apparent. The example also shows the ballast deleted. Since this particular locomotive chassis is of 1961-1966 vintage, Magnetraction eliminated the need for added weight. Incidentally, ballast was not used on 1952 models in spite of omission of the Magnetraction feature during that year. The same group of chassis is viewed from both rear and top (**Figures 22 and 23**) to show these three basic types of installations.

Being "deluxe" items, all Berkshire locomotives were equipped with smoke units. In 1946 the first models were produced with the marginally-performing 18-volt lamp-type smoke unit. The same lamp also provided illumination for the headlight. The unit used a wire "flapper shaft" to pump smoke. All locomotives to follow received a new resistance coil smoke unit with a stamped-metal smoke lever pump; this unit required the addition of a headlight socket to be attached to the smokebox door. A felt stack gasket sealed both old and new units. Occasionally, 1946 locomotives will be found with the newer smoke unit, since Lionel offered conversion kits to service stations for any owner wishing a conversion to the newer unit.

FIGURE 24: 1946 2426W *(top)*, 1950 2671WX *(second)*, 1952 2046W *(third)*, and 1961 736W *(bottom)*.

FIGURE 25: 1946-1949 2426W *(left)* and 1950-1966 2671WX, 2046W, or 736W *(right)*.

FIGURE 26: 1946-1949 2426W tender *(top)* and 1950-1966 2671WX, 2046W, or 736W *(bottom)*.

TENDER VARIATIONS

Since the Berkshires were sold as premium O Gauge locomotives, it was appropriate that their tenders be first class (**Figure 24**). All had motor-driven two-tone whistles. The first Berkshire of 1946 was sold with the highly desirable 2426W tender (A). This tender was lavishly detailed. Turned-metal stanchions guided wire railings around its deck. The all-metal die-cast body shell also had separate cast steps on its front and stamped-metal steps on its rear, as well as a plastic inlaid coal pile fastened by two screws. This tender, which weighed over two pounds, was rubber stamped "LIONEL LINES" in white serif lettering on its detailed flanks. Silver lettering also appeared on a small quantity of 1946 tenders. It rolled on six-wheel passenger car trucks and had a coil coupler. The same tender came with the celebrated 773 of 1950; after its discontinuance, its like would not be seen again until Fundimensions revived the tender type in 1981 with its Chicago & Alton Hudson passenger set.

A plastic "Pennsylvania"-type streamlined tender with a water scoop became the standard Berkshire tender in 1950

and thereafter (**Figure 24**, B, C, and D). This tender had several variations. The 1950 Berkshires were trailed by a 2671WX tender with "LIONEL LINES" widely spaced in small letters decorating its sides (B). The same six-wheel trucks and couplers were retained. The drawbar had two 45-degree bends within its length, compared to the two 90-degree bends on that of the earlier tender. The plastic body shell was retained by a screw at each end.

This tender received a new lettering treatment (C) and a new number, 2046W, in 1952. The expanded and larger "LIONEL LINES" is easily differentiated by an examination of the "O" in "LIONEL". It appears round on 1950-1951 models and flattened or elliptical on 1952-1960 tenders. This tender received four-wheel cast-metal freight trucks with a magnetically-operated coupler. A manual tab was added to the coupler in 1955.

The streamlined tender was altered again in 1961 (D). This time "PENNSYLVANIA" was heat stamped on its side in white letters, and it was renumbered "736W". This tender ran until the end of Berkshire production in 1966. It was furnished with cheaper plastic-sided AAR four-wheel trucks and a disc-operating coupler typical of Lionel's practice at this time with its freight cars. The cheapening of this tender was the sign of bad times to come; Lionel was declining rapidly towards the end of Berkshire production.

Lionel 726-736 Series Steam Locomotives

2-8-4 Berkshire Type (226 Boiler Derivative) — Variations Chronology, 1946-1966

MODEL YEAR	1946	1947	1948	1949	1950-1951	1952	1953-1954	1955-1956	1957-1960	1961-1966†
Cab Number	"726" Rubber-Stamped — Silver					"736" RS — Silver	"726" or "726RR" RS — Silver	"736" Heat-Stamped — White, Thinner Typeface		

ELECTRICAL

	1946	1947	1948	1949	1950-1951	1952	1953-1954	1955-1956	1957-1960	1961-1966
Motor	726M-1 "Atomic"	671M-1		681-100						
Drive	Horizontal, Dual Worm	30° Slant, Single Worm								
Brushes	Tubular Receptacles			Receptacles Integrated with Motor Backplate						
E-Unit	Horizontal, Spring Ret. Jack Plug	Vertical, Gravity Return, Lever through Top of Boiler								
Collector Assembly	4-Screw Cast Mount	2-Screw, Stamped Mount							1-Screw, Smaller Stamped Mount	
Smoke Unit	Lamp Type, 18V	Resistance Wire Heating Element								

WHEELS

Drivers	Zinc, Lettered "Baldwin Disc", Steel Tires				Sintered Iron, 1-Piece, Spoked					
Axles	Bottom Drop-Out	Through-Frame								
Traction Aid	None	Ballast Weight			Magnetized Drivers	None	Magnetized Drivers			
F & R Trucks	Cast-Metal Frames — Front and Rear							Rear — New Style Stamped Frame, Plastic Side Frames		
Pilot Plate	2-Screw Mounted	Staked to Pilot/Steam Chest Casting, Access Hole for Screw								

CASTINGS

Boiler	Short Dome, Open Detail	Long Sand Dome, Filled Valve Gear Hanger Detail, Cast Stanchion Posts								
Cab Windows‡	3- & 4-Window		4-Window		3- & 4-Window		3-Window		3- & 4-Window	
Frame	Open Bottom	Closed Bottom, Simulated Lower Boiler and Suspension Added			Magnet Cavity, Iron Side Plates	Cavity, No Side Plates	Magnet Cavity, Iron Side Plates			
Pilot	No Simulated Coupler	Cast, Simulated Coupler and Lift Pin Assembly								
Boiler Front	2 Small Mounting Lugs — Top and Bottom, 2 Notches Horizontally Opposite	1 Large Mounting Lug — Top Only, 1 Notch at Locking Snap								
Smokebox Door	No Head Lamp Brace, Hole in Head Lamp Baseplate						Cast Head Lamp Brace, Baseplate Hole Deleted			

HARDWARE

Side Rods	Notch in Eccentric Crank, Coupling Flat (nickel plated in early years; cadmium plated c. 1953-on)									
Handrails	Turned Stanchions with Nuts	Cotter Pin Attachment								
Flagstaffs	Hexagon Base (transition date unclear)							Round Base		
Head Lamp Lens	Flat Plastic Disc					Solid Lucite				
Draft Gear	Engine and Tender Close Coupled				Lengthened 1/4"					

TENDER

Frame Number	2426W				2671WX	2046W				736W
Body Style	Large Die-Cast Derivation of Prewar 2226W				1-Piece Plastic, Streamlined Pennsylvania type, with Water Scoop					
Misc. Details	Plastic Coal Pile, Turned Stanchions, Wire Handrails				3 Back-up Lamp Holes	Back-up Lamp Holes Filled				
Lettering	RS "LIONEL LINES", Silver or White in 1946, Silver only 1947-49				"LIONEL LINES" Small Type	"LIONEL LINES" — New Typeface, Larger				"PENN-SYLVANIA"
Trucks	6-Wheel, Plastic Side Frames				4-Wheel, Cast-Metal Side Frames					4-Wheel, All Plastic
Coupler	Electromagnetic				Spring-Loaded Plate (Manual Tab Added in 1955)					Plastic, Metal Disc, No Tab
Whistle	Cast-Metal Housing, Horizontal Motor Shaft	Plastic Housing, Vertical Motor Shaft								

MISC.

	1946	1947	1948-49		1950-51	1952 (2 varieties)	1953-54	1955-66		
Major Variants	1946	1947	1948-49		1950-51	1952 (2 varieties)	1953-54	1955-66		
Catalogue Price	N/A	$37.50	$42.50		$43.50 ($45.00 in 1956)				$47/$49	$50/$60

† Not manufactured after 1966, sold until 1968

‡ 3- and 4-window variations are known to exist in many (possibly all) 226 derived boiler/cab castings (i.e., 646, 726, 736, 2046, 2056)

FIGURE 27: 1946-1949 2426W *(left)*, 1950-1951 2671WX *(center)*, and 1952-1966 2046W or 736W *(right)*.

FIGURE 28: 1946-1949 2426W *(left)* and 1950-1966 2671WX, 2046W, or 736W *(right)*.

The tops and the front ends of these tenders are compared to illustrate the basic body design differences between the 1946-1947 and 1950-1966 tenders. Note the apparent massiveness of the earlier model. The 2426W tender looked expensive — and it was!

An interesting view of the three tenders shows back end variations (**Figure 27**). The 2671WX (center) had three small holes. These became back-up lights when the tender was sold with a small number of 1948 671 turbine locomotives.

The idea was never popular and was too expensive, so the holes were filled in for the years 1952 and afterwards (right). Another very subtle difference on the 2671WX can be seen at the top vertical tabs of the ladder (arrows), which

appear separated from the tender body shell. This separation was filled on all post-1951 models.

"Under the hood" of the tender, a pair of whistle mechanisms are compared (**Figure 28**). The mechanism of the 2426W (left), with its heavy die-cast metal housing, is mounted on its side. This mechanism produced a much clearer, more mellow sound than did its successor in 1950 and later (right), which was mounted in a "shaft-upright" position and made of marbled plastic in its earlier years and black plastic later on. The later mechanism's air intake used the water scoop for its air duct.

During the declining years of Lionel, the continued production of the Berkshires became a poignant reminder of the Lionel Corporation during its heyday. Today, the 726 and 736 stand as reminders of the excellence once achieved by the old Lionel Corporation.

It was inevitable, then, that Fundimensions would reintroduce the Berkshire, and, indeed, this occurred in 1980 with the production of the Chessie Steam Special and Union Pacific models. Two years later, a magnificent Berkshire was produced in Nickel Plate Road markings, this time with its original premium metal 2426-style tender. It is only fitting that these Fundimensions products represented what the original Berkshire was — the very best in steam locomotives. Indeed, the Nickel Plate Road Berkshire, with its electronic whistle and "Sound of Steam," might represent the ultimate in Berkshire production.

My personal need for a comprehensive but handy guide resulted in the chronology chart which accompanies this article. It is revised frequently as more data is discovered. Hopefully, the chart, coupled with the text and photographs, will enhance significantly the much-deserved interest in the fine Berkshire locomotive series.

LIONEL STEAM TURBINES

HOW DO THEY DIFFER? — *Pat Scholes*

Few postwar Lionel locomotives captured the imagination of the train-buying public more than did the Lionel model of the Pennsylvania Railroad's innovative S-2 steam turbine. From its introduction in 1946, the Lionel turbine was a runaway success; it was the first locomotive to be produced with Lionel's smoke units, and it included nearly every deluxe feature available.

This popularity has continued with collectors. Now, as then, the turbines have been excellent sellers, and many hobbyists still run them regularly as the best "haulers" in their operating collections.

How many variations of this impressive locomotive did Lionel produce from 1946 until its last year of production in 1955? Such a long production period would suggest that there were quite a few variations, especially in view of the popularity of the engine. In fact, no fewer than eighteen variants of this locomotive have been identified!

Variations may not be every collector's priority. However, tracing the turbine variations through the ten years of Lionel production gives a fascinating account of the attempts to "catch the eye" of children and adults interested in toy trains. Equipped with a prototypical 6-8-6 wheel arrangement, Lionel's turbine sported a total of twenty wheels! The sight of all this imagined power churning furiously down tinplate track has always been spellbinding and impressive indeed, especially when the turbine is coupled with the 1948 twelve-wheel tender.

The purpose of this article is to outline the progression and variations of the twenty-wheel steam turbine from its introduction in 1946 until its discontinuance in 1955. Some of the variations are quite subtle, while others are pronounced. Most of my observations are from examples which appear to have a history of not being altered after they left the factory. This, of course, can be very difficult to verify, but sometimes the originality can be inferred if the locomotive is purchased from original owners (or dealers who have bought it from original owners). In any case, much effort has been expended in examining many sets to arrive at the following information. Readers are asked to write with any additional information they might have so that the chart included in this article can be updated in subsequent editions. As with

automobiles, the turbines were changed on a "model year" basis. In the first four years of production, 1946 through 1949, there were three "lines" of turbines with three different number designations: 2020, 671, and 671R. With each year, a change in one of these lines was accompanied by changes in the others. In other words, the design changes in the 1948 2020 were the same as the design changes in the 1948 versions of the 671 and 671R. Since there were design changes each year in the first four years, this accounts for twelve variations (four years times three lines per year).

In addition to the engine number, some other characteristics to observe are:

- Presence or absence of thick nickel rims on the drive wheels.

- Presence or absence of thin blackened rims on the drive wheels.

- Extruded wheel weights on the drive wheels, as opposed to inset or recessed versions.

- Presence or absence of the E-unit lever protruding from the top of the cab.

- Presence of "ELECTRONIC" decals. These distinguished the radio-controlled 671(R) from the regular 671.

- Tender design. There were two basic types. One was the short, high 2466-type tender. It is different from those found on other locomotives of the period in that it has vertical handrails on all four corners. The second streamlined type was the long, low, water-scoop Pennsylvania tender, that was introduced in 1948 and was produced with six-wheel and later with four-wheel trucks.

There are two other distinguishing characteristics which are covered in the hobbyist literature in great detail. For completeness, however, both are included here:

- The position of the motor mounting (horizontal or slanted).

- The presence of additional valve gear linkage on the front drive wheels. This is found on the 682, along with a white stripe on the edge of the catwalk down each side of the engine.

Three different tenders that came with Lionel turbines. 2466-type *(left)* and two different versions of the long, low streamlined tender: 2671W *(center)* with twelve wheels and backup light holes and 2046W-50 *(right)* with eight wheels and filled-in holes. R. Bartelt photograph.

The long, low twelve-wheel tender with water scoop catalogued as 2671W and, later, 2671WX. We call this the streamlined tender. R. Bartelt photograph.

TENDERS

An examination of the tender varieties available with the turbine is an interesting part of a study of engine and tender variations. As mentioned earlier, the turbine was accompanied by two basic tender types: the high, short 2466-type, and the long, low 2671-type. An example of each type can be seen in the photographs. According to the 1946 catalogue, the 2020 came with the 2466WX tender which has no vertical handrails on the corners, as part of outfit 1413WS. All other 1946 engine and tender sets I have studied which appear to be original have had the tender with vertical handrails attached. In fact, the picture in the 1946 catalogue shows handrails on all the 2020 sets. All other sets in 1946 had the tenders with vertical handrails. These tenders were numbered 2020W, 671W, or 4671W, depending upon the engine number. Another complication is that the numbers were not stamped on the undersides of the tender in 1946, as they were later.

At Lionel, the tender variations from the basic design were sometimes denoted by adding or changing a digit in front of the number. Thus, the electronic tender in 1946 was numbered 4671W. Since the digit was "4", this leads us to conclude that the long, low Pennsy 2671W tender was on the drawing boards as the 1946 catalogue was being printed, even though it did not appear until 1948. The 4671W was produced unchanged until the electronic set was discontinued after the 1949 model year. It was basically a 671W

tender with chassis modifications to accommodate the radio receiver.

In 1947 none of the tenders were changed. In 1948, however, the 2671 Pennsylvania tender made its debut. Early production models had backup lights in the three portholes in the end of the tender, as did the prototype. There is some evidence that a few of these early models with backup lights were numbered 2671WX — the number which later denoted the same non-lighted tender with "LIONEL LINES" markings. The backup lights were soon discontinued, probably due to production cost compared to added value. The run was so short that the lighted tenders are, in my opinion, a prize all their own. (The feature is easy to install on non-lighted tenders, but original installations can be detected by the protrusion of three plastic knobs, part of the original plastic lens, out of the portholes. Post-factory additions would simply have a flat plastic lens glued inside the tender.) The light holes in the plastic tender shell were to persist through 1953, when they were finally filled in.

Another change to the tender occurred in 1948. Lionel was converting its couplers from the original coil-operated version to the mechanical flap-type coupler. Rolling stock which underwent this change and had a four-digit number was customarily denoted by changing the first digit from "2" to "6". Thus, the 2020W tender would become a 6020W. Oddly, I can find no evidence that the coupler was changed from coil to mechanical on the 6020W tender, despite the number change. It appears to have remained equipped with the coil coupler until it was discontinued after 1949. In fact, it may not have been planned to change the coupler on this

The short, high 2466-type tender was catalogued as 2020W, 671W, or 4671W. R. Bartelt photograph.

The streamlined tender later came with eight wheels. It was catalogued as 2046WX, but usually had "2046W-50" rubber stamped on its underside. R. Bartelt photograph.

A 1946 Lionel 2020 turbine with 2020W eight-wheel tender. The tender has vertical handrails at the corner. The locomotive does not have a reverse unit lever protruding through the boiler top; however, there are two receptacles on the brushplate for activating or disabling the E-unit. The drivers have thick shiny rims. H. Holden Collection, P. Bennett photograph.

tender, since the tender was due to be phased out. Since the 2671W tender had six-wheel trucks, it retained coil couplers because the mechanical coupler had not yet been developed for the longer trucks. Of course, the 4671W tender (and the other electronic cars) were forced to continue with coil couplers because they had to be activated from track power through the radio receiver; this would have been impossible with a mechanical coupler.

The last year for the production of the 2020 turbine — and its 6020W tender — was 1949. Likewise, the 4671W would not return in 1950; the electronic set was being discontinued. However, the 2671W was alive and well. In 1950 this tender continued to be pulled by a turbine, the new 681 model. (The engine number increased by ten when Magnetraction became a feature of certain locomotives.) The 681 was a redesigned 671 equipped with magnetized wheels for pulling power and stability. This combination remained until early 1952, when the Korean War caused magnetic materials to be in short supply. Because the 1952 engine reverted to 671 to signify the omission of Magnetraction, Lionel apparently took the opportunity to cut production costs on the 2671W tender. The company outfitted it with four-wheel trucks so that it was basically the same as the tender pulled by the 2046 Hudson, which was, of course, the 2046W. However, the Hudson's 2046W had "LIONEL LINES" on its sides instead of "PENNSYLVANIA". Therefore, the Pennsy eight-wheel tender was distinguished as a separate unit by numbering it 2046W-50, although it was referred to in the catalogue as 2046WX. This configuration remained through 1953.

In 1954 the turbine was modified and numbered 682. The tender remained 2046W-50, but it had a different plastic tender body shell. The backup light holes, unused since 1948, were filled in so that only an outline of the circles remained. The "PENNSYLVANIA" lettering on the tender was shorter, measuring 5-5/8" rather than the 6" length which existed from 1948 to 1953. There were no changes in 1955, the last year of production.

ENGINES

As previously mentioned, the steam turbine series was introduced in 1946 as the 2020, 671, and 671R. They had no E-unit lever protruding from the top of the cab. The round turbine housing had a flat outer surface. This is where the electronic decal was located on the 671R. The motor was horizontally mounted, and all eight drivers had thick and shiny nickel rims. The wheel weights were extruded, not inset (this characteristic would remain through 1949). A pair of receptacles on the brushplate was used to activate or disable the E-unit, depending upon which receptacle had the plug-in wire inserted into it. The tenders were not numbered, but they were the 2466-type with vertical handrails on all four corners.

In 1947 the cab casting and running gear were changed. This is the cab casting which would run through the end of production in 1955. The motor was mounted on an angle in the chassis to accommodate a single worm drive, rather than a double one as used in 1946. This slanted motor mounting continued through the rest of production. The cab casting had a slot in its top for the E-unit lever. The round turbine housing had a rounded outer surface. This necessitated moving the 671R electronic decal to a new position under, and

A 1947 chassis from a 671 with resistance coil smoke unit, vertical E-unit, and nickel rimmed drivers. The motor is stamped "LIONEL PRECISION MOTOR". R. Bartelt photograph.

The 671RR from 1952 had a space in the chassis between the first and second drivers where the magnets, if available, would have gone. Also note that the wheels do not have rims. R. Bartelt photograph.

Like the 1950 model, the 1951 model of the 681 did not have rims. It did have inset wheel weights and the Magnetraction magnet. It pulled the 2671W twelve-wheel tender. H. Holden Collection, P. Bennett photograph.

forward from, the engineer's window. All eight drivers still had nickel rims. The smoke unit was changed from the bulb-activated unit to a resistance coil unit which was to continue through the rest of production. Due to the presence of the E-unit lever, the receptacles on the brushplate were no longer needed, so they were discontinued from production of the 671 and 2020. However, the 671R retained them for connection from the electronic reversing unit in the tender. The tenders had the numbers stamped on the underside, usually in silver. The boiler showed extra piping detail just behind and below the smokebox, where the steam chest would be on a conventional steam locomotive. Because Lionel offered a conversion kit to install the new resistance coil smoke unit, some 1946 models will be found with a resistance smoke unit. Finally, a small number of early production locomotives had the numbers "671" or "6200" rubber stamped in silver on the boiler front Keystone instead of the more common red and gold decal. The exact manufacturing sequence for this change is not clear. Similar stampings are found in the 1947 production models of the 675 and 2025 locomotives as well.

In 1948 the 671 was coupled with the 2671W tender (or possibly in some cases the 2671WX). The 2020 was equipped with the 6020W tender, which was unchanged from the 2020W tender except for its number. All three turbines had thin, blackened rims on the front and rear pairs of drivers only; the two middle pairs had no rims.

The year 1949 brought little change. The main item of significance was that the rims on the drivers were discontinued completely.

In contrast to 1949, 1950 brought about many changes. The 2020 was discontinued, probably because Lionel wanted to concentrate sales of the turbine upon the O Gauge market (the 2020 had been marketed as an O27 locomotive).

The 671R electronic set was also discontinued. The 671 itself was fitted with Magnetraction and became a 681. In the process of designing and manufacturing the wheels to be responsive to the magnetic bar in the chassis, the drive wheel weights were inset rather than extruded, as they had been. The 681 pulled the 2671W tender, as had the 671 in 1949. No changes were made to the engine or tender in 1951.

The shortage of Magnetraction alloys in 1952 caused that feature to be eliminated shortly after production started. Although the 1952 catalogue was printed with the anticipation of materials shortages, some train sets were apparently produced with the 681/2671W combination. One of

my own train sets, purchased new in 1952, has the cars exactly as catalogued in 1952, but they are pulled by a Magnetraction 681! It was purchased as part of an unbroken set. In any event, Lionel soon had to cease 681 production and manufacture 671 locomotives, which were in reality 681 locomotives without Magnetraction. The firm apparently still had 671 cabs left over from 1949, so these were put on the non-Magnetraction 681 chassis. The 2671W was discontinued in favor of the less expensive eight-wheel tender, the 2046W-50. These 1952 671 engines can be distinguished from their 1949 counterparts, which also had no rims on the drivers, by the inset wheel weights and the hole through the frame between the first and second axles, where the magnet bar was omitted.

This year of 1952 eventually led to a further mixing of cab and number configurations. Lionel apparently exhausted its stock of leftover 671 cabs, so the company reissued them as 671RR (re-run). This number was the only change to the locomotive. The tender remained the 2046W-50. Still later, another 1952 variation emerged. Apparently, the magnetic materials for Magnetraction became available again before Lionel had used its complete stock of cabs marked 671RR. So, being prudent business people, they fin-

671 from 1952. Note opening in chassis behind first driver. R. LaVoie Collection, B. Greenberg photograph.

The 682 is distinctive because of the white stripe on the running board and its lubricator linkage attached to the first driver. R. Bartelt photograph.

The 671R electronic control turbine was numbered "671" beneath the window, but had distinctive decals on both the locomotive and tender. Note the radio receiver under the tender. H. Holden Collection, P. Bennett photograph.

ished their 1952 production by manufacturing some 671RR locomotives with Magnetraction! The example of this locomotive that I possess seems to be authentic. Although the Magnetraction 671RR is interesting from a historical point of view, I do not consider it particularly valuable because it would be simple to fabricate one by interchanging cabs. Early 1952 saw the end of the impressive 2671W twelve-wheel tender; it would not return.

So, the year 1952 saw four variations:

• 681/2671W with Magnetraction (same as 1950-1951)

• 671/2046W-50 without Magnetraction

• 671RR/2046W-50 without Magnetraction

• 671RR/2046W-50 with Magnetraction

SUMMARY OF STEAM TURBINES

1946	2020 / 2020W	All tenders are short 2466-type. No tender numbers. No E-unit lever. Receptacles for E-unit wire on motor brushplate. Smoke bulb. Thick nickel rims on all drivers. Extruded wheel weights. Horizontal motor, no Magnetraction. 671R has black electronic decal on round turbine housing.
	671 / 671W	
	671R / 4671W	
1947	2020 / 2020W	Tenders have numbers on underside. E-unit lever in cab. No receptacles for E-unit wire on motor brushplate (except 671R). Smoke heater unit. Slanted motor. Thick nickel rims on all drivers. No Magnetraction. 671R has black electronic decal moved to location under, and forward from, engineer's window.
	671 / 671W	
	671R / 4671W	
1948	2020 / 6020W	6020W tender is same as 2020W. Thin blackened rims on front and rear drivers. No rims on center drivers. Tender 2671W is long, low, streamlined water scoop-type. It has long (6") "PENNSYLVANIA" lettering, open light ports in back, and twelve wheels. 671R electronic decal same as 1947.
	671 / 2671W	
	671R / 4671W	
1949	2020 / 6020W	No rims on any of the drivers.
	671 / 2671W	
	671R /4671W	
1950	681 / 2671W	Has Magnetraction and inset wheel weights.
1951	681 / 2671W	Same as 1950.
1952	681 / 2671W	Same as 1951.
	671 / 2046W-50	No Magnetraction. No magnet in frame. Inset wheel weights. The 2046W-50 has eight wheels; otherwise very similar to 2671W.
	671RR / 2046W-50 (two variations)	Numberboard re-printed with "RR" under "671"; otherwise same as 671 above. Most 671RRs do not have Magnetraction; a few of them do.
1953	681 / 2046W-50	Same as 1950, except with 2046W-50 eight-wheel tender.
1954	682 / 2046W-50	Extra valve gear linkage. White stripe down side of engine. 2046W-50 tender has short (5-5/8") "PENNSYLVANIA" lettering and filled-in light ports in back.
1955	682 / 2046W-50	Same as 1954.

The year 1953 saw the re-emergence of the 681, this time with the 2046W-50 tender. Except for the tender, it was identical to the 1951 model.

In 1954 the 682 turbine arrived; this version has been the one most sought after by collectors. It is not as rare as other variations, but it is definitely in a class by itself because of the detail changes Lionel made to it. This locomotive had extra valve oiling gear on the front drivers and long, white striping along each side. The paint wore off quickly with handling, and it is difficult to find with the white paint fully intact. If you possess a 682, let me caution you against running it too much. A little bit of wear on the extra linkage can cause it to jam the drivers. The inertia of the engine is usually enough to break off the fragile linkage, and this seriously impairs the appeal and value of the engine. The 682 ran unchanged in 1955, which was the last year of production for the engine.

The chart included with this article summarizes the variation sequence, but if you have additions or corrections, please let us know.

The crowning irony of the Lionel S-2 turbine is that Lionel sold many thousands of these locomotives as toys, but their prototype was a coal-devouring prototype on the Pennsylvania Railroad, and the only one that was ever built.

But the story of the Lionel turbine was not over yet! After an absence of thirty years, Lionel's successor, Fundimensions, reissued the turbine as part of its Famous American Railroads series.

The new turbine, marketed in the spring of 1985, was the most spectacular version of this locomotive ever produced. Lionel's original turbines were a uniform black, but this one had Brunswick green upper works and a silver smokebox. In addition, the new model also had a big twelve-wheel tender with Sound of Steam and whistle, Magnetraction, white striping and whitewall drivers, smoke, the extra oiling linkage of the old 682 (reinforced, one hopes!), and even backup lights in the tender! This locomotive continued a long love affair with a truly magnificent tinplate masterpiece.

THE POSTWAR 1666 LOCOMOTIVES

Warren Blackmar

A comparison of two different postwar 1666 locomotives. Note the bell and hanger on the left locomotive and single-piece bell on the right locomotive. Also note the hatches on the top of the forward dome of the left locomotive. T. Riley Collection, R. Bartelt photograph.

Both of these 1666s have the rounded cab floor, but the locomotive in the top photograph has rubber-stamped numbers, and the locomotive in the bottom photograph has metal number plates. R. Bartelt photographs.

The 1666E, a 2-6-2 Prairie-type steam locomotive, first appeared in the 1938 catalogue in gray with the 1689T-type sheet metal tender. In 1939 it was painted black and came with the 1689T-type tender again. In 1940 some versions were equipped with a new plastic tender with coal pile. This combination continued with minor casting changes until World War II interrupted production of Lionel trains.

The 1666 was one of four prewar locomotives, two of which carried their old numbers, that reappeared as train production resumed. It is reasonable to assume that some engines were assembled with available parts and sold after the war, and that they are identical to the late prewar models with the exception of the tender trucks. The new die-cast trucks with knuckle couplers were used with the earliest units equipped with trucks having the "floating shoe" pickup.

Lionel did not catalogue the 1666 locomotive in 1945. It is possible that 1666s were assembled or manufactured and sold in 1945, but we have no data to support this supposition. However, Lionel did catalogue and sell the 1666 in 1946. The 1666 was not shown in the 1947 consumer catalogue or thereafter. However, it was included in a special

A comparison of the pilot trucks of an early postwar 1666 *(left)* and later 1666 *(right)*. The left truck is die cast while the right truck is stamped steel. R. Bartelt photographs.

A close-up of the number plate on the prewar 1666. Number plates are also found on the postwar 1666 locomotive. The prewar locomotive cab floor did not extend beyond the cab side walls. R. Bartelt photograph.

1947 spring promotional set, 3105W, shown on page 3 of the 1947 advance catalogue.

The 1666s manufactured after the war differed from the prewar 1666s in several ways. The cab floor end was rounded rather than straight across as on the prewar version. The postwar 1666 came with a 2466WX tender with staple-end trucks with coil couplers, while the prewar models had tenders with box couplers. The early postwar 1666 (probably manufacturered in 1946) was similar to the prewar model in a number of ways. It had number plates with "1666" in silver on a black background. The bell mechanism consisted of two parts. The first was a cast bell with a horizontal shaft mounted on a stamped-steel bracket. It, in turn, was fastened by a screw to the boiler. The pilot and steam chest were mounted by screws, which fit in drilled and tapped holes in the boiler casting; the front truck was cast; the center drive wheel on each side had slots to receive the nibs of the cast eccentric crank; the eccentric crank was at-

tached by a slotted screw; the rear truck mounting plate holes were drilled and tapped in the casting; and the headlight socket had a screw base.

However, later 1666s, probably manufactured in 1947, had noticeable changes. The two-part bell was replaced by a single-piece casting riveted to the boiler. The number "1666" was rubber stamped in silver on the cab beneath the windows. The steam chest pilot casting was peened to studs in the boiler casting. The front truck was stamped steel; the center drive wheel on each side had cast-in studs on which the steel eccentric crank was attached by a hex-head screw. The boiler casting had undrilled depressions at both the front and back that had been drilled and tapped on earlier engines.

As an active operator at that time, the first thing I did when the parts became available was to replace all of the trucks on my prewar rolling stock with the "new knuckle coupler" trucks in order to mate with the new equipment I was getting. I performed this upgrade on many tenders, as few people at that period were interested in maintaining factory originality. It is interesting to hear the contemporary speculation of factory variations and assembly techniques that may have resulted from conversions performed by myself and numerous other operators of the late 1940s.

A complete listing of 1666 locomotives and variations can be found in *Greenberg's Guide to Lionel Trains, 1945-1969, Volume I.*

THE 2400-SERIES PASSENGER CARS

Ralph Hutchinson

Freight cars, with their numerous variations and many colorful paint schemes, have starred in many fine articles. So have the large, aluminum-bodied passenger cars that Lionel made in response to AMT's competitive models. Yet, the smaller O27 passenger cars, which are of special interest to me, have not been so extensively studied. These cars were catalogued at various times as O Gauge, as well as O27 Gauge equipment.

In order to determine the origin of the various 2400-series O27 passenger cars, a history of their development is needed. Researching the catalogues and books written about Lionel led me to the conclusion that the catalogues were more accurate in their descriptions of these cars than they were with the freight cars. What follows, then, is as comprehensive a discussion of the development of the 2400-series O27 passenger cars as possible, given the current information available.

Through the years, the Lionel Corporation produced a large number of passenger cars, including the small metal prewar carry-over cars produced in green, brown, or blue finish; the ever-famous Madison cars (see Tom Rollo's article on these cars on page 84); the O Gauge streamlined cars first produced in 1952; and the O27 passenger cars. These last cars, however, did not originate as O27 cars, but as dual-gauge items.

The 2400 series made its debut in 1948 with the release of two Pullman cars and an observation car. These cars were painted green and accented with yellow trim, white lettering, and gray roofs; they were the 2400 Maplewood Pullman, the 2401 Hillside observation, and the 2402 Chatham Pullman. They came in an O27 set headed by the 2025 2-6-2 steam locomotive and in an O Gauge set headed by the 671 Pennsylvania turbine. The cars were offered for separate sale, and the same sets were offered again in 1949.

Some basic features about these cars should be noted:

- The cars were based upon a Pullman-Standard design.
- Both the coach and the observation cars were rich in rivet detail.
- The cars had metal interior framework, including the bulkheads, light sockets, and roof supports.
- All cars had two-bulb interior illumination with the lamps connected in series. They used the Q-90 (later 51-300) bayonet-based 6-8 volt bulb.
- The cars came equipped with a new AAR die-cast four-wheel passenger car truck with wire-wound (coil) couplers.

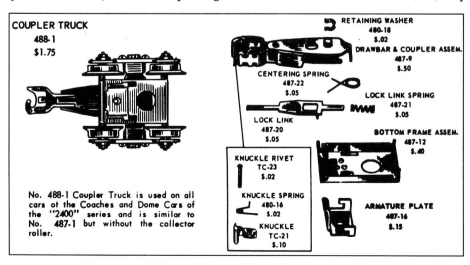

COUPLER TRUCK
488-1
$1.75

No. 488-1 Coupler Truck is used on all cars ot the Coaches and Dome Cars of the "2400" series and is similar to No. 487-1 but without the collector roller.

RETAINING WASHER
480-18
$.02

DRAWBAR & COUPLER ASSEM.
487-9
$.50

CENTERING SPRING
487-22
$.05

LOCK LINK SPRING
487-21
$.05

LOCK LINK
487-20
$.05

BOTTOM FRAME ASSEM.
487-12
$.40

KNUCKLE RIVET
TC-23
$.02

KNUCKLE SPRING
480-16
$.02

KNUCKLE
TC-21
$.10

ARMATURE PLATE
487-16
$.15

The 2400-series passenger cars featured the 488-1 coupler truck, which is basically a 487-1 without the collector roller. Further information on this truck design can be found on page 658 of *Greenberg's Repair & Operating Manual For Lionel Trains* as shown here.

Page 27 of the 1952 Lionel consumer catalogue shows "Lionel Streamline Coaches," all of the 2400 series.

One remarkable feature of this series is the construction anomaly which persisted from the introduction of the series through to its (slight) redesign for 1954 production. During this period, the roof was attached to the car by means of two large screw fasteners that were made to look like roof ventilators. When the roof was installed correctly, with the rain shield over the door end of the car, the holes for these screws did not quite match the screw receptacles on the car body. They only matched correctly when the roof was installed backwards, with the rain shield at the wrong end of the car. The misalignment was so slight that the cars still could be assembled either way. As a consequence of the misalignment, stress on the plastic bodies often resulted in hairline cracks in the body shells at their bottoms, where the ends joined with the sides. Since most of the cars were assembled correctly at the factory, this cracking is a readily observable phenomenon. Its absence is a virtual guarantee that the car has never been disassembled, even to change the light bulbs — and that the roof was mounted backwards at the factory in the first place! The phenomenon seems to be most common on the yellow Anniversary cars of 1950.

In the anniversary year of 1950, Lionel changed the color scheme and numbers of the cars. Introduced were the 2481 Plainfield Pullman, the 2482 Westfield Pullman, and the 2483 Livingston observation car; these cars had yellow-painted bodies and gray-painted roofs. The new cars came with a pair of matching 2023 Union Pacific Alco AA diesels. This set, commonly referred to as the "Anniversary Set," is the most desired of the 2400-series passenger trains. Another set of cars, the 2421 Maplewood Pullman, the 2422 Chatham Pullman, and the 2423 Hillside observation, were offered in an O Gauge set headed by the 681 Pennsylvania turbine steamer. These cars had a silver-painted finish with gray roofs, black lettering, and pin stripes above and below the window panels. All passenger cars had silhouettes in the windows in 1950, the first year this realistic feature was offered. The silver-painted cars were also offered for separate sale, while the yellow cars were not. Of the three names on the Anniversary cars, only the "Livingston" name would reappear on a later car.

The silver-painted cars returned in 1951. These cars were headed by a pair of 2023 Union Pacific Alco AA locomotives in matching silver, gray, and black. They were also offered for separate sale. For the first time, the cars did not appear in an O Gauge set; henceforth, they would be catalogued only as O27 equipment. There appears to have been

only one run of the black-lined, gray-roofed cars and these were probably unsold 1950 production items.

In 1952 the 2421, 2422, and 2423 cars were produced again, but this time they were painted entirely silver. They had black lettering, but lacked the pin stripes of the previous year's production. They were joined by a new Pullman, the 2429 Livingston. This car has not, to my knowledge, been seen in any other guise but its all-silver paint with black lettering. However, some collectors have speculated about the possible existence of a 2429 Livingston Pullman painted in the 1950 silver paint scheme with a gray roof and black pin stripes. The Lionel Service Manual, the Lionel catalogues, and all studies of these cars are silent about its existence. I have never seen this car; nor do I know of any collector who has reliably reported upon one. I believe that such a car was never made at the factory. However, a collector could add the 1950 features to the 2429 to make it match the 1950 series, since the gray roofs were available and the black lines could easily be added.

There were several production runs of the 2421 series during the years in which they were offered. This can be determined if one looks at the car stampings. I have found at least three different sizes in the "LIONEL LINES" logo on the cars. Differences can be noted in the thickness of the letters and the shape of the "O" in the word "LIONEL". The smaller lettering appears on the "LIVINGSTON" and its mates from 1952; it is most noticeable when the cars are placed next to an earlier car in the series. The lettering has not been centered between the top of the window panels and the row of horizontal rivets. The cars would have had a better appearance had the lettering been centered.

Two sets were offered in the 1952 catalogues, a four-car train headed by the 2056 Hudson steamer (a non-Magnetraction 2046 produced only in 1952) and a three-car set, excluding the 2429 Livingston, headed by the all-silver 2033 Union Pacific Alco AA pair. All four cars were also offered for separate sale.

In 1953 the all-silver-painted cars ran again in two sets with two changes: the 2429 Livingston was no longer offered in a set, and the steam locomotive was replaced with the 2055 small boiler Hudson. The 2429 Pullman was, however, offered as a separate sale item; it has become the scarcest car of this series because of its inclusion in only one set.

In 1954 there were some noticeable changes in the cars. Until this year, the trucks upon which the cars rolled had been equipped with the electromagnetic solenoid (coil) couplers, and each truck carried a light pickup roller. Because these cars were constructed in this fashion, the interior lights burned constantly; they did not flicker as the cars traveled over switches and crossovers. Sometime in 1954, however, a magnetic coupler replaced the coil arrangement; it was quite similar to that found on the larger O Gauge aluminum cars. Now, only one truck carried a light pickup roller. Thus, the lights in these new cars flickered like those in cabooses whenever the cars hit a dead spot on the track. Interestingly, the light sockets were still connected in series. This meant that a 6-8 volt No. 51 bulb was still needed, and if one bulb went out, the other would not light.

On the car bodies themselves, the numbers and colors changed once again. The Pullman coaches were now the 2434 Newark and the 2435 Elizabeth; the observation car became the 2436 Summit. The lettering on these cars was red, rather than black. For the first time since the series had been introduced, a new design appeared: the 2432 Clifton Vista Dome car. This car had the same body as the Pullman coaches, but the roof was altered to include a domed viewing area atop the car. The 1954 cars were offered in two three-car sets, one headed by the 2065 Baldwin-bodied Hudson (smaller boiler), and the other by the 2245 Texas Special F-3 AB single-motored diesel pair. All of the cars were offered for separate sale.

The same cars were offered again the next year separately and in three-car sets headed by the 2328 Burlington GP-7 and the 2245 Texas Special F-3 AB pair. There was also a four-car set headed by the 2065 locomotive and, curiously, the catalogue mentioned that the cars were "suitable for O Gauge operation." As has been pointed out in previous articles, 1955 was a year in which many strange things happened at Lionel. Set components were no longer mentioned; the line was cheapened; and, in the case of the larger O Gauge passenger cars as well as others, no effort was made to insure that cars within a set were of the same vintage.

In 1956 the silver-painted cars were offered for separate sale and in a three-car set headed by the General Electric locomotive commonly known to collectors as a 44-ton diesel, in this case the silver 629 Burlington model. A new set of cars was introduced this year: the 2442 Clifton Vista Dome, the 2444 and 2445 Newark and Elizabeth Pullman coaches, and the 2446 Summit observation. These cars carried new numbers because they had a painted red stripe running along the window areas for the length of the cars. These cars were offered for separate sale, as well as included in a set headed by the silver Burlington GP-7. This set did not include the 2445 Elizabeth Pullman; instead, it had two 2442 Clifton Vista Dome cars.

The next year, the red-striped cars were dropped from the line, but the silver-painted cars with red lettering were still available with one change. The name on the 2436 observation car was changed from Summit to Mooseheart. Once again, the 2435 Elizabeth Pullman was not offered in any catalogued set.

In 1958 the cars were offered once again. The Clifton and Mooseheart cars were available in a set headed by the 216 Burlington Alco A unit, and the same cars, joined by the Newark Pullman, were offered in a set headed by the 209 New Haven Alco AA diesels. Once again, the 2435 Elizabeth

Pullman was excluded from set offerings; this car has joined the Livingston as a scarce car in this series.

In 1959 only one set was offered, but it included three new cars: the 2412 Vista Dome, the 2414 Pullman, and the 2416 observation. These cars were headed by the 208 Santa Fe Alco AA pair. For the first time since the introduction of the series, they sported a name other than "LIONEL LINES" above the windows. Instead, they were now lettered for the Santa Fe in blue with a broad blue stripe running along the window panels. These cars were without specific names for the first time; this would be the case for the rest of the cars' run in the postwar years. In place of the name, these new cars only carried a number. The all-silver-painted cars were not offered, but the new Santa Fe cars were offered for separate sale in the catalogue. However, 1959-style orange perforated boxes for the 2432 and 2436 do exist.

In the following year, two Santa Fe Vista Dome cars and the observation car were offered in a set pulled by the 218 Santa Fe Alco AA pair with the famous red and silver "war bonnet" paint scheme. Since it was a Presidential campaign year, Lionel offered a set of campaign stickers for Presidential candidates. With these stickers, the purchaser could modify his passenger set into a political campaign train by adhering the stickers to the sides of the cars. The 2414 Pullman was offered as a separate-sale item only.

In 1961 a four-car set, including the 2414 Pullman, was offered; once again, the set was pulled by the 218 Santa Fe Alco AA. Similar sets were available in 1962 and 1963, with the cars being available for separate sale in all three of these years.

In 1964 three new all-silver-painted cars were introduced to the series. These cars were the 2404 Vista Dome, the 2405 Pullman, and the 2406 observation car. They were the cheapest cars Lionel created for the entire series. They lacked both the interior lighting and the detailed window stripes. This set of cars was headed by the 212 Santa Fe, and the same set was offered again in 1965. The cars still carried the Santa Fe logo. The photograph of the 2406 observation in the 1965 catalogue shows the car with one passenger truck and one freight truck at the boat end, and the car is shown with window stripes. Thus, the cars used for the catalogue illustrations were not the cars being produced that year.

In 1966 three new cars were introduced: the 2409 Pullman, the 2408 Vista Dome, and the 2410 observation. As in earlier years, these cars were illuminated and equipped with the window strip silhouettes. Their Santa Fe markings were meant to go with the 212 Santa Fe Alco in a set that year, and they were offered for separate sale as well. This was the last year for the 2400-series passenger cars in the postwar era; they did not return in the 1968 or 1969 catalogues. (Remember that there was no 1967 catalogue or production.)

No discussion of the 2400-series passenger cars would be complete without at least a brief mention of the subsequent revivals produced since the General Mills takeover of Lionel Trains in 1970. They first appeared in 1973 as a special set made for the Train Collectors' Association. One car was issued per year, beginning in 1973, and the locomotive, a new U36B, came out in the Bicentennial year of 1976. The cars were painted in red, white, and blue Bicentennial markings and had the same construction as their postwar predecessors, including the die-cast passenger trucks. The wheels were the only difference; they were the new Fundimensions tapered wheels rather then the postwar variety.

The second appearance of these cars in the Fundimensions era came in 1976. The Lake Shore Limited set featured two Pullman cars, the 6404 and 6405, a 6403 Vista Dome, and a 6406 observation, all in Amtrak markings and headed by the 8664 Amtrak Alco A unit. (An Alco B unit in Amtrak markings, the 8667, was available separately.) These cars were not offered for separate sale. They did not have the old silhouettes in the windows; however they were illuminated and equipped with plain frosted window strips to diffuse the light. In 1977 three more cars were offered as separate-sale items to expand the set: the 6410 and 6411 Pullman cars and a 6412 Vista Dome.

Despite their illumination and operating couplers, there are some significant construction differences between these cars and the earlier production. The two roof screws resembling vents on the 2400-series cars are absent on the Amtrak cars. The metal framework was also eliminated. The trucks on the Amtrak cars were taken from the wood-beam models used for the Fundimensions 9500-series passenger cars (ironic, since this design is much older than the design of the cars themselves). The operating couplers on these plastic trucks have a visible plunger apparatus (the "thumb-tack" design) which some collectors feel detracts from the appearance of the cars. Finally, the windows on the car doors have been filled in.

These cars also appeared in 1983 when Fundimensions issued its Quicksilver Express in Texas and Pacific markings. The cars came only in a set pulled by an 8318-8319 Texas & Pacific Alco AA locomotive pair; they were the 7200 Pullman coach, the 7201 Vista Dome, and the 7202 observation. These cars were constructed in the same fashion as the Amtrak cars. This set was an extremely brisk seller, no doubt because of the attractive dark blue and silver paint scheme.

In 1987 the cars were painted in a Pennsy scheme with tuscan sides and black roofs as numbers 16000, 16001,

16002, and 16003. They reappeared again in 1989 with a New York Central paint scheme. This offering included the 16016 baggage, 16017 combine, 16018 and 16020 coaches, 16019 Vista Dome, and 16021 observation.

Indeed, the original 2400-series cars have persevered. The names Lionel chose for these cars could tell an interesting story if we could be transported back into the past. Chatham, Clifton, Elizabeth, Hillside, Livingston, Maplewood, Newark, Plainfield, Summit, and Westfield were all names of northern New Jersey cities and towns in the metropolitan New York area. (So, for that matter, are Irvington and Madison.) Chances are this was Lionel's way of honoring the communities in which the executives and workers made their homes. In fact, some of the names had special meaning. Hillside was the location of the Lionel factory, and Clifton was the home of the Beacon Tool and Die Company, the firm which made the dies for Lionel's F-3 locomotive. During its earlier years, Lionel had a factory in Newark as well.

The only exception to this common denominator is the name Mooseheart. This car was named for the home for children maintained by the Loyal Order of Moose near Aurora, Illinois. Perhaps this was the favorite charity of one of Lionel's chief executives.

Another minor note: Lionel catalogued two other cars as part of sets containing 2400-series passenger cars. One was the 3428 operating U. S. Mail car. The other was the 6572 Railway Express refrigerator car. Lionel catalogued the 2400-series cars with only one F-3 diesel, the 2245 Texas Special AB pair; the rest of the sets were headed by the smaller Alco diesels. Personally, I have always favored the F-3 over the Alco for looks (as do most collectors), and an F-3 pair followed by one or both of the catalogued freight cars and four or five of the 2400-series passenger cars makes an attractive train, especially at "night," when the glow of interior lighting creates a fantasy of passengers patiently awaiting their arrival at some imaginary destination.

Because Lionel produced so many different cars in the series, the small postwar passenger cars can make an interesting and colorful collection.

OBSERVATIONS ON THE MADISON CARS

Thomas S. Rollo

Do you see the major difference between the two cars in the top right photo? Sorry — it is not the number! Nor is it anything as obvious as the different shade of tuscan paint — although those things do count. There really is no difference in the paint itself, although it might appear so. The particular paint Lionel used on the Madison cars was highly susceptible to mildew, and any perceived difference in the paint shade or gloss is the result of cleaning.

Study the lettering closely. On the 2627 Madison car at the top, the words "LIONEL LINES" are perfectly centered on the eight passenger compartment windows in the center of the car body. The name "MADISON" is then centered upon the words "LIONEL LINES". Because the words "LIONEL" and "LINES" each have a different number of letters, the car name is off-center in terms of the car body.

Now look at the lower car, 2625, which is exactly the opposite. The word "MADISON" is centered on the window post in the middle of the car, and the words "LIONEL LINES" are centered upon the name "MADISON". This means that the words "LIONEL LINES" are off-center on the car.

Both lettering formats are distinct and collectable, and their presence gives some insight into the finishing process. The cars were lettered and numbered in two different processes, the numbering first and the lettering second. The car numbers always appear in the same location. This explains the merry mix-up of names and numbers that appear on the prewar cars and the appearance of three different car names with the same number in the postwar cars in early 1947.

The question is: Which lettering format is correct? If you use a standard of judgment based on the prewar cars, neither one is correct! The lettering on the prewar cars is all properly aligned. The words "LIONEL LINES" are directly above the passenger compartment windows, and the car name is centered on the window post. Reflected light from the car body clearly exposes the areas of the car surface where rivets have been omitted to facilitate the lettering.

Photographs by Bill Kojis.

The "L" in "Lionel" on the early postwar format is in the riveted area. The car name is off-center in the smooth area under the windows of the later format cars. It is an awesome thought, but in terms of the prewar cars, all of the postwar cars are factory errors!

Well... not really. To be a true factory error, the lettering would have to be done unintentionally, and that clearly

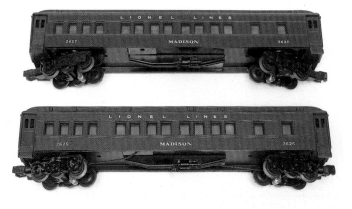

Take a look at the picture above. In fact, take a really *good* look.

Was Lionel responding to its own confusion? Here is a 2625 that came in a box marked "2625" and remarked "2628". The car dates from 1947.

is not the case with the postwar cars. The smooth painted bodies of the Madison cars did not hold their paint very well; as a result, many cars turn up with much of the paint flaking off.

This sad state of affairs has made the whole series a great candidate for restoration and repainting. Sometimes the repainting is done so well that it is impossible to distinguish the repainted car from the original without inspecting the lettering carefully to see whether it is heat stamped, as were the originals, or silk screened, as are most of the restorations. Generally, those who repaint the cars quite logically follow the absence of rivets as a guide for relettering the cars. That being the case, the collector can spot a repainted car right away if it is a postwar car. If the car has a postwar number and the lettering is right, it is wrong!

The 2625 Madison car in the photograph on the previous page and the 2625 Manhattan car illustrated with its box are both from early 1947; on both examples, the car name is centered beneath the windows. These photographs show that the numbers 2627 and 2628 for the postwar Madison and Manhattan cars were later assigned and used. The box shown was remarked by the factory to conform to the catalogue listing. Note that the number "2628" is rubber-stamped in the white band on the box flap next to "LIONEL", but the box contained a 2625 Pullman. It would seem unlikely that Lionel would make the same mistake twice, considering the prewar numbering and lettering mix-up. (In 1941 to 1942 Lionel produced a 2623 Irvington Pullman, a 2623 Manhattan Pullman, and a 2624 Manhattan Pullman. Lionel used the same number, 2623, for cars with different names — Irvington and Manhattan — contrary to their previous policy. Lionel also used different numbers — 2623 and 2624 — for the same car, the Manhattan Pullman. To add to the confusion, a 2624 Manhattan observation car was catalogued but never made, as far as is known.)

What has happened is a void between the decision-making and manufacturing processes. The 1946 cars (or those we generally regarded as 1946 cars) always appear with the lettering format of the two 2625 cars shown, but always with the name Irvington. Three known factory sets of these cars were studied for this article; all have the names and number mentioned, and all the body molds are in mottled colors of red, brown, and green specks. The body mold colors can be seen by looking at the bottom edge of the body. There are always four spots, two on each edge, which are never covered with paint.

This is caused by the rack upon which the body rested while in the paint-spraying booth. The dried miniscus is visible on either side of each unpainted area, proving that the spots are not paint chips.

Photographs of two other sets of cars bearing the same numbers and three different names were also studied: the three cars in black and white photographs on pages 146 and 151 of the 1987 edition of *Greenberg's Guide to Lionel 1945-1969*, and those pictured running behind a GG-1 on the outer loop of the 1948 Lionel showroom layout, perhaps the most photographed model train layout in history. By 1948 the three names, Irvington, Manhattan, and Madison, with three different numbers, 2625, 2627, and 2628, still appeared in the format of the 1946-1947 cars. It is difficult to identify 1948 cars specifically, since the catalogued sets for

1948 and 1949 were the same. One set studied was pulled by a 726 Berkshire with a tube-type brushplate and a simulated coupler and lift pin on the pilot, dating it as a 1948 product.

If you are fortunate enough to own either of the 1948 or 1949 sets in their original set and individual boxes, the dating is easy. The 1948 sets came in set boxes with a separately printed label pasted onto the box. The 1949 sets came in set boxes with labels printed directly onto the box.

Sometime in late 1948, Lionel began to tape the coupler coils to hide the bright copper characteristic of all coil couplers before that time. Most likely, the impetus to tape the coils was brought about by the introduction of the 2333 Santa Fe and New York Central F-3 diesel locomotives in that year.

The long coupler with a bare copper coil protruding through the pilot would have detracted from the appearance of these locomotives. Since coil couplers were being phased out on standard rolling stock due to the introduction of the magnetic coupler, more attention could be given to the coil couplers on premium units where the trucks could not readily be retooled for magnetic couplers or adapted to their use. Disguising the coupler coils by taping made the premium cars and locomotives which retained them look more like the rolling stock fitted with the new magnetic couplers.

The 2627 Madison car shown in the first photograph is a 1949 product. Although the most obvious reason is that there are no passenger silhouettes in the windows, there are two other, more convincing reasons. The first is that the car in the first photograph has grooves worn in the body mold under the paint at each end of the roof where the clerestory (raised portion) curves down and meets the roof line above the end train door. This is an indication of die wear.

The molding compound used to produce the Madison car body is granular in nature and is pre-formed into measured cakes. The pre-formed cakes are placed into the mold and the compression process is started. The material is pressed throughout the mold cavity at a temperature of 300 to 350 degrees Fahrenheit (your basic slow oven), and pressure of 2,000 to 5,000 pounds per square inch is applied for approximately eighteen seconds (not your basic pressure cooker!). In time, the friction produced by thousands upon thousands of repetitions of this process will cause a roughness on the mold surface, producing streaks or a pebble-like finish on the body shell. These effects can be seen in the finished casting of the 2627 in the first photo.

The second method for determining 1949 production is seen in different methods of wiring the lamp sockets. In the earlier cars produced in 1946 through 1948, the sockets are wired right through the lamp bracket. In 1949 and 1950 the socket is wired through a hole in the frame provided for that purpose directly behind the truck. For this change, the assembly procedure had to be modified. On the earlier cars, the truck and lamp sockets could be wired in advance, regardless of the presence or absence of the frame. However, when the wiring method was changed in 1949 and 1950, the truck, lamp bracket, and frame had to be part of the same assembly process, since the wire had to pass through the frame itself.

MADISON CAR SUMMARY

Year	Number	Names	Component Boxes
1946	2625	Irvington only	Art Deco without toy manufacturer's association logo
1947	2625	Irvington, Madison, Manhattan	Art Deco often restamped 2627 or 2628
1948	2625 2627 2628	Irvington, Madison, Manhattan	Individually type-stamped Art Deco boxes for all three numbers
1949	2625 2627 2628	Irvington, Madison, Manhattan	Early Classic boxes with San Francisco listed in the border
1950	2625 2627 2628	Irvington, Madison, Manhattan	Middle Classic boxes without San Francisco listed in the border

From the presence of two different lettering styles in 1949 and 1950, it could be concluded that the popularity of the cars had grown to the point that more than one production run was needed for each of the two final years the cars ran. In 1950, of course, the passenger silhouettes in the windows identify the year of production quite clearly.

Because authentic 1950 silhouette cars command premium prices (refer to Volume I for values), great effort in forgery takes place. Even genuine "pebble-grain" mylar silhouettes hardly prove 1950 vintage. No one seems to agree on the location of the "L" as being the true test, although many use this as a general guideline. Have you noticed that the nickel plating has a different brightness on the metal stamped plate on the underneath of 1950 frames as opposed to the same hardware on those of other years?

The Madison cars were popular items which are highly prized today by collectors. These cars, although they command stiff prices in excellent condition, show up more often than do the red-striped Santa Fe aluminum passenger cars or even the gold-striped Presidential passenger cars. With the exception of the 773 Hudson, the locomotives which pulled these cars in original sets turn up frequently as well. Since many collectors have made up sets of these cars and their locomotives, it is difficult to authenticate the manufacturing progression of these cars from 1946 to 1950.

Why hasn't Lionel reissued the Madison cars, either in the later postwar era, the Fundimension's age, or Lionel Trains, Inc.'s modern era? This issue is one of the great mysteries of the Lionel Corporation. Legend has it that the dies for the Madison cars were lost in 1951 or 1952, when the company accidentally included them in a shipment of scrap metal for the Korean War effort. That story has never been authenticated. However, other manufacturers, most notably the Williams firm, have produced a good number of Madison-style cars with considerable resemblance to the originals, even to the frames and later wiring method for the lights. The earlier Williams cars even have the opening vestibule doors of the originals, although the later versions lack this feature.

The initial Williams trucks were plastic units with non-operating couplers. Later cars had trucks with operating couplers. These cars keep the Madison car tradition alive.

For further insights into the production and premature discontinuance of the Madison cars, see "Breaking the Mold," an interview with Lee Price, on page 7.

ORDER OUT OF CHAOS

A SYSTEMATIC STUDY OF LIONEL'S 9-1/4" BOXCARS — *Robert Swanson*

One may make a case that the 2454 series and its offshoots are Lionel's anticipation of Rodney Dangerfield's comedy routine — they "don't get no respect!" These boxcars, which were manufactured by Lionel from 1946 through 1953, have been neglected far too long by Lionel collectors. On the larger side, they are overshadowed by the popular and more colorful 6464 series, and on the smaller side, they are outnumbered by the cheaper 6004 / 6014 / 6024 / 6044 series. Lionel's catalogues from this period did little to stimulate interest in the 9-1/4" boxcars,

TABLE 1
MAJOR VARIATIONS OF 9-1/4" BOXCARS

CATALOGUE NUMBER	ROAD NAME	YEARS MADE	BODY COLOR	LETTERING
2454(A)	Pennsylvania	1946 (early)	Lt. Orange	Black
2454(B)	Baby Ruth	1946-47	Lt. Orange	Black
3454	P R R Merchandise	1946-47	Silver	Blue
3464(A)	A T S F	1949-52	Orange	Black
3464(B)	N Y C	1949-52	Tan	White
3474	Western Pacific	1952-53	Silver	Black
4454	Baby Ruth (Electronic)	1946-47	Lt. Orange	Black
6454(A)	Baby Ruth	1948 (early)	Orange	Black
6454(B)	N Y C	1948 (early)	Orange	Black
6454(C)	N Y C	1948	Brown	White
6454(D)	N Y C	1948	Tan	White
6454(E)	A T S F	1948	Orange	Black
6454(F)	S P	1949	Lt. Brown	White (1)
6454(G)	S P	1950	Lt. Brown	White (2)
6454(H)	S P	1951-52	Red-brown	White (2)
6454(J)	Erie	1949-52	Brown	White
6454(K)	Pennsylvania	1949-52	Tuscan	White

NOTES:
1. Early herald, large letters.
2. Later herald, small letters.

since they are mostly incomplete or inaccurate concerning the boxcars that were actually produced. (Catalogued sets including these boxcars are listed in **Table 12** at the end of this article.) While several books and articles have been published in recent years which correctly identify the major variations, they seem to contain an increasing amount of confusing or conflicting information concerning the dates and details of minor variations.

The objectives of this article are threefold. First, I will try to establish some standard terminology and definitions that will permit consistent and efficient discussion. Second, I will identify and describe the "pieces of the puzzle," the major and minor variations. Finally, I will try to fit all the pieces together into a single consistent "big picture" of the development and production of the 9-1/4" boxcars.

Two basic definitions are necessary to get us started:

MAJOR VARIATIONS are differences in Lionel's car number, road name, herald, or painted body color. These variations were established at the time the car body was painted and heat stamped. Since there are only two body mold variations (with roof hatch for the operating merchandise cars and without it for all others), this feature plays no part in analyzing the development of the 9-1/4" boxcars.

MINOR VARIATIONS are car variations due to changes in components such as frames, doors, trucks and couplers, and plunger housings. Minor variations can be created or "faked" by interchanging components between two or more cars or by "repairing" a car with Service Station parts. With this in mind, the collector may find the information in this article useful in determining which minor variations are legitimate cars, which are plausible, and which are totally outlandish.

There are several methods of establishing the validity of minor variations. The first is by observing a significant number of absolutely identical cars. Another method is through determining the date of several individual components and then finding a period of common manufacture or availability of these components. Box and set information can be used, when available, to establish dates for cars and components. The greatest validity is established when all methods point to a single consistent conclusion.

Table 8, presented later in this article, represents a summary and consolidation of information gathered over the past twelve years. During this time, I have collected over a hundred of the 9-1/4" boxcars and observed the features and variations of perhaps a thousand more. Nevertheless, I am still making new observations and gaining new insights from

FIGURE 1: 9-1/4" boxcars manufactured in 1946 and 1947. *Top Shelf:* **2454(A)-1 Pennsylvania (orange door) and 2454(A)-2 Pennsylvania (brown door).** *Middle Shelf:* **2454(B) Baby Ruth and 4454 Baby Ruth electronic control.** *Bottom Shelf:* **3454 automatic merchandise car. R. Swanson Collection.**

Roundhead   Break in outer circle   Flathead

FIGURE 2: The early Southern Pacific herald (1949) has large letters and a small diameter inner circle. The outer circle almost always has a break between the "R" and the "N".

FIGURE 3: The later Southern Pacific herald (1950-1952) has smaller letters than the early one and a larger diameter inner circle.

other collectors. Should any readers have further information, please let me know so that this article can be updated.

MAJOR VARIATIONS

Table 1 contains a listing of the seventeen major variations of the 9-1/4" boxcars with a summary description. Color pictures of these cars are shown throughout this article.

Catalogue Numbers

The four-digit catalogue number assigned to these boxcars was a natural extension of the prewar numbering system. The semi-scale boxcar introduced in 1940 was numbered 2954. Most of the cars Lionel introduced in 1945 and 1946 with the new knuckle coupler were numbered in the 2400 series, so it was natural that the boxcar should be numbered 2454. Operating cars were numbered in the 3400 series, so the merchandise car was numbered 3454, and the electronic set with its unique radio-controlled couplers was numbered in the 4400 series; hence, the 4454 boxcar.

In 1948 Lionel changed the non-operating series number from 2400 to 6400 to reflect the introduction of the magnetic coupler, with the boxcar assuming the predictable number of 6454. Some boxcars produced in early 1948 carried the 6454 number even though they were equipped with the older coil couplers. Similar observations have been noted in studies of tank cars, gondolas, and hoppers. My own theory as to why this happened is very simple. There was probably a delay in the delivery of the tooling for the magnetic couplers. The coil coupler was still in production in 1948 for O Gauge cars and operating cars. Bodies and boxes for O27 cars had already been stamped with the 6400-series numbers. When production schedules called for the assembly of O27 sets, the couplers that were available were used to avoid shipping delays and inventory pile-ups in the factory. Since very few of the 6400 series cars came with coil couplers, the delay in magnetic coupler production was probably very short.

Non-operating 9-1/4" boxcars manufactured from 1948 to 1952 were stamped with five different road names, yet they all carried the same 6454 number. Dash numbers were never added to identify road names or color variations, as was done for the 6464 boxcars. This was because Lionel did not specify which boxcar would be included in which catalogued set. Lionel made the selection of road name from the cars in production at that time, not the customer. Obviously, the Lionel Corporation had not yet realized the potential for a highly differentiated boxcar market. In fact, the 1948 catalogue states on page 24 that the "...Lionel Corporation reserves the right to alter lettering or emblems on sides of its boxcars."

To make the job of identifying and discussing the major variations a little easier, I have added a single letter designation behind the catalogue number in Table 1. In Table 8, a number will be added behind the letter to identify the minor variation (e.g., 6454(B)-3). Hopefully, this shorthand notation will permit a concise identification of variations without a lengthy description of details.

TABLE 2
NEW DATES

ROAD NAME	CATALOGUE NUMBER	NEW DATE
Baby Ruth	2454, 4454, 6454	None
P R R Merchandise	3454	6-46
Pennsylvania	2454, 6454	6-45
A T S F	3464, 6454	None
N Y C	3464, 6454	9-44
Southern Pacific	6454	3-42
Erie	6454	None
Western Pacific	3474	1-52

The operating car introduced in 1949 was numbered 3464, since the 3454 number had already been used for the merchandise car. Again, two road names shared the same catalogue number. The choice for inclusion in sets was still Lionel's, not the customer's. It was not until 1952, when the silver 3474 Western Pacific operating car was introduced, that a boxcar with a specific road name was identified for inclusion within a specific set. While the 3474 was never offered in a consumer catalogue for separate sale, Lionel tried to promote the marketing potential of this car as part of a set and brought specific attention to the road name of this car on page 11 of the 1952 catalogue.

Road Names

Road names and heralds will be discussed in the chronology section under the year they were first introduced. However, I would like to pause for a minute here to discuss the "new" or built dates heat-stamped on some of the boxcar bodies. These "new" dates are associated more with the road name than the Lionel number, as shown in **Table 2**.

The new dates for two of these cars, the 3454 P R R merchandise car and the 3474 Western Pacific, follow Lionel's frequent postwar practice of indicating when the car was first made and catalogued for sale. However, that is where the pattern ends. None of the Baby Ruth, A T S F, or Erie cars ever had new dates, regardless of when they were produced. The Southern Pacific, N Y C, and Pennsylvania cars all had new dates from the time of World War II, when no trains were produced. Does this mean that Lionel made the heat stamp dies during the war in anticipation of postwar

production? Possibly, but more likely the Second World War new dates represent dates found on the real railroad boxcars which were the prototypes for Lionel's models. In its advertising, Lionel made much of the fact that its "realistic" trains were designed from real railroad blueprints. These blueprints (or associated photographs) were probably the source of all the graphic information — including the built dates. Why were not all the 9-1/4" boxcars done this way? No one knows for sure. This inconsistency shows that Lionel was not always obsessed with complete accuracy.

Colors

Another major variation in the 9-1/4" boxcars is the body color. Since all the bodies of these boxcars were painted, we are discussing the paint color, not the color of the molded plastic. Lionel could and did change the colors of the molded plastic, depending upon what plastic was available at the time. Several writers have pointed out that material shortages between 1946 and 1949 affected the body mold color quite a bit. The complex subject of Lionel's body mold colors is best left to its own article.

Before discussing paint color variations, I again feel that standard definitions are necessary for clear understanding. The eight separate and distinct colors used on the 9-1/4" boxcars are listed in **Table 3**. The objective here is to apply a color name to one and only one color, regardless of the number and road name of the car to which it is applied. In other words, all cars listed as brown should be the same color when placed side by side in the same lighting, no matter if they are N Y C or Erie cars. Likewise, the early Southern Pacific cars should all appear to be a lighter brown when compared with the brown N Y C or Erie cars. Interestingly, the later Southern Pacific cars have a definite red-brown color unlike the brown shade of the earlier Southern Pacific cars, which show no hint of red. The tuscan color found on the Pennsylvania cars can be described as a red-brown which also contains a trace of purple. The orange used on the 2454 and 4454 cars in 1946 and 1947 should be defined as light orange to distinguish it from the orange used on several 6454 cars in 1948 and on the 3464(A) A T S F cars made from 1949 to 1952. Tan is my name for the color between orange and light brown which has been called burnt-orange by some collectors. Why complicate matters with an eleven-letter hyphenated word when one three-letter word will serve just as well? Finally, silver is just that — silver.

At this point, I imagine that some collectors may feel that this color list is incomplete. At the least, they will point out that they have seen several orange, brown, and tuscan variations that I have not mentioned. There is no question that additional color and gloss variations can be found. However, I raise this question: Did all of these minor paint variations exist at the time these cars were manufactured? I do not think so. Dirt, cleaning agents, and fading can cause significant differences in the hue and gloss of the same paint on different cars. Several examples will illustrate this point clearly.

Consider first the question of fading. I have a 6454(K) Pennsylvania car which appears on one side to be a pure brown with no hint of the purple cast usually found in the tuscan color. The opposite side of this car has some damage,

TABLE 3
COLORS

Color name	Year Made	Catalogue Number	Road Name
Light Orange	1946-47	2454	P R R, B R
	1946-47	4454	B R
Orange	1948	6454	B R, N Y C, A T S F
	1949-52	3464	A T S F
Tan	1948	6454	N Y C
	1949-52	3464	N Y C
Brown	1948	6454	N Y C
	1949-52	6454	Erie
Light Brown	1949-50	6454	S P
Red-brown	1951-52	6454	S P
Tuscan	1949-52	6454	P R R
Silver	1946-47	3454	P R R Mdse.
	1952-53	3474	W P

but it is otherwise like new, and the paint is clearly the usual shade of tuscan. So is the inside of the car. (Unlike many of the 6464 cars, Lionel painted these bodies both inside and out.) I believe that this car was owned for several years by a collector who placed this car on a shelf with the damaged side against the wall. The brown side faced outward, where it was faded by sunlight or fluorescent lighting. Tuscan Pennsylvania and red-brown Southern Pacific cars seem to be particularly susceptible to fading, which can leave them a nondescript brown color. Opening the doors and looking inside the car will usually reveal the original color.

Dirt and cleaning can also affect the paint hue and gloss. Light orange Baby Ruth or Pennsylvania cars can appear much darker if smudged by newsprint or covered with years of attic dirt. A good cleaning will bring the car back to its original light orange color, but the cleaning agent will determine whether it is a dull orange or a slightly glossy orange. Cleaning with a mild soap solution will tend to leave a dull finish, while cleaning with furniture polish or any other cleaner containing a polishing agent will leave a shinier finish. If you try cleaning some of these cars yourself, you too can produce some of these reported minor paint variations!

There is, however, another source of minor color variation which deserves more study than is allowed by the scope of this article. This is the influence of the underlying body mold material upon the paint color. I have some cars with thin coats of paint over completely clear molded bodies. Particularly in bright light or with back lighting, these cars look significantly different from cars with opaque or heavily painted bodies. The body mold color which seems to have the most noticeable effect is the orange body molded in 1952. The brown, tuscan, and red-brown of the 6454 cars made with the orange body mold are all distorted to some degree by the orange mold material. Additionally, orange-painted 3464 cars which have orange bodies appear brighter than other orange-painted 3464 cars. On the other hand, cars with two coats of paint (a different color for each coat) do not appear to be affected by the color of the first coat! Mold material colors and multiple coats of paint obviously require more study and correlations with other datable features.

There is one final aspect of paint colors which merits some notice. During the four years from 1949 to 1952, Lionel was manufacturing three different, but similar, 6454 boxcars. Each road name had its own subtle color difference. The Southern Pacific cars were colored light brown or red-brown, the Erie cars were painted brown, and the Pennsylvania cars were painted tuscan. Incredibly, each of these cars came with doors painted exactly the same color as the body. After observing hundreds of these cars, I have never seen a car of one color stamped with the road name usually reserved for another color. Likewise, I have never seen a car in original condition where the door color did not precisely match the body color. This speaks volumes about Lionel's quality control, inspection, and general attention to detail. Remember that these three cars were produced concurrently through numerous production runs over a four-year period. It would have been very easy for a tuscan body to be stamped Erie or Southern Pacific. Brown doors could have easily been placed on a red-brown body — or vice-versa. Such "mistakes" would not have necessarily been intentional or due to carelessness, either. One of the most common

forms of color blindness or color weakness in human vision is an inability to distinguish between shades of red and brown. Obviously, Lionel kept people with this color deficiency away from the boxcar assembly and inspection lines. As a result, there are very few "wrong" color variations for collectors today. Some variations will be discussed in the last section of this article, "Prototypes, Color Samples, Factory Errors, Altered Cars, and the Future." However, none of the 6454 cars discussed involve paint color mix-ups.

MINOR AND COMPONENT VARIATIONS

To repeat the definition in the introduction: Minor boxcar variations are those due to changes in components. The components considered in this article are doors, frames, trucks and couplers, plunger housings (operating cars), merchandise car hatch pins, and door guide attachment pins.

Doors

Four distinct types of boxcar doors are defined in **Table 4** and shown in **Figure 6**. The first three types are die-cast metal doors originally designed for the prewar scale-detailed 2758 automobile car and also used on postwar 2758 and 2458 cars. The fourth type is a molded plastic door designed specifically for the 9-1/4" boxcars. Subcategories of the four major types are also defined in **Table 4** to identify color and/or surface treatment. These subcategories arise

---

**TABLE 4
DOORS**

TYPE 1: Metal, no pin on back, different right and left doors.
- 1-Y: Painted light orange, 1946
- 1-B: Painted brown, 1946-47

TYPE 2: Metal, short hollow pin on back of right door, no pin on back of left door.
- 2-S: Painted silver, 1946-47
- 2-B: Painted brown, 1947-48

TYPE 3: Metal, long solid pin on back of both right and left doors.
- 3-B: Painted brown, 1949
- 3-M: Painted to match car color, 1949-52
- 3-X: Chemically blackened, unpainted, 1949-52.

TYPE 4: Plastic, long solid pin on back of doors, all doors similar to right metal doors, no left doors.
- 4-M: Painted to match car color, 1952-53
- 4-U: Unpainted black plastic, 1952-53

FIGURE 4: 9-1/4" boxcars manufactured in 1948. *Top Shelf:* 6454(A) orange Baby Ruth and 6454(B) orange N Y C. *Middle Shelf:* 6454(C) brown N Y C and 6454(D) tan N Y C. *Bottom Shelf:* 6454(E) orange A. T. & S. F. R. Swanson Collection.

from applications to specific catalogue numbers and road names (see **Table 8**).

The highly-detailed metal doors were designed and cast as pairs for the double-door automobile car. (In this discussion, when the terms "right" and "left" door are used, we refer to the position of the doors on the sides of the automobile cars, not their positions on the 9-1/4" boxcars.) They look great when placed side by side in their original application. The right door looks fine when used by itself on the single-door boxcars, but the left door does not because it lacks a designation board and a latch handle. When this door appears on the single-door 9-1/4" boxcars, it looks like a mistake! However, since these doors were made in pairs, Lionel used them in pairs. Even when production of the double-door automobile car ended in 1948, Lionel continued to make right and left (wrong) doors for another three years! The three types of metal doors are distinguished by a pin or stud cast on the back side of one or both doors. Type 1 doors have no pins. Type 2 doors have a short hollow stud on the back side of the right door only. A drive pin inserted in this stud was the attachment point for the door-opening mechanism on the 3454 P R R merchandise car. These doors were subsequently used on non-operating cars. Type 3 doors are equipped with longer solid studs on both right and left doors for the door-opening mechanism of the 3464 operating cars. With pins on both doors, the body could be assembled onto the frame in either direction, and the operating mechanism would still open the door.

In 1952 Lionel finally developed new tooling for molding the doors out of plastic. These plastic doors, which are all right-side doors (apparently someone finally noticed the absence of the door latch!), have been designated as Type 4 doors. Notice in **Figure 6** that the plastic door has a second smaller designation board which is not present on the metal doors. In addition, the shape of the lower door slide housings has been changed from square to circular. However, the question which begs an answer is: Why did Lionel invest in new door tooling when significant production of the 9-1/4" boxcars would continue for only another year? Was the plastic door associated with the introduction of the 3474 Western Pacific car, which required a painted door on an operating car? The injection-molded plastic doors were undoubtedly cheaper to make than the die-cast metal doors, and they certainly improved the appearance of the boxcars (since the inappropriate left doors were not needed).

FIGURE 5: Operating boxcars manufactured from 1949 to 1953. *Top Shelf:* 3464(A)-1 — note brown door and 3464(A)-9 with black door. *Bottom Shelf:* 3464(B) New York Central and 3474 Western Pacific. R. Swanson Collection.

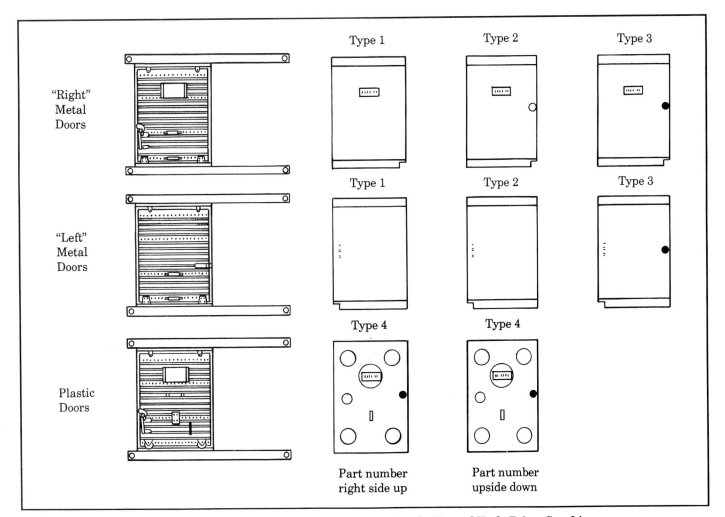

FIGURE 6: Doors used on 9-1/4" boxcars. Drawings by Konrad Koch, Prime Graphics.

TABLE 5
FRAMES

TYPE	STEPS	HOLE PATTERN	CATALOGUE NUMBER	YEARS MADE	SIDE FLANGE
1A, B	Yes	A, B (1)	2654	1946-47	A. Plain
			3454	1947	B. Indents (2)
			6454	1948	B. Indents
2A, B	Yes	A, B, C	4454	1946-47	A. Plain
				1947	B. Indents
3	Yes	D	6454	1948	Indents
4	Yes	D, E	6454	1949	Indents
4M (3)	Yes	D, E	3464	1949	Indents
5M A, B	No	D, E	3464	1950	A. Indents
				1950	B. Cutouts
6	No	A	6454	1950	Plain
7	No	E	6454	1951-52	Plain
7M	No	E	3464	1951-52	Plain
			3474	1952	
7P (4)	No	E	3464	1952	Plain
			3474	1952-53	

Notes:

(1) Hole pattern designations:

    A. Four holes; used for mounting the merchandise car mechanism.

    B. Two holes with slight drawing; probably planned for original mounting of electronic receiver but never used. One or both "B" holes in some early 1948 cars are not drawn and have a much smaller diameter than usual.

    C. Three holes; actually used for mounting and adjustment of electronic receiver.

    D. Four holes (three round, one narrow slot); used in operating milk car frame for mounting operating mechanism.

    E. Four holes (including large center hole); used for mounting operating plunger mechanism.

(2) Type 1B and 2B frames made in 1947 and early 1948 have side flanges with inch-long indentations which were required for door clearance on operating milk cars. All Type 3, 4, 4M, and a few 5M (5A) frames have these same indentations. The majority of the Type 5M (5B) frames have cutout sections in the side flanges which were required by the plastic doors used on milk cars beginning in 1950. Type 6 and 7 frames have neither indentations nor cutout sections.

(3) Frame types with an "M" suffix have been embossed around three of the Type E pattern holes for the mounting of the operating mechanism. The "M" indicates that the large center hole has been embossed to accept the metal plunger housing.

(4) Frame types with a "P" suffix have also been embossed for the operating mechanism, but the center hole has been prepared for a plastic plunger housing.

Frames

The published information on the frames for the 9-1/4" boxcars has probably been more incomplete and inconsistent than information on any other component of these cars. **Table 5** and the drawings in **Figure 7** are an attempt to set the record straight, once and for all. As it happens, the frames I have identified for the 9-1/4" boxcars have most of the same characteristics as the tank car frames identified by Bill Schilling. The frames made between 1947 and 1950 also contain some features required by the 3462 and 3472 operating milk cars, as detected by David Fleming.

All of the boxcar frames have six holes which are always used and whose purpose is well understood: four holes in the corners for screws used to mount the frame to the car body and two holes used for mounting the trucks. It is those

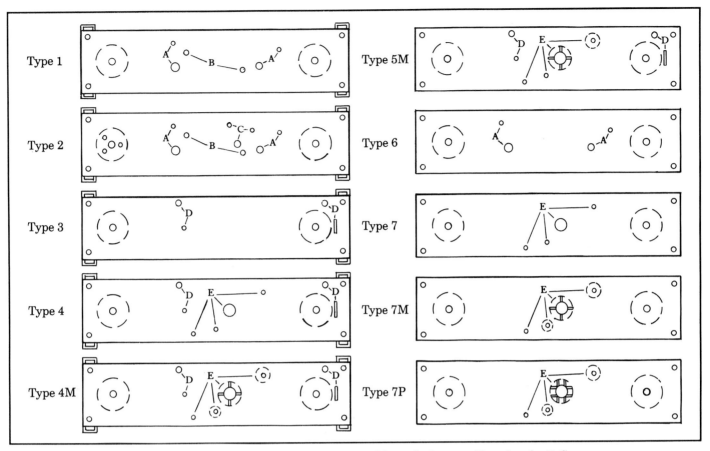

FIGURE 7: Frames used on 9-1/4" boxcars as viewed from the bottom. Drawings by R. Swanson.

mysterious extra holes in the frames which leave collectors perplexed. However, the extra holes can be grouped into five distinct patterns of two to four holes each, as explained in Note (1) to **Table 5**.

In the "A" pattern, the four holes are needed for the 3454 P R R operating merchandise car. The smaller pair of these holes is used for mounting the operating mechanism to the frame, while the larger pair of holes is used for passages bringing the wires from the trucks to the operating solenoid. These larger holes are also used for the same purpose in the 4454 boxcar with its electronic receiver. But, in the electronic boxcar, the larger holes are usually lined with rubber grommets to protect the wiring.

It is interesting to note that the two holes of the "B" pattern were not only pierced, but also drawn to accept self-tapping or sheet metal screws. Still, to my knowledge, these holes were never used on any boxcar, tank car, or milk car. The spacing and position of the "B" holes suggests that they were intended for mounting the electronic receiver inside the 4454 electronic boxcar. However, none of the 4454 cars I have observed have used these "B" holes. Instead, a Type 2 frame is used which contains an additional three-hole "C" pattern for an L-shaped receiver mounting bracket and access to the receiver tuning screw. Most of the Type 2 frames also have three embossed nubs around each truck mounting hole to insure a good electrical ground for the electronic receiver.

The four-hole "D" pattern, which first appeared on the Type 3 frames, is most often erroneously reported as "two small holes" because the third round hole and the slot are usually obscured by one of the trucks. The slot and the small hole near the center of the car are used for mounting the operating mechanism in the milk cars. The two holes near the side of the frame are used for clearance of two rivets which hold the milk car mechanism together. The round "D" hole located near the truck mounting embossment is usually egg-shaped instead of circular. This is because the "D" hole is pierced as a perfect circle that is then distorted when the truck mounting dish is embossed.

The four-hole "E" pattern is used for the operating mechanism of the 3464 and 3474 operating boxcars. These holes were punched during the main piercing and forming operation for the frames. Frames actually used in the operating cars required a secondary operation to prepare the large center hole for the plunger housing and to emboss the area around two of the smaller holes. The secondary operation was not required for the non-operating cars, so the areas around these holes are always flat on 6454 cars.

Note (2) in **Table 5** discusses the indentations and cutout notches found on the side flanges of some frames. These features were required for the door frames of 3462 and 3472 operating milk cars.

FIGURE 8: Non-operating boxcars manufactured from 1949-1953. *Top Shelf:* 6454(F) S P with early herald. *Middle Shelf:* 6454(G) S P (light brown) and 6454(H) S P (red-brown). *Bottom Shelf:* 6454(J) Erie and 6454(K) Pennsylvania. R. Swanson Collection.

TABLE 6
TRUCKS AND COUPLERS

All of the following are die-cast metal trucks.

TYPE 1: Staple-end truck, "whirly," deep-dished, or regular wheels with thick axles; early coil coupler design with "flying shoe"; 1945 and early 1946. Not known to be used on any 9-1/4" boxcars.

TYPE 2: Staple-end truck; with regular wheels and thinner constant-diameter axles, early coil coupler design with "flying shoe", early 1946.

TYPE 3: Staple-end truck with regular wheels and axles, later coil coupler with sliding shoe supported by metal plate attached to axles.

    (A) Coupler head attached to supporting plate by integral stud peened over, 1946.

    (B) Coupler head attached to supporting plate as in (A), except that the joint is strengthened by staking at four points, 1947 and early 1948.

TYPE 4: Staple-end truck with regular wheels and axles, magnetic-type coupler, no extra hole in activator plate, swaged end of rivet attaching activator plate is visible when observed from bottom of truck, 1948-1949.

TYPE 5: Staple-end truck with regular wheels and axles, magnetic-type coupler, extra hole in activator plate.

    (A) Swaged end of rivet attaching activator plate is visible when observed from bottom of truck, early 1950.

    (B) Round-headed end of activator plate rivet visible when observed from bottom of truck, late 1950-1951.

TYPE 6: Bar-end truck with regular wheels and axles, magnetic-type coupler, extra hole in activator plate, round head of rivet visible in activator plate as in 5(B), 1952-1953.

FIGURE 9: Type 3 trucks. 1946 production (left) without stake marks. 1947 production (right) had the knuckle attachment strengthened by the addition of four stake marks.

Trucks and Couplers

Postwar die-cast trucks with knuckle couplers are discussed in some detail elsewhere in this book. The only contribution I can add to this area is to point out that the Type 3 and Type 5 couplers can be divided into two easily distinguishable sub-classes.

As shown in **Figure 9**, the Type 3A couplers made in 1946 had the coupler head attached to the supporting plate by a single peened-over stud. This attachment was a weak point in the design, and the coupler head frequently became loose or separated. In 1947 the Type 3B coupler was introduced with a simple but effective means of strengthening the weak joint. After the stud was peened, a staking operation was added to produce a mechanical interlocking at four additional points, as can be seen in the right side of **Figure 9**.

The subdivision of Type 5 couplers is easier to see but harder to explain than the Type 3 subdivision. Production in 1950 began with the Type 5A coupler characterized by the activator rivet with the flared end down and visible from the bottom of the truck plate. For some reason, during the mid-

FIGURE 10: A comparison of a 1946 merchandise car without a visible roof hatch pin (left) and a 1947 car with a visible roof hatch pin (right).

dle of the 1950 production run Lionel changed the assembly of the coupler and the rivet was inserted from the bottom with the round head down, resulting in the 5B coupler. Since this change did not alter the operation or reliability of the coupler, one can only surmise that the change increased the efficiency of the assembly. There certainly must have been some advantage, because Lionel never returned to the earlier rivet orientation.

Plunger Housing

There was one change in the mechanism of the 3464 / 3474 operating cars during its production from 1949 to 1953. Early in 1952, the housing supporting the plunger and plunger return spring was changed from metal to plastic. A frame change was also required to accept the plastic housing; compare the center holes of Frames 7M and 7P in **Figure 7**. This change was probably a cost reduction.

3454 P R R Merchandise Car Hatch Pin

The hinge pin which supports the roof hatch of the 3454 P R R merchandise car is attached by either of two completely different methods. Cars manufactured in 1946 have a brass wire hinge pin which is bent at a 90-degree angle at both ends. The hinge pin is attached to the car body by two molded plastic posts which appear to be molded with slots that were heated and closed after the hinge pin was inserted laterally. This hinge pin is not visible from outside of the car at all.

The attachment method used in 1947 is identical to the method used on the 3462 milk car introduced that year. In this method of attachment, a steel or plated pin with a rounded head on one end is inserted through the end of the car body, as shown in **Figure 10**. The internal plastic posts now have holes instead of slots to support the pin. After the pin was inserted from the end of the car through the roof hatch, it was bent past the second support post to lock it into place. This second method of attachment eliminated the need for heat to close the open slots, but it left the car with an exposed pin head on the car end.

Door Guide Attachment Pin

The metal door guides of the 9-1/4" boxcars were all attached with short fluted drive pins having a head on one end. There are some variations in the length and fluting (straight vs. spiraled), but I have never removed enough pins to know for sure which was used when. However, there is a variation in head shape which is visible without disassembling the car.

Most of the cars have door guide drive pins with round heads. However, for some unknown reason, most of the cars made in 1950 used a flat-headed drive pin. The differences between these two drive pins can be seen in **Figures 2** and **3**. The use of the flat-headed pin in 1950 may have been caused by material shortages associated with the Korean War, or it may have been the result of a purchasing mistake.

FIGURE 11: The top two rows of boxes from 1946-1947 are much larger than those below. The large boxes were designed to contain a corrugated cardboard inner liner. The third and fourth rows are boxes from 1948-1949 except for the right-hand box in the fourth row which is early 1950. All boxes in the third and fourth rows are 10-1/8" long. The fifth and sixth rows contain boxes used from 1950-1953. These boxes are all 8-11/16" long.

Whatever the reason, the round-headed pins returned with the beginning of 1951 production.

A few 3464 (A) A T S F boxcars have turned up with flat-headed drive pins, yet these cars have many other components indicative of 1952 production. It is possible that some 1950 body assemblies were stored for use by the service department, but later assembled onto frames and trucks in 1952. I have seen four such cars in different parts of the country, so I do not think they are all Service Station repairs.

The Molded Human Figure

The molded human figure used in the production of the 3464 and 3474 operating cars comes in several variations. The most noticeable difference is that some have flesh-colored hands and faces, while others are entirely blue, as molded. The figures with the painted hands and faces were probably produced in 1949 and early 1950, while the solid blue figures represent 1950 or later production. The great frequency of cars with missing figures, the variety of reproduction figures readily available, and the ease in swapping figures between cars leads me to largely ignore the figure as a dating feature for the 9-1/4" operating boxcars.

FIGURE 12: Two Lionel Boxes. The top shelf has a box originally printed for a 2458 automobile car from 1946. The box was over-printed "2454" on all four sides and on both ends as well. The 2458 is a metal car which was packaged without a liner. The 2454 is a plastic car that Lionel, in 1946, usually shipped with a cardboard liner. The box came with a 2454(A)-2 Pennsylvania brown door. Was this a field trial to determine if plastic cars could be shipped without cardboard liners without damage or did Lionel simply run out of the right box and solved the momentary crisis by using another box?

Boxes

A study of the boxes used for shipping the 9-1/4" boxcars provides some interesting insights into the development of the series. Obviously, cars and boxes can be and often have been swapped through the years. Boxes cannot be used as a sole or conclusive dating factor for any specific car. However, when large numbers of cars in boxes are observed and careful comparisons between different boxes are made, some definite patterns do emerge. Through the years I have observed and collected twenty-four different boxes for the 9-1/4" boxcars. These boxes are listed with a brief description in **Table 7**.

The boxes designed for the 9-1/4" boxcars in 1946 and 1947 were large enough to contain a corrugated cardboard inner liner to protect the plastic body. I stress the idea of the plastic body because all-metal cars such as the 2458 automobile car and the 2457 caboose were packaged during this same period in smaller boxes with no inner liners. Apparently, Lionel believed that plastic bodies required more protection than metal bodies in these years.

After World War II Lionel continued a practice begun before the war in order to meet shipping demands and / or to adjust the firm's box inventory. Lionel would black out the original car number (and sometimes the description) on the box and then overprint another number and / or description. One box listed as Number 7 in **Table 7** is a 2458 double-door automobile car box that has been remarked to contain a 2454 boxcar. The car usually found in this box is a 2454(A)-2 brown door Pennsylvania boxcar, probably made in mid-1946. Notice in **Figure 12** that the original number and description have been obliterated, but the O Gauge designation has been left visible and unaltered. Was this reworked 2458 box used with the 2105WS set, the only O Gauge set to con-

TABLE 7
BOXES

LARGE SIZE: With cardboard inner liner, 1946-1947

1. 2454 boxcar, no ATMA logo, 11" x 3-3/4" x 2-5/8"

2. 2454 boxcar, ATMA logo, 11" x 3-3/4" x 2-5/8"

3. 2454 merchandise car, no ATMA logo, 11" x 3-3/4" x 2-5/8"

4. 4454 boxcar, electronic control, no ATMA logo, 11" x 3-3/4" x 2-5/8"

5. 3454 merchandise car, no ATMA logo, 11" x 4" x 3-3/4"

6. 3454 merchandise car, ATMA logo, 11" x 3-3/4" x 3-3/4"

7. 2454 boxcar, overstamped on 2458 box, no ATMA logo, no inner liner, 11-1/4" x 3-3/8" x 2-3/8"

MIDDLE SIZE: No liners, ATMA logo, 10-1/8" x 3-3/4" x 2-1/4"

8. 6454 boxcar, 1948

9. 6454 S P boxcar, 1 Lionel 1, 1949

10. 6454 Erie boxcar, 2 Lionel 2, 1949

11. 6454 P R R boxcar, 3 Lionel 3, 1949

12. 3464 S F boxcar, 1949

13. 3464 N Y C boxcar, 1949

14. 3464 N Y C boxcar, NYC overstamp of 3464 S F box, 1949

15. 6454 boxcar (6454 overstamp of 3464 S F box), 1950

SMALL SIZE: No liners, ATMA logo, 8-11/16" x 3-3/4" x 2-1/4"

16. 3464 N Y C boxcar, 1950-1952

17. 3464 S F boxcar, 1950-1952

18. 3464 S F boxcar, OPS ceiling price $5.50, 1952

19. 3464 N Y C boxcar (N Y C overstamp of S F), 1951-1952

20. 3474 W P boxcar, OPS ceiling price $5.50, 1952

21. 3474 W P boxcar, 1953

22. 6454 S P boxcar, 1950-1952

23. 6454 Erie boxcar, 1950-1952

24. 6454 P R R boxcar, 1950-1952

FIGURE 13: The case of the shrinking box. The top shelf has a 1947 box with the blue words "LIONEL" and "TRAINS" touching the blue band which surrounds them. This lettering was used in 1945-1947. However this box also has the "TOY MF'RS U.S.A" logo which first appears in 1947. This box was designed to accommodate a cardboard liner. The box on the second shelf is dated from the side view as either 1948 or 1949. Note the blue words "LIONEL" and "TRAINS" no longer touch the blue border. It is smaller because Lionel no longer used inner liners with plastic freight cars. The third shelf is a 1950-1952 box. Note that it is significantly shorter than the other two boxes. The reduction in length was achieved by removing the steps from the car frame and turning the trucks with couplers inward when inserted in the box.

tain a 2454 boxcar in 1946? Or was the box used with O27 sets as well, making the description a misnomer?

Another feature I have observed on some of the large boxes is the presence or absence of the American Toy Manufacturers' Association logo. I presume that the boxes without the logo were printed in 1946 and those with the logo were printed in the following years. All of the small and mid-sized boxes used for the 9-1/4" boxcars I have seen carried the ATMA logo.

The 3454 merchandise car came in two different boxes. The 1946 cars came in 4" wide boxes which did not have the ATMA logo, while the 1947 cars came in 3-3/4" wide boxes which did have the logo.

One of the more curious boxes is box Number 3 in **Table 7**, marked 2454 merchandise car. I have a number of these boxes, and I have always found them with 2454 P R R Baby Ruth boxcars inside. The car number on the box was correct; the description was not. The box does not have an ATMA logo, but the cars inside have been both 1946 and 1947 vintages, so I cannot date this box with any certainty.

In 1948 Lionel made a major change in boxes, along with the switch to magnetic couplers. The firm eliminated the corrugated inner liners; this permitted a substantial reduction in the size of the boxes used for the 9-1/4" boxcars. Instead of an inner liner, the box end flaps were cut and folded to create a protective pocket for the coupler which extended past the end of the car body. These intricate end flaps also protected the ends of the cars from damage.

FIGURE 14: Two examples of Box 13 from Table 7. The upper box is an early 1949 box and lists Lionel locations as "NEW YORK ... CHICAGO ... SAN FRANCISCO". The lower box is a late 1949 box (still a long box), which lists Lionel locations as "NEW YORK ... CHICAGO". Note that San Francisco is no longer included. R. Swanson Collection.

FIGURE 15: Two different 3474 boxes. Lower box has OPS ceiling price of $5.50 while upper box has no OPS price marking. OPS was Office of Price Stability, a Korean War government agency.

As we will see in the chronology section, there were five major variations of the 6454 boxcar produced in 1948, yet they all came in the same box, Number 8 in **Table 7**. This box contained no hint of the road name or body color of the car packaged inside.

In 1949 the policy of not designating the road name was completely reversed. The non-operating 6454 boxcars came in the same boxes as 1948, except that the end flaps were overstamped in black ink with the road name and a single-digit number on each side of the Lionel name. These are Boxes 9, 10, and 11 in **Table 7**. The 3464 operating boxcars introduced in 1949 had boxes containing the road name as part of the original end flap printing.

Road name markings on the boxes meant that the quantity of boxes with a particular name and number had to be coordinated with the quantity of that particular boxcar being manufactured. Since these quantities did not always agree, Lionel was once again forced to remark boxes to make them match the products already produced. Boxes 14 and 15 in **Table 7** are examples of such reworked boxes.

Box 15 is of particular interest because of the car it contained and the set with which it was shipped. As shown in **Table 8**, frames with footsteps are believed to have been phased out of production in early 1950. I have two Number 15 boxes, and they both contain 6454(K)-2 Pennsylvania boxcars. One of these cars is known to have come from a 1471WS set headed by a 2035 steam locomotive with Magnetraction catalogued in both 1950 and 1951. The Type 4 frame and the Type 5A trucks together point to early 1950 production. Lionel was probably using up leftover Type 4 frames with footsteps, and evidently the firm had run out of long 6454 boxes of any description. The expedient way to keep the production lines moving was to remark leftover long 3464 Santa Fe boxes, since the trucks of a boxcar with footsteps could not be turned inwards to fit the car into the shorter boxes.

Another change was made in boxes printed after mid-1949. At the suggestion of Tom Rollo, I started looking at the cities printed on the blue band on the box sides. All boxes listed in **Table 7** from Numbers 1-11 list the Lionel locations "New York...Chicago...San Francisco". Boxes 14

through 24 list only New York and Chicago, reflecting the termination of the San Francisco showroom agreement. Boxes 12 and 13 come in two variations, some with San Francisco and some without. This indicates two separate production runs, one in early 1949 and the other in late 1949. Boxes printed in late 1949 without the San Francisco entry appear to be the only mid-sized boxcar boxes carried over for early 1950 boxcars.

The elimination of frame footsteps in 1950 brought a second reduction in box size. By rotating the trucks so that the couplers were under the car body, the box could be shortened by about an inch and a half. Considering the quantities Lionel was dealing with, this reduction must have meant a considerable savings to the firm in warehouse space and shipping costs. For the operating boxcars, the change in length was indeed the only change from the earlier boxes. For the non-operating cars, the boxes were shortened and the end flap printing was revised to include the boxcar road name, as shown in **Figure 12**. (Note the disappearance of the Numbers 1, 2, and 3.) These boxes remained virtually unchanged through the end of the 9-1/4" boxcar production. Of course, the introduction of the 3474 Western Pacific boxcar in 1952 brought an appropriately marked box at that time.

The only box variation that I am aware of during the 1950 to 1953 period is the presence of OPS ceiling prices on some 3464 Santa Fe and 3474 Western Pacific boxes. The OPS price, when it appears at all, is usually printed directly onto the box. However, occasionally the OPS price was indicated by a white paste-on label. I recently had the opportunity to purchase a complete set of the OPS paste-on labels — sixteen pages of them! The labels came in an original Lionel envelope which had a message to dealers printed on its front. It said that the envelope contained OPS labels for all items listed in the 1951 catalogue. This leads me to believe that the OPS price marking was required during 1952. For the first five or six months of 1952, the only items the dealers had in inventory were leftover 1951 production items. These items had to be marked with OPS prices during all of 1952, so the paste-on labels were sent out to dealers. Items produced in 1952 were marked with the OPS price at the fac-

TABLE 8
SUMMARY OF 9-1/4" BOXCAR FEATURES

	1946	1947	1948	1949	1950	1951	1952	1953	Replacement Bodies
FEATURES									
Doors, non-operating	1Y	1B	2B		3M			4M	4U
Operating		2S		3B	3X			4U	
Operating — 3474								4M	
Frames, non-operating	1A		1B	3	4	6	7		
Operating		1A	1B		4M	5A / 5B	7M	7P	
Electronic		2A	2B						
Trucks and Couplers	2 / 3A	3B		4	5A	5B	6		
Drive Pin Head	Round				Flat	Round			
Plunger Housing				Metal			Plastic		
NON-OPERATING CARS									
2454 P R R, Lt. Orange	1 2 3								
2454 Baby Ruth, Lt. Or.		1	2 3	4					
4454 Baby Ruth, Lt. Or.		1	2 3	4					
6454 Baby Ruth, Orange			1 2						
6454 N Y C, Orange			1 2	3					
6454 N Y C, Brown				1					
6454 N Y C, Tan				1					
6454 A T S F, Orange				1					
6454 S P, Lt. Brown (1)				1	2				
Lt. Brown (2)					1 2 3				
Red-Brown (2)						1	2	3	4
6454 Erie, Brown				1	2 3	4	5	6	7
6454 P R R, Tuscan				1	2	3 4	5	6 7	8
OPERATING CARS									
3454 Merchandise, Silver		1	2						
3464 A T S F, Orange				1	2	3 4 5 6	7	8 9 10	
3464 N Y C, Tan				1	2	3 4 5	6	7 8	
3474 W P, Silver							1	2	
	1946	1947	1948	1949	1950	1951	1952	1953	Replacement Bodies

KEY:

Y - light orange
B - brown
M - match car
U - unpainted black plastic
S - silver
X - chemically blackened

Notes: (1) Early SP herald
(2) Late SP herald

tory, usually as part of the original box printing instead of a stick-on label. Still, the curious thing about the OPS marking is that I have observed it only on Santa Fe and Western Pacific operating boxcar boxes, not on the N Y C or any of the boxes containing non-operating cars. Does this mean that the OPS markings were required on items meant for separate sale, but not for items included as part of a set, where an OPS marking would have been on the set box? Or, was the OPS marking required on all the individual component boxes within the set? Additional reader information on this subject would be welcomed.

THE CHRONOLOGY: AN INTRODUCTION TO TABLE 8

Now that we have identified the major variations, component variations, and boxes, it is time to fit all the pieces of the 9-1/4" boxcar puzzle together into one integrated picture to explain the development and production of these cars. Table 8 is a graphical attempt to describe and date all the major and minor variations on a single page.

The distinctive component features are listed at the top of Table 8. A time line is then used to indicate the production sequence of the component variations. The identification codes for the doors were defined in Table 4, frames in Table 5, and trucks and couplers in Table 6.

The seventeen major boxcar variations are listed in the lower part of Table 8. A time line to the right of the road name indicates the most likely production dates for that variation. Minor variations are designated by a number indicating the production sequence. Each time there is a change in one or more components, a different minor variation is established. The specific components which comprise a minor variation can be determined by noting which component variations appear directly above the car production time line.

1946

Production of the 9-1/4" boxcars began with the 2454(A)-1 orange door Pennsylvania cars. The orange door cars are always found with Type 2 trucks and couplers (flying shoe design with regular wheels and axles). Since the doors were the same as the doors already being produced for the brown 2458 automobile car, except for the color, Lionel quickly realized that it could reduce its parts inventory by also using brown doors on these boxcars (2454(A)-2). Next came the abandonment of the flying shoe coupler design. The introduction of the Type 3A trucks and couplers led to variation 2454(A)-3. At this point, another major change was made. The Pennsylvania road name to the left of the door was replaced by the Baby Ruth logo (2454(B)-1). Curiously, the P R R logo and the printing to the right of the door remained unchanged.

The 4454 electronic control boxcar and the 3454 P R R automatic merchandise car were also produced in 1946, with both cars employing Type 3A trucks.

1947

Production of the 2454(B) and 4454 cars continued unchanged from the end of 1946, except that the 3B coupler with a stronger coupler head mounting was used instead of the weaker 3A coupler. Several other changes in components were made during the year.

The first mid-year change was the use of Type 2 doors painted brown on 2454 and 4454 cars. The short pin on the back of the right door served no useful purpose on these non-operating cars, but evidently the door mold had been modified in 1946 and Type 1 doors could no longer be made. The fact that this change did not show up until mid-1947 production indicates that a large inventory of doors was produced before the mold was modified.

The next mid-year change was a minor modification in frames (1B). The 3462 operating milk car, introduced in 1947, used a frame which was essentially a boxcar frame with some additional holes and slots. The milk car frame required slight indentations about one inch long in the side flanges. These indentations were required for clearance of the milk car door frames. For some reason, this milk car feature was incorporated into the boxcar frame tooling and not left to the secondary milk car frame tools. This side flange indentation appears on all boxcar frames until 1950, when several other tooling changes occurred.

Production of the 3454 P R R merchandise car apparently did not resume until later in 1947, since no early year variations have been found. All of the 1947 P R R merchandise cars I have examined contain all of the typical 1947 features: Type 3B couplers, Type 1B frames, exposed head for the roof hatch pin, and the slightly smaller Type 6 box. The current availability of the 1947 cars is substantially less than for the 1946 version and, of course, the 3454 was completely phased out at the end of 1947.

It is fun to speculate on the decline and fall of the 3454 P R R merchandise car, which had been so popular in 1946. I suspect that the major factor in its demise was the introduction of the immensely popular 3462 automatic refrigerated milk car. The buying public seemed to like the milk car better, perhaps because they perceived it as more realistic. It did have a man to toss out the milk cans and a special platform to receive them. With the merchandise car, there was no all-important human figure, and the little packing boxes came flying out the door at random, seldom falling into the unrealistic dump tray included with the car. Lionel probably liked the milk car better because of its higher profit margin. At $8.95 and ultimately $11.50, the milk car must have been considerably more profitable than the $5.50 merchandise car.

1948

The year 1948 brought many changes, both major and minor. As mentioned, the merchandise car was dropped from production. As I will explain later, I also believe that production of the 4454 electronic control boxcar ended in 1947. This left only plain, non-operating boxcars. Did this mean a dull inventory for Lionel's train sets? Not by a long shot! Almost everything but the size was new with the non-operating boxcars! There was a new number, 6454. The couplers were changed to the new Type 4 magnetic couplers. There was a new frame, the Type 3. There were new colors: orange instead of light orange, brown, and tan. Best of all, there were new road names: New York Central and Santa Fe. Even the boxes were new. Most of these changes were introduced at the beginning of the year, but a few were phased in after the inventory of older components was depleted.

Production began with 6454(A) Baby Ruth and 6454(B) New York Central cars, both painted the new shade of orange. The first cars produced in 1948 had Type 3B coil couplers, even though they were marked with 6454 numbers. Even more of the 1948 production had leftover Type 1B frames. By the time production of the Type 3 frames began, production of the Baby Ruth cars had already been phased out. Shortly thereafter, the orange N Y C car's color was shifted to brown and tan versions. I must admit that I have no way of telling which color came first, brown or tan; although the presence of the tan color on the later operating N Y C cars would suggest that tan was the later color. The orange Santa Fe boxcar was also produced during this period.

The new 1948 box was substantially smaller than the previous boxcar boxes because the cardboard inner liner was no longer used. All of the 1948 boxcars came in exactly the same box. It was only marked "6454 BOX CAR", with no mention of road name or color. Information to date has not shown any correlation between catalogued sets and the boxcars they contained. I have three 1427WS sets in boxes which contain the following boxcars: brown N Y C, tan N Y C, and orange A T S F. Lionel apparently used whatever boxcar was available when the sets were assembled and packaged.

I mentioned earlier that I felt the production of the 4454 electronic boxcar ended in 1947. I will point out two bits of evidence and let the reader draw his own conclusion. First, the use of light orange paint was discontinued on regular boxcars at the end of 1947 and a darker orange was introduced in 1948. It is doubtful that a darker orange 4454 boxcar exists; no one has ever confirmed one. Second, the box size changed in 1948, but I have never seen a smaller 4454 box. Assembly of 4454 boxcars could have continued in 1948 using leftover parts and boxes, but these cars would have been impossible to distinguish from 1947 production (4454-4). (We would like to hear from any reader who has evidence of 4454 component production from 1948 or later.)

There is another possible 1948 car that I have never seen, but have speculated might exist. Has anyone ever seen a 2454 N Y C boxcar? If you examine the X6454 number on the N Y C cars, you will notice that the "6" seems to be a little larger and lower than the other digits. Was the N Y C heat-stamping die originally made with a 2454 number and then modified to 6454 to reflect the new coupler design? If so, were any cars stamped before the "2" was changed to a "6"? It is curious that the 2454 boxcar listed for separate sale on page 28 of the 1948 consumer catalogue has N Y C markings! Verrrry interesting...!

1949

With all the changes made in 1948, one might expect that some or at least one of that year's cars would have car-

ried over to 1949 production. Wrong! Lionel must have felt that the boxcar line was too bland in 1948 without some kind of an action car, so the major push for 1949 was to overcome this deficiency. The introduction of the magnet in the 6019 and UCS operating tracks opened the possibility for a new series of low-cost operating cars. The 3464 operating boxcar was the first of this new series. Using a few stamped parts, wire springs, and a molded human figure, Lionel created a low-cost operating car which did not require a solenoid, special trucks, or die-cast parts.

Lionel must have been confident that its new operating boxcar would be eagerly accepted by the train-buying public, because the firm not only used the car to spruce up the O27 sets, but also as a replacement for the "scale-detailed" 2458 automobile car in O Gauge sets. Most people consider the 9-1/4" boxcar to be an O27 product, but between 1949 and 1952 it was the only boxcar made by Lionel, and it was included in no fewer than eleven catalogued O Gauge sets (see **Table 12**).

Production of the 3464 operating boxcar began in 1949 with an orange A T S F car, although it was soon joined by a tan N Y C car. Both of these cars must have been planned from the beginning because, for the first time, Lionel put the initials of the road name on the boxcar boxes as part of the end flap printing. Since both cars carried the same Lionel number 3464, how do we know which car came first? The main evidence is the existence of the 1949 brown door version of the A T S F car, while no legitimate examples of brown door N Y C operating cars from this time have ever been found.

The brown door A T S F 3464 represented a natural extension of Lionel's earlier policy: paint all doors brown regardless of body color. The single door color certainly simplified production and parts inventory. However, there was a problem on the operating cars with brown-painted doors. The painted door did not slide very well against the painted plastic body, causing sluggish operation. The chemically-blackened metal door was thus introduced as an engineering solution to reduce friction and improve the performance of the operating mechanism. The black door was introduced before the production of the N Y C car began, so all of the operating 3464 N Y C cars have black doors.

Although the non-operating 6454 boxcar was retained in 1949, it certainly did not get much promotion. It was not included in any sets shown in the 1949 consumer catalogue. The N Y C and A T S F road names used in 1948 were moved to the prolific 3464 series, and three new road names were introduced on the non-operating 6454 cars: Southern Pacific, Erie, and Pennsylvania. (The Pennsylvania name was actually a reintroduction, since it had been used on the 2454 in early 1946.)

Even though the three new 6454 cars are not shown in the 1949 catalogue (only a 1948 N Y C is shown), their introduction date can be well established by thorough, detailed examination of specific components. First, these cars always have Type 3 doors, which are distinguished by the long solid pin on the back side. (The 1952 cars have plastic doors, but that will be discussed later.) The Type 3 doors were developed for the 3464 operating cars which were not available before 1949. On the other hand, the earliest versions of the Southern Pacific, Erie, and Pennsylvania 6454 boxcars are all equipped with Type 4 couplers, the earliest magnetic couplers without an extra hole in the activation plate. Type 4 couplers were discontinued at the end of 1949 production.

There are two more pieces of evidence which tie the introduction of the three 6454 cars to 1949: frames and boxes. The Type 4 frame has been identified as 1949 production, since it was specifically designed to accommodate the new 3464 operating boxcars. In 1950 Lionel introduced the Type 5 frame, which lacked the steps of the Type 4. The hypothesis that the three new road names in the 6454 line were, in fact, introduced in 1949 is strongly supported by the fact that the earliest frame used with these cars is the Type 4. It should be noted, however, that the first 1949 S P 6454 cars were assembled with leftover 1948 Type 3 frames, but these cars still have other characteristics that strongly date them as 1949 products.

In my own mind, the boxes provide the clinching argument for the 1949 introduction of the three 6454 boxcars. The boxes used for the 6454 cars in 1949 were unique to that year. These were actually the same as the 1948 boxes, but the end flaps were overstamped in black ink with a road name and a number: "1-S P", "2-ERIE", and "3-PENN". This is the closest Lionel ever came to assigning hyphenated numbers to the 6454 cars, and this practice lasted for only one year. In 1950 the new shorter boxes contained the road name as an integral part of the blue lettering on the box end, and the 1, 2, and 3 numbers were never seen again.

There is one other detail peculiar to 1949 that must be mentioned at this point. There were two clearly different circular heralds used on the 6454 Southern Pacific boxcars. (See **Figures 2** and **3**.) The outer diameter of both heralds is about the same, but the letters are much larger in the 1949 herald, requiring a smaller inner circle. Another distinguishing feature of the 1949 heralds is a break in the outer circle between the letters "R" and "N" in the two o'clock position of the circle. This break was undoubtedly caused by a defect in the heat-stamping die, since it appears throughout the entire 1949 production run. The only herald known to be from 1949 which does not have this break appears on the black 6454 Southern Pacific boxcar which was part of the collection of the late Hank Degano. The defect in the stamping die was most likely the reason for the development of new tooling for the herald in 1950. That herald has smaller letters, no breaks in the circle.

1950

The year 1950 can be called a year of many minor variations. Besides the change in the Southern Pacific heralds discussed above, there were changes in frames (three), trucks (two), boxes, and the drive pins used to attach the door guides and brakewheels. These varied component changes were phased in at different times during 1950, creating as many as four different minor variations to a single car in one year!

The truck and coupler changes are probably the easiest to explain. The 1950 production began with conversion to the Type 5A coupler, which included a second small hole in the magnetic activator plate. This second hole permitted an easier, less expensive assembly and repair of the roller pickup version of the magnetic coupler and truck. Around mid-year, production switched to the 5B coupler, which is distinguished by the round head of the activator plate attachment pin showing instead of the flared end. This change was probably made to reduce assembly costs, but the specific reason is not known without exact knowledge of the assembly procedure and tooling.

Early in 1950 (but not right at the beginning of production), Lionel made another curious change in a very minor component — the drive pin used to attach the door guides and brakewheel to the plastic body. Instead of the usual round-headed pin used since 1946, a flat-headed pin which looks like a small carpet tack was used for the bulk of production in both operating and non-operating cars. This same drive pin found its way onto other cars in 1950, including stock and milk cars. As discussed previously, the use of these drive pins could have been a result of material shortages due to the Korean War, but the most likely explanation is a purchasing error. Whatever the case, Lionel did not like these pins because the firm returned to the round-headed design in 1951. The Lionel Service Manual, unfortunately, does not help solve the mystery. The 9-1/4" boxcars made from 1946 through 1948 used a door pin carrying the part number 45-70, indicating that this part was first used on the old 45 gateman made as early as 1935. There is no mention of a flat-headed pin anywhere in the Service Manual.

Let us proceed to a mystery we can solve! The most significant change Lionel made to these boxcars in 1950 was the elimination of the steps from the frame. If we can assume that Lionel began its 1950 production with the Type 5A trucks and couplers, then we can find that a few cars were assembled which used leftover 1949 frames with steps (P R R 6454(K)-2, A T S F 3464(A)-3, and N Y C 3464(B)-2). Once the leftover 1949 frames were used, the bulk of the 1950 boxcar production used frames without steps.

There is a necessary digression from our chronological narrative at this point. Our analysis of trucks, frames, and boxes can be used to solve other dating mysteries. We have observed that some 6454 Pennsylvania cars came with Type 4 frames with steps. We know that these Type 4 frames were superseded in 1950 by Types 5 and 6 frames without steps. The 6454 Pennsylvania car in question came in a Type 15 box (see **Table 7**), which is a 3464 A T S F medium-sized box overstamped "6454". The box was first made in late 1949 because 1949 was the first year of the 3464 A T S F car and because the box does not have San Francisco listed as a Lionel showroom. The San Francisco entry was dropped from Lionel's boxes in late 1949. The car has Type 5A trucks which were introduced in 1950 and replaced later in 1950 by Type 5B. From these characteristics, we can date this particular car as early 1950 production; no other dating fits all these characteristics. In this case, one might question the unusual combination of features. Our hypothesis is that Lionel had unfilled orders requiring boxcars and had available for assembly most of the components: bodies, trucks, and leftover frames. However, these components would not fit the new, shorter Lionel boxes. It is likely that there were unused long 3464 boxes in the warehouse, and Lionel was consequently able to make up a batch of cars using the old frames and box them to fill pressing orders. One Pennsylvania 6454(K)-2 came in one of these overmarked boxes with set 1471WS shown on page 15 of the 1950 consumer catalogue.

Lionel had two strong motives for eliminating the steps. The first was the material savings for the frame itself. If the car frames were stamped from coiled sheet metal stock, the width of the coil could have been reduced from 2-7/8" to 2-1/8", a material savings of twenty-five percent. With the old style frame, the material between the steps was cut out and discarded. The second source of savings came about because Lionel now had the ability to rotate the couplers inward when packaging the cars; this meant that the firm could use smaller car and set boxes and reduce its packaging, warehousing, and shipping costs.

Two completely different "stepless" frames with totally different hole patterns were used in 1950. The operating cars used the Types 5A and 5B frames, which were essentially 1949 frames with the steps cut off. In fact, close examination of these frames suggests that this is exactly how they were made because the side flanges near the end have some distortion lines caused by the punching of the steps. The A and B versions of this frame relate to the side flange detail associated with the operating milk car doors. The A version has indentations to accommodate the metal doors and their frames used from 1947 to 1949. The B version has cutouts to accept the plastic door frame used on milk cars made after 1949.

The non-operating 6454 cars used an entirely different frame in 1950, Type 6. These frames showed no traces of the steps. The Type 6 frames also contained none of the holes, slots, indentations, or cutouts required for operating boxcars or milk cars. Instead, they had four holes which had been required for the 3454 operating merchandise car made in 1946 to 1947! How — or why — did these holes reappear in 1950?

One possibility is that Lionel had two completely separate sets of tooling for stamping these frames. The first set of tooling was used for Types 1 and 2 frames made from 1946 to early 1948. These frames, with some off-line modification, were used in 1947 for the 3462 milk cars. As milk car production increased dramatically in 1948 (Lionel was to sell two and a half million of these cars between 1947 and 1955!), a second, more efficient set of tools could have been developed which was subsequently used to produce the Types 3, 4, and 5 frames. When the step elimination program came along for 1950, the production department may not have been in the position to release the efficient tool set so it could be modified, in view of the tremendous demand for the milk cars. This could have required the tool or engineering department to retrieve the older Type 1 tooling, which was then no longer in service. This tooling could have been modified some time in 1949 to be ready for 1950 production of Type 6 frames without disrupting any production schedules. The 3464 operating car frames could not be produced on the older tooling because there was no provision for the four holes required for the operating mechanism, particularly the large center hole. The experience and benefits gained from the modified tooling in 1950 probably justified the expense in developing a third set of tooling which was optimized for stamping the Type 7 frames which appeared in 1951.

The elimination of the steps in 1950 led to a whole new series of boxes. Since the trucks could be turned with the couplers facing inward, the box length was reduced from 10-1/8" to 8-11/16", a saving of almost 1-1/2" in space. The boxcar road name always appeared on the end flaps of these shorter boxes as part of the standard printing.

1951

Production of the 9-1/4" boxcars settled down considerably in 1951. The five basic cars introduced in 1949, two 3464s and three 6454s, all continued in production for a third year, with the only major variation occurring in the 6454 Southern Pacific. The light brown color used on the S P cars in 1949 and 1950 was dropped in favor of a red-brown color. The new Types 7 and 7M frames were strictly boxcar frames. For the first time in almost four years, they contained no milk car features. (However, with the additional punching of four square and two round holes, boxcar frames were still converted into tank car frames.) Doors, trucks,

---

TABLE 9
CONFIRMED MIXED VINTAGE VARIATIONS

NUMBER	ROAD NAME	CLOSEST CAR IN TABLE	DIFFERENCE FROM CLOSEST CAR IN TABLE	REMARKS
3464(A)-11	A T S F	3464(A)-10	Type 3X doors Flat-headed drive pins	1950 body on 1952 chassis
3464(A)-12	A T S F	3464(A)-9	Type 5B frame	Type 5B (1950) frames with Type 6 trucks; also reported by Schilling in tank car article
3464(B)-9	N Y C	3464(B)-8	Type 5B frame and metal plunger housing	Same remark as 3464(A)-12
3474-3	W P	3474-1	Type 5B frame	Same remark as 3464(A)-12

and boxes continued unchanged from late 1950 production. The round-headed drive pins for attaching door guides and brakewheels returned in 1951. All in all, it was a rather dull year for boxcar production. The year 1951 turned out to be the eye of a hurricane of change.

1952

Four component changes and the introduction of the first new road name and car number in three years made 1952 another year of many variations. The first change was in the trucks, with the bar-end metal truck replacing the staple-end variety. The next change was the replacement of metal doors with plastic ones.

The final component changes only involved the operating boxcars. The housing that supports the activator plunger and its return spring was changed from metal to plastic. Changes were also made in the frame so that the new plastic housing could be snapped into place. These changes obviously saved assembly time and production costs.

From the consumer's perspective, the most notable change for 1952 was the introduction of the colorful 3474 Western Pacific operating boxcar. This silver-painted car with its large yellow feather is quite a contrast to all the other rather drab orange and brown boxcars of the 9-1/4" series. All of the Western Pacific boxcars have plastic doors, although some of the early ones have metal plunger housings. Unfortunately for collectors, the Western Pacific has not held up too well to wear and tear; its silver paint lost its brilliance rapidly and the water-release decals used for decoration often chipped and discolored.

My best estimate of the introduction for the 1952 component changes is shown in **Table 8**. However, there have been a number of sightings of 1952 operating cars which do not fit the chart. Most of these "misfits" have a majority of components from 1952, but they also have one or two components from 1950. When I saw the first couple of cars with this mixture of components, I assumed that the cars had been repaired or upgraded by mixing parts from two cars. With time, however, I saw more and more cars with exactly the same mix of components, and these cars have been reported by other collectors as well. It could be that these cars were assembled after the decision was made to discontinue the 9-1/4" series. As components ran out in the production area, substitute parts from an earlier year could have been brought in from the service department. The mixed vintage cars which have had several confirmed sightings are listed in **Table 9**.

TABLE 10
9-1/4" BOXCAR
REPLACEMENT BODIES

PAGE NUMBER	PART NUMBER	DESCRIPTION	COMMENTS
9/15/47 Parts List:			
19	2454-9	Boxcar Body, stamped	P R R?
21	3454-3	Body Assembly	
1949 Parts List:			
31	2454-13	Boxcar Body, stamped	Baby Ruth?
34	3454-3	Body Assembly	
37A	3464-18	Boxcar Body, complete	Metal doors?
4/56 Substitute Parts List:			
5	2454-13	Obsolete, use 4454-6	Electronic
5	3464-18	Obsolete, use 3464-31	Plastic doors
8/59 Parts List:			
52	2454-13	Body ptd., sub. 4454-6	
57	3454-3	Body Assembly	
58	3474-2	Boxcar Body	W P
63	6454-6	Boxcar Body (brown NYC)	Tan?
63	6454-11	Boxcar Body (brown PRR)	Tuscan
63	6454-26	Boxcar Body (brown Erie)	Brown
63	6454-51	Boxcar Body (brown SP)	Red-brown

1953

According to the catalogues, the 3474 Western Pacific was the only 9-1/4" boxcar available in 1953. The availability of even this car was not widespread; the car was included in one inexpensive O27 set. Perhaps all production of 9-1/4" boxcars stopped in 1952, and the limited 1953 offering was to use up cars and parts already manufactured. It is important to remember that 1953 was the year of introduction for the larger 6464 series. If any cars were in fact manufactured during 1953, they are indistinguishable from 1952 production runs. After 1953 no 9-1/4" boxcar appeared in a Lionel catalogue of any kind for thirty-one years.

REPLACEMENT BODIES

Some confusion about minor variations has arisen because of the availability of replacement bodies through the service department. Replacement bodies were available as early as 1947 and were still available well into the 1960s.

The replacement bodies were painted, marked, and had doors and brakewheels installed. In most cases, the replacement bodies were exactly like the regular production. In all probability, they were leftovers or seconds from a regular production run.

However, some 6454 Southern Pacific, Erie, and Pennsylvania bodies were assembled, probably in the late 1950s, using black, unpainted plastic doors. I do not believe that black plastic doors were ever used on 6454 cars completely assembled at the factory. I have bodies with all three road names and black plastic doors which have never been mounted to frames. The complete cars with black plastic doors which I have seen always have components of several different years. In fact, several have been mounted on tank car or milk car frames. These cars usually show clear signs of post-factory assembly or repair.

Table 10 shows the part number and description contained in several Lionel replacement parts lists. The page numbers refer to the original pages of the Lionel Service Manual; some equivalent lists can be found in the Greenberg printing of the four-volume Lionel Service Manual pages.

PROTOTYPES, COLOR SAMPLES, FACTORY ERRORS, ALTERED CARS, AND THE FUTURE

Several references have been made throughout this article to some rare one-of-a-kind cars (or those few in number). These cars were not part of the regular production runs and do not yield significant information concerning the chronological development of the 9-1/4" boxcars. However, I think it is important to identify as many of these cars as possible and point out the possible pitfalls and blind alleys into which collectors may be led by them. These cars will be divided into four categories: prototypes, paint and color samples, factory

TABLE 11
ONE-OF-A-KIND OR RARE CARS

DESCRIPTION	SOURCE
A. Prototypes	
1. 2454 Baby Ruth, orange door	1946 catalogue, page 1
2. 2454 Alcoa, silver	McComas & Tuohy, *Lionel: A Collector's Guide, Volume. VI*, page 138
3. 3454 gray primer, no markings	Sold in 1982 by Don Shaw
4. 2454 clear, no markings	Formerly B. Eddins Collection
B. Paint and Color Samples; Salesmen's Samples	
1. 3454 P R R merchandise car, tuscan with white "PENNSYLVANIA" lettering	1946 catalogue, inside front cover
2. 3454 P R R merchandise car, brown with white "AUTOMATIC MERCHANDISE CAR" lettering	Sold in 1985 by Ed Prendeville
3. 3454 P R R merchandise car, silver with red lettering	J. Sattler Collection
4. 6454 S P, black	Formerly H. Degano Collection
5. 2454 P R R, silver with black lettering	1946 catalogue, page 1
6. Silver merchandise car, marked "2454 / Baby Ruth"	C. Adair Roberts Collection
7. 6454 Pennsylvania, orange, black lettering	Unconfirmed to date
C. Factory Errors	
1. 3454 merchandise car, silver, lettered on one side only	J. Sattler Collection
2. 3464 A T S F, orange, lettered on one side only	R. Swanson Collection
3. Orange body, no markings	A. Stewart Collection
4. Tan, no markings	R. Swanson Collection
5. 3464 A T S F, tan body, white lettering	R. Niedhammer, J. Sattler, A. Stewart, Margulies, and J. Smith Collections

errors, and post-factory altered cars. The article will conclude with a short discussion of the new 9-1/4" boxcar series first produced by Fundimensions in late 1983. For definitions of prototypes, paint and color samples, and factory errors, refer to the definitions in James M. Sattler's article on page 20.

Prototypes

Known and verified prototypes, color samples, and factory errors of the 9-1/4" boxcars are extremely rare. There are no known large groups or collections of these cars, as is the case with the 6464 boxcars. The prototypes I am aware of are listed in Section A of **Table 11**. Photographs in the 1946 consumer catalogue and some other Lionel photographs of the same period show some 2454 and 3454 cars painted brown or tuscan with white Pennsylvania lettering. The photographs appear to be taken on the prewar Lionel showroom layout, since the T-rail O72 track is clearly visible. Another car which appears in at least one of these photographs is a silver 2454 with Alcoa markings. I have no information at all concerning the current existence of any of these prototype cars shown in the Lionel catalogue or photographs.

Several years ago, I had the opportunity to examine a boxcar which supposedly came directly from the Lionel factory in Hillside, New Jersey. This was a 2454-type car painted dull gray primer not only on the body, but also on the doors, door guides, and frame. The first impression of this car was that it was a sloppy private repaint. However, after close inspection, it was apparent that the gray primer was a rather thin coat over a clear molded plastic body. One could look into the car through the open doors and see light in the corners where the paint did not completely cover the body. There was no trace of any other paint under the gray. Detailed examination also revealed no trace of heat-stamped markings which had been overpainted. The very poor condition of the car, along with the poor quality paint job, still left me with serious doubts about the validity of this car. Then, several months after seeing this unmarked gray car, I noticed a striking similarity between this car and a photograph of the 2454 Alcoa car. The door guides and the door guide drive pins on both cars had been completely painted. Perhaps this gray car was a legitimate Lionel prototype which for some reason had been discarded before being completely painted and lettered. The 2454 Alcoa car is shown on page 138 of McComas and Tuohy's *Lionel: A Collector's Guide, Volume VI*. It is evident from the photograph that the name "Alcoa" and the other letters and numbers were placed on the car with decals — a clear indication of a prototype.

Previous editions of the Greenberg Guides to postwar Lionel contained a photograph of an unpainted and unmarked clear plastic-bodied 2454 boxcar. I have never seen one of these cars directly, but several reportedly exist. Clear bodies which have not been painted for almost forty years will surely show signs of yellowing. (That, in fact, has happened with clear-bodied examples of the 2333 Santa Fe F-3 locomotives; these pieces are known to be genuine salesmen's samples.) On the other hand, painted cars which have been recently stripped should appear completely clear; they may also show faint signs of heat-stamped lettering and traces of paint in the corners and crevices.

Paint and Color Samples; Salesmen's Samples

Cars falling into this category include those cars that were made to allow decisions concerning the proper colors for mass production; they are identical to their mass-produced equivalent except for their color schemes. These cars are extremely rare because they represent color schemes which were ultimately rejected for mass production. Sometimes these cars were used by salesmen as demonstration samples.

Several color samples are shown in the 1946 consumer catalogue. The first is a Pennsylvania boxcar in brown instead of light orange. This may actually be a 3454 operating car since a roof latch seems faintly visible, but Pennsylvania lettering is identical to what was stamped on the early 2454 non-operating boxcars. This car also appears in the same picture as the Alcoa prototype in the McComas and Tuohy book.

Also, in the 1946 catalogue, a silver Pennsylvania boxcar with black lettering is shown in front of the coal elevator on page 1. The "Pennsylvania" lettering to the left of the door distinguishes this car from the usual silver 3454 cars which are lettered "Automatic Merchandise Car". The current whereabouts of these different colored Pennsylvania cars is unknown.

There are two color variations of the 3454 automatic merchandise car that have turned up recently. The first is painted the normal silver color, but all lettering and logos are stamped in red rather than dark blue. Several of these cars have been reported in various parts of the country, providing some evidence that possibly there was a limited production run of the red-lettered cars. Another 3454, which seems to be one-of-a-kind, is painted brown with white lettering. The "Automatic Merchandise Car" lettering is definitely heat stamped, but the line width appears somewhat thicker than the normal blue on silver lettering. Both the red-lettered silver and white-lettered brown cars which I have examined exhibited all the attributes of 1946 production (including blue wiring), making them closest to 3454-1 variations in **Table 8**.

I was also fortunate in being able to examine first-hand a black 6454 Southern Pacific boxcar owned by the late Hank Degano. This car is unique not only because of its black color, but also because it is the only Southern Pacific car with the early herald that I have ever seen that did not have the break in the outer circle at the two o'clock position. The markings on the car were definitely heat stamped, but evidently this car was stamped before the stamping die was damaged on the outer circle of the herald. Other features of this car included Type 4 trucks and couplers, Type 3M doors (the only **painted** black doors I have ever seen), and, surprisingly, a Type 1 frame. This car is clearly a color sample, not a prototype.

Another car I place into the Color Sample category is a silver operating merchandise car in the C. Adair Roberts Collection which is numbered X2454 and marked "Baby Ruth". This silver Baby Ruth is truly unique, but the most startling feature of this car is its Baby Ruth lettering. The letters are not solid, as they are on all the other 2454 cars. Instead, the letters are only outlined the way they are on the later 6024 Baby Ruth cars. This car has a Type 1A frame without side

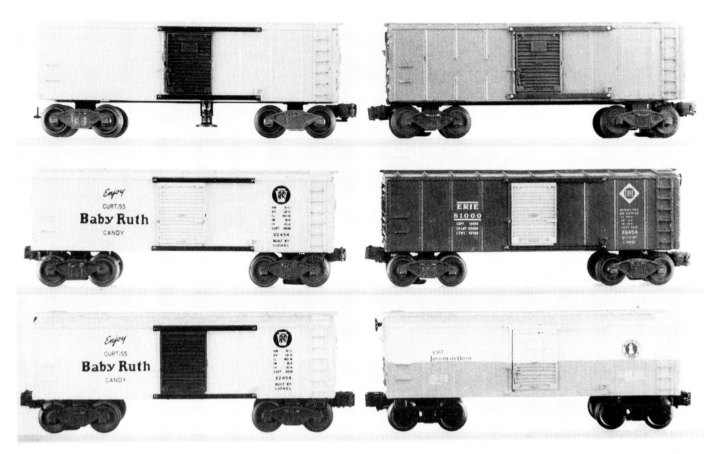

FIGURE 16: *Top Shelf:* (*Left*) 3464(A) Santa Fe operating car without printing on one side and (*right*) unnumbered, tan 9-1/4" car without printing on either side. (See Table 11, Factory Errors 2 and 4.) *Middle Shelf:* (*Left*) 2454 P R R Baby Ruth with orange doors instead of brown doors, but not confirmed as factory production and (*right*) 6454J Erie with post-factory-installed orange-painted doors. *Bottom Shelf:* (*Left*) snow white 2454 Baby Ruth boxcar which was produced by post-factory chemical alteration and (*right*) post-factory custom-painted Lancaster and Chester boxcar.

indentations, two blue wires, and no visible roof hatch pin — all features indicating 1946 production. On the other hand, the car has 3B couplers which are indicative of 1947 production. This car, which must have an awfully interesting history if it could only speak, was obtained as part of a set of trains from its original owner.

I would like to mention one final car in this section. There have been reports of an orange 6454 Pennsylvania car with black lettering. I have heard several unconfirmed reports that such a car exists, but I have never seen one or talked directly with an owner of such a car. One report indicated that this road name and color combination might have been a replacement body which was not shipped as a complete car. I would appreciate hearing from any collector with first-hand information about this car.

Factory Errors

Lionel's quality control department must have been very good during the late 1940s and early 1950s because very few production mistakes slipped through the inspectors and ended up with customers. I am aware of only two boxcars in this series where the heat stamping was left off one side of the car. One is a 1947 silver 3454 merchandise car from the

collection of Jim Sattler and the other is a 3464(A)-4 operating A T S F car in my own collection. There may well be others, of course.

Several other odd cars have turned up which have no lettering at all. I classify these as factory errors because they have bodies with very poor paint jobs which should never have left the factory. One tan car and one orange car in the Stewart Collection are known; both have identical features — a very unusual combination of component features, at that. First, they are mounted on Type 1 tank car frames (!) and are equipped with very rare double sliding-shoe trucks used only on the O Gauge 3854 operating merchandise car! Also, the door guides are attached with small, bright-headed drive pins which look like the type used on American Flyer boxcars made around 1950. It is quite possible that these rejected bodies somehow got out of the Lionel factory and were assembled into complete cars by another party, using repair parts. These cars do have an unusual combination of features, to say the least!

The tan 3464 A T S F cars with white lettering could be errors or they could be color samples. There are a number of these cars in collections, and there seems to be little doubt that some were included in sets shipped from the Lionel factory. I am aware of at least six of these cars and have unconfirmed reports of several more. The only one I have

FIGURE 17: A comparison of the Lionel 1946-1952 boxcar body on top with the 7910 Chessie boxcar (1985). The Lionel has a large body sprue in the middle of the roof underside for injecting plastic and also has four corner columns for the frame-mounting screws. These features were eliminated in the Fundimensions design which has a very small sprue at the brakewheel end *(right)* and one hole in each end for attaching the screws through the frame. The car has internal stiffening ribs which also serve as stops so that the frame does not go too far into the body.

inspected was clearly manufactured in 1949. It was identical to a 3464(A)-2 A T S F car in every detail, except that the car body was painted the tan color usually reserved for the New York Central cars. The best guess is that someone at the factory, perhaps new to the production line, put some tan bodies through the A T S F heat-stamping patterns before the error was discovered by a supervisor.

Altered Cars

One of the primary objectives of this article, as stated in the introduction, was to help collectors judge whether variations in boxcars which they observed at meets and shows were legitimate or not. I certainly do not claim to be the final authority on this subject. Nevertheless, I would like to pass along some examples and suggestions which may be helpful to other collectors as they are forced to wrestle with this question from time to time. Of course, be warned that the whole area of prototypes and factory errors is very risky, even for the most experienced collectors.

The most common alteration is probably the substitution of one or two components, such as trucks and couplers, in order to repair a damaged car. If identical original replacement components and the proper tools and procedures are used, the repair should not affect the authenticity of the car. On the other hand, lack of attention to details or the unavailability of exact repair parts may result in a repair job producing a purportedly minor variation. Each collector will have to decide for himself whether these homemade variations affect the collectability of the repaired car or not.

Some cars have been intentionally altered by operators in order to "improve" their appearance or performance. The 6454 Erie with orange doors and the blue and white Lancas-

ter and Chester (shown in **Figure 16**) are two examples of cars in this category. The orange doors on the Erie car are repainted Type 3M doors with long pins on their inner sides. The Lancaster and Chester car is an obvious repaint of a tan 3464(B) N Y C car. There was no attempt on the part of the seller to suggest that either car was a rare original Lionel variation.

Two other cars in this category are a different matter. An orange door 2454 P R R Baby Ruth could be an altered car made by taking the orange doors off a 2454(A)-1 made in early 1946 and installing them on a 2454(B)-1 car. If this is the case, whoever made this particular car also changed the trucks to the open shoe Type 2. On the other hand, since the trucks, doors, and all other component features are consistent with early 1946 production, this may be a very rare legitimate variation. It could possibly be the orange door Baby Ruth car shown in page 1 of the 1946 consumer catalogue, except that in this case the Pennsylvania logo to the right of the door does not seem to match the catalogue illustration exactly.

There is also a white 2454 P R R Baby Ruth car which has raised all kinds of questions — and controversy! Except for the body color, this car has all the component features of a 2454(B)-4 car, which would indicate mid to late 1947 production. The car surface has several small gray dots. When the gray dots were scraped, small amounts of orange paint became visible underneath with a ten-power lens. The gray dots had likely protected the orange paint underneath from chemical alteration. Since the car was purchased from a source known to have sold other chemically-altered white cars, it is highly likely that this car was also chemically altered. Moreover, several collectors familiar with chemical and dye processing have shown me 2454 cars they have made in colors such as red, blue, green, and (almost) white. *[The Train Collectors' Association has issued a warning about fraudulent pieces produced by just such a process, including white 3656 stock cars and white 3562-50 barrel cars. Collectors should exercise extreme caution in these matters — Ed.]* Needless to say, if a collector has the opportunity to

FIGURE 18: Side view comparison of the Lionel 1946-1952 boxcar body and the 7910 Chessie boxcar manufactured in 1985. Note differences in rib spacing and the lack of interruption in ribs to the left of the door on the Chessie boxcar. R. Swanson Collection.

buy an odd color car, he should consider carefully the possibility that the car has been altered from its original factory color.

THE PRESENT AND THE FUTURE: LIONEL TRAINS, INC.

When I first conceived this article in 1983, Lionel had not produced 9-1/4" boxcars for thirty years. Clearly, this

was a "closed" series which could be discussed and analyzed without fear that Lionel would ever rerun any of these cars. However, the 1984 traditional catalogue showed the folly of trying to outguess the makers of Lionel Trains! There, on page 12 of the catalogue, was a 7910 Chessie System boxcar which appears to be a direct descendant of the 9-1/4" boxcars!

When the 7910 Chessie boxcars were finally shipped by Fundimensions in August 1985, I immediately compared the new car with the old. The Chessie car is exactly the same size as the old ones, and the car even uses two metal door

TABLE 12 AVAILABILITY OF 9-1/4" BOXCARS ACCORDING TO LIONEL'S CONSUMER CATALOGUES				
YEAR	CAR NUMBER	SEPARATE SALE?	SET APPLICATIONS	
			O27	O
1946	2454	yes	1411W, 1413WS	2105WS
	3454	yes	1409, 1409W, 1415WS, 1421WS	
	4454	no		4109WS
1947	2454	yes	1435WS, 1437WS	2125WS
	3454	yes	1439WS	
	4454	no		4109WS
1948	2454	yes		
	4454	no		4110WS
	6454	no	1427WS, 1429WS, 1445WS	
1949	3464	yes	1451WS, 1453WS, 1445WS	2139W, 2151W
	4454	no		4110WS
	6454	yes		
1950	3464	yes	1457B, 1473WS	2159W, 2161W, 2167WS, 2175W
	4454	no		4333WS
	6454	yes	1471WS	
1951	3464	yes	1481WS	2167WS, 2175W, 2185W
	6454	yes	1471WS	
1952	3464	yes		2179WS, 2183W
	3474	no	1483WS	
	6454	yes		
1953	3474	no	1511S	

guides to hold the doors. However, the similarities end right there. The 7910 is obviously made from a completely new mold which differs from the old one both inside and out. The corner posts molded inside the old bodies which provided the attachment points for four self-tapping screws (and which were so fragile) are gone. The new body is attached to the frame by two sheet metal screws at the car ends. The mounting method and frame appear similar to those first used on the 6656 stock car in 1950.

The side ribs and rivets on the 7910 also have slightly different spacing than those on the original 2454-4 mold. The two rows of rivets immediately to the left of the doors are complete on the new cars, where there had been interruptions on the older cars for the heat stamping of the road name. That is an ironic reversal of the usual Fundimensions practice!

The doors on the 7910 are also different from any of the previous doors. The new doors are molded plastic, but they have external details similar to the right-hand metal die-cast doors last made in 1951. The new doors have no trace of any pin on the back sides and, like the bodies, they are not painted but are molded out of colored plastic.

The 7910 Chessie System turns out not to be the leader in the revival of the 9-1/4" boxcar series. In late 1983 Fundimensions made a special uncatalogued set for the Toys 'R Us stores which contained a 7912 Geoffrey's Star car, a giraffe car which was based on a 9-1/4" boxcar body with a hole in the roof. (Regular giraffe cars are based on the short stock car molds.) In July 1985 Lionel shipped a second set to Toys 'R Us; this one contained a 7914 "Geoffrey's Carnival Carrier" giraffe car. Both of these Toys 'R Us cars have molded white bodies and doors. They are identical to the 7910 boxcar except for the rectangular hole in the roof and the internal giraffe car mechanism. (The 7910 has a center hole in its frame filled with a plastic plug.)

Lionel (under Fundimensions management) has evidently developed new tooling and reintroduced the 9-1/4" box-

cars for their smaller, lower-priced Traditional series. The larger 9200/9400/9700 series boxcars will probably be kept for the Collector Series. It will be interesting to see if some of the old road names and color schemes are rerun in the 7900 series. [*Through 1990, no other examples have been catalogued — Ed.*] Because of the many mold and component differences, collectors need not fear any confusion between the new and the old cars.

A study of the 9-1/4" boxcars is almost the perfect case study in the Lionel manufacturing process for any collector. Very few of these cars are scarce, so any collector can acquire them and study nearly all the variations on a modest budget. These boxcars have been overshadowed by the more popular 6464 series, but they should not be ignored; they were a commendable attempt at realism when they were produced and they are, if not colorful, very interesting to collect and study.

ACKNOWLEDGMENTS

An article of this length and depth obviously cannot represent the efforts of just one person. Through the years, there have been many people who have helped me acquire these boxcars, given me information, and encouraged me with great persistence to write this article. For their help and encouragement, I would like to thank Harold Powell, Bruce Balsley, Tom Rollo, Charlie Pendergast, Barbara and Don Shaw, Ed Prendeville, Rand Washburn, Ralph Hutchinson, John Palm, Ron Niedhammer, C. Adair Roberts, Jack Smith, and the late Hank Degano.

Special words of thanks and appreciation are also extended to Barbara Houtsma, June Smith, and Nancy Wilczewski, who patiently and efficiently typed and proofread the original manuscript, which must have seemed to be a never-ending saga.

THE STORY OF THE 2456 AND 6456 HOPPER CARS

SAME CAR; DIFFERENT NUMBERS AND COUPLERS — *James M. Sattler*

The 2456 hopper car as shown on page 25 of the 1948 Lionel catalogue.

The story of the 2456 and 6456 hopper cars provides a curious footnote to Lionel's postwar history, because it provides an insight into the duality of the company's product line. From the beginning of its O Gauge line in 1915 Lionel offered two sizes of O Gauge rolling stock: a smaller, less expensive series and a larger, higher-priced series. In the early 1930s Lionel went a step further and offered three sizes of rolling stock.

In 1930 and 1931 Lionel introduced a special series of track to go with its less expensive line of electric trains. Called "O27", the new track was constructed with lighter material and lower profile rails, but the distance between the outside rails remained the same as that of the heavier O Gauge track. In 1931 Lionel introduced the term "O27" to de-

scribe the smaller, less expensive series of equipment. These O27 sets came with the O27 track.

In 1948 Lionel announced a new 9-1/2" hopper that appeared simultaneously in both the O27 (numbered 6456) and the O Gauge (numbered 2456) lines. Although the car bodies differed only in number, there were more important differences in the underpinnings. The most important difference was that the O27 version introduced Lionel's new "magnetic" couplers, while the O Gauge version continued the "electro-magnetic" couplers. The new magnetic couplers produced very large unit manufacturing cost reductions for Lionel, since the individual cars no longer had electromagnets with wound wire coils mounted on each truck. Lionel identified the change in rolling stock couplers from electromagnetic to magnetic by changing its rolling stock numbers from the 2000 series (i.e. 2456) to the 6000 series (i.e. 6456). There were several notable exceptions to this number change, such as some cars from the 3000 series.

Since Lionel's O27 production was much greater than its O Gauge production, substituting new couplers on its O27 line produced greater savings. As pointed out in the Lionel Service Manual, "Although, properly speaking, all Lionel re-

The 6456 hopper car shown as part of set 1425B on page 5 of the 1948 catalogue.

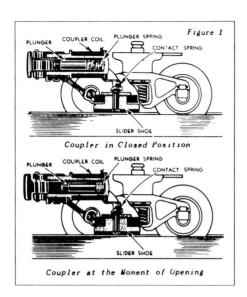

The 1948 O Gauge 2456 came with Type 3 trucks with coil-operated couplers. The operation of this coupler is shown here. The coil couplers were considerably more expensive to manufacture than the magnetic couplers introduced in the O27 line in 1948. In 1949 Lionel replaced the electromagnetic couplers on most equipment.

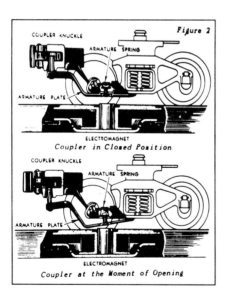

Most 1948 O27 Gauge 6456 hoppers came with the new Type 4 trucks. The operation of these couplers is shown in these diagrams. The coupler is operated by the magnetic pull of a coil mounted in the special uncoupling track.

mote control operating knuckle couplers work electromagnetically, i.e., through the medium of an electromagnet, whether on the coupler itself or in the uncoupling track section, the name 'electromagnetic' has been reserved for those couplers where the coil is wound on the body of the coupler itself."

The Service Manual also points out: "The designation 'magnetic' has been reserved for those trucks which do not have individual coils but are operated by an electromagnet located in the uncoupling track section. The coupler has no electrical connection to the track, but is opened when its movable armature plate is attracted by the energized track electromagnet."

Lionel's 1948 and earlier postwar 2000 series of rolling stock were equipped with "electromagnetic" couplers that had the electromagnet (which can be seen as the exposed copper wire coiled around the coupler shaft) as part of the coupler assembly. The "electromagnetic" couplers were activated by means of the 1019 (O27) or RCS (O) track sections. These sections had fourth and fifth rails, which, when activated, allowed electric current to pass through them to the sliding pickup shoes on the bottom of the trucks to activate the electromagnet and thereby uncouple the coupler.

The 6000 series of rolling stock had the newly-designed "magnetic" couplers, which were activated by an electromagnet in the remote-control track sections (6019 for O27, which was introduced in 1948, and the UCS for O, which was introduced in 1949), rather than in the coupler. When the electromagnet in the track section was activated, it physically pulled down a metal plate (which Lionel called the "movable armature plate" and which is sometimes called the "activator plate") that was attached to the underside of the truck. This plate held a pin which, in turn, held the coupler knuckle in its normally-closed position. When the electromagnet in the track was activated, it pulled down the activator plate, which then pulled the knuckle pin down and out of the knuckle, thereby opening the coupler.

The O Gauge 2456 hopper car has electromagnetic couplers (with the electromagnet in each respective coupler), which are activated by the five-rail, O Gauge RCS remote-control track that was introduced before World War II. The O27 6456 version has the then-new magnetic couplers which used 1948's "Brand new magnetic principle." It was offered with the new 6019 magnetic track that had an electromagnet in the center of the track section. See pages 26 and 27 of the

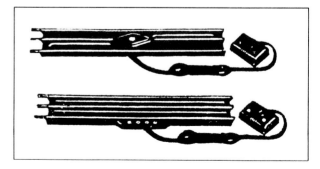

The 1948 Lionel catalogue illustrated the 6019 magnetic track and the RCS remote-control track. Note the presence of five rails on the RCS section.

Lionel 1948 catalogue for the two different remote-control track sections.

In the 1948 Lionel catalogue, the 6456 hopper car was shown and offered only with O27 set 1425B. It was not offered for separate sale. The 1948 catalogue showed and offered the 2456 hopper car in several O Gauge sets, all of which were supplied with the RCS remote-control track section. Except for their numbers and coupler mechanisms, both cars were identical, and both were only offered in black with white Lehigh Valley markings.

All O Gauge sets listed in the 1949 catalogue came with the new UCS track section, which replaced the RCS section. The UCS (the O Gauge version of the 6019) included an electromagnet in the center of the track section. The new UCS track permitted Lionel to use cars with the magnetic couplers in its O Gauge line. Consequently, all 1949 O27 and O Gauge sets that came with a hopper included the black 6456 Lehigh Valley hopper car with white markings. At the same time only the 6456 was offered for separate sale. The 2456 disappeared; it was not catalogued in 1949 or in any later catalogue.

Some 6456 hopper cars have been found with electromagnetic couplers instead of the later magnetic ones. Most of these cars are factory originals and came in boxes marked "New York ... Chicago ... San Francisco". There are several possible explanations for these cars. One is that Lionel could not get the new 6019 O27 remote track sections ready in time for all 1948 production of O27 sets; so, Lionel used the old 1019 O27 remote track with cars with matching electromagnetic couplers (perhaps Lionel did not have the new magnetic couplers available or perhaps they were simply depleting inventory). There are also 6555 tank cars, which were introduced in 1949, with electromagnetic couplers rather than magnetic ones (which gives credence to the depletion hypothesis).

The new 6456 and other 6000-series cars equipped with the new magnetic couplers would operate only on the new 6019 or UCS uncoupling/unloading sections. However, due to the additional fourth and fifth rails included on these track sections, these sections would also uncouple the earlier electromagnetic couplers on 2000-series cars.

Lionel created a minor marketing problem in 1948 by introducing 6456 hopper cars with magnetic couplers, which would not uncouple with the then-current O Gauge uncoupling tracks. To minimize the problem, Lionel included the magnetic coupler-equipped 6456 cars in only one O27 set, which had the new 6019 magnetic track. These cars were not available for separate sale while the 2456 was available. In 1949 the marketing problem was solved by providing both O and O27 uncoupling tracks with center electromagnets with their new O and O27 sets, respectively — Ed.

LIONEL 6362-SERIES FLATCARS

Ralph Hutchinson

To the novice, a train is a train. To a railroader, trains represent variety, with their many different colors, railroad names, and consists.

Even flatcars offer variety. They may have bulkheads or other devices to retain loads. They may be long or short, wood or steel. They may be used in busy freight trains or in seldom-used wreck trains.

Although real railroads used the fewest of their flatcars for wreck trains, Lionel offered an exciting selection of cars designed for wreck train service. In fact, wrecks were part of the fun on the most famous of miniature railroads: The Lionel Lines.

On the prototype the wreck or work train is typically composed of a crane, wheel, and truck cars; gondolas carrying pre-assembled sections of roadbed for temporary repairs; a water car; a tool car; and usually non-revenue passenger cars serving as bunk cars for work crews. These trains are assembled and run by the railroad's Mechanical Department.

Over the years, Lionel offered a variety of catalogued wreck and work trains, with the rolling stock patterned after actual wreck trains. One such car is the truck car, a model of which was introduced by Lionel in 1955. The prototype for the Lionel truck car is usually an older flatcar, no longer in revenue service, with rails mounted on the bed and trucks chained to the rails. Lionel could have created such a car by using the 6511 flatcar with rails mounted on the bed (as was done for the 6805 radioactive waste car), but chose instead to mold a new car body that contained the rails. It was mounted on a metal sill that ran the length of the car. This car, the 6362 rail truck car, along with the 3361 operating

The 6362 rail truck car was numbered 636255. In 1956 it had "LIONEL LINES" in sans-serif lettering.

log car, were the first in a series of cars using a body mold that would be catalogued in one form or another until the end of production in 1969.

While it has been previously pointed out that in 1955 Lionel management cheapened the line as a cost-saving measure, the 6362 car was by no means a "cheap" looking car. Rather, it featured rich rivet detail and finely-molded structural members. The car measured eleven inches from coupler to coupler and rolled on bar-end metal trucks, although these were held to the car frame by the sheet metal pins first introduced in 1955. The body itself was mounted to the frame by a tab and slot in one end and a screw in the other. The load consisted of three metal trucks.

The Lionel 1955 catalogue illustrated the 6362 with a raised brakewheel.

As was often the case with new Lionel creations, the first illustrations in the catalogue had little resemblance to the item which came off the production line. The cover of the 1955 catalogue gave no indication that the 6362 was to be introduced that year. The inaugural illustration on page 18 pictured the car in dark red — a color in which it was never made. When the car was manufactured it was molded in a bright orange with black rubber-stamped lettering on the sides. Since catalogue illustrations sometimes pictured a pre-production model, it is possible that such was the case for the 6362. The only other illustration of the 6362 that first year was on page 33 where the "new-in-1955" cars were displayed. Both illustrations show the car as having an elevated brakewheel like those on the earlier 2411/6411 flatcar, but the production model had the standard wheel riveted to the floor of the car. The car data as pictured by the artists shows the car carrying the logo "LIONEL" in the center of the body when in fact it came stamped "LIONEL LINES" in serif lettering. The number on the car, while shown in the correct position, was actually 636255, not 6362 as illustrated. The correct load was shown on the car, but the finished product carried the three trucks much closer together than the illustrations would have the reader believe. The trucks were kept in place by a bulkhead at each end of the car and by four indentations in the center of the rails, which held the center truck in exact position. There was no indication in the catalogue as to which set or sets included this car, since this was the year Lionel decided not to list set components. The illustration on page 18 hinted that the car was included in sets headed by the 2338 Milwaukee GP7 and the 682 Pennsy turbine, but in fact it came in only one set, 2235W, headed by the 2338. Although this car was new to the Lionel line, the company certainly did not give it much exposure this first year.

Lionel rectified the minimum exposure of this car by including it in three sets in the 1956 catalogue. While the artist's rendition now showed the car in its production color with the correct car data, the load was still not positioned correctly in all of the illustrations. The 1956 production run was identical to the previous year except that the lettering was sans-serif. The 6362 was included in sets headed by the 621 Jersey Central switcher, the 2338, and the 601 Seaboard switcher, as well as being offered for separate sale.

The car ran again in 1957 as a separate sale item only, with the load still incorrectly positioned in the illustration on page 40. The only change in the car was that it featured serif lettering once again. The sans-serif version of the car seems to be less common than the serif versions of 1955 and 1957. (A scarce variation of the car surfaced in 1957. It had serif lettering, but came in a distinctly flatter shade of orange that closely resembled the color of the orange 6119-25 work caboose.)

While the 6362 was manufactured for only three years, its sister fared much better. Usually after a new car was introduced into the line it would evolve into other cars in the series over a period of years. One example is the searchlight car which was introduced in 1949 as 6520 and evolved into the improved version 3520 in 1952. Therefore it was somewhat unusual to find two different cars using a common body mold appearing the same year (excluding the 6464 series), but that was precisely the case in 1955 as Lionel also introduced the 3361 log car.

The 3361 was almost structurally identical to the 6362 except that it came in unpainted gray plastic with black lettering. Introduced on page 23 of the 1955 catalogue and found as part of a set headed by the green GG1 and shown as a separate sale item on page 32, its illustrations suffered the same errors as its sister: red color with white lettering, in-

The 3361 has a dump tray activated by a solenoid mounted in the car. Note that "LIONEL LINES" is in serif.

correct brakewheels, and incorrect data. The body of the 3361 retained the features of the 6362 except that the center section was molded separately and acted as a dumping tray. The tray was held to the car by two molded plastic pins that were held in place by a long flat spring riveted to the car body. The dump tray had an extension which passed through the car body and rode upon an elevating cam that was fastened to the metal sill. This meant that Lionel had to stamp out two different metal frames, with that of the 3361 adapted to hold the electro-magnetic solenoid. This unit operated quite differently from that of the earlier log cars since it was mounted horizontally and had a return spring attached to the pawl. It also took seven movements to raise the bed to its maximum height. The solenoid itself operated through the then-current use of slide shoes mounted to the trucks. Like its sister, the 3361 came with serif lettering in 1955. The same stamp was used for both cars with only the number being changed. Although shown in the catalogue as carrying only the number 3361, the car actually carried the number 336155. There was a different placement of the numbers on the two cars however. On the 636255 the last "5" was 1-3/4" from the end of the car, while on the 336155 the last digit was placed 2-1/8" from the end. The 3361 came with five logs and a 160 trackside bin. The log car sold for $7.95 that first year, while the 6362 was offered at $5.95.

In 1956 the 3361 appeared in the series of four trains headed by the 2018 on page 17, the 665 on page 21, and the 2368 on page 23, as well as being offered for separate sale on page 28. The only differences in the 1956 production run were the sans-serif lettering and the finger on the bottom of the dump tray, which was lengthened to improve operation.

The 3361 continued unchanged in 1957. It appeared in four sets and as a separate sale item. In the 1958 production run the printing on the car returned to the serif version as it had been in 1955, but otherwise the car was unchanged. The car came as a part of three sets or individually. In each illustration the car data as portrayed by the artists was inaccurate.

By 1959, with the emphasis on the military and space cars, the 3361 was offered in only one set, headed by the 665, and for separate sale in an illustration in which the car lacks all markings. In 1960 the car disappeared from the consumer catalogue but was still available to dealers in the advance catalogue. This was a sell-off of the remaining stock. The car was unchanged. Both the 3361 and 6362 always came with metal trucks. As early as 1955 a 3361X was packaged with logs but without the bin, which was Lionel's usual method for packaging set components. The use of a smaller box made it possible to place the bin loose inside the outfit box, so that a cardboard filler was not required to hold the bin in place. As a separate sale item, the 3361 came in a larger box with only 3361 stamped on the end flaps. This larger box included a cardboard filler and the unloading bin.

In 1960 the first of the successor cars appeared as the 6361 timber transport car. For this car the 3361 body was molded in dark green plastic, and the dumping tray was removed. The car still retained the rails that had been used on the 6362 at each end of the body. The body bracing beneath the car bed was altered by cutting four square 3/16" notches in the plastic to hold the log chains in place. Since this was a non-operating car, Lionel used the frame from the 6362 car

YEARLY DEVELOPMENT OF THE 6362 SERIES

YEAR	CARS OFFERED					ROAD NAME	COLOR(S)
	6362	3361	6361	3362	3364		
1955	▓	▓				Lionel Lines	Orange, Gray
1956	▓	▓				Lionel Lines	Orange, Gray
1957	▓	▓				Lionel Lines	Orange, Gray
1958		▓				Lionel Lines	Gray
1959		▓				Lionel Lines	Gray
1960		(*)	▓			Lionel Lines	Gray, Green
1961			▓	▓		Lionel Lines	Green
1962			▓	▓		Lionel Lines	Green
1963			▓	▓		Lionel Lines	Green
1964			▓			Lionel Lines	Green
1965			▓		▓	Lionel Lines	Green
1966			▓		▓	Lionel Lines	Green
1967			▓		▓	Lionel Lines	Green
1968			▓		▓	Lionel Lines	Green
1969			▓		▓	Lionel Lines	Green

NOTES:

6362 carried three metal trucks as a load.

3361 carried four or five logs as load; came with 160 bin. (* Uncatalogued.)

6361 carried three real logs as load held by darkened brass or steel chains.

3362 carried three silver helium tanks; came without 160 bin.

3364 carried three stained or unstained logs; came without 160 bin. The car is actually stamped "3362", but is referred to as 3364 because of the load.

6362 and 3361 came only with metal trucks. 3362, 3364, and 6361 (and early 9300) came with Timken trucks;
   some 3362 and 6361 cars came with one operating coupler; 3364 only came with one operating coupler.

Various additional road names were created by Fundimensions, when it resurrected this series as their 9300 series.

once again with the current early AAR trucks riveted to the frame. This was one of the most realistic cars ever produced by Lionel because it carried three actual tree limb logs held by blackened brass chains that were held tight by a tension spring under the car body. The same rubber stamp was used for the log car as had been used on the 3361 and 6362. The white serif lettering and number were centered between the "LIONEL LINES" logo and the bulkhead near the end of the car. The timber transport car was introduced in the series of two sets, one headed by 2037 and the other by the 637. True to catalogue tradition, the illustrations were inaccurate. While the catalogue always referred to the 6361 as the "Timber Transport Car", the box in which it came was simply marked " 6361 Log Car". The car sold for $5.95 in 1960.

In 1961 the fourth car in the series appeared as the 3362 helium tank unloading car. For the operation of this car, Lionel had to make an additional change in the car body. For cost purposes, the operating mechanism used was a metal plunger which was attracted by the center rail electromagnet. A tubular projection was molded into the car body to hold the plunger, and the dump tray extension was changed from a narrow tooth-like projection to a square appendage holding a metal pin that was locked and released by the operating plunger. The dump frame on this car was raised by a spring. The spring was held to the body by a raised projection, and the dump frame was altered to hold the other end of the spring. Because of the elevating spring's tension, the long flat spring used to hold the tray on the 3361 could not be used and had to be replaced by a similar spring that had an angled end to counter the upward pressure and hold the dump tray hinge pins in their brackets. (Typically, the dump tray becomes warped and the load does not sit level on the car.) Because the plunger mechanism was different from that of the 3361, Lionel had to stamp out a new center metal frame for this car. The weight of this car was considerably lighter than the 3361 due to the plastic trucks.

The 3362 helium tank unloading car gave the load rough handling! Can you imagine the consequences of dumping a pressurized tank off a flatcar?

The 3362/3364 box with its dual number listing is probably unique among Lionel boxes. G. Halverson Collection.

The 3362 also used the same lettering stamp with serif-style white letters and appeared in only one outfit, headed by the 246 steamer, in 1961. It was also offered as a separate sale, but neither catalogue illustration was correct. This car sold for $5.95 when it was introduced.

Since the body mold had been changed for the 1961 production of the 3362, the 6361 timber car also made use of the new body and frame minus the dump tray and mechanism. The 6361 was not catalogued in 1962 or 1963.

The 3362 continued unchanged in 1962 and 1963, but it was upgraded to a set pulled by the 736 Berkshire. Each molding of this car produced a slight change in the green color, and while the car always came with rubber-stamped white serif lettering the position of the number did vary. While the majority of the cars were produced as pictured, some cars have the number printed much closer to the "LIONEL LINES" logo. The "2" of the number 3362 is 2-1/4" from the end of the car, but on the variant (probably produced in 1963) it is 2-3/4" from the end. Some 3362s came with one operating and one fixed coupler as Lionel continued to cut costs. The 3362 was the first of the dumping cars to come without the 160 bin. In 1964 the 6361 timber car returned, unchanged, using the 3362 body without the dumping mechanism. The 6361 continued structurally unchanged through 1969.

In 1965 the fifth and final car in the series made its appearance — the 3364 operating log dump car. This new car was simply the 3362 with a new load, and was stamped "3362". The 1965 and 1966 catalogue photographs showed the car still carrying the 3362 number. It was only offered in one set, the 11520, which ran for two years (1965-1966) behind the 242 locomotive; it was also catalogued as a separate sale item in 1965, 1966, and 1968, and came in an orange picture box with "3364" on the end flaps. The 3364 variation always came with one operating and one fixed coupler and carried three stained logs, which were the same size as the helium tanks but without the tapered ends. When the inventory of 3362 bodies was depleted and the mold was used once again, the car reappeared in 1969 as a completely unstamped example. The 1969 catalogue offered a unique double-numbered listing. On page 5 of the catalogue the car is shown as it had previously been produced. The copy lists the car as "3362 and 3364 operating dump car". The "Checkerboard" box in which these unstamped cars were sold was also marked with the double number as "3362/3364" operating unloading car. Because the 6361 timber transport car also used this body, it also appeared in 1969 without any lettering.

Of all the cars in the series, the 6361 timber car commands the most attention because of its realistic load. But the story does not end here, since the series has been continued into the "Modern Era" with structural differences. The most notable difference is the absence of the metal frame beneath the car body. When the 9300 Penn Central car appeared in 1970, the early production run came with three leftover helium tanks and the 3362 operating instruction sheet. Later that same year, the load changed to three unstained logs. The dump tray was no longer held by the long flat spring, but rather by interlocking pins and sockets molded into the car body.

The 6362 series is a relatively easy group to collect, with the possible exception of the unstamped 3362/3364 cars, since one or more of the series frequently turns up at train markets. For the modeler who operates a logging empire on his or her layout, a number of these cars loaded with tree limb logs taken from live trees (as on the 6361) can make an interesting as well as colorful train. The dump frames are easily removed, chain can be purchased at almost any hardware store, and small tree branches are in abundance. Why not begin now to collect this series of molded cars which are still available at reasonable prices? Happy Railroading!

NEW HAVEN AUTOMOBILE CARS

THE TALE OF THE 6468-25 — *James M. Sattler*

The 6468-25 New Haven automobile car as it appeared in the 1956 advance catalogue on page 22.

With their attractive orange bodies and two-tone "NH" logos, the 6468-25 New Haven automobile cars are certainly eye-catching. What makes them interesting, however, is the number of variations in which they can be found. Although establishing an exact chronology for the variations may be impossible, it is useful to study catalogue depictions to learn more about these cars. Unfortunately, catalogue illustrations can be arbitrarily misleading in color and detail. Therefore, this is a difficult and hazardous process at best.

Two kinds of Lionel catalogues were used for this review:

Advance Catalogue. The first is the February advance catalogue which is published in small quantities for dealer distribution at the New York Toy Fair. These catalogues are usually printed in black ink, sometimes with a second accent color. New items in these catalogues are often tentative and are based upon prototype models or factory mock-ups and often contain artists' sketches depicting proposed items in their early stages of development. In many cases, the depictions in the advance catalogues vary considerably from the way in which the items are later manufactured.

Consumer Catalogue. The second type of catalogue, published later in the year, is a full-color consumer catalogue which is made in large quantities. The consumer catalogues are usually more accurate than the advance catalogues.

An item is usually shown two different ways within each type of catalogue. First, as part of a set or multiple sets, and second, as an item available for separate sale. While the catalogue depictions of the 6468-25 New Haven automobile cars illustrate different features found on the different variations, the depictions themselves do not present a reliable timeline for these changes.

THE 1956 ADVANCE CATALOGUE

The 6468-25 first appears in the black and white 1956 advance catalogue as part of the 2350 New Haven set on page 22. It is also shown as available for separate sale on page 40. The black and white depictions on both of these pages show the car with a large black "N" over a large white "H", both without the left serif on the top of the large black "N". We will refer to this first color combination as the "black-over-white" version and the lack of the serif as the "half-serif" version. In the 1956 advance catalogue, the words "NEW HAVEN" and all technical data are shown in white. An actual car with all of these characteristics has not been observed.

THE 1956 CONSUMER CATALOGUE

In the 1956 consumer catalogue, the 6468-25 is also shown as part of the top 2350 New Haven set on page 19 and as a separate sale item on page 33. The colored depiction on page 33 shows a black-over-white logo with a complete serif, which we will refer to as the "full-serif" version, but it also shows the words "NEW HAVEN" in black and all technical data in white. Cars with all of these characteristics are available.

Interestingly, as the large black "N" shown in the 1956 consumer catalogue retained the full-serif at the top, the serif previously shown at the bottom of the "N" is now missing.

6468-25 NEW HAVEN AUTOMOBILE BOXCARS

	Variation:	(A)	(B)	(C)	(D)	(E)	(F)
"NH" Logo	Black-over-White	▓	▓	▓	▓		
	White-over-Black					▓	▓
"N" Serif	Half				▓	▓	▓
	Full	▓	▓	▓			
"NEW HAVEN"	Black	▓	▓	▓	▓		
	White					▓	▓
Data	Black					▓	▓
	White	▓	▓	▓	▓		
Doors	Black	▓	▓	▓	▓	▓	▓
	Tuscan						
Frame	Type 1	▓					
	Type 2		▓	▓	▓	▓	▓
Trucks	Bar-End	▓		▓	▓	▓	▓
	AAR		▓				

The 6468-25 New Haven automobile car as it appears on page 9 of the 1957 advance catalogue.

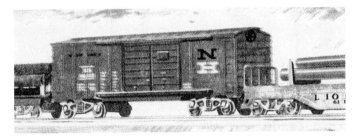

The 6468-25 as shown on page 12 of the 1957 consumer catalogue.

THE 1957 ADVANCE CATALOGUE

In the 1957 dealer advance catalogue, the 6468-25 car appears as part of the 2037 set on page 9, but now in the half-serif, white-over-black configuration with the words "NEW HAVEN" in white and all other technical data in black. The car also appears on page 39 for separate sale, but in this second depiction, the car appears in the same color combination as in the 1956 consumer catalogue, with a half-serif, black-over-white logo and all other lettering, including the words "NEW HAVEN", in white. No cars have been observed in this latter configuration. The depiction on page 39 of the 1957 dealer advance catalogue appears to be merely a reduced version of that on page 22 of the 1956 advance catalogue.

THE 1957 CONSUMER CATALOGUE

In the 1957 consumer catalogue, the car appears as part of the 2037 set on pages 12 and 13, this time in the half-serif, black-over-white version, with the words "NEW HAVEN" in black and all other technical data in white. Examples of such a car have been found. The car is also offered for separate sale on page 41 in the half-serif, black-over-white version with all other lettering, including the words "NEW HAVEN", in white. No such examples have been observed.

THE 1958 ADVANCE CATALOGUE

The 1958 dealer advance catalogue shows the 6468-25 New Haven car as part of set 2507W on pages 20 and 21, in the half-serif, black-over-white version, with all other lettering, including the words "NEW HAVEN", in white. The car in the same configuration is also shown for separate sale on page 37. No such examples have been observed.

THE 1958 CONSUMER CATALOGUE

In the 1958 consumer catalogue, the car appears as part of set 2507W on pages 28 and 29, and also for separate sale on page 29, this time in the full-serif, black-over-white version with all other lettering, including the words "NEW HAVEN", in white. No such examples have been seen.

SUMMARY

Because of the discrepancies in the catalogue depictions, it is not possible to state, with any high level of assurance, the actual chronological order of these cars. The sequence of cars found with all of the characteristics as depicted in any of the catalogues are first, the full-serif, black-over-white version; and second, the half-serif, black-over-white version.

The cars have been listed in what appears to be the most reasonable and logical sequence based upon all observable data. Current values can be determined by checking the latest edition of *Greenberg's Guide to Lionel Trains, 1945-1969, Volume I.*

6468-25 NEW HAVEN: Catalogued 1956-58, double-door automobile car, Type 2B body (has faint ice hatch lines across roof near the brakewheel end, as on 6352-1), orange unpainted plastic body, four black plastic doors, bar-end trucks with magnetic tab couplers, unless noted, "BLT 3-56", single brakewheel. There are two frames: Type 1 has two non-functional holes, while Type 2 has none.

(A) Large black "N" over large white "H", black-over-white, with full-serif, black "NEW HAVEN", white technical data, Type 1 frame. J. Sattler Collection.

(B) Same as (A), except with early AAR trucks with disc couplers. J. Sattler Collection.

(C) Same as (A), but four tuscan brown-painted doors (same as on 6468-1(A)), Type 2 frame, assembled by Madison Hardware from parts. J. Sattler Collection.

(D) Same as (A), except with half-serif and with lighter, semi-glossy orange body and Type 2 frame. J. Sattler Collection.

(E) Same as (D), but with completely reversed colors of lettering, white-over-black. J. Sattler Collection.

(F) Same as (E), except with lighter, flat orange body. J. Sattler Collection.

Note: The early navy and tuscan automobile boxcars (Type A) show no roof line marks because they were made prior to 1955 before the dies were modified to accommodate the hatch on the 6352 ice car. The later 6468-25 Type B boxcars have faint lines across the roof on the brakewheel end which show that the die had been filled in after provision was made for the ice hatch.

REEFERS AND INSULATED PLUG-DOOR BOXCARS

SIMILARITIES AND DIFFERENCES — *Norman E. Anderson*

Hobbyists who take part in the world of scale model railroading are usually very careful with the terminology they use to identify rolling stock, in keeping with the philosophy of realism they strive to achieve. The world of tinplate railroads and toy trains is, however, not so precise at times, and misunderstandings can result when various types of rolling stock are given erroneous designations. Therefore, in an attempt to clarify terms for tinplaters, I will try to define the characteristics of two frequently mismodeled and misnamed types of cars — plug-door insulated boxcars and refrigerator cars or "reefers."

REEFERS

There are some similarities between reefers and insulated plug-door boxcars in that both cars have insulated sides and ends for temperature and environment control, and flush-fitting (plug) doors. However, reefers differ in that they have either ice bunkers or refrigeration units to keep the inside temperature low to preserve the produce, etc. being shipped in the car. Insulated plug-door boxcars do not have these features.

Basically, there are three types of reefers: (1) original design wood-sided reefers with ice bunkers; (2) steel smooth-sided reefers with ice bunkers; and (3) steel smooth-sided reefers which have mechanical (diesel-driven) refrigeration units. Visually, the first two types should have plug-doors on the sides and four ice hatches in the four corners of the roof. The mechanical reefer should have plug-doors, louvered side doors at one end of the car on both sides (for air entry to the refrigeration unit and maintenance), and a roof exhaust stack.

The recent 5700 wood-sided reefers produced by Fundimensions are close to correct for Type 1 reefers, except that they lack the roof ice hatches. A check of Athearn or

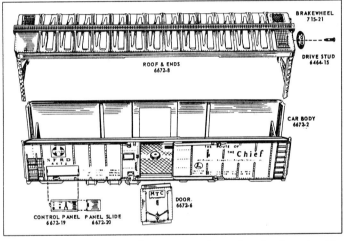

The 6672 refrigerator car has a control panel and exhaust grille on the side. These details are helpful in identifying mechanical refrigerator cars.

other HO reefers will show this missing detail. The 6352-1 Pacific Fruit Express reefer built by Lionel (and its Fundimensions 6700 revival) is the Lionel attempt at a Type 2 reefer. This car totally misses the mark, however, since it has a standard boxcar door and no correctly positioned roof ice hatches — even though it is set up to receive ice blocks from the icing station accessory. The New York Central (NYMX 0000) mechanical reefer illustrated in the prototypes chapter is the closest car I can find to a Type 3 reefer. (The 6572 Railway Express and 6672 Santa Fe reefers are also similar to this car. The 6572 is illustrated in Volume I.) Louvered doors are indeed present, and the underframe-mounted items, which could be diesel fuel tanks, might qualify it as a Type 3 reefer. These reefers represent the closest Lionel gets to detailing a Type 3 reefer. As far as I can tell, Fundimensions has not duplicated this car exactly, al-

REFRIGERATORS AND INSULATED BOXCARS — SIMILARITIES AND DIFFERENCES			
Car Type	**Body Details**	**Underbody Details †**	**Lionel Version(s)**
Original wood-sided reefer (Type 1 refrigerator)	Ice hatches in each corner on roof	None	5700 series (Modern Era)
Steel-sided with ice bunkers (Type 2 refrigerator)	Ice hatches in each corner on roof	None	Postwar 6352-1
Steel-sided, mechanical (Type 3 refrigerator)	Louvered ventilators on sides, exhaust stack on roof	May have generator and/or fuel tank	6572 REA and 6672 ATSF
Insulated plug-door boxcar	Flush-fitting "plug" door	None	Standard O billboard cars (Modern Era) ‡

† Any of the cars discussed may have basic underbody details such as bracing and brake gear; our discussion relates only to the appearance of special equipment on the underside.

‡ Although these cars are insulated plug-door boxcars, they are commonly identified by Lionel and collectors as "reefers." This type of misunderstanding is exactly what the author would like to eliminate!

though I notice that some 9800-series billboard reefers appear to have the same underframe detail — which would be incorrect.

In summary, although attempts have been made to produce reefers, these cars appear to be the most poorly reproduced examples from prototypes made by either Lionel or Fundimensions.

INSULATED PLUG-DOOR BOXCARS

Insulated or plug-door boxcars have been made for the real railroads in various lengths, with 40-, 50-, and 60-foot versions being the most popular, both in single and double door versions. Usually, they are equipped with some sort of inside load restraining gates or bars. In the early days of these cars, large markings advertised these special load-protecting features, such as DF Load Dividers. Sometimes cars simply sported large initials, such as "DF" (Damage-Free) or "PC" (Protected Cargo). More recently, however, these features have become so commonplace that mention of them is less conspicuous, if they are mentioned at all. Probably part of the confusion resulting in these cars being mistaken for reefers is brought about by the Association of American Railroads' car designation "RBL". Since the cars are different from ordinary boxcars, they carry a special designation

code. Apparently they were thrown into the general category with reefers, since both types were insulated. The "RBL" designation stands for Refrigeration Box with Load dividers, even though the cars are not actually refrigerated, just insulated. The Standard O "refrigerator" cars produced by Fundimensions and Lionel Trains, Inc. are modeled after this type of insulated boxcar, but they should not be called "reefers."

CONCLUSION

Hopefully, the foregoing explanations will clear up the problems associated with the naming of these Lionel and Fundimensions products. Remember, refrigerator cars are those that are *refrigerated* to keep perishables from spoiling. The details on these cars should reveal the means of refrigeration used — either ice hatches or vents and/or mechanical gear. Boxcars with plug-doors (which close flush with the surface of the car side) tend to have less internal temperature variation than other boxcars, but they are not refrigerated.

Even if liberties are taken with the names of these cars, one must remember that Lionel and Fundimensions, being makers of toy trains, should be held accountable only to a certain degree and no more.

LOOKING AT THE LIONEL OPERATING MILK CARS

David Fleming

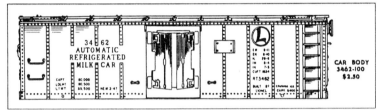

The 1947-1949 milk car had metal doors.

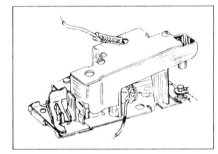

The 1947 car had the Type I brass-based mechanism.

Ask a person who remembers a childhood of the early and middle 1950s what he or she remembers about Lionel trains. You will likely be told one of two things: "the little white pills you would drop down the stack to make the engine smoke" or "the little white car that delivered the milk cans."

That "little white car" was the Lionel automatic refrigerated milk car, which became the most popular accessory ever made by the Lionel Corporation.

Although it was produced in such huge quantities that it is common today and sometimes overlooked by collectors, in its heyday the automatic refrigerated milk car was "most everybody's grocery-getter," delivering its contents on demand with the simple touch of a small red button.

Despite the omnipresence of the milk car even today on train sellers' tables, certain variations of the car are not very well known at all. In an examination of the milk cars in my own train collection, I turned up an early 1947 brass-based mechanism model which had not been described by anyone up to that time. For that matter, Lionel never documented the first form of this car, the 3462 early production model, or the last form of the car, the 3482, in any of its service literature. Therefore, a close examination of all the varieties of this car can turn up some interesting variations.

Artwork by Jerry Schuchard.

The automatic refrigerated milk car was introduced in 1947 with a 3462 number designation and a clear plastic body painted cream, with a first-run variation in glossy cream paint. The car was equipped with a brass-based mechanism, Type I, from which the milkman slid out on a small square slide. The brass base was attached to the car frame by three (and later, four) tabs which fit through slots. This

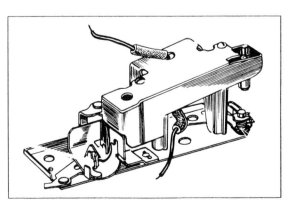

The 1948 car had a revised mechanism, which we call Type II.

CHRONOLOGY OF VARIATIONS — 3462 / 3472 / 3482 MILK CAR

YEAR:		1947	1948	1949	1950	1951	1952-1953	1954	1955
CAR NUMBERS:		3462		3472				3482	
BODY	Color	Gloss White	Flat White or Cream Paint	White or Eggshell Plastic				White Plastic	
	Doors	Aluminum		White or Eggshell Plastic				White Plastic, Notched Opening	
	Hatch	Small, Painted Cream		Large, White or Eggshell Plastic				Large, White Plastic	
	Miscellaneous	"RT 3462"		"RT 3472"				"RT 3482"	
MECHANISM	Type	1947, Type 1	1948, Type 2	1950, Type 3				1954, Type 4	
	Miscellaneous	Has Slide	Swing Plate has Triangular Hole in Arm	L-Shaped Hole in Arm, Boss for Can Sweep				Large Plunger, Removable Coil, Large Solenoid	
	Return	Hairpin Spring		Small Coil Spring				Large Coil Spring	
	Material	Brass Base	Nickel-Plated Steel		or		Cadmium-Plated Steel		
FRAME	Type	3462 Side Dents		3464 Operating Holes		3472 and 6472		3482 Ribbed with Cutouts	
	Miscellaneous	Has Tab Slots	No Slots	Side Dents	Door Frame Cutouts			Tab and Screw Mount	
TRUCKS	Design	Staple-End						Bar-End	
	Coupler	Coil		Magnetic, No Tabs					
MISC.	Major Variants	1947, 2 Var.	1948	1949	1950-53			1954-55	
	Catalogue Price	$8.95	$9.95			$11.50		$10.50	

was probably the design concocted by inventor Richard G. Smith, a carpenter in upstate New York, who invented many of the accessories marketed by both Lionel and American Flyer. Other accessories credited to Smith are the Lionel barrel car, log dump car, log loader, icing station, and forklift platform. For American Flyer, Smith invented a flatcar which unloaded a vehicle and a baggage car which picked up or dropped off a mail sack.

In 1948 the milk car received its most significant design change of its nine-year run with the Type II mechanism, which was made of parts less delicate than the original brass-based model, with fewer folds and shapes. Thicker metal was used, and the overall design was simpler. Instead of being guided by a square slide, the milkman now pivoted out of the car on a swinging plate. The sweep arm which moves the man out of the car now had a large triangular hole be-

hind him. This version kept its 3462 number designation and retained its original coil couplers.

In 1949, when Lionel introduced magnetic couplers for most of its rolling stock, the milk car number changed to 3472. Additional holes of no significance are found in the frame, and when one compares this frame to the 3464 operating boxcar, it is apparent that 3464 frame blanks were used to form the frames of the 1949 and 1950 milk cars. The first versions of the 3472 retained the short hatch on the roof and the aluminum doors of the 3462, but the car body was either painted eggshell or, more commonly, was made of unpainted white plastic.

In 1950 the milk car received the most visible changes of its evolution. It had new plastic doors (along with a new method of attaching them to the body), a larger loading

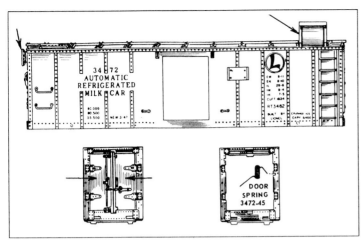

The 1950 model featured a new plastic door assembly.

hatch, and a slightly revised mechanism, Type III. The Type III mechanism used a coil spring return to pull the man back inside the car and better load the next can out of the chute leading from the loading hatch. The sweep arm to which the man was attached now had an L-shaped slot which replaced the triangular hole. Additionally, a cast boss was formed on the can rack to hold the can sweep arm, which had been previously riveted to the solenoid bracket. Lionel also began the production of plastic doors which clipped onto the body rather than being folded onto it. These plastic doors were so easily broken or lost that they currently represent one of the big markets for replacement parts manufactured today. Changed along with the doors was the frame, which now had side cutouts instead of side indentations. These allowed the car frame to clear the door frame. It is of minor note that some of these frame alterations appear as variations of the 6454 boxcars, which used the same frame blanks.

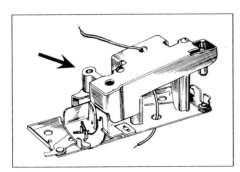

The 1950 mechanism with the new cast boss to hold the can sweep arm.

In 1951 the milk car ran unchanged from the preceding year. It also reached the apex of its popularity; the incredible total of 180,000 units were sold at $11.50 per copy. Lionel earned about a million dollars from gross sales of nearly $2,700,000, and inventor Smith, who earned two percent of the wholesale gross, realized a tidy $20,000 royalty from Lionel — a considerable sum in those days. In the 1951 catalogue a full page was devoted to the milk car, and in thousands of American homes the milkman, immaculately

dressed in white, was "getting his job done." In these postwar years, Lionel rode the crest of toy train technology with this "state of the art" product.

Only one change was made in 1952; the staple-end metal trucks on the milk car were replaced by bar-end metal trucks. This change provides collectors with a means of differentiating the very similar cars made between 1950 and 1953.

In its final development, as Lionel's corporate attention was being diverted to the design of the larger 11" pneumatically-operated 3662-1 O Gauge milk car, the company saw fit to revise its little white marvel one more time. The Type IV mechanism employed in this revision incorporated a larger solenoid plunger, probably for a different and smoother action in the operation of the milkman. In addition, all previous versions had attached the body to the frame by means of two spring clips on the car underside. In the 1954 final revision, this method of attachment changed to the more common slot and tab on one end and screw on the other. To designate cars with these changes, the car was renumbered 3482.

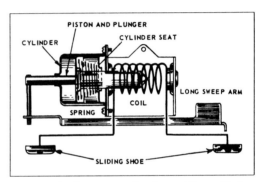

The 3662 had a new mechanism with a cylinder and piston to provide a smoother action.

In the 1954 change, Lionel had initially forgotten to renumber the small reporting marks on the side of the car; early production kept the "3472" while the large number read "3482". This oversight was corrected in the 1955 run of the 3482. Production of the small white milk car ceased after 1955 in favor of the bigger 3662-1 O Gauge milk car, which had its own variations. This big and very attractive car came with dull brown and bright brown roofs; in its later years, it had the less expensive AAR plastic trucks instead of bar-end metal trucks.

A chart of variations is included with this article for the 1947 to 1955 production of the milk car. Readers are requested to write to us if any further changes are discovered.

These, then, are the developmental details of the most popular car of Lionel's operating fleet. The automatic refrigerated milk car kept many fumble-fingered youths of the 1950s busy learning the significance of the push button. It even gave Joshua Lionel Cowen himself an excuse to pretend he was a mere spectator in his own showroom. This man-boy, who had been making trains for over half a century, would enthrall himself for hours with his little white wonder, telling his customers, "Marvelous, isn't it?"

A STRING OF ORANGE

A STUDY OF LIONEL'S BOXES — *Thomas S. Rollo with the assistance of Paul V. Ambrose*

This article was written in two parts. As originally published in the 1988 edition of Volume II, it covered the years 1945-1959. Now, thanks to a fantastic reader response and some additional discoveries, the article has been expanded to describe the development of Lionel boxes from 1960 through 1969.

One of the first new discoveries came out of an almost uneventful trip to a swap meet in March 1989. Armed with my notebook for recording anything of interest for this article and the upcoming Greenberg's Guide to Lionel Accessories, 1945-1969, *I attended a monthly swap meet at Grays Lake, Illinois. This was one of those swap meets where there was nothing new. As the meet wore down I was standing at one seller's table while he was packing. One item still on his table was a 1956 6257 caboose — a 6257-50 to be exact. The caboose was boxed in the customary Middle Classic box, which is the only reason why it caught my attention. I picked it up and looked it over. Just then the seller said, "two bucks and it's yours." I gave him two dollars and went on my way. Just before pulling out of the parking lot, I decided to give it another look. This time I unknowingly opened the wrong end of the box.*

This is the end without the coupler flap. The box part number was printed on this flap and the number was "12-11".

That struck me as strange since according to Lionel's part numbering system (see pages 130-131), the part number for an item made in 1956 should have been 6257-XX. What did come to mind were the box part numbers used on the paper boxes printed in the late 1960s. These were generic boxes with their contents rubber stamped onto the box flap. All of these have box numbers with the root number "12". Looking over the printing on this box, the box contents were entirely rubber stamped. It is the only all-rubber-stamped box that I have seen. The type style and alignment were so perfect and so much like printed boxes, that at first glance it did not look like rubber stamping. The "50" suffix is positioned in the white band on either side of the Lionel name and is in perfect alignment.

Originally my research pointed to the early corrugated boxes Lionel used after the war, and the boxes from 1966 through 1969 as the only generic boxes Lionel used. This discovery indicates that these types of boxes may have been used off and on during the postwar period.

Merchandise Cartons — that is what Lionel called their trademarked orange and blue boxes. For a youngster interested in electric trains, the sight of the box evoked as much fantasy as the Lionel catalogue or a well-equipped, often crowded, display layout.

A Lionel dealer's store in the 1940s and 1950s was an unequaled thrill. Store windows were jammed with as many pieces as space would allow. Often, a Lionel diesel horn was rigged to sound as the door opened, announcing the arrival of customers. There was usually an operating layout on one side of the sales floor and a long counter on the other side. Above the counter, on shelf upon shelf, were sets, locomo-

tives, and individual rolling stock on display. On lower shelves were cascades of orange and blue boxes.

These boxes tell many stories. First, the boxes tell the story of a company coming to terms with conditions of post-World War II, then of a company doing all it could to maintain a high level of production, and finally a story of a company which lost its marketing direction and merchandising leadership. The purpose of this article is to tell those stories and give identity to the different types of boxes that Lionel used.

This study of Lionel boxes is also helpful in dating the pieces inside the boxes (assuming they have not been switched). The boxes, among other data, give insight into one of the most fascinating events in the day-to-day activities of the company: the manufacturing cycle. Far fewer boxes have survived than the trains that were inside. With

Photographs by Bill Kojis unless otherwise noted.

FIGURE 1: This photograph shows examples of the many styles of paper boxes used during the postwar period. (For further descriptions of paper-type boxes, see Table 1 on page 154.) *Top to bottom, left to right:* **(1) side view, Art Deco; (2) side view, Early Classic; (3) side view, Middle Classic; (4) top view, OPS Classic; (5) side view, Late Classic with the stock number deleted from the sides; (6) end view, Bold Classic; (7) end view, Late Classic; (8) top view, Perforated Picture; (9) bottom view, same for both Orange Perforated and Orange Picture; (10) top view, Orange Perforated; (11) top view, Orange Picture; (12) bottom view, Cellophane Front; (13) top view, Cellophane Front; (14) side view, early version of Hillside Orange Picture that showed only the new corporate name "The Lionel Toy Corporation"; (15) side view, standard version of Hillside Orange Picture; (16) top and bottom views, same for both Hagerstown and Hillside Checkerboard; (17) end view, Hagerstown Checkerboard; and (18) end view, Hillside Checkerboard. M. Sokol Collection, B. Greenberg photograph.**

the accumulation of more data we will eventually be able to define the "proper" box for each Lionel item.

Lionel's boxes were printed by many box manufacturers located in New Jersey, New York, and eastern Pennsylvania. Some manufacturers dated their products and others did not. We have identified numerous manufacturers, including the Berles Carton Company, St. Joe Paper Company, Gibraltar, Allcraft Container, Gair Bogota, Demson Banner, National, Express, Star, Mead, and Kieckhefer Container.

But first, a word of caution: until now, little attention has been given to the boxes, beyond the relative value of the item (if boxed or not). This study will illustrate the value of the box in dating an item. For example, Lionel's orange and blue paper boxes underwent some form of change almost every year from 1946 to 1958. If the Lionel student considers the boxes, instruction sheets, and known variations of the contents, it is possible to chronicle each year's production of common pieces (eg., the 151 semaphore, 153 block signal, or the 154 crossing signal).

At a recent swap meet, an antique dealer was offering Lionel trains on a consignment sale from the trains' owner. From the items being offered, it was clear the owner was not a collector but had merely bought a number of train items be-tween 1946 and about 1960. All of the pieces for sale were in their original boxes and there were many trackside accessories. Among them was a 151 semaphore in a box that was clearly printed in 1947, the first year the semaphore was catalogued.

This accessory is structurally similar to the 153 block signal, both of which use the same base casting and post stamping. In the 1947 consumer catalogue, the semaphore is illustrated with a green base rather than the black base with which it is usually found. Knowing Lionel's pattern of using parts from mass-produced items in mock-ups, this is not surprising. In fact, there are regular production semaphores with green bases from the earliest 1947 production. I picked up the semaphore in the 1947 box, opened the lid, and looked down inside. The contactor and instruction sheet were in their bag, and there at the bottom of the box was a bright green base looking up at me. My better judgment prevailing, I simply closed the lid and asked for a price. The salesman told me "fifteen bucks" and I handed him the money. Later, at my sales table, the fellow with me said, "You look like the cat that just ate the canary." I replied, "meow-tweet-tweet." You see, knowing Lionel's boxes is very helpful!

THE "DOT AND YEAR" DATING SYSTEM

The box dating systems that follow are easy to identify. The names given these systems are my own and are arbitrary. There are four systems noted, and there could conceivably be others. The first and most common dating system in the postwar era is the "dot and year" system. This system was used by more than one box manufacturer. However, the corrugated boxes manufactured by the St. Joe Paper Company are the most common. Lionel used the St. Joe boxes between 1950 and 1958. This system uses a number line (1-12) to represent the months of the year. Some manufacturers use dots, stars, or other symbols.

The numbers or symbols may be in a line on either side of the year, or in a semi-circle surrounding the box manufacturer's certificate. A close friend of mine in the printing business describes this method as a function of the rotogravure printing process. In this process, a printing plate is cast which contains the box certificate with year and dateline. The plate is cast with stars, dots, or other symbols. As each month passes, a dot (or star, etc...) is ground off the plate. This leaves the remaining characters to represent the current month.

All of the boxes in **Figure 2** are for the Lionel Berkshire steam locomotive. The box on the left is for a 726 Berkshire as is evidenced by the box part number "726-86". In Volume I of *Greenberg's Guide to Lionel Trains, 1945-1969*, some contributors refer to this number as a "flap number" because it is found on the tuck flap of the orange and blue paper boxes.

The term "flap number" is misleading since these numbers were printed on the sides or ends of corrugated boxes long before they appeared on the flaps of paper boxes. The

number is clearly derived from the part numbering system and should be called the box part number. The box on the left is not dated. Although we cannot "zero-in" on the exact year, the range of years 1946 to 1949 can be determined in another way. The 726 was only manufactured from 1946 through 1949 and in 1952. The gummed paper tape used to seal the box is the orange and blue "LIONEL CORPORATION" custom tape. The company used this sealing tape generously before World War II and occasionally after the war. No post-1950 boxes that have been sealed in this way have been observed.

The box in the middle is also for a 726 Berkshire; however, this box is dated. Following the dot and year system, the numbers present are 4 through 12 (1 through 3 are missing). Below the number line is the year 1952, thereby leading to the conclusion that the box was manufactured in April 1952. Using other item-dating methods, one expects that the locomotive in the box is numbered "726RR", that it is fitted with sintered-iron wheels, and that it does not have Magnetraction. Any other Berkshire variation found in the box would be other than the original.

The box on the right is for the more common 736 Berkshire with flaps that fold and tuck into the center. This design was introduced in 1955. Note that the sealing tape has been peeled back to reveal a "7". We can deduce that the year was 1957 for the reason that this style box was not available prior to 1955. The position of the number on the box and the box design are the clues. (If the history of the Berkshire is a bit cloudy to you, study the article by Ron Greisbeck on page 61.) If seven is the year, then you obviously have two choices: 1957 or 1967, but 1967 is immediately eliminated because St. Joe was not a box manufacturer used in the mid-1960s era. The supplier during that era was usually the Mead Company. Therefore, 1957 is the only logical year for this box.

There are box manufacturers who express the years on a number line. The numbers 85, 86, 87, 88 would appear on the box. The lowest number, 85, is the current year of production and each year would be eliminated as it passes. This dating technique is found on MPC and Fundimensions boxes. It has not been observed on postwar Lionel boxes.

THE "MONTH-YEAR" DATING SYSTEM

The second method of box dating is the simple month-year method. This is the same method you use when writing down a date, such as 3-54 or 11-57. The box for the 132 station shown in **Figure 3** is dated in this fashion. Note the date is "5-50" (May 1950).

The month-year method can also be found on paper boxes. In fact, this is the only dating method found on the paper boxes. In contrast, corrugated boxes used many different methods in the postwar era.

The box in **Figure 4** was photographed to show the box part number; notice that the root number is "6660", meaning this is the box for the 6660 boom crane car, which was only catalogued in 1958. The oval logotype reveals that the box was manufactured by the Berles Carton Company, Inc.,

FIGURE 2: Three different boxes for Berkshire locomotives. *Left to right:* **726 (1946-1949), 726 (1952), and 736 (1957). T. Rollo Collection.**

FIGURE 3: This 132 station box was made in May 1950 and shows this date. T. Rollo Collection.

FIGURE 4: This 1958 paper box shows the date, manufacturer, and box part number. B. and S. Schneider Collection.

Paterson, New Jersey. On the opposite flap is the date: "BC583", (Berles Carton, March 1958). The "9" on the next line is probably a particular production line.

THE "JULIAN" DATING SYSTEM

The third dating system is the Julian dating system. Unless you recognize this dating system, you could mistake it for some other code; it is a simple string of numbers. The Julian calendar does not recognize the months by name. Instead, it treats the days of the year in numerical order from 1 to 365 or 366 (leap year). For example, the date May 1, 1988 would be 88121 or just 8121 (May 1st being the 121st day of the year).

THE "WAGON WHEEL" or "CLOCKFACE" DATING SYSTEM

The fourth dating system is the "wagon wheel" or "clockface" dating system. As with the Julian system, this is very common to Lionel boxes manufactured after 1969. It is easy to spot and interesting, because there are so many variations and each one is a challenge to figure out. Basically, this system involves a clockface (a circle with twelve numbers). The numbers, however, are not hours but months. Sometimes the current month is represented by a missing number or the current month is the lowest number showing, as in the dot and year dating system. At other times, there may be tick marks next to the numbers and the current month is the missing tick mark. In any case, the year is expressed in two digits and is shown in the middle of the clockface or directly outside of the circle. See **Figure 5**.

1945-1946

Like most trains and accessories offered in 1945 and 1946, the box design was a carry-over from the prewar years.

The design of the orange paper boxes is clearly from the late 1930s. The tops and bottoms of the bold blue letters contact the bold blue bands. This design is known as Art Deco. (If you have ever been to Manhattan and walked around Rockefeller Center, not in the plaza itself, but around the perimeter, the lettering above the store fronts and at Radio City Music Hall is very similar.) The majority of these boxes also included a formed cardboard liner to protect the contents. If you own any boxed 6464 boxcars, slide one out of the box and observe the latch receiver part of the body casting to the left of the door. You will likely find that the paint has rubbed off the side. The packaging does not completely protect the contents, but the early Art Deco boxes were Lionel's finest packaging. To date, only one example has been found with a box part number: the tiny No. 88 controller which had assigned part number "88-6" on the box. Examples of the Art Deco boxes are shown in **Figure 6**.

The corrugated boxes used to package large, bulky, or fragile pieces are shown in **Figure 7**. Each of these boxes included a part number and a separately printed contents label pasted on the outside end. The label format was the same in most cases, differing only slightly for large transformers offered for separate sale. The transformer boxes had the words "Trainmaster Transformer" where the word "Electric" appears in **Figure 7**.

Another interesting observation about these labels is that the line in the white band states the box's contents in a typeface that is different from any other print on the label. This separate printing of the contents line left an impression on the label, which is easily detected by running a finger back and forth across the label. This evidence indicates that a blank or generic label was printed first, and the contents printing added later. This is certainly not true for all of these labels, but it is likely that the generic label was printed by an outside firm and the contents line was added by Lionel as needed. At this point, no pattern has been determined for those with added contents information.

In both of the examples in **Figure 7**, Lionel Corporation sealing tape was used to seal the boxes. Although optional, it was replaced from time to time with paper tape. Note that

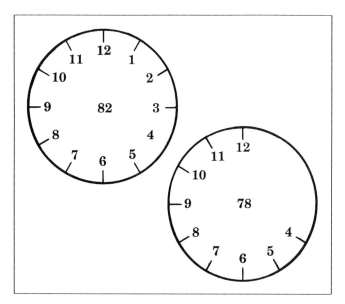

FIGURE 5: This drawing illustrates the "wagon wheel" and "clockface" dating system. The number in the center is the year. Hence, the left wheel is April 1982 (since the tick is missing from the 4) and the right is either March 1978 (the highest number missing) or April 1978 (the lowest number present).

the top box in **Figure 7** is a unit or shipper box. Boxes of this type can definitely be described as rare. The 64 lamp posts were individually packaged in orange and blue paper boxes. The box shown in the illustration contains one dozen of them. This box would probably have been discarded by

the dealer once the contents were sold, unless one buyer purchased all twelve of them at one time (which seems unlikely). Unit boxes also tell collectors whether or not a piece of rolling stock was available for separate sale, as opposed to being included in sets only. A case in point is the 3474 boxcar. This car was catalogued in 1952 and 1953 as part of one O27 set each year. No mention is made in the Lionel catalogues of the car being offered for separate sale, yet it frequently turns up apart from the other set components. We can assume that the 3474 was offered for separate sale, but a unit box would be positive proof.

The box for the 115 passenger station has another story connected with it. I purchased the station new in 1959 from a dealer who just happened to have some left, nearly ten years after the station was catalogued! The retail store, located on the west side of Chicago, was called the West Towns Hobby Shop. Although its doors have been closed for many years, West Towns' price tags still turn up on Lionel boxes found at Chicago-area swap meets. In fact, the little fantasy that appears at the beginning of this article takes place in that store.

My first trip to West Towns was shortly after Christmas 1955. Inside my new milk car, a milk can had become stuck crossways in the chute and had to be dislodged. The salesperson, who also repaired trains, solved the problem. After it was repaired, I was cautioned not to pick up the milk car while the cans were inside. While this was going on, I saw an unusual-looking station in a corner, behind the sales counter. It was big and beautiful, with gorgeous sconce lights on either side of the doors. "LIONEL CITY" appeared above the clock over the doors, and propped up on its roof

FIGURE 6: (Left to right) 2411 flatcar and 2454 merchandise car with their liners and 2461 transformer car and 2411 flatcar in their liners. T. Rollo Collection.

was a white card with a price of $15, which was a good bit of money at that time.

Four years passed before I was able to purchase it. My mother decided that we should drive in but wanted to phone the store just to make sure that the station was still there. The answering salesperson said "Oh yes, we've marked them down to $7.50 to get rid of them. They are really a collector's item at this point."

The packaging was as interesting as the station. While unpacking it, I attempted to get the station out from the opposite end of the package, so as not to disturb the outside label. As you can see in **Figure 7**, this was to no avail. The station was wrapped in three sheets of wrapping paper, causing such a tight fit that it required pushing and pulling from each end to get the station out of the box. The skylight piece was wrapped separately in three smaller sheets and surrounded by crushed paper to prevent it from moving around the roof area.

The frosted lamps intended for the sconce fixtures were packaged in individual boxes and placed between the wrapping paper and the station wall, on the opposite side of the sconces. I recall unwrapping the station with the sconces facing me and being startled by the absence of the bulbs from their sockets.

There were two corrugated liners under the wrapping paper at each end of the station. The liners were folded at the top and bottom so that they would be held in place by the roof overhang and the station base. One liner was notched to provide clearance for the three thumb screw terminals, while the other was not. These two liners were doubtlessly intended to protect the enameled finish, should the person opening the box attempt to do so with a sharp object.

Lionel's attention to packaging with these liners suggests that box liners were cut and folded from corrugated sheet stock at Lionel, rather than being prepared by the manufacturer. If the manufacturer had made the liners, it would have made more sense to notch all of them, rather than only half. The brown envelope containing the instruction sheet, two CTC lockons, three connecting wires, and four fiber pins (two O Gauge and two O27 Gauge) was placed between the sconces.

The instruction sheet is dated August 1948, and both it and the information on the outside of the envelope were printed in red ink. The station, however, was not packaged until 1949. The box part number is 113-1, and comes from a prewar version of this station which was painted a different color and did not have the train control feature. This was manufactured prior to 1935. Another interesting note is that the envelopes for the peripherals included with the 132 station and the 153 block signal in this period were also printed in red. All of them contain CTC lockons and deal with train control. Sometime in the postwar era, Lionel offered CTC lockons packaged in large brown envelopes of fifty. Presumably, these were meant for dealers but probably could wind up in consumers' hands if that many were purchased at once. The lettering on these envelopes is also red.

The set boxes in these years also were identified with paste-on labels; the label can be seen in the 1945 set article "The Real Beginning of the Postwar Era" on page 51.

FIGURE 7: Corrugated boxes for 64 lamp posts and 115 station. T. Rollo Collection.

After studying many paste-on labels from this period, it appears that the set number on some of the boxes was printed after the label was printed and follows the same practice as the corrugated accessory boxes discussed earlier.

1947

The corrugated boxes, both for sets and accessories, remained unchanged in 1946. The Art Deco paper boxes, however, underwent one small change; they included the Toy Manufacturers Association logo on the wide, flat surface to the right of the blue Lionel Electric Trains rectangle. After studying the box for the 2411 flatcar in **Figure 6**, you will find that it is actually a 1947 box because "Toy Mfrs." logo is present. The question is "When did this change occur?"

You might think January 1; after all, that is the beginning of the year.... Wrong!! The Lionel Corporation's fiscal year began on March 1 of each calendar year. Fiscal year change is the time most corporations make new plans and corporate America has the option of choosing their own year. The absence of the cardboard liner in the majority of boxes could have been a cost-cutting move.

FIGURE 8: The Type S transformer box from 1947. T. Rollo Collection.

The 1947 box is an adaptation of the 1945-1946 Art Deco box with the "Toy Mfrs." logo. Another box was simply printed with block lettering and no color at all. Boxes like this one will not be given a name or number of their own. The box in **Figure 8** contains the Type S transformer, and although the box is not dated this is clearly a 1947 product. Note that the box picture shows "80 WATT" while the 1947 catalogue describes the transformer's output as 75 watts. The transformer actually produced 80 watts!

As a side note, in 1948 the 313 bascule bridge came in a box lettered the same way as the 1949 Type S transformer box. I have noted the two following examples, both of which have "1948" printed directly below the box certificate. I. D. Smith has observed that the red indicator light on top of the bridge structure changed from smooth to fluted on this acces-

sory with the introduction of the VW and ZW transformers as well as the 26 bumper that used this new indicator light cap. Based on the 313 bascule bridge box, this observation is confirmed!

1948

Once again, the corrugated accessory and set boxes remain unchanged. The paper boxes, however, underwent drastic changes. The exterior was completely redesigned into what is perhaps the best remembered Lionel package of the postwar era, the Early Classic box with smaller lettering, the stock number printed on all four sides, and the city names New York, Chicago, San Francisco. This is the first of many box variations that occurred in the following eleven years.

The New Frisco boxes are 1948 and early 1949, and there are no box part numbers. The change is demonstrated in the two boxes shown in **Figure 9**. On the left is the scarce 2456 hopper car still in a 1947 Art Deco box with liner. On the right is a 6454 boxcar that is also a 1948 product. Note that the box is a New Early Classic type. The car inside the box is a Santa Fe, and its date can be determined by the frame, trucks, and couplers.

Lionel students have argued about the 2456 hopper car, some claiming that the car was produced in January and February 1948 (fiscal year 1947), as well as the first of the 2257 and 2357 Southern Pacific cabooses. In reality, both factions are correct. The hopper car was produced in fiscal 1947 or calendar 1948, depending on your point of view. On the car body's side is "NEW 1-48". It is not the purpose of this study to go into "NEW" dates and "BLT" (built) dates in any detail. It is true that Lionel left these dates on the sides of rolling stock many years after their initial runs.

In the case of 9-1/4" boxcars, some have "NEW" dates that occurred during World War II when Lionel was not producing trains. One thing can be said with reasonable certainty about them, however; a piece of rolling stock bearing these dates was not manufactured earlier than its "NEW" or

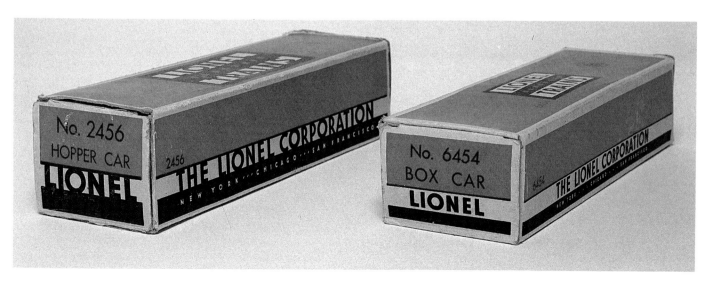

FIGURE 9 *(left to right):* 2456 hopper car in Art Deco box and 6454 boxcar in the New Early Classic box, both from 1948. T. Rollo Collection.

FIGURE 10: *(Left)* **1948-1949 2333 Santa Fe master carton with component 2333P and 2333T boxes. Note that the 2333P comes in a corrugated cardboard carton.** *(Center)* **2367 Wabash F-3 from 1955 in a master carton.;** *(Right)* **O27 master carton containing 204P and 204T boxes. Even the 200-series Alcos came in master cartons when available for separate sale. M. Sokol Collection, B. Greenberg photograph.**

"BLT" date. Another point that fixes the introduction of the "new" Early Classic box at the beginning of the fiscal year is the pattern of catalogue numbers that appear on them. The O27 sets produced in 1948 also introduced the new magnetic couplers and the 6000-series catalogue numbers assigned to non-operating rolling stock.

Operating cars retained their 3000-series numbers, with the coupler change being reflected by a change in the tens digit. In my three years of research, I have found only two 6000-series numbers appearing on Art Deco boxes. They are the 6257 SP caboose and the 6419 work caboose: these are very scarce boxes. Not long ago, I received a letter from Fred Davis of Audobon, New Jersey that contained photos of a 6419 caboose in an Art Deco box. Now the question arises, why this car? Was this one of the first of the 6000-series cars to be produced? A possible answer to the second question lies in a recollection of Bob Swanson's. A boyhood friend of his received a Lionel freight set for Christmas in 1947. The set was catalogued with a tinplate Pennsylvania caboose, but the set his friend received came with the work caboose. Bob's hypothesis is that the supply of Pennsylvania cabooses had been depleted and the new Southern Pacific cabooses were not ready for packaging, thus the work caboose had been substituted. This would have caused a premature use of the supply of work cabooses, making it among the earliest 1948 production. The question at this point is, were there any other examples?

There are also overstamped Art Deco boxes with 6000-series numbers. However, these were leftovers. Re-marked boxes will be discussed at length in the 1954 section. Earlier, when discussing the dating systems, the Scout-type cars came in boxes dated March and April of the year. We also

know from the lamp replacement charts published during that time, that items to be included in O27 sets came before those designated as O Gauge.

There is one other condition I have used to determine box design changes. I have held off discussing it until now, because 1948 is the best year in the postwar era for demonstration. After studying the packaging of those items that were new in a particular year, they would obviously be packaged in the latest box designs, whatever they were. Because of the coupler changes, the 6000-series rolling stock can be considered all new, in a manner of speaking. This does not imply that boxes for the items would have changed at the same time. Lionel would have used whatever supplies of boxes were available until they were exhausted.

A case in point is the 364 lumber loader which was first catalogued in 1948 and came in an early corrugated box. It continued to be packaged in this box as late as 1954! Several years ago, I was invited to a private train sale. Among the items for sale was a 364 lumber loader in an early box that was sealed. Unfortunately, there were a number of water stains on the exterior of the box, and the box lid had begun to warp due to exposure. There may have been a piece of "mint rust" inside. The price was reasonable, so I decided to take a gamble, which turned out to be a good one. The accessory was beautiful, and there was a glossy paper folder listing authorized Service Stations for the 1954-1955 season. The instruction sheet was dated April 1954, and the load of logs were stained dark brown. Other researchers have noted the dark logs first appearing with the green 3461 lumber car catalogued in 1954 and 1955.

With the introduction of the Early Classic boxes, the use of the cardboard liners was greatly reduced. The work ca-

FIGURE 11: The paper Early Classic box, dated 1948, for the 45N gateman. T. Rollo Collection.

booses and the transformer cars, for example, continued to include corrugated liners. The latter ran only through 1949, but it needed the liner to protect the tall insulators on top of the transformer. The work cabooses kept their liners through 1955 when the tall die-cast chimney on the roof was replaced with a short one that eliminated the need for full wraparound liner protection.

Among accessories, there was a movement away from corrugated packaging in favor of paper boxes. The 156 station platforms produced through 1947 came in corrugated boxes with liners. The box was so thick and heavy that it weighed only four ounces less than the accessory for which it was made. Both Roland LaVoie and myself have noted examples of this accessory in corrugated boxes dated February 1948 (fiscal year 1947). In fiscal 1948 the box changed to a cubic, paper Early Classic type with a very thin liner similar in style to the type shown in **Figure 11**.

1949

There were some changes in 1949. The orange and blue paper boxes continued as before; however, "San Francisco" was eliminated from the blue band along the narrow side of the box. There were still no box part numbers on this box, which will be called Middle Classic. "San Francisco" had not appeared on some earlier corrugated boxes, such as the Type S transformer box shown in **Figure 8** and some of the tiny paper boxes used to package replacement lamps. For example, the tiny pea lamp used in the work cabooses came in boxes with and without "San Francisco" between 1946 and 1949. However, these occurrences were the exceptions. Note also that on the label on the 115 station box in **Figure 7** "San Francisco" is absent. "San Francisco" disappeared from the label with the closing of the showroom there.

When the earliest versions of the operating boxcar surface (X3464 Santa Fe or New York Central), they are found in Early Classic boxes and are furnished with instruction sheets dated March 1949. Although this seems to indicate that the Early Classic boxes continued longer than they ac-

tually did, the truth is that during the period between World War II and the Korean War the span of time between a dated box and the related instruction sheet could be as long as six months. Gradually this gap narrowed until 1950 and after, when instruction sheet dates fell in or around one month as related box dates.

At that time, there was a new item in Lionel's product line that is helpful in understanding box changes from one year to the next: the Scout set.

Scout sets were unique items because the truck and couplers were not compatible with other rolling stock of the same period (1948-1952). Furthermore, the set contents were not offered for separate sale, since Scout couplers were not compatible with regular Lionel couplers. When I observed a boxed Scout set made during this period, the orange and blue paper boxes followed the expected year box changes to the letter.

The accessory and set corrugated boxes underwent interesting changes as well. **Figure 12** illustrates a 1949 set box and the corrugated box for the 30 water tower. The 1950 version of the corrugated box for the 30 water tower on the top of the set box is included here for comparison purposes. The most noticeable changes are the labels which are printed on the box. This had one important advantage for Lionel because it passed the process of marking corrugated boxes on to the box manufacturer.

Note in **Figure 12** that two different procedures were required to pack the boxes for the water tower. The 1949 version was packed by inserting the tower base first into the narrow side which, in this case, is the top. The later 1950 version was packed by inserting the tower sideways into the long side of its box which became the top. The 1949 version took much longer to pack.

The changes from corrugated to paper boxes in 1949 gave the same result. Corrugated boxes required gluing or taping while paper boxes were secured with simple tuck flaps.

There is another point that may have influenced these changes, although it has not been discussed by other writers. This point has to do with changes in Lionel's total manufac-

FIGURE 12 *(left to right)*: 1949 set box (1447WS), 30 water tower (1950 version) and 30 water tower (1949). T. Rollo and R. Lemke Collections.

turing trends. In the prewar era, Lionel offered more products that were structurally similar and ran in the consumer catalogue concurrently. The 115 and 117 stations are examples, the latter not being equipped with the sconce lights. This practice lent itself to the use of generic boxes with unique labels. This analysis was aided by a box for the 83 traffic signal that Roland LaVoie discovered during my research. The box contents were rubber stamped on what would have been a blank early Art Deco box. Beginning in 1935 with the introduction of the steam whistle, Lionel began offering train sets with or without whistles and equipped with the appropriate transformer. The sets were identical in every other way and illustrated only once in the consumer catalogue. After 1947 this practice was discontinued.

On pages 84-86 is an article discussing Lionel's Madison cars. During the editing period that followed submission of the article, the question was asked "How can we tell the difference between the 1948 and 1949 cars?" At least one way lies in the study of the set box. The 1948 cars came in set boxes with paste-on labels, while the 1949 cars came in boxes with labels printed directly onto the box (assuming the supply of paste-on labels had already been depleted).

1950

The second half-century was underway and with it came new innovations from Lionel and new boxes. Before getting into a discussion on specific changes, however, the box changes and instruction sheet dating offer another important discovery.

I recently purchased set 1469WS. This set was first catalogued in 1950 and continued in 1951. All of the set's components were intact and in beautiful condition. What was odd about this set is that it was packed in a 1949 box. The box was not dated but followed the format shown in **Figure 12**.

Below the box label, the price was preprinted as $39.95, the price of the 1950 version. In 1951 the price was increased to $48.50. The price difference between 1950 and 1951 supports the identification of this set as a 1950. At first, it appeared that Lionel continued the previous year's box design. The instruction booklet furnished with the set is the 1949 edition.

There is a fragment of the back cover stuck in the bottom of the box that came in contact with wet glue that had oozed between the box flaps and there is a corresponding tear in the back cover of the booklet.

Three items in the set came with their own instruction sheets: 1033 transformer, 6019 remote-control track, and the 2035 steam locomotive. Two of the instruction sheets were dated January 1950, while the third was dated February 1950.

The set box design is left over from 1949. Instruction sheets are all fiscal 1949 (dated January and February 1950; fiscal 1950 started in March 1950). Other researchers have determined that an early form of Magnetraction was introduced on the 622 and 6220 diesel switchers in 1949, although not catalogued. Magnetraction in a more marketable form was catalogued for the first time in 1950. The 2035

steam locomotive in the set is equipped with the 1950 version.

Often firms will push projects through to completion if they are coming in under budget, rather than show surplus money. This may be the case here. I have noted earlier the box dating of the boxes for the Scout-type cars in 1953 and 1954. This, together with the introduction of the Early Classic boxes, with the start of the Scout sets in 1948 and the dated Scout set instruction sheet (3-48), established the fact that the least expensive sets were produced early in the fiscal year. This pattern is broken by the 1469WS set. This is a more expensive set and was produced at the end of fiscal 1949 instead of later in fiscal 1950 as it should have been. It took Lionel years to develop the whistle and the smoke pellet, and Magnetraction simply took less time. Lionel was able to finish Magnetraction in 1949. As you put the analytical techniques to work for yourself, doubtlessly, you will find that there are exceptions to what is discussed here.

One of these is the case of the 2035 motor unit. It was fabricated from naturally-colored pieces of aluminum that were not chemically darkened. The shiny aluminum motor sides detracted from the locomotive's overall appearance by drawing visual attention to the unrealistic motor mechanism rather than the boiler details. Years later, in financial distress, Lionel returned to shiny motor sides for its bottom-of-the-line equipment. Hence, the 2035 locomotive looks like the inexpensive steamers produced years later. The hopper car packed in that set was maroon, not black as catalogued.

The interesting piece in that set was the 6465 tank car. It came packaged in a Middle Classic box of the necessary length to accommodate a car with footsteps. The footsteps, however, had been omitted. The blanking die used to stamp out the frames had been modified so that the four corners of the frame were slightly turned out. There are no stub ends and the body of the car is not the typical bright aluminum, but a metallic gray.

The Middle Classic boxes had no exterior changes on them. Out of view, there was one noticeable change; the box tuck flaps now included a box part number. This change was made across the product line. A scarce box for the 2460 crane surfaced in 1950. It was a Middle Classic (not Art Deco) box and had part number 2460-45 printed on the inside lip of the end flap. These boxes were probably ordered to update the look of existing finished 2460 inventory. By this time, the Art Deco boxes looked antiquated. Box part numbers were printed on the paper boxes henceforth.

The accessory and set corrugated boxes also changed. **Figure 13** illustrates three accessory boxes. This simplified the printing process somewhat, but each time a different color was printed on the box, it was put through the press again. The 1949 corrugated boxes used the same number of colors (two), but they required more care to align the printing correctly. There is blue within the blank areas framed by orange.

The 1950 boxes simply consisted of an orange field printed on the box directly first, followed by blue lettering within a frame printed last.

This is the first year Lionel used boxes from the St. Joe Paper Company, making dating easy. Note that the 125 whistle station and the 256 freight station were both new in

FIGURE 13 *(left to right):* **256 freight station, 145 automatic gateman, and 97 coal elevator from 1950.**   T. Rollo and D. and S. Erich Collections.

1950. The 1950 season was the last year for the 97 coal elevator and the 30 water tower (**Figure 12**), and Lionel had new style boxes manufactured for them. Lionel apparently had inventory on hand that did not have boxes, so new boxes were printed for those two accessories. The next section of this report will offer evidence that there is no production of many items during the last year of cataloguing. The final appearance in the consumer catalogue was merely to get rid of existing stock.

Before we move on, there is one other Lionel item that needs comment. For years, collectors have discussed the production dating of the yellow 6656 stock car. Was it manufactured in 1949 or not until 1950? Although we currently have less information than with the previously discussed 2456 hopper car, it is suspected that the stock car followed the same box pattern as the hopper car did. The car has been observed in Middle Classic boxes (fiscal 1949), but it was not catalogued in 1949. It was first catalogued in 1950. When more research is done on this car, perhaps we will find it was manufactured in January or February 1950.

1951-1952

The celebration of Lionel's anniversary year was over.

Although the Korean War started in 1950, it did not visibly affect Lionel's train production until this time. The Service Manual notes part substitutions due to Korean War shortages. The prewar carry-over pieces were gone, as were a number of the better items, such as the GG-1.

The boxes for the corrugated set and accessory boxes underwent a small modification. The orange field present on the 1950 version was omitted, leaving only the blue block lettering surrounded by a blue square.

As discussed earlier, this simplified the printing process by reducing the need for one pass of the press. The orange and blue paper boxes (Middle Classic) remained essentially the same as in 1950 except for OPS modifications.

The period between the end of World War II and the Korean War was one of high inflation. The price of a telephone call from a public pay telephone in many areas increased from a nickel to a dime. Gasoline stations across the country began showing gasoline in cents per gallon instead of a quantity of gallons for $1.00. Gas went from five gallons for $1.00 to 22 cents per gallon. The impact of inflation is also visible in the changes in Lionel's pricing. Between 1950 and 1951 the price for an identical train set, 1469WS, increased from $39.95 to $48.50. This is an increase of 21.4 percent.

During 1951 all of Lionel's packaging became subject to efforts by the United States government to curb inflation. Consequently, the Economic Stabilization Agency, Office of Price Stabilization, set forth guidelines for price ceilings for manufactured products. The full particulars of these guidelines can be found in docket number 4007-042-750-P for those interested in further study.

For our purposes, we will deal only with how this impacted Lionel. On August 10, 1951 the company issued a four-page folder titled "Statement of Considerations" to distributors and dealers. The third paragraph is important to this study of boxes.

"The special order contains provisions requiring each article to be marked by the applicant with the retail ceiling price established by the accompanying special order. The applicant and intermediate distributors are required to send purchasers of the articles a copy of this special order, a notice listing retail ceiling prices for each cost line, and in special cases of subsequent amendments of this order."

In the above paragraph, "applicant" refers to Lionel and "purchasers" refers to the retailer, dealer, or service station, not the consumer. Since it was now August, much of Lionel's product line was already in production. Some pieces were finished, packaged, and awaiting shipment. Others were already on their way to retailers. Lionel had to provide for the marking of OPS ceiling prices on products in each of these stages. The usual procedure was for the box to be marked with the retail price along with "OPS". The inset list identifies five marking methods. The following discussion covers each method in more detail.

The Factory

1. Rubber stamping. The LTC lockon box shown in **Figure 14** is an example of this method. This would have been used on those items packaged and ready for shipment. I expect that it was used for the most part on small items, but in at least one case, rubber stamping turned up on a larger piece. A 3464 Santa Fe operating boxcar is also marked in this way. Rubber-stamped boxes have lighter markings than do boxes with metal type.

2. Marking with metal type. This involves the same process as re-marking to change the box contents identification. On larger paper and corrugated boxes the format was the same as that shown on the 2422 illuminated Pullman car box also shown in **Figure 14**. However, those re-marked in the factory were marked with black ink. On some, the "S" in the dollar sign and the digits of the price had serifs. The exact position on the box and the impression left by the type varied from one box to another. The important point is that the boxes marked in this way were flat, having yet to be packed with merchandise.

3. Paste-on stickers (smooth edge). The 145 automatic gateman shown in **Figure 14** is marked with a smooth-edged sticker.

The example in the photograph is worn; however, the sharp edges of the sticker clearly have no perforations. During the last few years I have noted a total of seven examples of this accessory labeled in this way. In every case the smooth-edged sticker was affixed in exactly the same position on the box. All of the boxes were St. Joe boxes dated April 1951, and, for those interested, the accessory inside had a bright red roof instead of the usual maroon. Uniform placement of the sticker would have been possible only if the packaged accessories were labeled at the same time, in the same place — the factory. This will be more clear when we discuss the next marking method.

FIGURE 14: 1951-1952 OPS Classic boxes; LTC lockon, rubber-stamped OPS; 2422 illuminated Pullman car, box manufacturer preprinted OPS and 145 automatic gateman, paste-on OPS sticker (smooth edge). T. Rollo Collection.

Marking of OPS Prices on Boxes

THE FACTORY (1951)

1. Rubber stamping.
2. Marking with metal type.
3. Paste-on stickers (smooth edge).

THE DISTRIBUTION CHANNEL (1951)

4. Paste-on stickers (perforated edge).

FUTURE PRODUCTION (1952, possibly late 1951)

5. Box manufacturer, preprinted.

FIGURE 15

The Distribution Channel

4. Paste-on stickers (perforated edge). These are perhaps the most familiar to collectors. These stickers were issued to distributors and retailers in perforated sheets. An example of one page of the sticker set is shown in **Figure 16**.

Each set contained sixteen pages, with as many as thirty stickers per page. The page with stickers for track sections had instructions to affix the sticker to the packing carton. Distributors and retailers slapped these on boxes any which way rather than uniformly as Lionel did with the smooth-edged stickers. At a glance it is easy to differentiate between the two different paste-on stickers. The edges and the position of the sticker on the box are what to look for. Sometimes pieces in 1950 corrugated boxes turn up with these stickers on them. These are 1950 items leftover in the distributor's or dealer's inventory. The one item noted most frequently is the 125 whistle station. This was not a glamorous accessory, rather strictly functional. No doubt sales of that accessory were very flat.

Future Production

5. Box manufacturer, preprinted. This method is just as its name states. When new boxes were printed after the OPS price ceilings were in effect, the box printing included the required information. This was likely the least expensive way of meeting the government rules. The 2422 illuminated Pullman car shown in **Figure 14** and the 2031 Rock Island diesel locomotive box shown in **Figure 17** are both examples. In both cases the ink color and the printing process for the OPS markings were the same as the other type on the box. This was the rule in 1952. In fact, the 2031 Rock Island box was photographed in order to show the box date, September 1952. In the years of research that have gone into this project we have not found a box marked in this manner that could be dated prior to 1952. We cannot rule out the fact that if Lionel's supply of boxes for only one item had

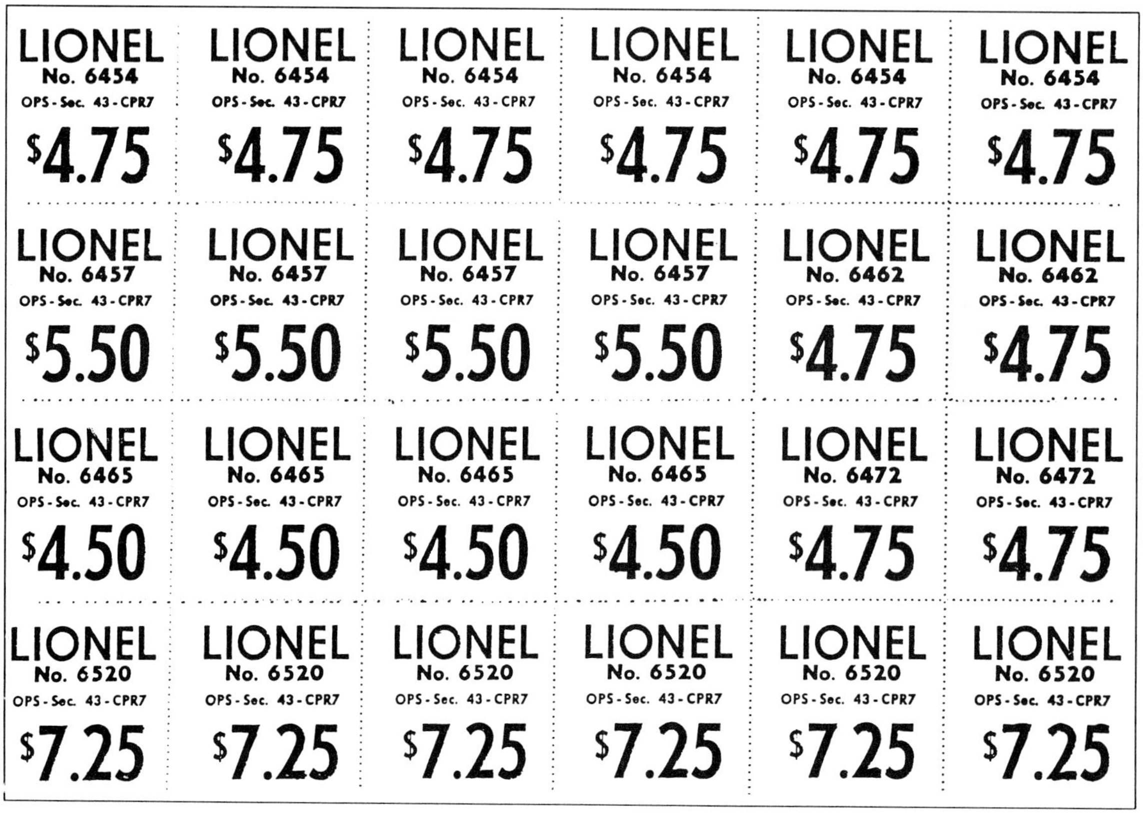

LIONEL No. 6454 OPS-Sec. 43-CPR7 $4.75	LIONEL No. 6454 OPS-Sec. 43-CPR7 $4.75	LIONEL No. 6454 OPS-Sec. 43-CPR7 $4.75	LIONEL No. 6454 OPS-Sec. 43-CPR7 $4.75	LIONEL No. 6454 OPS-Sec. 43-CPR7 $4.75	LIONEL No. 6454 OPS-Sec. 43-CPR7 $4.75
LIONEL No. 6457 OPS-Sec. 43-CPR7 $5.50	LIONEL No. 6457 OPS-Sec. 43-CPR7 $5.50	LIONEL No. 6457 OPS-Sec. 43-CPR7 $5.50	LIONEL No. 6457 OPS-Sec. 43-CPR7 $5.50	LIONEL No. 6462 OPS-Sec. 43-CPR7 $4.75	LIONEL No. 6462 OPS-Sec. 43-CPR7 $4.75
LIONEL No. 6465 OPS-Sec. 43-CPR7 $4.50	LIONEL No. 6465 OPS-Sec. 43-CPR7 $4.50	LIONEL No. 6465 OPS-Sec. 43-CPR7 $4.50	LIONEL No. 6465 OPS-Sec. 43-CPR7 $4.50	LIONEL No. 6472 OPS-Sec. 43-CPR7 $4.75	LIONEL No. 6472 OPS-Sec. 43-CPR7 $4.75
LIONEL No. 6520 OPS-Sec. 43-CPR7 $7.25	LIONEL No. 6520 OPS-Sec. 43-CPR7 $7.25	LIONEL No. 6520 OPS-Sec. 43-CPR7 $7.25	LIONEL No. 6520 OPS-Sec. 43-CPR7 $7.25	LIONEL No. 6520 OPS-Sec. 43-CPR7 $7.25	LIONEL No. 6520 OPS-Sec. 43-CPR7 $7.25

FIGURE 16: One of sixteen pages of perforated price stickers sent to distributors and retailers by Lionel. R. Swanson Collection.

been exhausted by year end, the reordered boxes would have been marked in the "new" way. The orange and blue paper boxes are termed OPS Classic. The re-marked boxes from 1951 are not given specific identity because of the possibility of stickers appearing on boxes produced earlier than 1951 due to leftover inventory as stated.

Lionel's statement of compliance with the OPS pricing guidelines was printed in the 1951 and 1952 consumer catalogues inside the front cover beneath the copyright note.

Before we move on there is one other point about pricing on boxes that must be discussed. As early as 1950, and with the 1951-1952 outfit 2190W, and again in 1953 and 1954, Lionel had prices printed on some of the corrugated boxes used to package sets and accessories. These prices are not related to the OPS issue. Other Lionel writers have noted that the company was beginning to have difficulty enforcing its fair trade pricing policy. These prices are believed to be an effort on Lionel's part to enforce fair trade practices. When a price label refers to OPS that reference is stated somewhere in the price label. Because of its problems with discounters, Lionel probably would have welcomed OPS regulations if they had prohibited discounting.

The elimination of footsteps on most 1950 rolling stock also brought about an important change in the paper boxes. Rolling stock could be packaged by turning the trucks around so the coupler was under the car frame. Consequently, Lionel eliminated the coupler flaps and shortened

FIGURE 17: 2031 Rock Island diesel locomotives in an OPS corrugated master carton from 1952, D. Fisher Collection; 2032 Erie diesel locomotives in a 1953 "Circle-L" blue and red ink on brown box. J. Kraemer Collection.

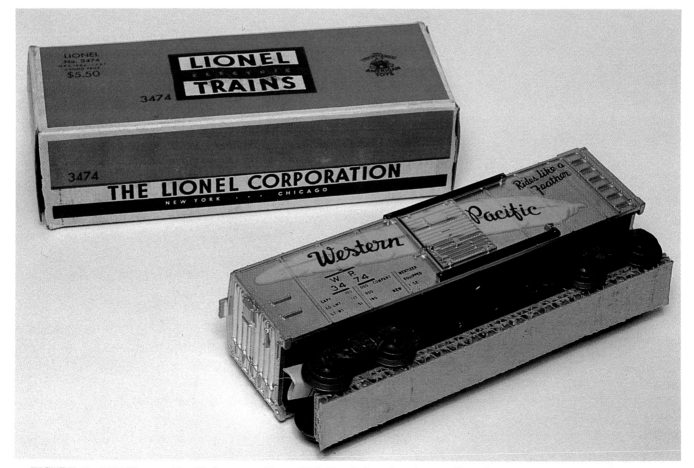

FIGURE 18: 3474 Western Pacific boxcar with an OPS Classic box showing cardboard strip maintaining truck position.

FIGURE 19: Assorted corrugated boxes. The Circle L logo was introduced in 1953 while the 2031 Rock Island master carton dates to 1952 because of the OPS stamp. T. Rollo, D. Fisher, and D. and S. Erich Collections.

the boxes. In order to keep the truck from twisting as the car was placed into the box, a thin corrugated strip was placed on the inside of the wheels running the length of the car. The 6454- and 3464-series boxcars utilized this cardboard strip. The 3474 Western Pacific boxcar in **Figure 18** is another example. The cardboard strips were usually lost, as they did not stay wedged between the wheels for long.

Collectors who own a number of pieces from this period know only too well what happens after the strip is gone. The boxes become tattered from the inside out from the trucks twisting as the piece is returned to its box.

1953

When the Korean War was concluded, Lionel returned to normal production. The 1953 product year started out with the loss of one of Lionel's greatest assets, Arthur Rafael who was the Vice President of Sales. During his career with Lionel, he instinctively put to work certain principles that in recent years would have been included in college-level business school curricula. These principles include such things as focus group studies which ask: Who buys our product and why? Rafael also practiced trend analysis, observing consumer buying patterns. Demographic and psychographic analysis were among his many other talents (these two concepts deal with buyers' characteristics and their preferences). Had Rafael lived longer, dramatic changes would have taken place in Lionel's merchandising, which included packaging. Changes in packaging necessary to meet changing markets would not materialize until late 1958. Over the next five years we will see Lionel make a number of poor packaging decisions.

The corrugated set and accessory boxes changed in 1953. A new, more colorful design was introduced. These were the first of the "Circle L" boxes. The first variation is blue and red ink on a brown box. Although this box involved printing with two colors, the colors did not overlap as with the 1949 and 1950 boxes. The printing process was still uncomplicated. An example of the set box is shown in **Figure 20**. The set box in the illustration is actually a 1954 set; however, Lionel followed this format both years. In 1953 both types overlapped. In my research I have noted a set of O42 manual switches in a 1951-1952 box dated as late as September 1953, while the earliest of the Circle L boxes is March 1953.

The orange and blue paper boxes were unchanged in basic format from the year before. The OPS price ceilings had been removed so those preprinted prices were dropped. There was an addition to the information printed on some of the paper boxes, but not all. In 1953, for the first time, Lionel introduced a planned series of rolling stock that required an individual identity for each piece. This was the 6464 boxcar series. There had been series-like attempts in the past, such as the 6454 9-1/4" boxcars, but no organized system of unique numbers for each car had been adopted.

In his article about 9-1/4" boxcars, Bob Swanson has provided a photograph of the boxes that came with these cars. In 1948 there was no unique identity at all. In 1949 the numbers "1", "2", and "3" were used to denote the three differ-

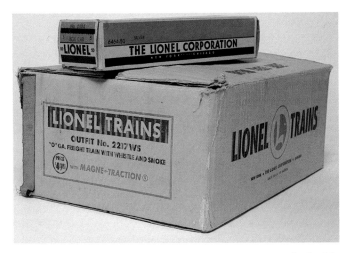

FIGURE 20: A 1954 set box and 6464-50 box re-marked with "Silver" and overprinted to obliterate the road name. This box actually contained the 6464-175 RI boxcar. T. Rollo Collection.

ent road names of the non-operating boxcars. In subsequent years the road name provided the only unique identity.

The 6464 boxcars made use of a suffix number following the catalogue number. This is parallel to the part numbering system and the lamp numbering system prior to 1953. With one exception, suffix numbers ending in "0" or "5" were fully assembled products, while suffix numbers ending in other digits were parts.

The exception is the suffix "1". Lionel began printing the suffix codes on boxes beginning in 1953 to denote each item in the series. The suffix codes were printed apart from the catalogue number, in the white margin on each side of the Lionel name on the box flaps. On the sides of the box, the suffix number was printed next to the catalogue number separated by a hyphen. The exception is, again, the suffix "1". This number was understood and did not appear on the box. The 6464 Western Pacific boxcar was the first in the series. Only the number 6464 appears on the box for this car. Subsequent boxes in this series, -25, -50, etc., had their suffix numbers printed as described. This practice left the first box in the series uncomplicated in the event a planned series did not develop. During my research on this project, I discovered one box for the 6464-75 Rock Island boxcar without suffix numbers on the box flaps. It appears that this is just an error in the box manufacturing process and not some policy change at Lionel. There may be other examples. What is also important here is that the road name in addition to the complete number including the suffix was printed on the box.

1954 THE HUMP YEAR

If anyone were to ask me the question "What was Lionel's greatest year in the postwar era?", I would have to answer "1954" — not because the products manufactured that year are the most desirable in terms of their value, but in terms of total quality and variety of output. The years between the end of World War II and the Korean War can be characterized as years of quality and quantity. Lionel's total income peaked in 1953.

Although sales would fall off in 1954, the company did not know that when the 1954 product line went into production. For this and reasons to follow the characteristics of quality and quantity gain a third characteristic, variety. It is no wonder Ron Hollander in his book *All Aboard — The Story of Joshua Lionel Cowen and His Lionel Train Company* copied pages 30 and 31 from the 1954 catalogue. On those pages are pictured Lionel's finest manufactured offering of diesel locomotives.

The variety of road names in each locomotive style reached its peak. The better Alcos were still available in three road names. The General Motors F-3 A-B-A combinations came in three combinations, including the 2356 Southern. The first and best detailed of the single-motor F-3s, the 2245 Texas Special, was introduced. The 623 Santa Fe and the 624 Chesapeake & Ohio NW-2 diesel switchers were joined by the 6250 Seaboard. To top it all off, the first of the Fairbanks-Morse Trainmaster locomotives, the 2321 Lackawanna, made its debut.

The offering of products in series (same car with different road name or color) broadened in 1954. In addition to four more 6464 boxcars, the 3562 barrel car was introduced in black and another in gray. Both bore Santa Fe markings, however the black car had suffix "1" and came in a box with only the catalogue number "3562" on it. The gray car, on the other hand, had the suffix number "25" in the position on the box already described. This was the second cargo-carrying operating car after the milk car to carry a human figure. In the consumer catalogue that year the popular milk car was upstaged. There were more barrel car listings than milk car listings!

However, it was status-quo in box designs at Lionel. No new box designs were introduced this year. There is one box that tells a story about Lionel's re-marking practices, and it is the keystone of my hypothesis about where re-marked boxes originated. Study the boxes in **Figure 20**. The set box is the box for the 682 steam turbine freight set. On top is the Middle Classic paper box for the silver 6464-175 Rock Island boxcar that was included in the set. The box was originally lettered for the 6464-50 Minneapolis and St. Louis boxcar. The road name has been overstamped and the only additional marking to uniquely identify the contents is the word "Silver".

Let us stop for a moment and consider the implications of the re-marked 6464-50 box. Imagine yourself as a sales clerk in a retail store that sold Lionel trains in the mid-1950s. Would the re-marking tell you what was in the box? No! In 1954 three silver boxcars were offered: 6464-1 Western Pacific, 6464-100 Western Pacific, and 6464-175 Rock Island. It is true there were some large Lionel dealers that knew the product as well as we know the product today. But considering the types of retail outlets Lionel targeted for sale of their products (hardware stores, variety stores, even some sporting good stores, to name only a few), it seems that these knowledgeable dealers were in the minority. Now put yourself in the position of the consumer. Would you trust what was in the box? Probably not. You might have wondered if the contents were shop worn. Were they used for display purposes? The likely answers to these questions were not re-

assuring. If you were Lionel and you had odd boxes left over, how could you make use of them and avoid all of these potential problems? Very easy, bury them inside set boxes. The re-marked or over-stamped boxes came from sets. Over the last three years I have noted carefully every re-marked box and the item that it actually contained, if that could be determined. Each piece of rolling stock was available in a set. In the same time period I have noted only two accessory boxes that were re-marked. One contained 022 switches in a box originally lettered for the short-lived 022A switches. The other was for the 348 manual culvert unloader catalogued in 1966. This corrugated box was originally lettered for the uncatalogued 346 manual culvert unloader offered before 1966 in the Sears set pulled by the coveted 2347 Chesapeake & Ohio GP-7. This box was re-marked with a paste-on label. So far these are the only two.

The No. 50 gang car was new in 1954, the first year the car was packaged in a Middle Classic box with a formed cardboard liner. By 1956 the car had moved to a corrugated Circle L box with a one-piece tuck flap that became the liner once the car was placed inside. There is no question that this was a big seller, because it offered a great deal of play value for its price.

A question I have for readers concerns the outfit box for set 2234W catalogued in 1954. It is a typical corrugated box; however, the colors are reversed. This was probably done to highlight the top-of-the-line set. Are there any copies of this set in boxes printed in the standard format?

1955 THE TRIP DOWNHILL

The Middle Classic boxes carried on into 1955 but with some changes in size and shape. Protective box liners were eliminated from tenders and the 2500-series passenger cars. The work caboose, crane, and diesel switcher were given less complex inserts. The corrugated set and accessory boxes also continued the Circle L design. However, the labeling on the set boxes did change. This year the words "1955 Outfit" were printed on the ends. Lionel attempted to confuse and mislead retail customers by issuing two different but corresponding series of outfit numbers. The traditional four-digit numbered boxes were reserved for the wholesale distributors while the three-digit numbers were relegated to department stores and chains. Fair trade pricing had ended and the sets offered in the consumer catalogue were not listed item by item. This was also the first use of a generic box since the 1948 catalogue year. Generic packaging in some form would remain in use through 1969. In 1955 Lionel also introduced an inferior version of the NW-2 diesel switcher. This, together with a decline in 1954 profits, is generally regarded by researchers as the turning point after which Lionel began to cheapen its product. It could be argued that the use of generic packaging was at this time a cost-cutting move. In the past, the use of generic packaging dealt more with efficiencies resulting in increased output. Empty set boxes were available to dealers. With the cancellation of fair trade pricing, Lionel also allowed dealers to make up sets on their own and encouraged them to include accessories!

1956 FROM BAD TO WORSE

The Circle L boxes used to package accessories continued without change. There were major changes in both the set boxes and the orange and blue paper boxes.

The set box design introduced in 1956 was a radical departure from what Lionel had been using since the end of World War II.

Until now every format the company had chosen was a basic brown corrugated box with a label either separately printed and pasted onto the box or printed directly on the box by the box manufacturer. An example of the new design is shown in **Figure 21**. The lettering and illustrations were printed in one color on a background field printed in a different color. The background resembled a loosely-woven basket pattern. Hence, it is referred to as a basket weave box. This format would remain in use in some form through 1960. Through these years the box color would change along with the color of the lettering. The typeface and format would remain basically the same. Note in **Figure 21** that this example does not show the typical four-digit set number followed by "W" indicating whistle, "WS" indicating whistle-smoke, or "B" indicating bell. The set number has been replaced by a three-digit code. We will discuss the significance of this later. First, we will take a look at the changes that took place in the orange and blue paper boxes.

The Classic boxes changed in 1956. The contents information was drastically reduced. The catalogue numbers now appeared only on the box flaps. The use of road names was eliminated also on many boxes; the most notable of which were the 6464 boxcars. A box printed during or after 1956 stated "6464-400 / BOX CAR" on two lines. "Baltimore and Ohio" or "B & O Timesaver" were nowhere to be found. This is the Late Classic box.

Study the boxes in **Figure 22**. Moving from left to right the change can be easily seen. The 3359 dump car box was printed in 1955, the year the car was introduced. On the right, the 601 diesel switcher box is for the red and black Seaboard, introduced in 1956. There is no road name on the

FIGURE 21: Conventional-type O or O27 Gauge basket weave set box that was introduced in 1956. T. Rollo Collection.

box. The two 2436 observation car boxes show the span of change. Note the catalogue number appears on one box from 1954 or 1955, and not the other from 1956 and later.

What is the significance of these changes? To answer this question, let us relate two personal incidents to you. In 1956 the author's family was living in Wheaton, Illinois. One of Wheaton's four Lionel dealers was a hardware store located in a 1950-style strip mall on the north side of the city. I had no idea they sold Lionel. One day I went there on an errand for my father, and, as I parked my bicycle in front of the store window, I noticed a 153 block signal all by itself among the hammers, screwdrivers, window shades, and Revere Ware. After I found what I wanted, I went over to see what the store had in the way of Lionel trains. The boxes, mostly accessories and individual rolling stock, were all in disarray, spread over the shelves in no order at all. Many of them had been opened with torn flaps. A little boy about seven years old had a 6262 wheel car box in his hand and was busy prying the outer flap open. This car has a load of wheel sets which were held in place by a rubber band stretched the length of the car passing through the coupler jaws at each end. The rubber band had slid to one side and the wheels were loose inside.

FIGURE 22: The transition of Middle Classic to Late Classic boxes illustrating the changes from 1955 to 1956 as the stock numbers were deleted from the four sides. T. Rollo and D. and S. Erich Collections.

FIGURE 23: Shades of 1957 and 1958 Late Classic boxes: 6646 stock car in orange tone box, 6424 automobile flatcar, 6818 flatcar with transformer, and 89 flagpole in red boxes. T. Rollo and R. LaVoie Collections.

When the box came open the wheels came tumbling out, rolling up and down the aisle. An elderly female sales clerk was at one end of the aisle and saw this happen. With the wheels rolling all over the place, she put her hand on her hip and said in a voice that could be heard all over the store, "Oh! honestly" and shook her head. The little boy looked up at her and with a look of anguish as if he was about ready to burst into tears said, "I just wanted to see what it was." If ever an epitaph is written, in as few words as possible, to describe Lionel's merchandising techniques (or lack of them), it should be those words.

Several months passed and again I was in that store with my father. The shelves where the trains had been were now bare. The store owner waited on us and at the appropriate moment I asked where the trains were. The gentleman said they were all put away and that another store was interested in buying them. He said that he bought a small pack-

age deal, probably referring to the $300 dealer package, and that there were too many single pieces and no way to display them.

Another recollection involves a television program in which contestants were given shopping sprees in a toy store. Each contestant won the chance to run through the store for five or ten minutes and could keep all of the toys that they could cram into a shopping cart. As each participant ran through the store an off-camera voice commented on the items being chosen. One of the participants came to the Lionel train sets, which were in the basket weave boxes and stacked like cases of motor oil in a present day discount store.

One fellow picked up a set and the announcer commented, "Now he's picking up a set of those wonderful Lionel trains." What was it? Was the set an inexpensive O27 outfit? Was it the top-of-the-line Congressional passenger set? Nobody knew.

What these two incidents tell us is that the retail environment was changing. Self-service merchandising was becoming the rule, and it was no longer confined to grocery and five and dime stores. The fact that Lionel's packaging was

FIGURE 24: (Top) 3356 operating horse car and corral in a 1958 Bold Classic box; (bottom) 3366 operating circus car and corral in a unique Orange Picture box. M. Sokol Collection, B. Greenberg photograph.

FIGURE 25: Bold Classic boxes printed in 1958. T. Rollo and B. and S. Schneider Collections.

less descriptive than before actually put the product further away from the consumer at a time when sales assistance was declining. The problem of Lionel's declining sales was compounded by the lack of appropriate packaging. Display packaging would have helped prevent this. It is surprising in that packaging of this type was not new to Lionel. The prewar State set came in a large flat display box that was very bulky. At that time, display packaging throughout the toy industry was commonplace.

1957 LIONEL'S "INDIAN SUMMER"

As Lionel collectors and researchers learn more and more about the company, its products, and manufacturing, the product line of 1957 becomes more and more mind boggling. Never in the postwar era was Lionel's product line as varied as it was in that year. Unfortunately there were no merchandising improvements to promote the product.

The Circle L corrugated boxes for accessories continued unchanged. The basket weave set boxes also continued as they had before for O and O27 Gauge. One additional set box was introduced. This had the same format as the basket weave box but was printed on a brown field and had motive power scenes added to the four sides. This design was developed exclusively for Super O sets. Along the side of the box was an illustration of a Denver & Rio Grande F-3 in a panoramic view, as if it had been lifted from the consumer catalogue. The illustration used the same ink colors as the rest of the lettering on the box, making the level of detail rather poor.

The Late Classic boxes continued with a new and unusual variation. Some of the boxes produced in 1957 were red instead of orange. Actually the red boxes were used with one piece in 1956, the 6436 Alcoa covered hopper car. The one in my own collection is in a red box, as is one owned by another Milwaukee area collector.

Roland LaVoie once found one packaged in a red box and called to tell me about it. The 6436 hopper was offered in 1956 only. This is the only datable piece from 1956 that has turned up so far in a red box. The vast majority of red boxes occur in 1957, which is why we are covering it here. This was not intentional; it was some fluke in the inks used in the printing process. This is evidenced by the box for the 746W Norfolk & Western tender. Two 746W boxes have been spotted that appear red on one box flap and two sides. Flip the box over so the opposite flap and the other two sides are showing and the box is orange. You no doubt recall the tale of the Pied Piper of Hamlin? Well, this is the "Pied Box of Lionel." The occurrence of both red and orange on the same box supports the idea that this was an accident. **Figure 23** shows some examples of red boxes. An orange box for the 6646 stock car is shown for comparison. The orange box was available only in 1957. While this photograph was being set up, the photographer, Bill Kojis, who also owned Lionel trains as a child said, "Those boxes aren't orange, they're red." I told him, "That's exactly why we're taking this picture of them."

Roland LaVoie is actually responsible for naming 1957 Lionel's Indian Summer. Considering the fact that a number of the instruction sheets issued that year and in 1956

were printed on canary yellow paper with brown ink and the red boxes, he is right.

One last point concerning red boxes. When the customary orange boxes are exposed to moisture for a period of time, the orange tends to develop a reddish look. This could occur when boxes are stored in a damp basement. These can be distinguished from the 1956-1957 red boxes in that the moisture also causes warpage and sometimes a fuzzy surface.

1958 MODERATE REVISIONS

The set boxes continued virtually unchanged with one addition. A slight variation of the Super O box appeared. This version had a slightly reddish tint to the otherwise tan field. O Gauge sets were no longer being offered and would not appear again until 1964.

The Circle L corrugated accessory boxes also continued in 1958. There was a new variation in the Circle L boxes, which is not dated. However, the color change places it between the Circle L boxes as I have discussed thus far and a datable color change in 1959. The lettering that had been blue was changed to black. The box was the same as the early Circle L box in every other respect. Thus far, the only example of this variation that has been found is a box for the 736 Berkshire and tender. This was unusual in that the locomotive and its tender were packaged together in the same box separated by a liner. This unusual box was similar to the box design used to package the twin Alco locomotives between 1950 and 1954. It is more common to find the Berkshire and its tender in separate boxes. In 1958 Lionel offered the Berkshire as a separate sale item for the first time since its introduction in 1946. This is the only explanation that comes to mind for such an exceptional box.

The orange and blue paper boxes continued into 1958. A new version was introduced this year, the Bold Classic box. **Figure 25** shows two examples of this box. Note that the lettering on the box flap is chubby and bold, similar to the Art Deco boxes of 1945-1947. Many of the Bold Classic boxes are dated, and those that are have 1958 dates. The box for the 6670 boom crane car is an overstamp. It was originally printed for the 6660 version of the same car with outriggers made in 1958 only. This box came from set 1617S and was the only catalogued set offered that year to include this car.

Another version of the Classic box also appeared. This is the Glossy Classic box. These were the same as other Classic boxes, only they were made with coated paper. They were not very common in the product line. Thus far, the glossy version has turned up for packaging Lionel Plasticville, LTC lockons, 260 bumpers, some very late 167 whistle controllers, and an occasional 3424 Wabash brakeman. These are easy to spot because the use of coated paper made the orange and blue colors more vivid.

Late in the year a new and entirely different paper box made its debut. This was a solid orange box, which came in a total of five variations and would be the mainstay of Lionel's paper box packaging from now through 1965. Widespread use of this new design did not occur until 1959; however, we do know it was introduced in 1958, as one collector I know owns an 868 accessory promotion assortment. He has

FIGURE 26: These are the unique outfit boxes for two advance catalogue sets. The graphics on 1109 (bottom) were used in 1960 only while the Texas Special artwork (top) was introduced in 1959 for outfit 1105. B. Myles Collection.

dated the contents from the ads on the billboards included in the package. At last Lionel began using display packaging. Cellophane see-through windows were added to some accessory boxes. Like the introduction of HO scale trains and the development of Super O track, it was too little, too late. The damage Lionel did to itself the previous three years, together with changes in leisure time activities, could not be corrected. Lionel betrayed its awakening in another way. In 1958 set content detail returned to the consumer catalogue after an unfortunate absence of three years.

1959 THE CHANGE COMES

The variations of new issue solid orange boxes will be discussed here. Four of the five types are shown in **Figure 27**. The Orange Picture box on the lower right is dated to 1961.

These boxes have several characteristics in common which identify them as a series. All of them were solid orange on coated paper. The lettering style and format on the box flaps and narrow sides were the same on all five variations.

1. Variation A: This was not a display box at all. Instead of a display window, the long flat sides simply contain the words "Lionel Electric Trains" in blue and white letters. The box for the 214 plate girder bridge shown in **Figure 27** is an example.
2. Variation B: (Not shown in **Figure 27**.) This type is the same as above, except one side had an illustration of the contents. The 260 bumper came in this box.

3. Variation C: Cellophate See-Through. This is the earliest known version beginning in late 1958. This box was confined to small, lightweight accessories. The box of 76 teardrop lamps shown in **Figure 27** is an example. This box required the use of a colored liner (either yellow or white) to hold the accessory in the proper position.
4. Variation D: This type, called the Orange Perforated box, is the one that raises the most questions. The tear-out was a perforated window much like the opening in a box of facial tissues. In 1959 Lionel began offering the sets in display boxes. The dealer might tear out the windows on one set to be used for display purposes, show the contents, and yet make it clear to the prospective buyer the items had not been handled. Many of the boxes were made by the Berles Carton Company and dated 1959. The 6119-100 work caboose box shown in **Figure 27** is an example. For a long time I was certain this box was produced in 1959 only. However, early in 1987 I was invited to a private train sale in a Milwaukee suburb. The first thing that jumped out at me when I arrived was a 6475 pickle car in a box with a tear-out display window. The 6475 pickle car was first catalogued in 1960. Well, that shoots that theory! The Orange Perforated box is dated 1959-1960.
5. Variation E: Called the Orange Picture box, this type does not appear until 1961, but it is part of the same series. This box was the same as the Orange Perforated box without the tear-out perforated window. In its place was a white block showing a panoramic view of two approaching locomotives. One was a Santa Fe-type Hudson and behind it the Santa Fe F-3. Many of these boxes are a lighter shade of orange. The 6464-725 New Haven boxcar box shown in **Figure 27** is an example of this type. Note that this is the famous mislabeled box: the catalogue number is shown as 6464-735. On this box the coupler flaps were omitted. This required turning the couplers underneath the car in the same manner as the cars on the 9-1/4" frames in the early 1950s. This was something the 6464 car bodies were not designed to do. Turning the coupler around requires enough force to damage the skirt on the car body.

One question that comes up is why were there so many box variations at the same time? There is no sure answer to this. In the case of the 214 plate girder bridge, a display box would have been useless, showing only the base plate of the bridge and the bumper was too heavy to accommodate a box with a cellophane window. Why not use a cellophane window for rolling stock? The theory on this situation involves cost. Cutting out a window and then gluing in a sheet of cellophane is much more involved than cutting a perforation. This can be done at the same time the box is being cut from sheet stock.

The Circle L boxes in 1959 continued with some new variations. The box field color changed from brown to yellow. Those used for accessories had a simple illustration of the accessory on the tuck flap.

The Super O set box also changed to a yellow field version still with motive power illustrations on the four sides.

As mentioned earlier, display-style set boxes started in 1959 (see **Tables 4** and **5** on page 156). These, too, had a yellow field. The box lid was perforated and could be creased to

FIGURE 27: An array of orange: A 1959 accessory box for the 214 girder bridge; a Cellophane Front accessory box that would later be adapted for rolling stock and passenger cars in 1966; and a 1959-1960 Orange Perforated box on top of a 1961-1964 Orange Picture box. T. Rollo Collection.

permit the illustration on the lid to stand up above the edges of the lid. The 1800 General Gift Pack offered in 1959 was the first to be offered without track and transformer. All three types of flat pack display-style boxes were utilized for the O27 line and set components were placed unboxed inside of the outfit box for Types A and B packaging. The better O27 outfits came with component boxes in a conventional-type box also on a yellow background.

1960

The Orange Perforated component boxes continued unchanged from 1959 in 1960. Display style outfit packaging was still the norm for the O27 line. 1960 was a combination year that included some outfits with Type A, B, and C yellow background display-style boxes the same as in 1959, and others with new half-orange, half-white graphics that included a sketch of a 4-6-2 Pacific steam engine on the upper portion of the lid.

The Super O outfit box was changed. It retained the same motive power scenes as in 1957, but the background was solid orange-coated stock.

1961

The Orange Picture box appeared for the first time in 1961. The picture occurred three ways. The most common is the one shown in **Figure 27**. The other two are easy to identify without a photograph. In one version the locomotive illustrations repeat with two steam and two diesel locomotives. The length of these boxes is not a factor in whether or not the illustrations repeat. The third is a little more subtle. The white picture has more rounded corners.

The rerun of the 6572 REA refrigerator cars manufactured for Madison Hardware Company came in these boxes. There was one very scarce oddball box in 1961. This is a cross between the Orange Perforated and Orange Picture boxes. The white picture along the side of the box was printed on a perforated tear-out panel. This is referred to as a Perforated Picture box.

O27 outfits came in varying style boxes. The low and moderate sets were packaged the same as 1960 with the half-orange, half-white graphics in Type A or B only, while the better sets were packaged in a conventional-type solid orange box. The advance catalogue sets came in a Type A display-style box on a white background with deep red print and graphics that were later adopted for the 1963 line.

The Super O outfit box also underwent a change. The motive scenes that were part of the original 1957 design were eliminated, but the box still retained a solid orange color.

1962-1963

There was only one notable change in 1963. The paper boxes took on a noticeably darker orange color. Many of these darker orange boxes are dated. The 214 bridge box in **Figure 27** is darker than the others. This particular box is dated April 1963.

In 1962 Lionel changed its set numbering system. The new system was described in detail in the advance catalogue. The reason for the change was to identify a train set from other non-train products Lionel was manufacturing at the time. The new system used a five-digit number and no letters. The "WS", "W", and "S" suffix letters, that had been so characteristic of Lionel's set numbers, to indicate whistle and smoke, whistle, or smoke were discontinued. The pat-

1962 Numbering System

First digit — Item is a train set.

Second through fourth digits — Actual set number.

Fifth digit —Type of packaging used.

The **fifth digits** are broken down as follows:

    1 — Display pack.

    2 — Display pack.

    3 — Display pack.

    4 — Display box with component packaging.

    5 — Conventional non-display.

    6 — Conventional non-display.

    7 — Conventional box with component packaging.

    8 — Conventional box with component packaging.

FIGURE 28

tern of using even-numbered set numbers to indicate a passenger set and an odd number for a freight set was broken. The new numbering system is listed in **Figure 28.**

Following this system set number 13068 is a train set number 306 and is packaged in a conventional box with component packaging. The new numbering system covered more types of packaging than the company was actually using at the time. In 1962, of the regularly catalogued sets, "5" was not used at all and only one set, the Plainsman, was assigned a number ending in "6". However, the last digit "5" was used on several 1963 outfits in which some of the contents were component boxed while others were packaged unboxed. Lionel had also experimented with the type of packaging in the mid-1950s.

The 1962-1963 Super O outfit boxes were the same used in 1961, but the O27 outfit boxes underwent a change in 1963. The low and moderate outfits came in a Type A display style with *new* orange and white graphics. The box lid pictured a small Hudson-type steam engine and a Santa Fe F-3. The better sets were packaged in a conventional-type tan corrugated box.

1964

Lionel changed its corporate identity during 1964 from The Lionel Corporation to The Lionel Toy Corporation. The famous address of 15 East 26th Street, New York gave way to Hoffman Place, Hillside, New Jersey. The only connection Lionel maintained with New York was a showroom at 200 5th Avenue. This was the beginning of the Robert A. Wolf administration at Lionel. Wolf would have the last positive

impact on Lionel's packaging and merchandising efforts, but not until later in his tenure.

The paper boxes made a noticeable change this year. The shiny finish on the box surface was much more dull than it had been in the past and the shade of orange was lighter. Although the corporate name changed, this change was not reflected on the boxes. Boxes continued to be lettered with The Lionel Corporation.

The set numbering system that Lionel instituted in 1962 was slightly changed. It continued to be a five-digit number, however from now until the end of production in 1969, all of the set numbers ended in zero. It is important to note here that the company appeared to be unable to develop a system and stick to it.

O Gauge was reintroduced in 1964 and only one Super O outfit was offered. It was the reissue of the 773 Hudson in outfit 13150. Refer to **Tables 3, 4,** and **5** on pages 155-156 for information pertaining to these outfit boxes.

1965

This was the last year Orange Picture boxes were issued. The new picture box reflected the corporate name change. The lettering along the side of the box changed to The Lionel Toy Corporation, Hillside, New Jersey. The phrase, "The Leader in Model Railroading" was added. These boxes are extremely difficult to find. The product line changed so little from the previous year that an existing supply of boxes could last for well more than one year's production.

The O27 outfit box underwent a change (see **Figure 29)**. It was a Type D display-style box with Hillside logo and new graphics. A 2037 steam engine pulling a string of freight cars was now pictured on a white background.

The solid white O Gauge outfit box was the norm for all sets offered except outfit 12800 which came in a Type D display-style box that used the same graphics as those for the O27 line. The Hudson freight set was the only outfit offered in Super O and it still came in a conventional tan box.

1966 LIONEL'S SWAN SONG

The outfit boxes remained the same as those used in 1965, but there were many changes and improvements to Lionel's other boxes in 1966. Thomas Wolf had brought the company back to a better financial position and it was clear that the budget for production, advertising, and packaging was much more generous than it had been in the recent past. The consumer catalogue returned to its traditional sideways layout with full-color photographs of the train sets, rolling stock, and some accessories. The previous three years what was offered was shown with surrealistic black and white illustrations that were really quite pitiful.

New paper boxes were introduced for rolling stock and passenger cars. All of these boxes had a cellophane see-through window. For the first time Lionel was using a box that the company should have introduced at least ten years earlier. These boxes brought to the model train line a new trademark that Lionel had introduced with the slot car racing sets in the consumer catalogue in 1963. The letters spelling out the name Lionel were block letters leaning forward much like the "Forward Look" the Chrysler Corporation had named the automobile design introduced in the late 1950s. The letters were within an oval line with two arrow points following or chasing each other. These boxes were generic. The end flap had a solid white band where the catalogue number of its contents was rubber stamped. I am surprised Lionel didn't attempt this much earlier. This must have been a cost savings and it would have made much more sense to use generic packaging than cheapen the contents. This practice would have eliminated the need to re-mark boxes that was common place ten years earlier.

Another style of packaging was introduced this year. This was blister packaging. Blister packaging came two ways: the blister box or shadow box. This type of box was used to package accessories such as signals. The accessory and related track contactor were held in place within a clear plastic sheet with a pocket or blister fashioned slightly larger than the pieces. The background was an illustration of the accessory in use. All of this was enclosed in a cardboard frame that had been punched to permit the box to be hung from a peg board. The second blister pack was a plain cardboard sheet with the blister glued onto it. The latter was used for lighter weight pieces that did not require track contactors. The cardboard backing also functioned as the instruction sheet and a promotion for other Lionel products. This is the first time, since the counter top displays for lamps, lubricant, smoke pellets etc., that Lionel used packaging intended to address impulse buying. It is interesting to note that such elaborate packaging was used to sell accessories that were the items most poorly illustrated in the catalogue. There is a bit of an irony here. The small track side signals were treated so elaborately while corrugated boxes for items like the 348 culvert unloader and the 133 station were packaged in plain boxes. The culvert unloader came in a leftover 346 box that was used for Sears and was now re-marked 348 with a paper sticker over the catalogue number. The station came in a plain white box with orange lettering.

1967

Lionel did not issue a consumer catalogue this year and there was no 1967 production. The question here is why nothing was produced when there was such a splash of progress the year before? With all of Lionel's merchandising improvements, there should have been some positive impact. Wolf introduced a marketing strategy that was actually the forerunner for exactly what for Lionel, in the modern era, would be a success after 1969. Why didn't it work now? Wolf had a great strategy; the problem was that the timing was terrible. The mid to late sixties was a time of great social turmoil. The baby boomers who had enjoyed Lionels during the golden era were now for the most part undergraduates or just finishing high school and working hard to stay one step ahead of the draft. The Vietnam War was gathering momentum. The interstate highway system was in its greatest period of development. Automobiles were cheap and so was gasoline. There was no time or need for indoor leisure time activities. Certainly no time for playing with trains. The fuel shortages of the early seventies was one event that would bring everyone back inside again.

FIGURE 29: 1965-1966 Type D display style outfit box with lift-off top. Note the channel construction. M. Kaye Collection.

FIGURE 30: *(Top)* A late edition accessory box for the 110 trestle set and *(bottom)* front and back views of the 1966 Cellophane Front component box.

1968-1969 THE BITTER END

Lionel's train production moved to Hagerstown, Maryland in 1968. Only one set was offered this year. Collectors refer to this as the Hagerstown Set and for that reason we will refer to its set box as the unique Type D Hagerstown box.

The paper boxes changed again. The well-planned cellophane see-through boxes and the blister packaging were dropped. The Checkerboard component box was introduced. The name comes from the pattern of the lettering on the box sides. "LIONEL" is repeated with girdled letters overlapping one another. When viewed from a distance these boxes do resemble the New Haven railroad's checkerboard logo. Another very similar box was issued for packaging accesso-

ries. This is solid orange with Lionel on the broad side. Some of the solid boxes were fitted with a die-cut cardboard liner to hold the contents in place. The end flaps were the same on both versions, with a white band to rubber stamp the box contents. The lettering across the lower band read either "The Lionel Toy Corporation Hagerstown, Maryland" (1968) or "Hillside, New Jersey" (1969). This is why the final two years of production are being treated together. Most rolling stock, even SP-type cabooses, were also issued in generic boxes sized for the 6464 cars. However, not all of these were generic. The boxes for the 6560 crane car and the 260 bumper were printed because their use was restricted to a single item.

The set box in 1969 was also different. The display packaging had been discontinued completely. All of the sets of-

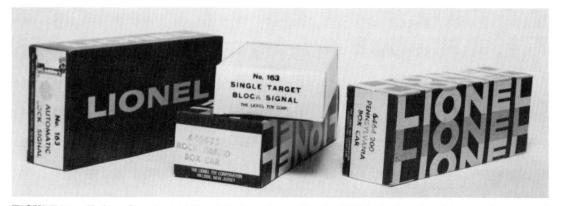

FIGURE 31: *(Left and center top)* Two late issue boxes for the 163 block signal and *(center bottom and right)* the 1968 and 1969 versions of the Checkerboard component boxes. The Hillside, New Jersey *(center bottom)* was 1969 issue while the 6464-200 boxcar *(right)* came in a leftover Hagerstown box. T. Rollo Collection.

fered in 1969 were packaged in a plain white box with the color photograph used in the catalogue pasted on the end of the box, something which Lionel should have done years before. No component packaging was used, just cardboard dividers.

The last box was the "bitter end box". It was just plain white with the contents rubber stamped in the ends. The white box for the 163 single target block signal shown in the photograph is the most common. 260 bumpers also turn up in these boxes as do Presidential passenger cars. A rather sorry end for a once great company.

In the end Lionel was also using whatever the company had left over. Even some Orange Picture boxes turned up with 1969 pieces in them.

CONCLUSION

The Lionel Corporation was a well structured company with a firm sense of order. This study of boxes has shown that. Lionel emerged from World War II and followed closely a strict fiscal planning cycle. When changes occurred in the marketplace that changed the demand for its products, the company attempted to change its marketing direction, but never found the right direction. The company made many attempts to regain its position but sadly never made it.

Now that we have studied Lionel's postwar boxes, the question that might be asked is, "OK, now what?" The marketing and manufacturing implications are interesting, but how can this be of value in collecting? Let's consider three Lionel pieces: the 022A switches, the 71 lamp post, and the 1045 flagman. Why these three? They certainly are not glamorous. In fact the 71 lamp post is downright common.

FIGURE 32: An end view of two 1969 outfit boxes. Lionel finally did what it should have done a score of years sooner — pasted a picture of the set, for identification purposes, on the exterior of the outfit box. M. Sokol Collection.

When a person faces the fact that he or she is a collector, one instinct has developed in that person's personality. A sense of order. Other more complex pieces can be put in order with the help of the Service Manual. Studies of the Berkshire locomotive and the milk cars are accurate without question. The point is that boxes help put other pieces in some form of order, through at least part of the time they were offered.

TABLE 1
Nomenclature for Postwar Paper-type Boxes

ART DECO
The original postwar component box with bold blue lettering that touched the tops and bottoms of the blue frames and outlines.

EARLY CLASSIC
The most notable box of the postwar era introduced in 1948 for the O27 line with smaller lettering; the city names "New York", "Chicago", and "San Francisco"; and with the stock number printed on all four sides.

MIDDLE CLASSIC
Same as Early Classic, except the city name of "San Francisco" was eliminated. It was used from mid-1949 through 1955.

OPS CLASSIC
Same as Middle Classic, but with the inclusion of the OPS stamp. It was used in 1952.

LATE CLASSIC
Same as Middle Classic, except that the stock number was eliminated from the four sides. It was used from 1956 through 1958.

BOLD CLASSIC
Same as Late Classic, but with a much bolder-faced print on the end flaps. It was used for part of the 1958 product line.

GLOSSY CLASSIC
A scarce box that surfaced in 1958. It was made in the Classic design, but was printed on coated stock similar to what was introduced in 1959. The 3424 Wabash brakeman, for example, occasionally came in this type of box.

ORANGE PERFORATED
A dramatic change in graphics that was a total departure from the classic design. The box was orange coated stock that had a tear-out perforated front panel. It was used in 1959 and 1960.

PERFORATED PICTURE
This box occasionally surfaced in 1961 and 1962. It was not regularly used, but was simply a means by which to deplete unfinished, perforated-front "raw" stock. It sometimes appears with a rolling stock item, but its use was most prevalent for early issue Presidential passenger cars.

ORANGE PICTURE
A variation of the Orange Perforated without perforations and with a picture of a steam and F-3 locomotive on the front, and the city names "New York" and "Chicago". It was used from 1961 to 1964 and included the phrase "The Lionel Corporation".

HILLSIDE ORANGE PICTURE
Similar to Orange Picture, but "Hillside" replaces "New York" and "Chicago". It was used for part of the 1965 product line and included the new corporate name, "The Lionel Toy Corporation".

CELLOPHANE FRONT
This was Lionel's attempt to make package contents visible by adding a cellophane window to the front of the box. The stock number was no longer printed on the end flaps as part of the manufacturing process; it was now rubber stamped and was used in 1966.

HAGERSTOWN CHECKERBOARD
Another dramatic change in graphics. This 1968 box had a Lionel checkerboard pattern with "Hagerstown" printed at the bottom of the end flaps and a rubber-stamped stock number.

HILLSIDE CHECKERBOARD
Same as Hagerstown Checkerboard, except that "Hillside" replaced "Hagerstown" in 1969.

HILLSIDE SOLID
End flap format is similar to Checkerboard, however these boxes had solid orange sides with "Lionel" appearing only once.

BLANK
Plain white box with contents and company name rubber stamped on flaps was used in 1969.

Note: See page 129 for a photograph of all of these boxes except the Hillside Solid and Blank.

TABLE 2

Dating Rolling Stock Boxes

1945:	Art Deco type with bold lettering. Many boxes were overstamped prewar issues.
1946:	Art Deco type with bold lettering.
1947:	Same as 1946, but with Toy Manufacturers Association logo.
1948-early 1949:	Introduction of the Early Classic box of the postwar era with smaller lettering; the stock number printed on all four sides; and the city names "New York", "Chicago", and "San Francisco".
Mid-1949-1954:	Same as 1948 to early 1949, but "San Francisco" eliminated.
1952:	Same as mid-1949 to 1954, but with the OPS stamping.
1955:	Same as mid-1949 to 1954, but with some major design, size, and liner changes.

> A. Liners eliminated from all steam engines, not to reappear until the reissue of the 773 Hudson in 1964.
>
> B. Liners eliminated from all tenders.
>
> C. Liners eliminated from all the F-3 power and tender units.
>
> D. Liners eliminated from all the 2500 series passenger cars.
>
> E. Redesigned smaller single-piece cardboard insert for the 6419 work caboose and for the new-issue 6119 series work cabooses.
>
> F. Wraparound liner eliminated from the diesel switchers in favor of two small cardboard filler pieces.
>
> G. Redesigned, less complex single-piece cardboard insert for the 6560 cranes.

1956-1957:	Same as 1955, but the stock number was eliminated from the four sides.
1958:	Same as 1955, but some with bolder-faced type on the end flaps.
1959-1960:	Solid orange with tear-out perforated front.
1961-1964:	Orange and white with picture of a steam and F-3 locomotive on the front, and the city names "New York" and "Chicago". Earliest issues were a distinctly darker orange.
1965:	Same as 1961-1964, but "Hillside" replaces "New York" and "Chicago" and with the new corporate name, "The Lionel Toy Corporation".
1966:	Cellophane see-through front.
1967:	No production.
1968:	Lionel checkerboard pattern with "Hagerstown" on the end flaps.
1969:	Same as 1968, but with "Hillside" on the end flaps.

TABLE 3

Dating O Gauge Outfit Boxes

1945	Conventional tan with paste-on label.
1946	Same as 1945
1947	Same as 1945.
1948	Same as 1945.
1949	Conventional tan with orange and blue printing directly on the box.
1950	Conventional tan with an orange field framed in blue with blue printing and most with the retail price.
1951	Conventional tan with blue frame only and blue printing, either with or without the OPS price stamping.
1952	Same as 1951.
1953	Conventional tan with red frame, blue printing, a large circled-L, and the retail price.
1954	Same as 1953.
1955	Same as 1953, but without the retail price and the phrase "1955 Outfit" either within or outside of the blue frame on box end.
1956	A dramatic change — the introduction of the tan-gray basket weave look.
1957	Same as 1956.
1958-1963	No production.
1964	Conventional tan with black rubber-stamped number, and the early release of the 1965-style box.
1965	Conventional type, solid white with orange lettering, except outfit 12800 which was packed in a Type D display-style box.
1966	Same as 1965.
1967-1969	No production.

TABLE 4
Dating O27 Gauge Outfit Boxes

(O27 and O outfit boxes were the same for all years 1946 through 1957.)

1958	Tan-gray basket weave look that originated in 1956.
1959	Introduction of the attached perforated-lid Type A, B, and C display boxes on a yellow background for the low and moderate outfits. Better outfits were packaged in a conventional-type box (also on a yellow background), while the advance catalogue sets came in a unique Type A display-style box on a white background.
1960	A combination year that included some outfits with Type A, B, and C yellow background display-style boxes the same as in 1959, and others with new half-orange, half-white graphics that included a sketch of a 4-6-2 Pacific steam engine on the upper portion of the lid.
1961	Low and moderate sets were packaged the same as 1960 with the half-orange, half-white graphics in Type A or B only, while the better sets were packaged in a conventional-type solid orange box. The advance catalogue sets came in a Type A display-style box on a white background with deep red print and graphics that were later adopted for the 1963 line.
1962	Same as 1961.
1963	Low and moderate outfits came in a Type A display style with *new* orange and white graphics. The box lid pictured a small Hudson-type steam engine and a Santa Fe F-3. The better sets were packaged in a conventional-type tan corrugated box.
1964	The same artwork as 1963, but now the top was completely unattached and lifted off. This is referred to as the Type D display box.
1965	Type D display-style box with Hillside logo and new graphics. A 2037 steam engine pulling a string of freight cars was now pictured on a white background.
1966	Same as 1965.
1967	No production.
1968	Type D display-style box with special Hagerstown graphics.
1969	Conventional two-tier type on white background with red and blue printing and a picture of the outfit pasted on one end.

Description Key for display-type boxes:

Type A — Perforated attached top with interior channels or cardboard dividers.

Type B — Perforated attached top with one-piece die-cut interior filler.

Type C — Perforated attached top with no interior channels but with component boxes.

Type D — Lift-off top with interior channels.

TABLE 5
Dating Super O Outfit Boxes

1957	Conventional-type, two-tier, tan-brown basket weave look with motive power scenes on all four sides.
1958	Same as 1957.
1959	Same motive power scenes as 1957, but on a solid yellow background.
1960	Same motive power scenes as 1957, but on a background of solid orange coated stock.
1961	Same coloration as 1960, but the motive power scenes were deleted from the four sides.
1962	Same as 1961.
1963	Same as 1961.
1964	Outfit 13150 only in a conventional tan box.
1965	Outfit 13150 only in a conventional tan box.
1966	Outfit 13150 only in a conventional tan box.
1967	No production.
1968	No production.
1969	No production.

Note: Occasionally a nondescript tan conventional-type outfit box surfaces with a regular production set number in years that it should not. One can assume that these may have been special packing requests by a customer, such as a company that did mail-order business, or the limited numbers packed did not warrant the special ordering or reordering of a standard outfit box. Also, flat-pack or display-style boxes were used for a few 1959-1960 sets, namely outfits 2527, 2528WS, and 2547WS.

HALF A CENTURY OF ENTERTAINMENT

LIONEL'S AUTOMATIC GATEMAN — *Linda F. Greenberg and Roland E. LaVoie*

"The most unusual model railroad accessory ever conceived!" thundered Lionel's 1935 catalogue on page 31. The descriptive text went on to describe the action of a sheet metal trackside shed containing a gateman figure with a little red lantern. This colorful little fellow darted out of the shed, swinging his lantern to warn pedestrians and autos alike, until the train passed. Then he retreated back into the shed, closing the door with a metallic clank. His house had a little white chimney sitting perkily atop a red roof, and a pole adjacent to the house had a brass railroad warning sign. The gateman himself was nattily attired in the traditional railroad blue uniform, with a blue cap, white shirt, and black tie.

In those years Lionel was never known for exact truth in advertising, often becoming trapped in its own hyperbole. However, this is one time when the catalogue's glowing prose may actually have understated the brilliance of an accessory. Who at Lionel could have guessed that the life span of this accessory, in one form or another, would run continuously from 1935 to 1984 — a span of fifty years? That must be some sort of record for any toy; in fact, the toy industry is notorious for the short life span of its products. Such was the fascination of the public for the Lionel automatic gateman that it became Lionel's longest-lived accessory, and few toy train layouts were without it. The gateman had the perfect combination of features — low price, attractive construction, and fascinating action. It was also ruggedly constructed, using the durable and dependable solenoid coil for its action. Significantly, it was also the first accessory to make use of a human figure in its action, and perhaps that feature more than any other explains its popularity. Even when it was reintroduced in 1987 in new colors, it became a big seller once again.

If the long life span of Lionel's automatic gateman is not enough to convince the reader of the accessory's popularity, perhaps another significant fact will do so. The Lionel gateman was easily the most copied and imitated accessory Lionel ever made. In the late 1940s the Colber Company of South Orange, New Jersey, long a manufacturer of lamp posts, bridges, and other trackside accessories, put out its own version of Lionel's gateman. Colber's gateman was much smaller

Should we call him "Comrade Gateman"? Shortly after World War II, a Soviet toy manufacturer copied the popular Lionel design. The Russian gateman sports a heavier overcoat than his American counterpart, but his housing and job duties are very similar to those of a Western gateman. R. Clement Collection.

The history of the Lionel gateman is shown on three shelves. *Top Shelf:* All three houses have brass diamond warning signs which were used from 1935 to 1938. The left gateman has a lattice-work post adapted from the 068 crossing sign, dating it as 1935 only. The center gateman is a 1936 product which has a solid pole and the word "THE" added to the brass sign. The gateman on the right has an embossed toolbox lid and has been dated 1938. *Middle Shelf:* All three pieces utilize the die-cast crossbuck. The left house, with its decaled toolbox lid, is dated as a 1940 product because of its gray post and black cap. The center house features a sans-serif "45N" stamping on the underside of its base and is dated 1947. The right house is a 1949 product; its green base is darker and its crossbuck is in the low position. Compare the middle house (mid-position) and left house (high position). *Bottom Shelf:* The gateman house on the left is the 145 model produced from 1950 through 1966 with either red roof (early) or maroon roof as shown. The middle house is a Fundimensions 2145 model from 1972. Later Fundimensions products had brown-red roofs, doors, and toolbox lids. Note also the much darker green base. The right house is the Lionel Trains, Inc. model 12713 of 1987-1988. R. LaVoie Collection.

than Lionel's and it lacked an illuminated lantern. However, the Colber version worked by solenoid, just as did Lionel's. The Colber gateman inhabited a little red brick lithographed house, and, of course, sold for less than Lionel's gateman.

In the early 1950s Marx put out its version of the Lionel gateman, and this version was truly amusing. Marx, in its fashion, cut costs as much as possible. Instead of the gateman figure coming out the door, Marx had the figure glued to the inside of the door, which was the only operating element of the house! Today, the Marx figure looks ludicrous when it operates, but in its day the accessory made money for Marx.

Perhaps the most interesting imitation of all is a version made in the Soviet Union, which was first described in Ron Hollander's *All Aboard!* The "Russian gateman," as some collectors now call him, was apparently copied shortly after World War II. The Soviet version lacks the pole and warning sign, and its gateman figure is dressed in a Russian overcoat rather than an American trainman's

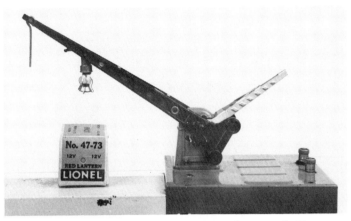

This is the 47-73 "lantern" lamp used on the 46 and 47 prewar crossing gates. We think the mysterious 45-75 lamp mentioned in the 1946 lamp replacement chart might have been very similar to this bulb. R. LaVoie Collection.

uniform, but in other respects it is just like Lionel's design, right down to the little chimney on the roof. This fascinating piece has been on exhibit at the Toy Train Museum in Strasburg, Pennsylvania; it is from the collection of Richard Clement (illustrated on previous page).

There is another side to the story of Lionel's automatic gateman which is not too well known and which might be revealed here for the first time. There is some circumstantial evidence that Lionel may have made efforts to light the lantern held by the gateman, rather than illuminate the lantern from below by a hidden light bulb. Chances are that Lionel, despite all its efforts, found this procedure to be too delicate because the wiring would have had to move with the figure, too costly to manufacture, or too time-consuming in the manufacturing process to meet the huge demand for this accessory. However, we are reasonably certain that at least the

thought crossed Lionel's corporate mind to make several attempts at a lighted lantern. It would not have been the first time Lionel tried something super-realistic; just after World War II, the Lionel engineers made the 38 water tower with real pumping water at Joshua Lionel Cowen's stubborn insistence. One can imagine Mr. Cowen demanding to know why the lantern itself would not light!

There are two critical pieces of possible evidence for this hypothesis. One — admittedly quite speculative — comes from the language of the catalogues themselves. Whatever the "hype," Lionel always tried to describe the action of its accessories as accurately as possible in order to stimulate sales. In the 1935 and 1936 catalogues, the action of the accessory is described perfectly. The catalogues state that the lantern is "illuminated by a beam of light focused on it from the base." That is exactly how all the Lionel gatemen from 1935 through 1949 were manufactured. However, the catalogues for 1937 through 1939 state that "the gateman rushes out swinging an illuminated lantern." That change in language may be a little too precise to be regarded as coincidental. If the correct description had been in the previous catalogues, why did Lionel feel the need to change the language? One possible answer, of course, is that during these years Lionel tried several times to make this lantern light, possibly experimenting with several different methods. However, if Lionel did indeed experiment, the firm was unsuccessful, and the accessory continued to be made as before.

The experiments, if any, were probably abandoned by the time of the 1940 catalogue, because the language changes again. In the 1940 and 1941 catalogues, we are simply told that the "gateman rushes out swinging a lantern." Except for a mention of the bulb, there is no reference to illumination. (The bulb used for all these prewar gatemen was Lionel's 616-13, a 12-volt clear screw-based bulb.) The 1942 catalogue says that the lantern is lighted "by a beam of light reflected from a concealed lamp." That statement is, of course, an accurate description of the accessory as actually produced. It is probable that no gatemen were made in this year because of war shortages, but the accessory was cer-

CHART OF REPLACEMENT LAMPS

LAMP No.	PRICE	DESCRIPTION	USE WITH CATALOG NOS.			
Q-90	$.25	8V Clear	Q, R, V, Z			
27-3	.25	12V Clear	221, 224, 1121, 1654, 1666, 2440, 2441, 2442, 2443			
28-3	.25	18V Clear	56, 115, 132, 137			
28-6	.30	18V Red	022C, 025, 391, 1025			
39-3	.30	12V Frosted	58			
45-75	.30	12V Red	45N,			
64-26	.40	12V Opal	64			
152-33	.30	12V Red	152			
3-23	.30	6-8V	153			

This is the Lamp Replacement Chart from the second 1946 instruction booklet. Note the reference to the never-made 45-75 bulb in the sixth line. Note also that lamps are listed for other pieces which were never made, notably the 391 circuit breaker, illustrated in this booklet, and the semi-scale 703 Hudson.

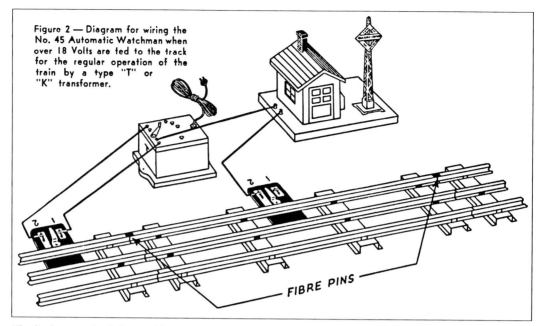

Figure 2 — Diagram for wiring the No. 45 Automatic Watchman when over 18 Volts are fed to the track for the regular operation of the train by a type "T" or "K" transformer.

FIBRE PINS

The lockon on the left provides track power to operate the train. The lockon on the right connects one wire to the outside insulated rail which is the negative side of the circuit. A direct wire from the gateman to the transformer provides a lower voltage for the positive side. The fiber pins insulate the outside rail so that it is only powered by the passing train.

tainly available. All of the catalogue illustrations, perhaps in a classic case of wishful thinking on Lionel's part, showed the lantern actually illuminated.

Admittedly, all of these arguments can be dismissed as speculation, although there is a strong temptation to believe the story. However, the second piece of evidence for Lionel's attempts to light the gateman's lantern is real and tangible, because it exists on paper. In late 1946 Lionel put out its second instruction booklet of that year (green and orange covers), this time with a revised lamp replacement chart. In that chart is a reference to a lamp numbered 45-75 — a bulb which was never produced. Lionel's practice at the time was to assign a number to a lamp based upon the first accessory to use it. For example, Lionel issued an 8-volt bayonet-based lamp, calling it the Q-90 because it was first used in the Type Q transformer in 1938. Therefore, whatever the 45-75 bulb was, it was meant to go with the 45 gateman, replacing the 616-13 bulb. (Curiously, the 616-13 is still listed in the chart as well.)

What kind of bulb would the 45-75 have been? We cannot know for sure, but we do have a good clue to that from the bulb numbered 47-73, which was actually produced. This bulb was a red-enameled, sub-miniature screw-based lamp used with the 46 and 47 prewar crossing gates. Later on, the number would change to 47-40 with a change in voltage to 18 volts. Significantly, it was boxed with a little, hand-soldered clip-on metal piece which, when clipped onto the glass globe, gave the appearance of a little lighted lantern. One cannot escape the conclusion that the 45-75 lamp would have been identical except for the voltage, and that it was meant for the gateman but never issued. (For the full story of Lionel's use of light bulbs, see Tom Rollo's article in this edition.)

Jim Sattler, a well-known collector, recently wrote something in a letter to Bob Swanson that is appropriate to the lighted lantern. In the letter, Jim explained that he had been reading an article about studies done on the Dead Sea Scrolls, and he said that conclusions about these religious artifacts could only go so far; they would "remain forever tentative." The phrase "remain forever tentative" aptly describes our hypothesis about the lighted lantern for the 45 gateman — unless someone happens to run across a legitimate prototype by some miracle! Still, the subject is fascinating, even if it is just idle brainstorming.

A systematic study of the Lionel automatic gatemen is necessarily divided into two sections: the sheet metal 45, 045, and 45N versions produced between 1935-1942 and 1946-1949, and the plastic and metal postwar 145 version produced from 1950-1969 and its similar successors, the Fundimensions 2145 produced from 1970-1984 and the Lionel Trains, Inc. 12713 model introduced in 1987. In this study, we will examine first the instruction sheets, proceeding to a discussion of the critical variables for both versions. Finally, we will provide a comprehensive listing for all prewar, postwar, Fundimensions, and Lionel Trains, Inc. versions of this accessory.

THE INSTRUCTION SHEETS

The first instruction sheet we were able to obtain is dated January 1936. It is headed "INSTRUCTIONS FOR OPERATING LIONEL AUTOMATIC WATCHMAN NO. 45 AND 045". When the accessory was numbered 45 it was meant to operate on a Standard Gauge layout, while the 045 version was meant for O Gauge. The only difference between the two accessories was the type of insulated track in-

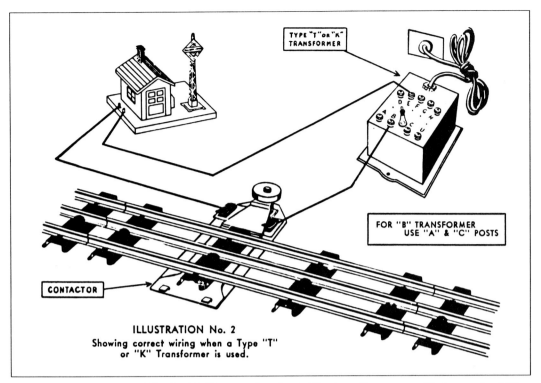

ILLUSTRATION No. 2
Showing correct wiring when a Type "T"
or "K" Transformer is used.

This illustration appeared in the 1937 instruction sheet. The transformer supplied a constant 12 or 14 volts to the accessory. The voltage to the accessory did not vary with track voltage as it did when insulated track sections were used. Note that the warning side girder is perforated.

The 1940 instruction sheet (45N-2-KPEX-2-40) showed the 45N gateman hooked up to the transformer using the 41C contactor. With this arrangement, power to the gateman was a constant 12 or 14 volts — it did not vary with track power. The 41 contactor has only two posts. Note that the gateman shanty is shown with a chimney in this illustration.

cluded within the box. The O Gauge version came with a piece of O Gauge straight track with an insulated outside rail, while the Standard Gauge version had a similar section of Standard Gauge track. Pages 2 and 3 of this instruction sheet show two diagrams. One is meant to show how to hook up the gateman to a separate voltage source when it was used with Standard Gauge. This was because the Standard Gauge trains operated with a much higher voltage than did the O Gauge trains — too high for the accessory.

The next significant change in the instruction sheets came about with a sheet dated March 1937. This was done when the special insulated track was abandoned in favor of the No. 41 contactor, which had been introduced the year before. Now, the weight of the train would activate the pressure switch, causing the accessory to operate. The instruction sheet showed wiring instructions for the Type T and K transformers and noted that different transformer posts should be used with Types A and C. The front cover changed to "INSTRUCTIONS / LIONEL AUTOMATIC GATEMAN / No. 45N". Lionel assigned the suffix "N" to the 45 gateman to indicate that it was designed for use with either gauge and with the 41 contactor.

The change to a weight-activated contactor meant better inventory and shipping control for Lionel because the big 1935-1936 packing boxes could be replaced with a much smaller box. The weight-operated contactor worked well with a

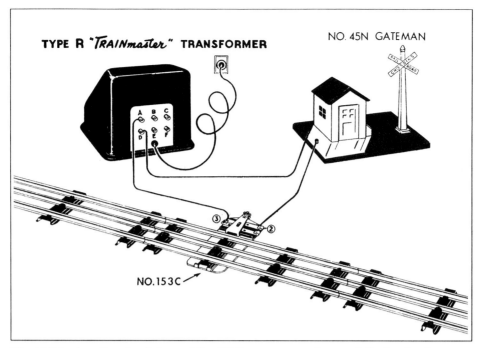

The 1942 instruction sheet showed the 153C contactor and several distinctive features, such as a gateman shanty with no chimney and a transformer with an AC line to wall outlet. Courtesy W. Holden.

track fastened to a table as long as the track section under the 41 contactor and the track on either side of the 45N was unfastened.

By February of 1940 the instruction sheet had changed to a two-page leaflet, and the instructions were simplified once again. This time, the wiring diagram for the gateman showed a hookup for the newer Trainmaster transformers, in this case the Type R, which was first catalogued in 1938. On the back of the sheet, Lionel placed a chart showing the proper operating posts for both the older and the newer transformers.

Lionel substituted the 153C contactor for the 41, probably in 1941. The 153C contactor was introduced with the 153 block signal in 1940. William Holden has provided a copy of the 1942 instruction sheet (part no. 45N-2-KXJX-1-42TT), which shows the 153C installed with the 45N gateman. The instruction sheet shows the 45N gateman without the chimney on the roof.

Another two-page instruction sheet from October of 1945, the first postwar instruction sheet for the 45N gateman, is identical to the 1940 sheet except for the postwar substitution of the all-purpose No. 153C contactor instead of the No. 41, which had been discontinued after World War II. Only the No. 2 and No. 3 posts of the No. 153C contactor were used for the 45N gateman. True to the actual production of the accessory, the 1945 wiring diagram omits the chimney from the roof of the accessory. The transformer chart on the back page was changed to reflect postwar production as well, even though the posts for the older prewar transformers were also given. This was the last instruction sheet devoted solely to the 45N gateman.

By March of 1946, just a few months later, Lionel issued another instruction sheet, this time devoted to the No. 153C contactor and all the accessories it operated. To save printing costs, Lionel went to a generic instruction sheet for the 45N gateman, the 152 crossing gate, and the 153 automatic block signal, all of which used this contactor. The 45N wiring diagram on page 1 of this generic sheet was identical to that on the separate sheet from October of 1945. However, there is one very curious notation on this sheet. Just above the diagram, Lionel gave the replacement lamp as the clear No. 616-13 lamp; the 1945 sheet had not given lamp instructions. The postwar versions of the 45N gateman had abandoned the use of a red acetate insert in the lamp hole and were using the No. 1449R 12-volt screw-based lamp in red. This reference to the prewar light bulb could be an error in the instruction sheet — or it could mean that the earliest postwar 45N gatemen were made without chimneys but with the red acetate insert. The instruction sheet error is the most likely possibility. However, the reference is repeated in the next instruction sheet dated November 1946, so there is a distinct possibility that some 1946 versions of the 45N gateman were produced with red acetate inserts.

The next instruction sheet is dated March of 1948; it adds the No. 151 semaphore to the three previous accessories operated by the No. 153C contactor. This time, the 45N diagram is gone completely; the sheet gives wiring instructions for the No. 152 crossing gate and tells the reader that the 45N is operated in the same way. From this point onward, the instruction sheets show no significant changes as far as the 45 gateman is concerned. The last instruction sheet to mention the 45 gateman is dated October of 1949, the last year of production for the sheet metal version of the gateman.

THE 45, 045, AND 45N: CRITICAL VARIABLES

Over the half-century life of the Lionel automatic gateman, by far the most variations are found in the 045, 45, and 45N sheet metal versions produced between 1935-1942 and 1945-1949. Sometimes these variations follow a clear and steady pattern; at other times, there is no discernible pattern to the changes. However, there is enough logic to the changes so that the pieces are datable.

The first variable collectors need to know is whether a particular 45 gateman is a prewar piece produced from 1935-1942 or a postwar piece produced from 1945-1949. The most reliable indications for prewar and postwar pieces are the presence or absence of chimneys on the roofs and the presence or absence of red acetate in the hole the lamp shines through on the base. As far as we know, prewar 45 gatemen have the chimneys and the red acetate inserts, while postwar examples lack these features. The light bulb itself may be convincing proof of the piece's age. If the lamp is clear, marked "12 v", and especially if it is embossed with the legend "MAZDA" up near the globe's junction with the base, it is unquestionably an original prewar light bulb. No postwar lamps are known to carry the "MAZDA" legend. On the other hand, if the bulb is red and is marked "1449", it is definitely a postwar light bulb. Of course, this assumes that the bulb has never been changed — but a surprising number of 45 gatemen in fine condition still carry their original light bulbs.

A word of caution is necessary at this point. Lionel introduced the No. 76 warning bell and shack in 1939; this accessory was made very much like the 45 gateman except for its colors. This accessory had a roof identical to that used on the 45 gateman, except that it had no chimney. Therefore, it is possible for a few late prewar 45 gatemen to have been made without chimneys, though we have yet to observe such a piece. In addition, the first two 1946 instruction sheets for the 45 gateman specify the old 616-13 clear 12-volt screw-based light bulb as a replacement for the accessory. We think this is an error, but we cannot rule out the possibility that some early postwar pieces from 1945 and 1946 may have been made without chimneys but with the red acetate lamp inserts. We would like our readers to search their collections for examples of interesting hybrids, if they exist.

1. The Warning Sign and Post

One indicator of 45N dating is to note whether the post is painted light gray or silver. Early 45s have silver posts which indicate prewar pieces, 1941-1942 posts have light gray-painted posts, while silver posts also indicate postwar pieces; (though it is likely some 1945-1946 pieces were also painted light gray). According to Charles Weber and Bob Sell, Lionel likely switched from silver to light gray paint because of an aluminum shortage. The aluminum was powdered to make silver paint. Aluminum was a critical war material and in short supply by 1941. The finial cap on the post is brass on the earliest examples, silver-painted or chromed on later prewar pieces and all postwar pieces, and black on some pieces from 1940-1942. The warning sign begins as a brass diamond sign in 1935. In this year only, the

The earliest gateman has a latticework post with brass diamond-shaped warning sign and an embossed toolbox lid. J. Kotil Collection.

black lettering reads "LOOK OUT FOR LOCOMOTIVE". In 1936 and later versions of this sign, the wording changes to "LOOK OUT FOR **THE** LOCOMOTIVE".

There are two versions of brass warning signs with "THE". One version has "MADE IN U. S. A." at the top of the diamond in tiny letters and the other version does not.

The diamond-shaped metal warning signs persist through 1938. Some of these signs may have been issued in

The 45 gateman shown has a chimney and red acetate in the hole in the base which dates it as 1942 or earlier. The gateman also has a die-cast crossbuck which was introduced in 1939. The die-cast crossbuck is mounted on a stamped-steel post that does not have the latticework found on the earlier version. Hence this example was made between 1939 and 1942.

This is the first version of the 45 gateman's warning sign. Note the absence of the word "THE" at lower left and the latticework post, identifying this as a 1935 piece. The 1936 and later versions added "THE" after "FOR" at the lower left. J. Kotil Collection.

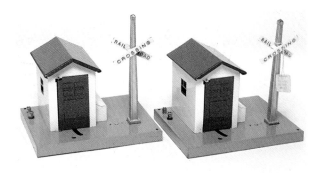

The 45N gateman on the left is a 1949 product; its crossbuck is in the low position and the house is painted a cream color. The 45N with the original price tag still intact is from the previous year, 1948. It is identical to the 1949 version, except that it is painted a bright white, not cream. Note the darker green color base which is particular to these two years of production. T. Rollo Collection, W. Kojis photograph.

aluminum with black lettering, although no such prewar examples showed up in our research. If these are genuine signs (they are, after all, easily switched from the 1045 flagman, which used the same post and sign), they are probably 1938 products. The aluminum and black warning sign did not show up on the 1045 flagman until 1947.

In 1939 the 76 warning bell and shack was introduced. This accessory had a die-cast crossbuck sign painted white with the word "CROSSING" in front of "RAILROAD" in black letters. The smooth feel of the paint on the sign fools many collectors into thinking the sign is made of Bakelite, but as far as is known all prewar and postwar examples are die cast in one piece. The fact that they are one-piece castings is important for another reason. The crossbucks were mounted on the poles by simply shoving the signs down on the poles until they would go no further. Until 1940 all such signs are found in one position, about half an inch down the pole. At that time, the 154 highway flasher and the 153 block signal were introduced — and these used poles of different thicknesses. Thus, after 1940 the crossbuck can be found in three different positions on the poles, depending upon their relative thicknesses; apparently Lionel used whatever poles were available. This is especially true of postwar pieces. In the high position, the sign is almost at the very top of the pole; we have found one example from 1946. In the low position, very common in 1949 which was the last year of production, the crossbuck is well over an inch and a half down the pole.

2. The Gateman's Shack: Colors Used

Over the life of the 045/45/45N gateman, the gateman's shack always had red window inserts divided into three small sections and one large section. The doors were painted

to match the color of the house, except for red doors, which seem to be most common in postwar pieces. The house itself was painted either a rich cream color (brownish-white) or a bright white. Since many white examples have become dulled through age and dirt, it is not always easy to tell the difference unless one sees a cream-painted house in excellent condition. The earliest examples in 1935-1936 were, as far as is known, all done in the cream color. In later years, it is likely that both colors were produced in the same year. The 1949 postwar houses appear to be mostly done in the cream color, though a few white ones have turned up. For a complete breakdown of the year-by-year paint schemes, see the listings at the end of this article. Without exception, the roofs on the pre- and postwar sheet metal gatemen were bright red. Prewar chimneys always matched the house color.

3. The Lionel Identification Labels and Stampings

The 045, 45, and 45N gatemen were identified in one of three ways. The earliest examples from the first four years of production had an embossed toolbox lid. In fact, the first two years had two kinds of identification: the embossed lid, and a number — 045 or 45, depending upon the track supplied — stamped in black ink on the underside of the base within the indentation holding the pole. Only in 1935 and 1936 did this stamping show serif numbers. On the first 1935 production examples, the numbering was very small in size. Other rubber-stamped examples show up in the very late prewar and most postwar examples. In some this takes the form of a rectangle stamped in black on the underside of the base. In other examples, the sans-serif number "45N" is stamped within the pole indentation. In well-used examples, these rubber stampings are nearly illegible. A third type of identification follows the pattern established on the 76 warning bell and shack and was probably used only in 1939 and 1940. This was a silver and blue water-release decal which was affixed to the toolbox lid. In the 1939 examples the numbers on this label were done in sans-serif style, but in 1940 (and perhaps later) these numbers had serifs.

Here are the two types of silver and blue water-release decals used on the 1939 and 1940 versions of the 45 gateman. They are somewhat hard to find in intact condition. The top version with sans-serif numbers comes from 1939, while the bottom version with serif type is from 1940. A careful study of these decals will reveal other, more subtle differences.

4. The Accessory Base

Nearly all the bases on the 045, 45, and 45N gatemen, whether pre- or postwar, are painted a yellow-green which has come to be known by collectors as "45N Green." The only variation of this occurs in the 1948 and 1949 production, when the green shade is distinctly darker and has far less of a yellow cast to it. There is a large chromed rivet next to the pole; in some examples this rivet is rounded and on others it is flat. Other than the presence or absence of the red acetate insert beneath the light bulb hole, there are no further significant differences in the bases.

5. The Gateman Figure

Two distinctly different types of gateman figures were used on the production of the 045, 45, and 45N gatemen. The earlier figure was used on examples made between 1935 and 1938. This early figure, somewhat crude by later standards, was molded of a composition material which has a grainy appearance and feel. The early figure had a large hat, a thin face, and a rather fancy paint scheme. Most often, the early figure is found with a flesh-painted face and flesh-painted hands. He often has a white shirt and a thin black tie under an old-fashioned high collar. He also has black shoes mounted on a black-painted base and is secured to the operating mechanism by means of a rivet. The back of this figure is solid with a slot accepting a separate arm piece. In this early figure, both arms are free to pivot.

In 1939 Lionel changed the figure, possibly because the earlier figure was too easily broken. This later figure would last throughout the remainder of the prewar and postwar run of the 45. Like its predecessor, this figure was secured to the operating mechanism by a rivet. However, that is where the similarity ends. The later gateman figure was made from a far less grainy composition material. As a result, this figure is much smoother in appearance and has a

This is the early version of the gateman figure. Note that both arms pivot; note also the thin face with highly detailed paint and the relatively rough surface of the casting, giving the figure a crude look.

This is the later figure used on the 45N gateman beginning in 1939, when the accessory underwent some minor design changes. Note the attached left arm and the swinging right arm when this figure is compared with the early model, pictured above. The more polished look is readily apparent. J. Kotil Collection.

more finished look. The later figure has a fuller face and a smaller hat than its predecessor. The flesh-colored hands and face are detailed as before. The figure's tie is wider and is sometimes painted white on a blue shirt. In other examples, both the shirt and the tie are blue. The back of this later figure is hollowed out, perhaps for ease of assembly. The most important difference is that the figure's left arm is part of the main casting, while its right arm is attached to the figure by a small drive pin. Thus, only the figure's right arm swings with the lantern. This made for better swinging action, since the older figure's arms would bind periodically. It is a more durable figure than its predecessor.

Now that the major critical variables of the 045, 45, and 45N automatic gatemen have been analyzed, we can proceed to a fairly complete year-by-year breakdown of the varieties and changes in this accessory. The following listings are not necessarily complete; we feel that there are more varieties to come, and we would appreciate reports from our readers.

THE POSTWAR 145 AUTOMATIC GATEMAN

In 1950 Lionel implemented an ambitious program to redesign nearly all of its accessory offerings. By the time the first 1950 catalogue was printed, it was obvious that Lionel was not standing still on its 50th Anniversary. Gone were all the prewar carry-over accessories made of sheet metal and compression-molded plastics. Lionel wanted to take ad-

This is the 145 automatic gateman, which was to change very little during its long production run. Note the reflection of the light bulb just behind the gateman figure, the fragile crossbuck, and the plastic door strips, which are often missing when the accessory is found today. J. Algozzini Collection.

vantage of new injection-molding technology which would allow the firm to turn out a product faster and more economically than before. In addition, Lionel introduced a raft of new accessories in 1950 to consolidate its lead in the toy train field. These redesigned or new accessories would allow Lionel to become the largest toy company in the world during the next five years, rightly known as the Golden Age of Toy Trains.

As part of these changes, the quaint 45N gateman disappeared from the Lionel lineup. It was replaced by a totally redesigned accessory with a new number — the 145 automatic gateman. The only surviving part from the old 45N was the return spring! Yet, if toy train enthusiasts would no longer hear the clank of a little metal door closing, they could not deny that the new 145 gateman had a charm of its own. Lionel had come up with another winner!

The 145 gateman's shack was situated upon a metal base painted the same darker green as its 1948-1949 45N predecessor, but there was no hidden light bulb beneath the base. Instead of a green-painted metal base bottom, the 145's base was an unpainted galvanized metal. The shack itself was no longer metal. Instead, it was a durable injection-molded piece in bright unpainted white; it was molded to look like old-fashioned clapboard siding, true to the archaic spirit of the gateman. (On real railroads, few gatemen were left by 1950.) As before, a toolbox on the outside of the shack hid the operating solenoid from view. The shack had a separately cast roof which lifted off to provide the owner with access to the wiring connections. The toolbox had a separately cast hinged roof which matched the shack roof only part of the time. Above the two-paneled plastic door was a red and gold sticker to give the gateman his proper home: "LIONEL-VILLE".

Frosted plastic window and door inserts gave a bright feel to the lighting, which was substantially changed. On the 45, the light only worked when the accessory was operated, and it only lit the lantern. For the 145, the lighting of the lantern was dropped in favor of constant lighting of the shack itself. This was an astute decision on Lionel's part.

With the shack constantly lighted, the toy train operator could, with a little imagination, visualize the gateman propping up a chair against the shack wall, reading a favorite magazine, until duty called him and he rushed unfailingly out of the shack with his lantern.

The electrical connections for the 145 gateman were quite different from those of its 45 predecessor, which had two thumbnuts built into one edge of the base. There were now three connections, one for the ground wire, one for the solenoid, and one for the lamp, and they were reached by lifting off the roof and connecting the wires to three large Fahnstock clips. The lamp, always a No. 431 large-globed clear bayonet-based 14-volt lamp, hung suspended into the shack by a strip of spring steel attached permanently to one of the clips. The wires could be routed into the shack by means of three small holes in the shack casting at the top rear. Lionel also created an alternative routing, to completely hide the wiring. It seems likely that Lionel created the alternative routing after devising its initial method, but we lack hard evidence to support this. A hollow column was molded into the shack casting in such a way that the wires could be brought straight up from the bottom of the accessory. The same shack without the lamp was used with a different base for the 125 whistle shack. (Indeed, every once in a while a shack with the lamp attachment would sneak onto a whistle shack.)

As a final touch, a small and rather fragile crossbuck on a thin pole was attached to the base by means of a die-cast sign base fastened with two small screws. Many of these signs are missing or broken when the 145 gateman is found today — perhaps the only unfortunate part of the design.

The human figure, of course, was still present. The figure used for the entire run of the 145 gateman was patterned after the later figure used on the 45N; like that figure, it was molded, but this time of injection-molded styrene instead of cellulose acetate. The hands and face were flesh-colored and still hand-painted for most of the production run. As before, only the right arm was free to pivot with the lantern; the left arm was part of the main casting.

Lionel often changed equipment in its first year or two of production. However, the gateman manufacturing process and gateman operation were apparently so satisfactory that Lionel made no changes in 1950 and 1951. The roof and toolshed lid were red in the first year, 1950, but after that the roof was always molded in maroon, even though the toolbox lid sometimes remained red. Like any efficient factory, Lionel used the parts on hand. Hence it is possible that some gatemen departed the factory with a roof of one color and a door of another. About 1952 Lionel made a small design change to the toolbox lid, giving it little plastic "ears" on its attachment arms where they fit into slots in the toolbox housing. This was done to prevent the toolbox lid from falling off the shack too easily.

The new gateman worked so well that there was little reason for Lionel to change it. The 145 used a sturdy rack and pinion system to open and close the door, eliminating the occasional jamming experienced with the old 45N when the metal door was bent. Lionel experienced a little trouble with the bottom of the door rubbing against the base in early 145 models, but the firm soon solved that problem by using a spacer washer between the door and the base. The gateman figure was attached to its base by a stronger nut and bolt system, making it less likely that the figure would become detached from the base, as it sometimes did with the peened rivet used in the 45N. The drive pin attaching the figure's right arm to the body was also strengthened, as was the drive pin holding the lantern to the hand. As a result, the system was seldom changed.

That very lack of change poses problems for collectors in dating the pieces. The best way to tell the exact date for the 145 gateman is through the date coding on the original boxes. Several different codes were used, but the most frequent code involved the year of manufacturing and a series of numbers on the outer rim of the test circle on the box. As each month went by, the number of that month was eliminated from the ink stamping used on the box. For example, if the year reads 1951 and the first number is 4, the box was made during the month immediately preceding that number, in that case 3, which would be March of 1951.

In 1958, when things had begun to go awry for Lionel, the firm introduced a 1047 crossing watchman accessory, essentially a gateman without the shack. This accessory was made with the same base as the 145 gateman, but with a cheapened green cardboard base bottom instead of a galvanized metal base. (Of course, the galvanized base had its own Achilles' heel. That base was tabbed onto the top part and, in time, the tabs would break once they were bent to allow access to the inside.) The change was just one more example of a general cheapening of the Lionel line as sales fell. The embossed legend on the galvanized base wore away completely during the accessory's first years of production, and Lionel did not bother to re-work the embossing tool. As a result, the 145 gatemen produced after about 1955 do not as a rule show embossed lettering on the underside of the galvanized base. In addition to that change, the gateman figure began to be issued without the charming hand-painted work of the past; instead, the figure was all blue, including the face and hands. The hand-painted figures would never return, even during the Fundimensions era.

The 145 gateman was probably last manufactured in 1966, although the accessory was certainly available right up to the end of production in 1969. We would like to hear from readers who possess late examples of the 145 gateman in the later all-orange Lionel boxes, the late boxes with cellophane windows, or (this would be a real surprise) the checkered Hagerstown boxes of 1968-1969.

LISTINGS

145 AUTOMATIC GATEMAN: 1950-66, white plastic clapboard-sided house on medium green-painted metal base, red and gold "LIONELVILLE" sticker atop door, small white plas-

Two examples of box codes used on the 145 gateman boxes. The left picture shows a 1950 box, month undetermined. The right picture shows a box made in January 1951. Note the intact row of numbers and the year below the seal. J. Algozzini Collection.

tic crossbuck warning sign with black lettering attached to main base with die-cast rectangular base secured by two small screws, red door, two windows with red plastic inserts, plastic window and door pieces, three Fahnstock clips for wiring hidden by detachable roof, lamp socket secured by spring steel strip, takes No. 431 large-globed bayonet-based clear lamp.
(A) 1950, galvanized base bottom, red roof and toolbox lid, blue-suited gateman figure with flesh-painted face and hands. J. Algozzini and L. Bohn Collections.
(B) 1951, same as (A), but maroon roof with red toolbox lid. G. Wilson, J. Algozzini, B. Greenberg, and G. Cole Collections.
(C) 1952-57, same as (B), but spacer washer added to door post at bottom, "ears" added to toolbox lid to prevent its falling out of shack structure, maroon or red toolbox lid. G. Wilson Collection.
(D) 1957-66, same as (C), but all-blue unpainted gateman figure. J. Kotil and G. Wilson Collections.

THE FUNDIMENSIONS SUCCESSOR: THE 2145 GATEMAN

When General Mills took over the train inventory of the Lionel Corporation in 1970, the vast stock of spare parts enabled the fledgling train company to assemble many accessories and package them under its own name, even though the pieces were essentially postwar era leftovers. That is precisely what happened to the automatic gateman in 1970 and 1971. The gateman is not pictured in the catalogues, but it certainly was available. Glenn Halverson reports that the accessory was listed under 2145 on the dealer order forms of 1970-1971. Several pieces identical to late postwar production have shown up in early Fundimensions Type I boxes.

By 1972 Fundimensions was ready to market its own version of the automatic gateman, numbering it 2145 to match its own numbering system. In most ways, the accessory produced from 1972 to 1984 was identical to its late postwar predecessor. It had the non-embossed galvanized metal base and the unpainted blue gateman figure. However, there were some noteworthy color changes. The bases for the accessory were painted a shade of pea green which is referred to by collectors as Penn Central green. This shade is not as glossy as the brighter green of postwar 145 units. The roof, window inserts, and door were changed to a shade of reddish-brown instead of the maroon of the postwar pieces. Fundimensions also returned to the 153C contactor; the postwar examples had been packed with the accessory's own two-pole 145C contactor.

From 1972 to 1978 the accessory was essentially unchanged except for its boxes. True to the economizing of its postwar predecessors, Fundimensions used the same shack structure for its ill-fated 2125 whistle shack of 1971, the later 2126 whistle shack, and the 2127 diesel horn shed. In 1979 there was one further minor change. The door, which had two large window openings, was subdivided with cross-hatching so that the two large window openings became twelve smaller windows in two groups of six. The accessory was made with this door until 1984. Its production finally ceased in 1985 after an uninterrupted fifty-year period of availability. In 1987 Lionel Trains, Inc., the successor to Fundimensions, revived the automatic gateman with a five-digit number (12713) and completely new colors — butternut yellow shack; bright red door, window, and roof; and light gray base. The following manufacturing changes were made to the accessory: green cardboard base rather than galvanized base, a cardboard insert was added to prevent light from bleeding through the walls, and a small doorstop bump added to metal base. The story of the automatic gateman had begun again!

LISTINGS

2145 AUTOMATIC GATEMAN: 1970-84; Penn Central green-painted metal base, unpainted galvanized metal base bottom, all-blue unpainted gateman figure, white shack structure, essentially similar to late postwar production except for colors.

(A) 1970-71, maroon roof and red or maroon toolbox lid, medium green-painted metal base; came in Type I early Fundimensions boxes. These are postwar carry-over pieces assembled and sold by Fundimensions. G. Halverson Collection.

(B) 1972, dark translucent maroon roof, door, and toolbox lid; dark flat green-painted base, came in Type II Fundimensions horizontal box with cellophane display window. Came with instruction sheet and 153C contactor packed in separate compartment above accessory.

(C) 1973-78, dark red-brown roof and toolbox lid; came in Type II square Fundimensions boxes without cellophane window, insert, and separate compartment. G. Wilson and R. LaVoie Collections.

(D) 1979-84, same as (C), but door window openings divided into twelve small windows instead of two large ones. Same changes made to 2126 whistle shack and 2127 diesel horn shed. R. LaVoie comments.

12713 AUTOMATIC GATEMAN: 1987-88, butternut yellow shack; bright red door, roof, and toolbox lid; light gray-painted metal base; all-light gray man. R. LaVoie Collection.

CONCLUSION

Each version of the Lionel automatic gateman, whatever its variety or age, seems to have special appeal. There is no mistaking the quaintness of the 045/45/45N versions, with their bright enamel and old-fashioned look. The 145 and 2145 versions are beautifully lighted and realistic with their clapboard appearance. The automatic gatemen are relatively trouble-free, even in the oldest versions. Significantly for the collector, it is not hard to build a substantial collection of these little gatemen because all of the versions are common and available at reasonable prices at any train show or shop, even brand new. The only really difficult version to secure is the 1935-1936 045/45 with the original large boxes.

However, the real marvel of the Lionel automatic gateman is that the accessory retained its brisk sales and attractiveness to the train-buying public for such a long time. Who can say why one small item in the perilously short-lived toy industry could last that long? Perhaps the answer is that the Lionel automatic gateman had a superlative concept and design in the first place — something to think about when toy manufacturers find themselves faced with the task of designing a new "Mr. Machine" every year to keep the public from getting bored with their product offerings. The Lionel automatic gateman is an authentic legend — and a great plaything, too.

FROM PERSIAN GODS TO SMOKING LOCOMOTIVES

LIONEL'S MINIATURE LAMPS — *Thomas S. Rollo*

Let the lamp affix its beam.
The only emperor is the emperor of ice-cream

— Wallace Stevens

In 1935, just as the Lionel Corporation was beginning to recover from the Great Depression, the company introduced a new and revolutionary trackside accessory, the 45/045 automatic gateman. Right away, the importance of the moving human figure made toy train history. A few years later, another human figure emerged with the production of the 1045 flagman. Amid Lionel's movement towards scale detailing, the Goliath size of the flagman would have made him more at home collecting pigeons on a park pedestal rather than at trackside. Still, he represented human action. Then a white-clad human figure climbed aboard Lionel's milk car in 1947, and the human figure became a fixture on the Lionel layout.

Collectors and operators alike have fond memories of these figures on their layouts. With similar fondness, they also remember the little smoke pellets, which had so much appeal that steam engines ran many more miles on tinplate track than did their counterparts on real trackage. But there was a third alluring feature of the "toy of toys" which made them irresistible, and little attention has been paid to the importance of this feature.

To identify that feature, go back to your childhood. (Perhaps, like many train buffs, you have never really left it!) Do you remember what fun it was to turn off all the lights in your train room, letting just the layout lighting illuminate the rail scene? Look at the lights in the locomotives, passenger coaches, houses, lamp posts, etc. Observe all the trackside warning devices, the bumpers and switches as they changed color; eerie red, green, and white glow reflecting off the tracks and the roads. Without question, the miniature light bulb was just as important as any human figure or smoke pellet. You noticed the importance of a miniature lamp only if it were suddenly absent — the electrical equivalent of the faithful family dog.

After all, what would a steam locomotive (or any engine) be without a headlight shining down the tracks? Lionel tried the production of locomotives without headlights in 1950 and quickly recognized its error. What would a sleek passenger train be with darkened windows, or a passenger station without elegant sconce lights on either side of its doors? The answer is: Nothing! Because of that, the toy train industry must rank among the largest consumers of miniature lamps, not to mention those used by scale modelers.

Lionel's use of miniature lamps was not always aesthetic. The lamps told operators when there was a short circuit, when the transformer was left plugged in, what position the switches were in, or when the rails of the transfer table or turntable were properly aligned.

The objective of this article is to explain the development of Lionel's use of miniature lamps through their nomenclature. This development will result in an analytical tool which will give the collector the ability to understand the chronology of lighted (or *illuminated*, to use Lionel's buzzword) accessories and rolling stock when other identifying factors may not be helpful. In time, light bulbs do burn out, and they may or may not be replaced with a bulb identical to the original. For that reason, the basis of this study is taken from pieces which are mint, like new, or excellent in condition. Logically, these pieces still would be equipped with their original lamps, since their condition would indicate that they have received little or no use.

Additional research and commentary by Bruce Stiles.
Photographs by Bill Kojis.

FIGURE 1: The two bulbs shown above are No. 63-11, but they are not prewar bulbs. The bulb on the right was made some time before 1950; the one on the left was made in 1952 or later. In 1960 the author wrote to the Lionel Service Department to purchase some heart-shaped bulbs for the bracket lights on the No. 115 station. Lionel replied that these bulbs, No. 40-3, were still in stock at 50 cents each. The No. 63-11 lamps were sent in error, but what is significant here is that even at this late date, Lionel continued to stock lamps manufactured before World War II.

THE LAMPS OF THE PREWAR ERA

To understand better what took place in the postwar era, we have to begin our study by looking over our shoulder at the prewar era to review briefly the development of Lionel's use of miniature lamps. Between 1920 and 1926 Lionel offered a total of nine different lamps, each given its own catalogue number. Descriptions were given for each lamp, including shape and size. On some lamps, the description changed from one year to the next. For example, in 1923 "globe" probably meant that the bulb was painted white rather than clear, since it was intended for use on lamp posts. In 1924 the same bulb was listed as "pear-shaped." During these years (1923-1927), Lionel offered its dealers a "No. 111 Lamp Cabinet" containing an assortment of 50 replacement lamps packaged in round, labeled wooden containers. (In the postwar era, the number 111 would be used for the elevated trestle set introduced in 1956.)

In 1927 the catalogue numbers of the replacement lamps were changed to 27, 28, 39, and 40. These numbers and lamps would remain part of Lionel's lamp offerings in some form all the way to 1969! In the case of the 39 and 40 lamps, leftover supplies would be used in the Fundimensions 2156 station platform as late as 1971.

It is unclear exactly why the catalogue numbers of these lamps changed in 1928, but it is likely that this was the first use of lamps manufactured by the General Electric Company. In the 1928 catalogue, the 111 lamp cabinet is shown in a cardboard box with each lamp packaged in a smaller car-

ton rather than a round wooden container, as before. This type of packaging would continue through 1952.

In 1929 the Nos. 27 and 28 lamps became available in red or green in addition to clear. The colored bulbs were denoted by suffix letters "R" and "G".

In 1931 a new lamp post was catalogued, the No. 53. The 53 was an Ives design originally catalogued as 305 and later catalogued as No. 1882 during Lionel's production of Ives. The replacement lamp for this accessory was not catalogued until 1932. Instead of assigning a unique catalogue number to this lamp, Lionel started something new in its lamp classification system. The catalogue number for the replacement lamp included the accessory number in this, the first bulb to use it, the No. 53-8 replacement bulb. This is the beginning of a lamp numbering system which would not change until the year 1953.

Originally, it was suspected that this numbering system had its origin with the practices of Ives. Further research has disproved this hypothesis. The Greenberg library contains a copy of an instruction booklet included with the Ives sets produced during this time. The Ives lamp numbering system simply uses the Lionel number with "19" in front of it; thus, Lionel's No. 40 lamp is Ives No. 1940, etc. From this time onward, each new lamp Lionel used would be assigned a catalogue number including the number of the first piece to use it.

In 1933 Lionel catalogued two more new lamp posts, Nos. 52 and 63. For these, Lionel had General Electric design a new lamp which was assigned the catalogue number 63-10. This was a large urn-shaped bulb which was a replica of a globe made by General Electric for city street lighting systems. The prototype bulb was sold under the trade name Novalite-Luminaire. General Electric used that trade name for a variety of incandescent street lamp globes, and the bulb made for Lionel was a dead-ringer for one of them. When one thinks about it, it is an amazing fact that General Electric produced a model of its own product for use by the Lionel Corporation! In 1935 the number of this bulb was changed to No. 63-11 for no apparent reason. Usually, a change in the suffix number indicated a change in voltage or color, but there is no evidence of that in this case.

New lamps were added as needed to the lamp replacement chart as Lionel introduced new products requiring different sizes, shapes, colors, or voltages. In 1939, with the introduction of the Trainmaster series of transformers, Lionel used the first bayonet-based lamp in its history. Taking its number from the first product off the drawing boards to use the lamp, the Type Q transformer, Lionel assigned the catalogue number Q-90 to the lamp. This was a 6- to 8-volt lamp; its operating voltage range betrays its intended use as an automotive lamp. (Most automobiles in those days used a 6-volt electrical system.) Lionel's decision to use a bayonet-based lamp can be attributed to the fact that transformers vibrate and a screw-based lamp would ultimately work its way loose in its socket. Prewar collectors know quite well what happens to screw-based lamps inside passenger cars; it is not unusual to pick up a prewar passenger car and find the bulb rattling around inside the car. Lionel's use of bayonet-based lamps would continue to grow. By 1950 this type of base would be dominant.

In 1939 other changes took place to make the cataloging system uniform. The original six lamps from 1927 were re-numbered to conform with the system begun in 1931 with the introduction of the No. 53 lamp post. The clear bulbs, Nos. 27 and 28, were assigned the suffix "-3" and so were the frosted, pear-shaped Nos. 39 and 40 bulbs. The 18-volt red lamp numbered 28R was re-designated 28-6. By now, so many different pieces used these lamps that going back to the first piece which used the lamp would have been confusing and a waste of time. The 28G green lamp was an exception to this, however. This bulb's number became 408-45, tracing its origin to the 408E Standard Gauge locomotive which used this green lamp in pairs as running lights on the front of the cab. The 12-volt red lamp numbered 27R was assigned a new number, 79-23, taking its number from the old 79 crossing signal.

THE MAZDA TRADEMARK

With the advent of World War II, General Electric changed the manufacture of all its light bulbs, miniature or otherwise, by dropping an ancient trademark which today is all but forgotten as an adjunct to lighting, but is perpetuated by an automobile — the trademark Mazda. In the prewar years, this trademark was used by General Electric, Westinghouse, and even Western Electric. Its presence on a light bulb always denotes the bulb as a prewar product.

The origin of the name Mazda is interesting and quite in keeping with American advertising traditions and naming. For example, Mercury, Neptune, Vulcan, Thor, and Hercules are American brandnames based on gods from mythology. Mazda can be traced back through General Electric's history to Thomas A. Edison himself. General Electric came into being as a result of the reorganization of Edison's consumer product interests and the trademark came with that reorganization. The name goes back to the ancient Persian religion of Zoroastrianism, organized in the sixth century B.C. by the prophet Zoroaster. The religion was characterized by worship of Ahura Mazda, God of Light. We expect that either

Edison or a member of his staff had heard of the god Mazda, since high school students of the nineteenth-century frequently studied mythology.

General Electric's lamps were marked "MAZDA" in the following manner: screw-based lamps were marked by embossing the "MAZDA" at the very top of the base. The 18-volt bulb on the extreme right in **Figure 2** is marked in this way. Sometimes the bead of solder connecting the lead to the base obscures part of the word, but some letters are always visible. The small colored lamp is rubber stamped; it reads "G.E. / MAZDA 51 / G-8V". This is the earliest known use of an industry standard number (51) appearing on a lamp base. Lionel never used the green version of this lamp, only its clear equivalent, the Q-90 of transformer fame. It is included here to illustrate the marking method. The type of coloring used on this lamp is also of interest. When General Electric colored the lamps, opaque colors were used. The presence of a translucent color on a lamp usually indicates that Lionel colored the lamps within its own plant. The other clear bulb in the photograph is of the same rating as the Mazda lamp, but is many years newer. In my research, I have yet to find a known postwar product equipped with a lamp marked "MAZDA". Most likely, Lionel continued to furnish replacement lamps to dealers, service stations, and customers throughout the war years, depleting whatever stock the company had on hand. The information about the deletion of the name Mazda after World War II came from a former neighbor of mine who was an executive at General Electric.

This now brings us to the postwar era and perhaps the most useful part of this study. The presence or absence of the Mazda trademark is one more factor — perhaps a decisive one — in making a definite separation between prewar carry-over pieces and true postwar production. The presence or absence of the trademark may answer such questions as whether any 165 cranes were produced after World War II or if the 137 station was made as well. The 137 station was included in the instruction booklet's lamp replacement chart through 1948, and this station was used on the 1948 showroom layout in the very center on the mountain division.

THE 1946 LAMP REPLACEMENT CHARTS

Between the years 1946 and 1949, Lionel discontinued furnishing a lamp replacement chart in the consumer catalogues, so we must turn our attention to the instruction booklets provided with train sets. In 1946 two different booklets were used. The earlier of the two had a two-tone blue cover — a dark blue field with lighter blue lettering. This early edition was nothing more than a reprint of the prewar 1940-1942 booklets, with certain key changes concerning the automatic merchandise car and the new knuckle couplers. The lamp replacement chart is on page 32 of this booklet; item for item, it is exactly the same as its prewar predecessors.

The newer 1946 edition of the instruction booklet is much more interesting because it was extensively revised. It has a dark green cover with orange lettering. The lamp replacement chart was still on page 32, but now it listed only those items produced since the resumption of production

FIGURE 2: General Electric placed the name "MAZDA" on each and every lamp the company made before World War II. This figure shows the methods of marking the lamps.

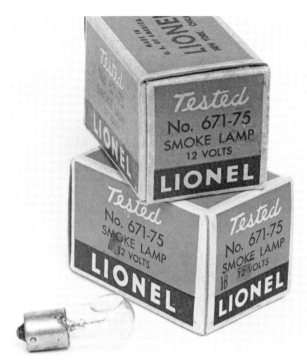

FIGURE 3: In 1947-1948 replacement charts listed only the 18-volt version of the smoke lamp. Both of these boxes have 18-volt lamps despite the number. These boxes date after mid-1949, since there is no San Francisco reference. The lower box has been re-marked to show an 18-volt lamp. After 1946 the company exhausted its lamp stocks, reprinting only one box and ignoring the lamp numbers. These lamps were purchased from a dealer in 1961.

after World War II. This is, of course, less than one calendar year. Needless to say, this chart lists far fewer pieces than the earlier edition, but what is revealing is the number of errors in this edition. The chart lists the 703 locomotive, which was never produced, as well as a 2626 Sager Place Madison-style observation car, which was never made. The other errors involve the accessories. The chart lists a 391 circuit breaker which was never produced. The 45N gateman is listed twice. One of the listings shows the accessory using a clear 12-volt lamp, No. 616-13. (Note the number — this bulb was first used on the Flying Yankee locomotive.) The other listing shows the 45N using a new lamp numbered 45-75. Late prewar versions of the 45N are equipped with a red acetate window in the accessory base; hence, these versions used a clear lamp. Early postwar versions omitted this acetate piece and thus used a red lamp numbered 154-18.

Roland LaVoie has advanced the theory that the presence of the mysterious 45-75 reference in the second 1946 lamp replacement chart may have indicated that Lionel was making an attempt to light the lantern in the 45N gateman's hand, rather than have the lantern lit from a concealed bulb below the base. For a full discussion of this hypothesis, see Linda Greenberg's article on the Lionel gateman on page 157.

This is a highly significant piece of information because it gives us our first glimpse of Lionel's manufacturing cycle. It is unknown what the 45-75 lamp was, or if it even existed, which is doubtful. The chart is telling us that the change in bulb was planned for, but had not taken place yet! New or

carry-over O27 items are listed correctly in the late 1946 lamp replacement chart, as well as unchanged accessories. However, items of O Gauge rolling stock to be included in O Gauge sets or otherwise designated as O Gauge pieces, as well as new or redesigned accessories, are listed incorrectly. Since this was the second edition of the instruction booklet, the conclusion is inescapable: O27 Gauge sets were already in production, but O Gauge sets and accessories were still in the planning stages. Therefore, Lionel began its manufacturing year by producing the better-selling O27 items and only then produced O Gauge items later in the year.

Further evidence of this manufacturing cycle exists elsewhere. In an early edition of the 1952 consumer catalogue, one page lists steam locomotives for separate sale. The steamers designated as O27 Gauge are all numbered correctly, as seen by the non-Magnetraction 2056, a renumbered 2046. The locomotives designated for O Gauge are another story. In this catalogue, the locomotive eventually marketed as a 671RR because of its loss of Magnetraction is numbered 670. Similarly, the 726RR is listed as 725 and the 675, which kept its original number, is listed as a 674. These proposed numbers had to have been dropped before production, indicating that this early catalogue came out after the O27 locomotives had gone into production, but before the O Gauge locomotives had been produced.

THE LIONEL SMOKE LAMPS

We cannot move on in this study without discussing Lionel's smoke lamps. These were the most significant lamps in Lionel's history, since they enabled the company to secure a competitive edge over other toy train manufacturers in 1946. Most likely, this was the last custom-designed lamp Lionel commissioned General Electric to produce.

In keeping with prewar tradition, two different lamps were produced: a 12-volt lamp, No. 671-75, and an 18-volt lamp, No. 703-10. In the prewar era Lionel equipped Standard Gauge items with 18-volt lamps, O27 items with 12-volt lamps, and O Gauge items with both. This was done to match the usual operating voltages for the particular equipment; Standard Gauge items used a great deal more current because of their size and weight. The year 1946 was the last year Lionel made a distinction between one set of rolling stock as O27 Gauge and another line as O Gauge, although certain pieces would be designated as O Gauge only in future years. The 12-volt version was intended for use in one of the new steamers to be equipped with the smoke feature, the 2020 and its O Gauge version, the 671. The 18-volt version of this bulb was assigned the number 703-10, taking its designation from the 703 Hudson which was never made. The fact that this lamp number has a suffix of 10 means that the 703 had developed through some level of planning before it was abandoned; possibly, a prototype was made. In any event, the 703-10 lamp was used in the 1946 version of the 726 Berkshire locomotive. When Lionel's lamp designation numbers changed in 1953, these bulbs, still available, changed part numbers. The 671-75 lamp became the 797-300, while the 703-10 lamp became the 799-300.

Production of this lamp required extremely close coordination between Lionel and General Electric. The lamp is held in the smoke chamber by a clip with two notches at the rear-most end. These notches hold the tabs on either side of the lamp base. The notches are so positioned that when the clip is inserted into the smoke chamber, the tabs on the lamp base are about three degrees off horizontal. With the lamp base in this position, the smoke pellet cup in the glass bulb is positioned straight up. This meant that the bulb had to be cemented onto the base in exactly the right position when it was manufactured. Standard miniature lamps, as well as regular 120-volt lamps for home use, have bases with glass bulbs which are cemented in place anywhere. However, multiple-filament automotive bulbs equipped with large bayonet bases and optical projection lamps are manufactured to the same exacting specifications as the Lionel smoke bulbs. These bulbs are similar to the Lionel bulbs in overall size as well. My hypothesis is that once Lionel's engineers decided that a light bulb was required to melt the smoke pellet, they submitted their requirements to General Electric. That firm came back to Lionel with its design, saying to Lionel that if General Electric were to produce this lamp, these would be its mandatory specifications. In turn, Lionel's engineers designed a lamp housing to fit General Electric's specifications. This sounds like a classic case of the tail wagging the dog! Nonetheless, it also illustrates Lionel's determination to be in first place in the world of toy trains.

LAMP REPLACEMENT CHARTS: 1947 AND BEYOND

In 1947 the lamp replacement chart was error-free. However, there was one glaring (or should we say glowing?) error in the 1948 chart. This was the entry for the 2026 steam locomotive, which was new that year. The chart shows the locomotive using lamp No. 151-51, which was introduced the year before in the 151 semaphore. For this locomotive, Lionel actually chose a new lamp and assigned it the number 2026-58. Once again, it was a bayonet-based lamp designed for 18 volts. The manufacturer's number was 1445. This lamp has been the all-time favorite among collectors and operators since its introduction, since regardless of the equipment, the lamp's higher voltage rating allows it to burn

FIGURE 4: The lamps in this photograph are all examples of Lionel's lamp No. 315-20. The lamp at right was taken from a 245 caboose made in 1947. The second lamp from the right comes from a 1948 2357 caboose. The third lamp from the right comes from a 1950 132 station. The lamp at left is a replacement lamp from a 1952 122 lamp assortment set.

FIGURE 5: Top lid of No. 122 lamp assortment of 1952.

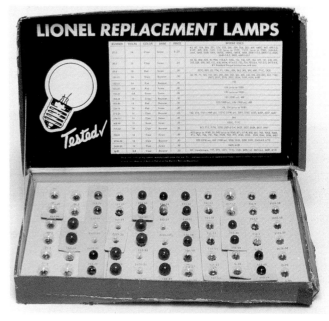

FIGURE 6: This is the No. 122 lamp assortment set of 1952, which contains sixty-six randomly assorted lamps. Note that overlays have been added to the cardboard liner to indicate changes in bulbs. If the overlays are removed, the lamp configuration would have been the same as the 1949 assortment found in the Bruce Stiles example of this set.

cooler at lower voltages. For this reason, damage in the form of warped or melted plastic is unlikely.

In 1949 Lionel had finally caught up to its own lamp usage. The listings in the lamp replacement chart were all correct. There was, however, one new twist — lamps formerly shown as 12-volt lamps, were listed in this chart as 12-to 14-volt lamps. This reflected a change made by General Electric in lamp designation, but there were no changes in the lamps themselves.

By 1950 Lionel referred to the 315-20 lamp as a 14-volt lamp. As can be seen in **Figure 4**, prior to 1949 General Electric designated the same lamp as a 12-volt lamp. This is significant because pieces produced prior to 1950 use what were known as 12-volt lamps, and the lamps found with the pieces will be marked accordingly.

The year 1950 was a turning point for the Lionel Corporation. Gradually, the company's use of bayonet-based bulbs consumer could substitute a 14-volt 154-18 lamp for the red lamp and a 616-13 clear lamp for the green lamp; this bulb, suggested the manual, could be painted with green nail polish. I cannot help but wonder how many women were wearing green nail polish (and perhaps matching green lipstick) in the late 1940s or early 1950! The fellow who wrote that note in the Service Manual must have moved around in some strange social circles!

The lamp replacement chart returned to the consumer catalogue in 1950. The list included lamps for currently available pieces, as well as those recently discontinued. One piece listed which was never mass produced was the 4681 electronic control Pennsylvania S-2 turbine with Magnetraction. Only one of these locomotives is known to exist, but the number of that locomotive remained in the catalogues' lamp replacement charts through 1953. There were no changes to note in 1951; production was being scaled down because of the Korean War.

The 1952 catalogue listed four new accessories: the 445 switch tower, the 450 signal bridge, the 356 operating freight station, and the 157 illuminated station platform. From a study of Lionel's instruction sheets, it is evident that as a general rule accessories which were new in a given year were not manufactured until late in the manufacturing cycle. In fact, production of the 445 switch tower did not begin until early in 1953. This fact is stated in the Service Manual and can be verified by the first-run box dated February 1953 and the instruction sheet dated January 1953. This instruction sheet, No. 445-55, neglected to show lamp replacement information which by now had become commonplace. The same was true of the 356 and 450, both of which had instruction sheets dated October 1952.

However, the 157 station platform was somewhat different. No instruction sheet was furnished with this accessory. Instead, the instructions (such as they were) and the lamp replacement information were engraved into the die core which forms the inside of the station base. (The predecessor 156 station platform was also done this way.) The lamp replacement information read: "Use Only General Electric No. 51 6-8 Volt Lamp For Replacement." This is one of the few times Lionel used another vendor's name on one of their products. (Two other occurrences come to mind: in the Service Manual's instructions for repair of smoke units, Lionel recommends Saureisen Electrical Cement to glue the smoke unit cap into place, and a 1925-1927 lubricating instruction folder, which recommends 3-N-1 Oil.)

From these four accessories, it is clear that a change in Lionel's light bulb system was imminent. That change came about in January 1953. The instruction sheet for the 2343 "Lionel Twin Diesels For O Gauge Track," Form 2343-60, listed the replacement lamp for this locomotive as "Lionel No. 2026-58 (General Electric 1445)." By March 1953 the conversion of Lionel's bulb numbering system was complete. A page in Lionel's Service Manual dated March 1953 contains the following information: "To improve the availability of replacement lamps for Lionel equipment and to reduce their price whenever possible, Lionel has standardized its lamps with the general lamp industry. The lamps will be packaged in standard packing of 10 lamps. The new prices and stock numbers under which Lionel Replacement Lamps will be billed appear below. Key to Stock Numbers: The

number before the dash is the industry number which appears on the base of the lamp. The last figure indicates color. 0-clear; 1-red, 2-green, 3-white, 4-yellow."

The instruction sheets, of course, followed suit. The one for the 260 bumper (Form 260-11) stated the replacement lamp as L363. The new designation simply used the manufacturer's number preceded by the letter "L". The manufacturer's number also included the suffix letters "R", "G", and "W", indicating red, green, or white. The reason for the change will be dealt with in the discussion of the lamp assortments. The old numbering system was, in Lionel's own words, a "catalogue number." This number was derived using the part numbering system used with other component parts and listed with them in the Service Manual. The new lamp part numbering system used the manufacturer's number without the "L" prefix followed by a three-digit suffix which, as shown above, indicated the color of the bulb. This is the numbering system used by Fundimensions and Kenner-Parker, and currently by Lionel Trains, Inc.

Lionel was taking a bit of a risk by exposing the manufacturer's number, since dealers and the public alike could now go directly to lamp makers or distributors, bypassing Lionel. However, it is probable that the sale of replacement light bulbs did not form much of the profit margin for Lionel; more likely, the bulbs were regarded as a service to the consumer rather than a large profit source.

General Electric packaged lamps specially designed for Lionel for direct sale, as is evidenced by the 797 and 799 smoke lamps in General Electric boxes in the Bruce Stiles Collection.

In 1953 the company introduced two new lamps which would ultimately dominate the product line. These were the No. 53 and No. 57 lamps, small and large globes, respectively. The two new lamps were both rated at 12 to 16 volts. Right there, the intended use of these bulbs becomes obvious. They were designed for use by the automotive industry to satisfy the impending conversion of cars from a 6-volt operating system to a 12-volt one. This conversion was complete by 1955. There were a number of advantages for Lionel in deciding to use these lamps. First, with the automotive industry using these lamps, the manufactured quantity would be large enough so that price and availability would be favorable. Second, both lamps consumed less current than did their predecessors; the No. 53 was rated at .1 amp and the No. 57 at .2 amp.

Gradually, the 53 lamp worked its way into the product line, replacing the 363 (151-51). The 57 lamp was used to replace the 431 (315-20) to some extent and to replace totally the 1456 (717-54). After the conversion, the 1456 was listed only in the Service Manual, not the replacement charts. The pieces using this lamp were transferred to the No. 57 in the consumer lamp replacement charts. By 1954 the 363R (153-50) and the 363G (153-48) were replaced by 53R and 53G lamps, respectively. The first year's production of the 140 banjo signal, new in 1954, used the new 53R lamp. The first year's production of this accessory can be verified by the instruction sheet dated August 1954, Form 140-58. Subsequent production used a generic instruction sheet, Form 145C-51S or 145C-56, entitled "Accessories Operated By 145C Contactor." Lionel used up the remainder of the 363R and G lamps in the 450 signal bridge and the related 450L signal light head. This signal bridge and extra light head turn up more often with the 363R and G lamps. The pieces added to the author's collection in 1954 were so equipped.

In 1955, for the first time, Lionel offered the O27 1122E remote-control switches separately as 1122RH or 1122LH. Before this time, they had only been sold in pairs equipped with a twin switch controller, 1122-100. For the separate sale, the company used the 022C single controller. This posed a problem. The 1122E was designed so that the lamp in the twin controller was wired in series with the switch motor. The low current rating of the No. 53 lamp inside that controller had no effect upon the switch motor. The large 18-volt red and green lamps normally supplied with the 022C controller, No. 432R (28-6) and No. 432G (408-45), passed enough current so that their use would either cause the 1122E switch to buzz constantly or, worse, operate unexpectedly. To solve this problem, Lionel introduced a new lamp, No. 52. This was likely the last standard miniature screw-based lamp the company requested from a manufacturer. Electrically, the lamp was the same as the No. 53. For the red and green effect, the fluted caps used on the ZW transformer and elsewhere fit the openings in the 022C shell perfectly.

The importance of this fact for the present-day train operator is significant. Today, perfectly usable 1122E switches turn up inexpensively, but the controllers are broken, missing, or corroded. The 1121-100 and 1122-100 controllers are ancient and difficult to find, but 022C controllers are available from many sources, including the current Lionel division. Additionally, Lionel's Service Manual never explained this use of the No. 52 light bulb — never! The bulb was completely overlooked in the text of the Service Manual, the 1122E instruction sheets, and the lamp replacement charts. The No. 52 lamp was finally listed in the consumer catalogues in 1956 — but the listing was wrong! The listing gave the number 1122-100, the number of the twin controller. By 1957 Lionel finally corrected the listing.

In 1956 Lionel began the use of pin-based lamps for the first time. The first use of the pin-based lamps was in the No. 253 block signal with its "train-stopper" feature. (Actually, the train-stopping feature had been transferred from the No. 132 station, last catalogued the year before.) The first year's production used 6-volt lamps Nos. 12R and 12G and a resistor to permit operation at higher voltages. Subsequent production of the 253 used 14-volt pin-based lamps and the resistor was dropped. The lamp replacement charts in the Service Manual were never revised to reflect this change, but the changes made on the listings inside the lamp assortments were revised. The pin-based lamps streamlined production for Lionel a bit further, since they had only to be pushed into the very fragile sockets. The lamps themselves were much cheaper to make, as was the 253 itself, being made almost entirely of plastic. It was the mid-1950s, and the quality which had been Lionel's hallmark was waning as profits diminished. This is one example of that decline.

In the 1956 catalogue, the old pre-1953 "part number" type of catalogue reference returned, now shown in parentheses next to the corresponding "L" number. Often, the 1953, 1954, and 1955 catalogues turn up where someone has penciled in the old numbers. The most noteworthy addition, however, was at the top of the catalogue's lamp replacement chart. For the first time since 1928, a replacement lamp assortment was catalogued.

In 1957 the only notable change was the further inroads made by the new pin-based bulbs. This time, these bulbs made their way to a top-of-the-line item, the 746 Norfolk and Western Class J steam locomotive.

Prior to 1958, flashing lights were produced by separate bi-metallic blinker units or, in the case of the 154 crossing signal, a clever split-contact track contactor. With the introduction of the 52 firefighting car, a neat motorized bump-reverse unit, and the 199 microwave relay tower, that situation changed. Now the bi-metallic strip was actually part of the lamp itself. (The 52 used the bayonet-based No. 257, which Lionel termed optional, suggesting that the use of the No. 57 lamp in the flash unit was not desirable.) The 199 microwave relay tower used a tubular lamp, No. 402, which had no base at all! The bulb and the pigtail wires on its bottom were held in place by a peculiar-looking convex gasket. This is ironic because the handwork necessary to replace this lamp is very awkward, and this was part of the assembly process at the factory.

One of the most coveted pieces of the postwar era was brought out in 1958: the 6557 smoking caboose. This piece used a special lamp, Lionel's No. L55. The lamp is rated at 7 volts and, like many others the company used, was an automotive lamp. In fact, this lamp can be found lighting glove compartments and dome lights in General Motors cars of the 1940s and early 1950s. In this caboose, the lamp was wired in series with the smoke generator. This meant that the smoke generator was also rated at about 7 volts. The lamp and the smoke generator acted as ballast for one another. If any other lamp was used, the electrical series might be thrown sufficiently out of balance to damage the smoke generator permanently. Lionel issued warnings about this fact, and the company really meant business! Since this was the one and only application of the No. 55 lamp in Lionel's product line, finding the lamp might be very difficult at hobby retailers or swap meets. However, automotive dealers who specialize in parts for older cars will have plenty of these lamps.

In 1959 Lionel produced the 1862 and 1882 General locomotives. Because of the physical constraints of the box headlight on these locomotives, Lionel used a midget flange-based light, No. 191. This lamp had been used earlier in Lionel's HO Gauge line, and this was its first and only application to the O Gauge products.

The year 1960 was the last year a replacement lamp assortment was catalogued; it was also the last year the pre-1953 "old catalogue" number appeared in parentheses on the lamp replacement charts. One interesting footnote: there in the 1960 consumer catalogue, next to the lamp numbered L432G, was the old number 408-45, derived from the lamp's first application as a running light for the majestic 408E Standard Gauge locomotive of the 1920s. A remnant, a faint glimmer, of Lionel's past glory made it into the 1960s!

Between 1961 and 1969 no new miniature lamps were issued. The lamp replacement charts contained only reruns or adaptations of previously manufactured items. The catalogue continued to carry a list of replacement lamps through to the end of the postwar era in 1969.

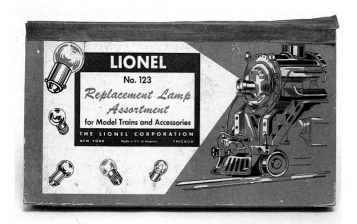

FIGURE 7: Top lid of the No. 123 replacement lamp assortment set.

FIGURE 9: This is the No. 123 lamp assortment set of 1958. This assortment contained eighty lamps in eighteen varieties.

FIGURE 8: This is the No. 123 lamp assortment set from 1955. The new "L" lamp numbers are in place, as well as the new lamp coloring. This assortment contains ninety-two lamps in eleven varieties.

which had no base at all! The bulb and the pigtail wires on its bottom were held in place by a peculiar-looking convex gasket. This is ironic because the handwork necessary to replace this lamp is very awkward, and this was part of the assembly process at the factory.

One of the most coveted pieces of the postwar era was brought out in 1958: the 6557 smoking caboose. This piece used a special lamp, Lionel's No. L55. The lamp is rated at 7 volts and, like many others the company used, was an automotive lamp. In fact, this lamp can be found lighting glove compartments and dome lights in General Motors cars of the 1940s and early 1950s. In this caboose, the lamp was wired in series with the smoke generator. This meant that the smoke generator was also rated at about 7 volts. The lamp and the smoke generator acted as ballast for one another. If any other lamp was used, the electrical series might be thrown sufficiently out of balance to damage the smoke generator permanently. Lionel issued warnings about this fact, and the company really meant business! Since this was the

FIGURE 10: This shows two other boxes of replacement lamps. The large boxes on either side contain a dozen 153-48 14-volt green lamps each. The box in the center has ten L-19 pin-based lamps, offered in 1957 or later.

one and only application of the No. 55 lamp in Lionel's product line, finding the lamp might be very difficult at hobby retailers or swap meets. However, automotive dealers who specialize in parts for older cars will have plenty of these lamps.

In 1959 Lionel produced the 1862 and 1882 General locomotives. Because of the physical constraints of the box headlight on these locomotives, Lionel used a midget flange-based light, No. 191. This lamp had been used earlier in Lionel's HO Gauge line, and this was its first and only application to the O Gauge products.

The year 1960 was the last year a replacement lamp assortment was catalogued; it was also the last year the pre-1953 "old catalogue" number appeared in parentheses on the lamp replacement charts. One interesting footnote: there in the 1960 consumer catalogue, next to the lamp numbered L432G, was the old number 408-45, derived from the lamp's first application as a running light for the majestic 408E Standard Gauge locomotive of the 1920s. A remnant, a faint glimmer, of Lionel's past glory made it into the 1960s!

Between 1961 and 1969 no new miniature lamps were issued. The lamp replacement charts contained only reruns or adaptations of previously manufactured items. The catalogue continued to carry a list of replacement lamps through to the end of the postwar era in 1969.

LAMP ASSORTMENT SETS

Lionel last catalogued the No. 111 lamp renewal cabinet in 1931. At that time, the illustration in the consumer catalogue showed a large cardboard box with a hinged lid containing lamps packaged in smaller boxes. At this point in the research, the first evidence of another replacement lamp assortment does not come until seventeen years later, in 1948. In Volume VI of McComas and Tuohy's *Lionel: A Collector's Guide and History*, a page from a dealer folder is shown on page 135 which advertises a dealer display No. 10M. From the listing of the train sets and the early 397 coal loader in the foreground of the display (a mock-up or prototype showing a light-colored generator housing and the No. 70 yard light), the year can be easily identified as 1948. The same coal loader was used for the illustration in the 1948 consumer catalogue. The No. 122 lamp assortment set is shown at the lower left corner; it is packaged in the same manner as the version in the 1931 catalogue. The design of the box has changed from the prewar "picture" box to the familiar orange and blue design.

In 1949 the individual boxes within the No. 122 lamp assortment set were eliminated; they were replaced by a solid sheet of yellow cardboard with pointed holes punched into it to hold 66 lamps. Bruce Stiles owns an example of this 1949 lamp assortment; he has determined the methods for dating the sets precisely. The following procedure can be used to zero in on the exact year:

(1) Scan the catalogue numbers on the box lid, noting the years when the pieces were introduced. In Bruce's example, he notes the 6420 work caboose as having been introduced in 1949.

(2) Next, check for specific numbers of pieces introduced in the following year: the 455 oil derrick, the 2330 dual-motored GG-1, the 773 Hudson, etc. If these numbers are absent, the 1950 product line had not been created.

The listing of lamps in the Stiles assortment makes his particular set datable to 1949. The February 1950 edition of the instruction sheet for the 154 crossing signal (Form 154-20) listed the replacement lamps as 153-50. These were the new bayonet-based lamps. The assortment in the Stiles example does not include this lamp number at all.

Figures 5 through **9** are examples of lamp assortments produced between 1952 and 1958. All were purchased from the original dealers between 1956 and 1959. The story of the acquisition of these pieces is of some interest. In 1955 the author's family moved to Wheaton, Illinois where the population at that time was 20,000. There were four Lionel dealers in Wheaton in 1955, and in neighboring Glen Ellyn (population 13,000) there were another two. Six dealers for a total population base of 33,000 people! Only one of these was an approved Lionel Service Station. In 1955 Lionel dropped the fair trade pricing from its catalogues because of adverse court decisions and lost its battle against discount retailers. After only one year of discounting, one by one, every Lionel dealer sold out his stock in 1956, often at up to forty percent off the list prices. By 1959 the Service Station in Glen Ellyn was the only Lionel dealer left.

After all the trains were sold out of the five stores going out of business, you can imagine what was left — No. 40 reels of hook-up wire, SP smoke pellets, greasy tubes of 925 lubricant — and the lamp assortments. I bought the lamp assortments because I found them to be extremely educational. At the age of twelve, it was hard for me to identify all of the catalogue numbers inside the lids. The No. 122 lamp assortment shown in **Figures 5** and **6** was complete. The dealer was glad to get rid of it! He said that the 2420 bulbs (the small bulbs used in the work caboose searchlights) were "dead stock." Some lamps had been sold out of the two 123 lamp assortments shown in **Figures 7**, **8**, and **9**, but over the years I have replaced them with the correct bulbs. It is interesting to note that the years when these dealers were selling out were the very years directly related to the decreasing availability of Lionel products. The blue or red tape on the outside box cover hinge has been added. Unfortunately, the boxes have become a little tattered over the years, having survived five changes of address.

Two of the more common lamps in the 122 lamp assortment set can be seen in **Figure 6**. The large red 152-33 (431R) lamp was used only on the now discontinued 152 crossing gate. There are eight of these bulbs in the assortment. Similarly, there are eight 2420-20 (1402) pea bulbs used in the 2420 and 6420 work cabooses, also discontinued items in 1952. Why so many of these bulbs if the items were discontinued? This lamp assortment set was prepared in the last year of the old numbers and the old transparent lamp coloring. Using the logic outlined by Bruce Stiles, I have been able to pinpoint the year as 1952. The 57 station platform and the 2345 Western Pacific locomotive are not listed, since they were brought out in 1953. My hypothesis is that this oddball assortment was used to get rid of what Lionel overstocked.

The red and green lamps in the No. 123 pictured in **Figure 8** show the new translucent coloring (which is sometimes erroneously referred to as "opaque"). Once again, the date is determined by the lamp chart. The new No. 415 diesel fueling station is listed, as is the No. 155 ringing highway signal. However, the numbers for the lighted 628 and 629 44-ton center-cab diesel switchers, as well as the 2341 Jersey Central Fairbanks-Morse, are absent.

By 1958 pin-based lamps were part of Lionel's lamp offerings; they came in 6- or 14-volt versions in red, green, or clear. This added six different lamps. The presence of these six lamps designates this assortment as a 1958 product.

The green lamps in the large boxes shown in **Figure 10** (153-48) were not introduced until 1950, when the lamps changed from screw to bayonet base in the 153 block signal. After 1952 this lamp became the L363G, which was superceded by the L53G in 1954. In all of this author's years of research, he has yet to find boxes such as that in the center with old lamp numbers (such as 153-48) on them. The physical design of the center box in **Figure 10** is intended to be compatible with automatic packaging equipment and has the same overall dimensions as those used by General Electric when the lamps are sold by that company. The only difference in the boxes would be the colors, which in General Electric's case would be the familiar yellow and blue.

The preceding observations have led me to an interesting hypothesis. Prior to 1953, Lionel colored and packaged the lamps themselves. The transparent film on Lionel's older colored bulbs is sometimes very pale and sometimes very intense; it is not very consistent. General Electric did use this type of coloring for some miniature lamps used in non-train related toys, but when General Electric did the lamp coloring, it was always consistent.

The translucent colors were consistent with those found on General Electric's Type C-6 series-burning, 15-volt bulbs used on Christmas tree lamps produced during that time. The white lamps, however, were in fact painted by General Electric. The white paint matches that found on General Electric's "G" ball-shaped standard lamps, some of which are produced to this day under the trade name "Flair."

Beginning in 1953 Lionel furnished General Electric with empty boxes, and General Electric did the packaging.

This would explain the change in the numbering system, regardless of what Lionel said in its Service Manual. Numbers such as 153-23, Q-90, etc., were meaningless to General Electric. However, 1445, 57, 53R, and other numbers with an "L" in front of the number identified the bulbs as Lionel's, but they also told the lamp manufacturer what went where. We can further hypothesize that Lionel's Service Manual claim was right in its statement about cost reduction because having General Electric do the packaging freed employees for other, perhaps more important duties. It is important to remember that Lionel's peak years in volume were 1952 and 1953.

There is one other point worth mentioning. The lamp assortments offered after 1952 included less variety than Lionel was actually using at the time the products were manufactured. The 123 lamp assortments of 1955 and 1958, for instance, do not include the L431 (315-20) lamp, even though this lamp was used in all versions of the SP and N5C cabooses. The lamp replacement charts in both No. 123 assortments state that the L57 lamp "may be used in place of the L431 lamp in the following"; then the chart lists numbers. Miniature lamps tend to be components of more types of finished products than are other standard lamps; in other words, they have more potential applications. Therefore, companies using miniature lamps may order great quantities of one type of lamp so that they are in place at the time production begins on the many products which use them. This means that Lionel had to compete with other users, such as automotive companies, for these miniature lamps as raw materials. Therefore, Lionel ordered and acquired in bulk. The lamp assortments, however, could be sorted and packaged at a more leisurely pace when the right quantity of suitable lamps was available at the best price.

The "little things" of toy trains...what stories they can tell us about the trains we all know and cherish! Who would have guessed that an examination of a plain, mundane light bulb could tell us a great deal about Lionel's manufacturing and production cycles, for example? Think about that the next time you plug in your transformer and your street lights glow softly. Better yet...check the lamps in your accessories and rolling stock. They may have great stories to tell you!

S. A. M. A. T.

LIONEL SPACE AND MILITARY ACTION TRAINS — *Gordon L. Wilson*

Hong Kong Fly-Apart! Cheap plastic! Rinky-dink trash! Garbage! Scrap heap rejects! Which derogatory term did you use to describe the Lionel movement into the Space Age? Regardless of what you said or thought, one fact is very clear: Lionel's military rockets got further off the ground than some of the early real rockets at Cape Canaveral. The variety of gadgetry was endless. It included everything from a pencil sharpener to a two-stage rocket that actually worked.

From hauling rockets to launching helicopters, Lionel's space and military action toys added a new twist to the company's traditional line of realistic toy trains. The 6175 shown here carries a chunky missile.

Many of the items produced, if used by the real railroads, would today result in massive marches and protest rallies. For instance, how would you respond to a flatcar going through your town carrying radioactive waste material, flaunting that fact by having viewing windows so you could watch the fission process? Many a Lionel layout was certainly contaminated for all time by the 6805 flatcar with radioactive waste disposal canisters. Or how about a boxcar full of highly volatile explosives parked on a siding near your home? Nervous breakdown time, huh?

Conversely, Lionel engineers did manage to manufacture a few railroad military items which were reasonably close to believable. The uncatalogued 6651 "Big Bertha" cannon car was similar to the German World Wars I and II weapons of the same name. It also resembled the U. S. Army's "Atomic Cannon" of the 1950s. The United States military did transport many military vehicles from place to place via the rails during World War II. The 6800 series military flatcars did likewise. In the San Diego area, the U. S.

Navy transported their "mini-subs" on flatcars, and in northern New Jersey, near Dover, prototypes like the 42 switcher really cavorted around the Picatinny Arsenal. However, it is hard to imagine real helicopters being launched from flatcars and boxcars.

Why did a quality toy train company deviate from the standard line of relatively realistic toys to inexpensive plastic gadgetry? There is probably no single answer, but rather many contributing factors, not the least of which is the date

---

EXCLUSIVELY MILITARY POWER UNITS

41	U S Army turbine switcher — black / white, 2-4-2
42	Picatinny Arsenal turbine switcher — olive / white, 2-4-2
44	U S Army mobile missile launcher — blue / white
45	U S Marine Corps mobile missile launcher — olive / white
51	U S Navy turbine switcher — blue / white, 2-4-2
52	Fire car — red / white, 0-4-0, automatic reverse
57	A E C turbine switcher — white / red, 2-4-2
59	U S Air Force Minuteman turbine switcher — white / blue-red, 2-4-2
203	Armored locomotive — gray or olive drab, rotating two-gun turret, 1917-21, 0-4-0
212	U S M C Alco diesel — royal / white
221	U S M C Alco diesel — olive / white
221	Santa Fe Alco diesel — olive / white
224	U S Navy Alco diesel and dummy B unit — blue / white
229	M & St. L Alco diesel A unit — olive (rare) pre-production sample
240	Locomotive — Scout-type 2-4-2 with smoke, black plastic; special Sears item
1625	Switcher — die-cast 0-4-0, black

MILITARY / SPACE SETS

YEAR(S)	SET(S)	COMPONENTS
1917-1918	213, 214, 215	
1919-1921	214, 215	
1958	1595	"Marine Battlefront Special": 1625LT, 6804, 6808, 6806, 6017 (gray)
	1591	"U S Marine Land and Sea Limited": 212, 6809, 6807, 6803, 6017-50
	2505W	Super O Virginian Rectifier Freight: 2329, 6805, 6519, 6800, 6464-500, 6357
1959	2717W	Super O Rio Grande Diesel Freight: 2379 A & B, 6519, 6805, 6800, 6434, 6657
	1625WS	2037LTS, 6636, 3512, 6470, 6650, 6017
	2527	44, 3419, 6844, 6823, 6814, 943
	2545WS	"Space Freight": 746LTS, 175, 6175, 6470, 3419, 6650, 3540, 6517
1960	1629	225, 6650, 6470, 6819, 6219
	1633	"Land-Sea-Air": 224 AB, 6544, 6830, 6820, 6017-200
	1805	"Land-Sea-Air": 45, 3429, 3820, 6640, 6824
	2527	44, 3419, 6844, 6823, 6814, 943
	2549W	2349, 3540, 6470, 6819, 6650, 3535
1961	1643	230, 3509, 6050, 6175, 6058
	1647	"Freedom Fighter": 45, 3665 3519, 6830, 6448, 6814
	1650	"Guardian": 2037LTS, 6544, 6470, 3330, 3419, 6017
	2572	"Space Age": 2359, 6544, 3830, 6448, 3519, 3535
	2574	"Defender": 2383 AA, 3665, 3419, 448 w/ 6448, 3830, 6437, 943
1962	11212	"Cyclone": 633, 3349, 6825, 6057
	11232	"New Haven": 232, 3410, 6062, 6413, 6057-50
	11252	"Texas Special": 211 AA, 3509, 6448, 3349, 6463, 6057
	11268	"C & O": 2365, 3619, 3470, 3349, 6501, 6017
	11288	"Orbitor": 229 AB, 3413, 6512, 6413, 6463, 6059
	11298	"Vigilant"": 2037LTS, 3419, 6544, 6448, 3330, 6017
	12512	"Enforcer": 45, 3413, 3619, 3470, 3349, 6017
	13008	"Champion": 637LTS, 3349, 6448, 6501, 6119
	13018	"Starfire": 616, 6500, 6650, 3519, 6448, 6017-235
	13028	"Defender": 2359, 3665, 3349, 3820, 3470, 6017-100, 943
	13058	"Vanguard": 2383 AA, 3619, 3413, 6512, 470 w/ 6470, 6437
1963	11341	"Space Prober": 634, 3410, 6407, 6014, 6463, 6059-50
	11361	"Shooting Star": 211 AA, 3665, 3413, 6470, 6413, 6257
	11385	"Space Conqueror": 223, 218C, 3619, 3470, 3349, 3830, 6407, 6257
	13108	"Santa Fe": 617, 3665, 3419, 6448, 3830, 3470, 6119
	13128	2383 AA, 3619, 3413, 6512, 448 w/ 6448, 6437
1964-1965	No complete military sets for sale; only individual military / space rolling stock and accessories	

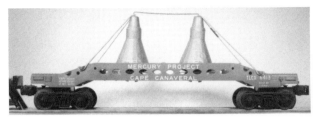

One of the non-warfare items in the series, the 6413 flatcar peacefully carries a pair of Mercury capsules.

October 4, 1957. How often have we heard "It's a Communist plot"? Well, if you are familiar with history, you know that on that date Sputnik I went into orbit around the third planet in our solar system. American public school curricula changed overnight to an emphasis on the sciences. The movie industry began to turn out countless films on invasions from outer space. People everywhere built bomb shelters, for "doomsday" was now a reality. Plastic model corporations, such as Aurora and Revell, switched their marketing emphasis from model cars to model rockets. To compete in an already declining market, Lionel had little choice but to enter the "space race." Coupled with the fact that the basic Lionel philosophy for years had been to provide action toys as a part of their train outfits, it was only natural to develop rocket and satellite launching cars. In 1961, to further ensure the development and exploitation of the military-space marketing campaign, Lionel hired General John B. Medaris as President of the Corporation. His entire background was totally immersed in the military way of life.

Unfortunately for all concerned, there were some serious drawbacks to this program. Much like the ill-fated Girls' Set, which was produced in 1957 to attract female interest in toy trains, the military items, because of their unrealistic quality, bombed just as miserably. Everyone knew that satellites and rockets were not launched from railroad flatcars, but rather from elaborate complexes at Cape Kennedy. (There was a prototype for a missile-launching boxcar, but it was abandoned as impractical.) Another drawback fell into the area of safety. Lionel's marketing philosophy stated unequivocally that they were making "sane" toys that did not kill or maim. Perhaps they did not kill, but the sharp tips of the plastic rockets could certainly wreak havoc on one's eyes if a person were not careful.

Undoubtedly another reason for the decline in sales can be attributed to the fact that the children who grew up during the "Golden Age" of Lionel were now entering college, the service, or the business community. Consequently, their change in life styles dictated a change in their buying habits. Electric trains were toys; toys were for kids, and they were no longer kids. Nonetheless, Lionel persisted in manufacturing gadgets. The few serious collectors of the time disdained the items and refused to buy the cheapened-quality product.

The many persons who did purchase Lionel military / space material did so, in all likelihood, strictly for inexpensive play value. As a result, many of the items, when located today, are broken or missing their loads. However, despite the high mortality rate of the military units, some of them are surprisingly easy to collect today, such as the 3349, 3419,

OPERATING ROLLING STOCK

(3309)	Turbo missile firing car — unlettered, olive, varying coupler and missile combinations
(3309)	Turbo missile firing car — red plastic, fixed couplers or one fixed and one operating coupler
3330	Flatcar with submarine kit — blue car
(3349)	Turbo missile firing car — red plastic, two missiles, operating couplers
3409	Flatcar with yellow helicopter — blue car, advance catalogue
3410	Flatcar with yellow helicopter — blue car
(3413)	Mercury capsule launching car — red plastic car, gray superstructure
3419	Flatcar with gray helicopter — blue car (in various shades), with large and small launcher, gray helicopter with two or four blades and counter-balancing pods
3429	U S M C automatic helicopter car —olive-painted with U S M C helicopter
3470	Target launching car — blue / white superstructure
3509	Satellite car — green, manual operation
(3510)	Satellite car — red, manual operation, advance catalogue
3512	Fire extension ladder car — silver or black ladders
3519	Automatic satellite launching car — green
3535	A E C security car — red / white, rotating spotlight
3540	Operating radar car — red plastic
3619	Helicopter reconnaissance car — light yellow or dark yellow, split black roof
3665	Minuteman missile car — light blue or dark blue split roof
3666	Minuteman cannon car — light blue split roof, part of Sears set
3820	U S M C flatcar with removable submarine — olive-painted
3830	Flatcar with removable submarine — blue
6448	Exploding boxcar — white / red plastic or red / white
6470	Exploding boxcar — red plastic
6480	Exploding boxcar — red plastic, advance catalogue
(6512)	Cherry picker car — black flatcar with manually-operated silver spaceman
6544	Missile firing car — blue plastic
6630	I R B M launcher — black plastic flatcar, advance catalogue
6640	I R B M launcher — U S M C olive-painted
6650	I R B M launcher — red plastic flatcar
6651	Cannon car — olive-painted flatcar, uncatalogued
6805	Atomic disposal flatcar — red plastic

Note: Items in parentheses are not stamped with number.

MANUAL ROLLING STOCK

702	Supply car — gray or olive drab
900	Ammunition car — gray or olive drab
(1877)	Unmarked gray flatcars — one with moss green tank, one with Jeep and Howitzer; some have AAR trucks, others have arch bar trucks
6017	Lionel Lines caboose — gray with black letters
(6017)	Caboose — unlettered, olive
6017-50	U S M C caboose — dark blue
6017-200	U S Navy — light blue
(6076)	Hopper — unlettered, olive
(6112)	Hopper — unlettered Scout-type, olive
6175	Flatcar with 175 rocket — red or black car
6407	Flatcar with pencil sharpener rocket — red car
6413	Mercury capsule carrying car — light blue car
6463	Two-dome rocket fuel tank car — white / red
6500	Flatcar with red / white Bonanza plane — black car
6519	Allis Chalmers atomic generator carrier — light or dark orange body
6530	Fire safety car — red plastic body, white doors
6800	Flatcar with Bonanza plane — red car, yellow / black or black / yellow plane
6803	Flatcar with vehicles — U S M C, tank and sound truck
6804	Flatcar with vehicles — U S M C, anti-aircraft gun truck and sound truck
6806	Flatcar with vehicles — U S M C, hospital truck and radar truck
6807	Flatcar with vehicles — U S M C, DKW load
6808	Flatcar with vehicles — U S M C, searchlight truck and two-gun tank
6809	Flatcar with vehicles — U S M C, hospital truck and anti-aircraft gun truck. **Note:** These trucks are gray with U S M C (sometimes U S Navy) insignia. They were NOT made by Lionel but for Lionel by the Pyro Manufacturing Company, Union, New Jersey. All of the same trucks, in olive green with a white star on the sides, were issued separately well before Lionel came out with them in 1958.
6814	Rescue unit caboose — white-painted plastic; also, variation produced for Sears with no load
6819	Flatcar with gray helicopter — red car
6820	Flatcar with gray helicopter — blue car
6823	Flatcar with I R B M missiles — red car
6824	U S M C rescue unit caboose — olive / white
6830	Flatcar with non-operating submarine — blue car, gray submarine
6844	Flatcar with six "Little John" missiles — black or red car

Note: Items in parentheses are not stamped with number.

3665, and 6650. Unlike other areas of Lionel, there are very few truly rare and super-expensive items. The military trucks made for Lionel by Pyro are hard to find unbroken. The balloons for the 3470 target launcher also suffered. Over the years the rubber has fused together, causing the balloons to be uninflatable. The truly "rare" pieces are the unstamped olive SP-type caboose, 6407, and the 3429 U S M C helicopter car. Some items, such as the Sears military set with the 3666 cannon car and 347 cannon launching platform, are hard to find, *but* they can be found if one looks hard enough.

Even more fascinating than the items produced were the pre-production artists' renderings or mockups which appeared in the advance catalogues. A few of the items with more obvious changes are the 6175 rocket carrying car, the helicopters, the 44 mobile missile launcher, the 470 I R B M missile launching platform, and the 462 derrick platform set.

The 6175 rocket carrying car first appeared in the 1958 advance catalogue. It is missing the "U S NAVY" identification, but has instead some illegible printing near its base. It also looks more like a high-powered rifle shell (bullet) than it does an intercontinental rocket. Strangely, in 1959 and later years, catalogues pictured the missile just as it appeared in the 1958 advance catalogue, despite the fact that it was produced in a different shape.

The helicopters first produced in 1959 look like real Chinook helicopters used later in Vietnam for rescue missions. There is no clear plastic bubble on the front. They all have four rotors, as well as what appears to be an operating rear blade. The rear sections are raised in a graceful curve. There are no markings to identify which branch of service the helicopter is from. On the flatcar, the support piece for the tail is not notched to accept the tail, but rather is flat and protruding.

Perhaps the item most altered between the advance catalogue and actual production was the 44 mobile missile launcher. First, it is not identified with any branch of the service — it did not even have a number other than the one under the picture. It is pictured with a whip antenna on the right front and a radar-scanning disk on top of the cab. On the rear quarter of the unit is a large five-point white star, which presumably identifies it as American, since the Russians use a red star. Finally, to the rear of the control panel man is a seat and what appears to be a clear plastic shield held in place by a bar parallel to the railroad tracks.

The 470 I R B M missile launching platform also changed radically from the 1959 advance catalogue. The launch mechanism is totally different. The original one is streamlined and sleek, while the actual one has a latticework configuration. Instead of a Quonset hut building, it is shown as a complete wall-like "block house" with two microwave disks on top. These are the same disks that appear on the 199 microwave tower. Beginning at each end of the block

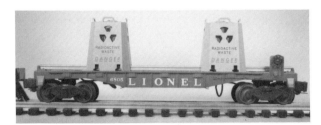

Whoa! — not in *my* neighborhood! Imagine the horror of residents in Lionelville when the 6805 flatcar and its load of blatantly-marked radioactive waste passed through town!

building is a single-rail fence that surrounds the entire missile-firing area.

Finally, the 462 derrick platform set is pictured with the boom derrick magnetically hoisting a radioactive canister. The description even makes reference to a magnetically-operated hoist. When it finally appeared, the derrick boom assembly was exactly the same as that on the 6670 boom derrick car.

This military equipment was less than realistic, but Lionel continued to make the material. Yet on the rear of the 1959 advance catalogue, a major step in railroad realism was made — all the unrealistic military items appear on realistic two-rail track. There is a message in there somewhere.

What many people do not realize is that the military units are essentially both a beginning and an end of the old Lionel Corporation's O Gauge production. Nearly everyone attributes the demise of the Lionel Corporation to the cheapened and unrealistic quality of the trains and accessories of the 1960s. However, in 1917, as the "Great War" was taking place on the European continent, Lionel went into the military business. The 203 self-propelled armored locomotive with a two-gun turret pulling two 900 ammunition cars marked Lionel's entry into the military train market. This set and a more expensive version with two 702 supply cars were among Lionel's best selling sets from 1917 through 1921. These sets came in two colors, gray and olive drab, and were first catalogued in 1918. The promotional hype was not very subtle, as it encouraged the young engineers to "Play War! Bring up siege guns on tracks."

Some twenty years later Lionel would once again join the military, only this time as a manufacturer of precision navigational and nautical instruments for the U. S. Navy. Today, both of the World War I sets, as well as the World War II navigational equipment, are highly desirable items eagerly pursued by collectors.

When Fundimensions began Lionel production in 1970, they catalogued a satellite launching car. However, this car, like several others shown, was not produced in that year. It was not until 1980 that vestiges of the past started to reappear, with the reissuing of the Allis Chalmers car and the radioactive waste disposal car.

In 1981 Lionel began what appeared to be a serious plunge back into space and military items with the vigorously promoted "Land and Space Early Reaction" set, or "L. A. S. E. R." to use its acronym. This set ran again in 1982. Following closely upon the heels of this set was yet another radioactive waste car and then, in 1983, the Commando As-

ACCESSORIES

175	Remote-control rocket launcher
175-50	Rocket for rocket launcher
197	Rotating radar antenna — orange or gray superstructure
199	Microwave relay tower
347	Cannon launching platform — olive (uncatalogued)
394	Rotary beacon — air driven, various colors
413	Countdown control panel
419	Heliport control tower
448	Missile launching platform
462	Derrick platform set with radioactive waste containers
470	Missile launching platform
494	Rotary beacon — vibrator driven, various colors
943	Exploding ammo dump

sault set. It was in camouflage colors and contained a rather curious piece — a brown / green / black camouflage cruise missile. Perhaps this cruise missile crawled rather than flew? Only Lionel engineers know for sure! Lionel offered an optional uncatalogued display case and board for this set. The case was made of clear acrylic plastic and fit over the display board in the manner of an inexpensive terrarium. Supposedly, one could then run this DC-powered set under the acrylic dome — but only supposedly. The track came too close to the sides and caused the train to derail in each of its four corners. This was hardly an effective Commando Assault unit, and promotion of the display case was soon abandoned.

The year 1984 saw the introduction of the last military trains of the decade. The Commando Assault set ran for the last time. Added to the traditional catalogue was a new locomotive: a U. S. Marine Corps SW-1 in camouflage colors. Also in the same catalogue was a searchlight car and a Marine Corps bunk car, both in camouflage colors. Then, just as rapidly as the military and space items had reappeared, they disappeared. In 1985 the Marine Corps SW-1, bunk car, and searchlight all ran again. Since then, nary a piece of S. A. M. A. T. has made an appearance. The last decade of the century is now upon us and where events of late 1989 and early 1990 made it seem as though disarmament of the Super Powers might be a real possibility, doubts yet remain. One can only hope that Lionel will soon disarm its military trains. Only time will tell.

Many of the exciting space and military action trains, including variations, are illustrated in full color in Greenberg's Guide to Lionel Trains, 1945-1969, Volume I — *Ed.*

THE 1945-1946 TRUCK AND COUPLER

Robert Swanson

The interruption in toy train production during World War II gave Lionel the opportunity to step back and analyze some of its design and marketing strategies. The scale 700E Hudson and the 700-series freight cars introduced in the late 1930s were engineering masterpieces incorporating a wealth of detail. However, because of their relatively high price and the requirement for 72-inch diameter track, they were not big sellers.

Notice two wires

FIGURE 1: Type 1A flying shoe truck and coupler with whirly-backed wheels and thick axles. This design bears no relation to the tinplate prewar trucks and box couplers.

Early in the war, Lionel decided the key to large post-war profits would be to incorporate as much detail and realism into their popular-priced toy trains as possible. Experience had shown the market for toy trains to be far greater than for expensive scale models. The emerging technology in injection-molded plastics, which developed rapidly during World War II, provided an inexpensive way to produce highly-detailed car bodies. These cars went well with the series of die-cast steam engines that Lionel developed in the late 1930s (i.e. 224, 225, 226, 1662, 1666, etc.). The final item to be upgraded was the truck and coupler assembly. The prewar tinplate trucks and box coupler obviously did not meet the new requirements for realism.

Some Lionel memos reproduced in the January 1983 issue of the *Train Collector's Quarterly* show that Lionel

---

TABLE 1
COMPONENT VARIATIONS

(1) Axles (1-4 are thick axles)

1. Short center section, splined ends (fixed wheels)
2. Short center section, smooth end sections (free wheels)
3. Long center section, splined ends (fixed wheels)
4. Long center section, smooth end sections (free wheels)
5. Regular postwar axle (thin axle)

(2) Support Fiber

1. Black with extra round hole
2. Black
3. Brown (dark)
4. Tan (light brown)

(3) Coil Termination to Shoe

1. Two strands of coil wire, black tape on coil
2. Copper strip, black tape
3. Braided wire, black tape
4. Fiber board with eyelet, no tape on coil
5. Fiber board with eyelet, black tape

(4) Coil Ground Termination

1. Soldered, tab protruding right
2. Soldered, tab protruding down
3. Not visible
4. Grounding terminal bent forward

Note: Used in designation code, 1A (1) (2) (3) (4)

started development of the new trucks and coupler assembly early during the war years. The result of this early development was introduced in set 463W, the only set produced for Christmas 1945. The four-page 1945 catalogue claimed that the die-cast trucks and automatic knuckle couplers had been perfected. . . a Lionel exaggeration!

Examination of the flying shoe trucks and coupler design (see **Figure 1**) shows that it bears no relation to the prewar tinplate trucks and box couplers at all. The tinplate truck sides, journal boxes, and wheels have obviously been replaced by more realistic solid metal components. What is not as obvious is that constant diameter axles with swaged points to control wheel gauging (a standard practice for 25 years) had been replaced by larger diameter steel axles, machined on the ends to a smaller diameter. It is even more surprising that Lionel abandoned the successful axle-mounted coil sub-assembly after so many trial-and-error design attempts at automatic coupler designs during the late 1930s.

The flying shoe design seems less surprising if the prewar scale freight car trucks are considered as a point of reference, rather than the tinplate trucks. In actuality, the postwar trucks seem to be a combination and compromise of the two prewar designs.

There are three types of evidence indicating that Lionel's 1945 claim of knuckle coupler perfection was premature:

1. Lionel published seven repair bulletins by April 1946 to help Service Stations cope with a rash of customer problems.
2. The existence of a very high percentage of broken and non-operating couplers when found today.
3. The existence of many design variations in the components of the flying shoe truck.

Apparently, Lionel tried to solve its coupler problems through a series of continuing changes, but the coupler components were so fragile that by mid-1946 Lionel completely redesigned the knuckle coupler. Both the initial flying shoe design and the more common axle-mounted coil designs are illustrated in Frank Pettit's Patent No. 2,658,629 which was filed November 16, 1946 (issued November 10, 1953 and assigned to the Lionel Corporation).

DESCRIPTION OF COMPONENT VARIATIONS

Lionel spent considerable effort in developing and refining its initial flying shoe truck and coupler design. During this development process, they made many changes to various components, a number of which found their way onto trains sold to the general public. The most obvious variations were in the wheels and axles used in these trucks. Less obvious variations are found in the central fiber mounting strip and the details associated with termination of the "hot" end and the grounded end of the coupler coil.

Some truck and wheel definitions and conventions have been established in prior publications and will be utilized

TABLE 2
OBSERVED COMBINATIONS OF VARIATIONS

Type 1A	Qty.	Type 1B	Qty.
1A1111	5	1B3111	1
1A1111R	3	1B3131	4
1A1121	5	1B3131R	1
1A1131	2	1B3232	5
1A2111	1	1B3232R	1
1A2131	2	1B3243	2
1A22..R	4	1B3243R	3
1A2232	18	1B33..R	1
1A2232R	8	1B41..R	2
1A2331	1	1B42..R	3
10 Variations	**49**	1B4232	12
		1B4232R	1
		1B4242	4
		1B4242R	1
		1B4243	26
		1B4243R	2
		1B4254R	1
		1B4343	3
		18 Variations	**73**

Type 1C	Qty.
1C21..R	1
1C2243	8
1C2244	4
1C23..R	1
1C2344	1
1C2344R	1
1C24..R	2
1C2454	1
1C2454R	3
9 Variations	**22**

Type 2	Qty.
2C5354	26
2C5354R	4
2C5454	32
3 Variations	**62**

TOTALS

Trucks observed	206
Variations	40

here. Type 1 trucks have thick axles and Type 2 trucks have thin or regular postwar axles. A letter designation has been established for the wheel:

A — Whirly Backed.

B — Dished. (The dished area comes in two sizes, as shown in **Figure 2**. Both sizes were apparently manufactured concurrently since they are frequently mixed on the same truck, even the same axle. The large dish wheel is more common than the small dish by a ratio of about 5:1.)

FIGURE 2: Wheels used on early postwar trucks: A, whirly; B, dished (large and small); and C, regular with built-up area around axle hole.

FIGURE 3: Six axles showing five different axle types. 1 — thick axle with splined ends, used with whirly-backed wheels. 2 — thick axle with smooth ends for free-turning wheels. 3 — thick axle with splined ends used with fixed-dish wheels. 4 — thick axle with smooth ends for free-turning dished wheels. 5 — regular (thin) postwar axle.

C — Regular postwar wheel with built-up area around axle hole. (There are some variations in the regular wheel that show up during the 1950s and 1960s, but for all practical purposes, the regular wheel was constant during the 1946 to 1950 period.)

A four-digit detailed description number will now be defined to identify variations in:

1. Axles.
2. Support Fiber.
3. Coil (hot side) Termination to Shoe.
4. Coil Ground Termination.

When these four digits are added behind the truck type, a six-character truck and coupler identification code is established which can be used to identify all variations (i.e., 1A1234). A summary of the component variations is presented in **Table 1**. A listing of component combinations observed on 206 trucks is presented in **Table 2**. An "R" after the six-character identification code indicates the truck has a center-rail pickup roller. A dot (or period) is used as a place holder for trucks lacking certain features, such as front trucks on tenders which have no couplers.

Five different axle variations (shown in **Figure 3**) have been observed on flying shoe trucks: four different thick axles on Type 1 trucks and the regular thin axle on Type 2 trucks. Short center-section axles were first used on the trucks equipped with whirly-backed wheels. Lionel first

made these axles with splined areas on the machined small-diameter end sections, so that wheels pressed onto these axles would not rotate relative to the axle. The axle and both wheels rotated as a unit between the truck's side frames, just like real trains. Since the wheels had a flat (constant diameter) tread, there was no differential action as the trucks went around the sharp curves of tinplate track. This caused drag, which significantly slowed trains through curves, so Lionel soon removed the splines and allowed the wheels to rotate freely on the axles.

Lionel replaced the whirly-backed wheel with the dished wheel. The dished wheel was thinner than the whirly-backed wheel in the center, where the axle went through. Hence Lionel lengthened the large-diameter center section of the axle to maintain proper wheel gauging, by shortening the turned-down end sections. For some unexplainable reason, Lionel experimented again with wheels fixed to the axles, even though trucks with these wheels have greater drag. Consequently, there are two variations of the long center-section axle: splined and non-splined.

Lionel then developed and produced what we today call the "regular" postwar wheel with a built-up area on the backside around the axle hole. To mate with this wheel, Lionel returned to the short center-section axle. However, only the non-splined variation was manufactured. Apparently, Lionel engineers finally learned their lesson about fixed wheels, and once realistic wheel details were sacrificed to production and operating realities, the thick axle was clearly an unnecessary extravagance. Lionel then reintroduced the constant-diameter (thin) axle with swage points to control wheel gauging, which had been its standard for twenty-five years before the war.

Several variations have been observed in the phenol-fiber strips which support the flying shoe and roller pickup (if so equipped). The most obvious variation is color. Most 1945 items are found with black fiber strips, while most 1946 items are found with brown or tan fiber strips. However, the correlation is not one hundred percent (as shown in **Table 2**). A more subtle variation is the presence of one or two small round holes in a very few of the black strips (see **Figure 4** with hole and **Figure 5** without hole). These holes are usually found with Type 1A trucks which have whirly-

FIGURE 4: Type 1A1111 truck showing extra round hole in black fiber strip.

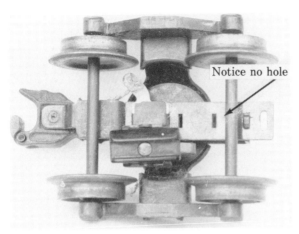

FIGURE 5: Type 1B3232 truck without extra round hole in black fiber strip.

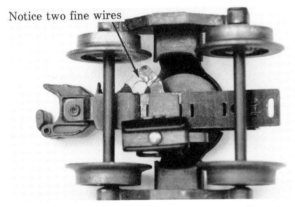

FIGURE 6: Type 1A1111 truck showing two fine strands of wire connecting coupler coil to shoe termination. (See Table 1 for code definitions.)

FIGURE 7: Type 1A1121 truck showing copper strip connecting coupler coil to shoe termination.

backed wheels pressed onto splined axles. One round hole is fairly visible under the axle, farthest away from the coupler. The second round hole, if it exists, is almost impossible to see because it is directly under the flying shoe support bracket. The only time the second hole can be observed without disassembling the truck is on the front truck of tenders, where there is no flying shoe, and the fiber is required to support only the roller pickup.

TABLE 3
APPLICATIONS OF
TYPES 1 & 2 TRUCKS

CAR NAME	1A	1B	1C	2
2466W tender (1945)	5, 1	5, 1		
2452 gondola	5, 1	9, 1		
2755 tank (open frame)	7, 1	9, 3	1, 4	
2758 automobile car	4, 1	11, 1	2	
2457 caboose, red (2 couplers)	4, 1	8, 1		
2457 caboose, brown (2 cplr)	2, 3	2, 3		
2466W tender (1946)		1	1	1
2466T tender		1, 1	1, 1	
2452X gondola			2	9
2454 boxcar (PRR)			1	5
2465 tank (2 domes)			1	6
3454 merchandise car				?
3559 dump car				5
2472 caboose, red (1 coupler)			1	4, 1
2457 caboose, red (1 coupler)			3	
2555 tank (closed frame)			2, 1	4, 1
2440 Pullman, green			4	
2441 observation, green			2	
2442 Pullman, brown			2	
2443 observation, brown			2	
1654T tender				1
221W/T tender			?	?
2458 automobile car				4
2430 Pullman, blue			2	
2431 observation, blue			1	

Many very subtle variations have been observed in the termination of the coupler coil, both the "hot" side to the flying shoe and the ground side. As originally produced, there was no terminal on the coil to mechanically "tie-off" the final turn of the very fine coil wire. The black friction tape was the only thing that prevented the coil from unraveling during the assembly process. **Figures 6, 7,** and **8** show different methods of completing the electrical connection from under the tape to the "flying shoe." When a small terminal board was added to the back of the coil, the black tape around the coil was, at first, eliminated (**Figure 9**), but eventually, it returned, possibly to protect the coil as well as for aesthetic reasons (**Figure 10**).

Changes in the grounding of the inner end of the coupler coil are perhaps the most subtle of all the variations in these

FIGURE 8: Type 1A2232 truck showing the braided wire connecting coupler coil to shoe termination.

FIGURE 9: Type 1B4243 truck showing coupler coil terminated into fiber board with eyelet; no tape on coil.

FIGURE 10: Type 2C5454 truck showing coupler coil with fiber terminal board and tape around coil. The tape protected the coil and gave a better appearance. Each of the changes shown in these photographs represented Lionel's attempt to improve the truck design.

FIGURE 11: Type 1A1121 truck showing coil ground termination soldered to tab protruding to the right (from the viewer's perspective).

FIGURE 12: Type 1A2232 truck showing coil ground terminal soldered to tab protruding down.

FIGURE 13: Type 1B4243 truck showing no soldered ground termination of coupler coil. (Ground termination is internal and not visible.)

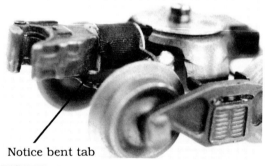

FIGURE 14: Type 2C5454 truck showing coil end plate tab bent forward.

trucks. I can offer no explanations for these variations. They are only presented in pictures (**Figures 11** to **14**).

1945-1946 TRUCK APPLICATIONS

The observed application of these trucks is a story unto itself, maybe more interesting than the actual detailed variations. Basically, the flying shoe trucks were applied to tenders and cars made in 1945 and early 1946. But which items had which trucks and why? First, remember that Lionel was a profit-making organization and trains were toys being made for children, not collectors. Production and profit were the prime motivators. All the trucks available were used to meet production objectives. With this in mind, let us examine the available evidence.

Table 3 lists all the cars and tenders that I have observed with flying shoe trucks. The items are presented in three groups, based on the catalogue in which they first appeared. Group 1 items are illustrated, although quite inaccurately in some cases, in the 1945 catalogue as part of set 463W. Group 2 items were introduced in the rare and elusive spring 1946 catalogue. In fact, I have observed at least two examples of every rolling stock item in the spring 1946 catalogue equipped with flying shoe trucks, except for the 3454 operating merchandise car. The final group of cars and tender were first shown in the 1946 advance catalogue.

The number of cars and tenders that I have observed, equipped with the four major subcategories of flying shoe trucks, are indicated in Table 3. The number to the left in each column (in front of the comma) represents the number of cars with both trucks of the indicated sub-category. The second number (to the right of the comma), represents the number of cars which had only one of the indicated trucks (the other truck being a different sub-category of the flying shoe type).

Some patterns and trends, but very few absolutes, can be observed from the data in Table 3. First, Types 1A and 1B were **primarily** used in the 463W set produced in 1945, while Types 1C and 2 were **primarily** used in the spring 1946 production. While the data is admittedly very limited, the tinplate passenger cars (including all three series: blue, green, and brown) appear to be the most consistent application for Type 1C trucks, while the greatest numbers of Type 2 trucks are found on O27 freight cars. Except for three plastic freight cars (2452 gondola, 2454 boxcar, and 2465 two-dome tank car), the flying shoe couplers are always found on items which are carry-overs of prewar designs.

In trying to establish which sets were assembled in the Lionel factory using flying shoe trucks, the data is very limited and sometimes misleading.

Very few complete sets from 1945 and early 1946 have survived intact to the present time. The few complete sets from this period which are found often contain one or more Type 3 coil coupler trucks. Were sets shipped from the factory with this mixture of trucks or is the mixture evidence of a forty-year-old repair? Many times it is impossible to tell.

Given this rather shaky data base, Table 4 represents nothing more than a "guesstimate" as to which sets had which trucks. One generalization does appear fairly safe. Lionel's use of the flying shoe truck appears centered on the sets appearing in the 1945 and spring 1946 catalogues. (As mentioned earlier, the 3454 operating merchandise car is the only car in either catalogue which has not been found with any version of the Type 1 or 2 truck. Even the brown 3454 mentioned in my 9-1/4" boxcar article in Volume I was equipped with Type 3A trucks.)

Besides the sets in these two catalogues, three additional sets have been observed equipped with flying shoe trucks: set 1400 (blue passenger cars headed by a gray 221 steam locomotive), set 1401 (a small O27 freight set headed by a 1654 steam locomotive), and set 2103W (a three-car O Gauge freight set). These sets are all shown for the first time in the 1946 advance catalogue.

TABLE 4
SET APPLICATION OF
TYPE 1 & 2 TRUCKS

Truck Type	Set Number	First Catalogued
1A	463W	1945
1B	463W	1945
1C	1400(W) tender?	advance 1946
	1402(W)	spring 1946
	2100(W)	spring 1946
2	1401(W)	advance 1946
	1405(W)	spring 1946
	1409(W) merchandise?	spring 1946
	1411(W)	spring 1946
	2101(W)	spring 1946
	2103(W)	advance 1946

The 2103W set contains a 3559 dump car, the only operating car which has been observed to date with the early coil couplers. The 1409W set is listed in the catalogue with a 3559 dump car and also a 3454 merchandise car, but since the merchandise car has never been observed with early couplers, early 1946 production of the 1409W set cannot be firmly established. I have a complete 2103W set in my collection with a mixture of Types 1C and 2 trucks. Steve Ferman of St. Louis sent me detailed pictures of a second 2103W set equipped with all Type 2 trucks. The 2103W set may therefore be the only source of 3559 operating dump cars with early coil couplers. Or, does someone have a 1409W set with some other car substituted for the missing 3454 merchandise car? Reader comments are invited.

In closing, one final observation is made. Flying shoe trucks are generally not found in 1946 sets containing a smoking locomotive. While there may be a few cars which represent individual exceptions, Lionel appears to have discontinued their use before the "New for 1946" smoking locomotives were ready for shipment. In fact, the use of flying shoe couplers on 221 tenders (the 221 locomotive was new in 1946), has never been firmly established, even though the use of these couplers on blue 2430 and 2431 passenger cars is well documented. Were the blue passenger cars with early couplers and silver rubber-stamped markings made early in 1946 along with similar green and brown cars, and then held until the new 221 locomotives and tenders were ready? Or, were early blue passenger cars shipped with available 1666 locomotives and 2466 tenders in an uncatalogued set? There are still many unanswered questions concerning early postwar Lionel production.

FROM STAPLE-END TO BAR-END TRUCKS

Joseph Kotil

When looking for the reason that Lionel changed from staple-end to bar-end type trucks, the only conclusion that can be drawn is cost reduction. Since material cost is unchanged, the savings have to be in labor costs, an important consideration with increasing volume. Both truck types have stood the test of time and are intact on otherwise destroyed trains. The following analysis of the manufacturing sequence is based on my never having seen nor having any firsthand information about Lionel's operation.

To upset the staple ends the bolster and the side frames would have to be assembled, probably by hand, and inserted into a crimping fixture. The circular vertical area where the bolster rises was necessary so a bar on the fixture could back up the dual punches used to spread both staple ends. The bolster would have been clamped down and the staple ends spread automatically. At another station this assembly would have been fitted with wheels, probably by an operator putting wheels on axles and springing them into the truck frame.

By crimping the side frames onto the bolster as in the bar-end truck, no clamping is needed since the crimping is vertical. Looking at the wheel and axle assembly, the logical reason for the wheels to be retained by the outer crimps is to save assembly time. Vibratory feeders would orient and deliver wheels and axles to an unattended assembly machine which would press on the wheels and crimp the assembly. This reduces the number of parts at final assembly from six to two. The operator at the side frame-bolster assembly station could now insert two wheel-axle assemblies between the side frames and eliminate the entire second operation of springing the wheel and axle assemblies into the side frame and bolster assembly.

With assistance from Dan Johns.

Lionel introduced the staple-end truck in 1945. We call it a staple-end truck, because the fastening of the bolster bar to the side frame resembles a staple.

The bar-end truck was introduced in late 1951 by Lionel.

The preceding analysis is of course hypothetical. Obviously Lionel could not have come up with the ultimate cost reduction which was the injection-molded truck with integral coupler in 1945, so each gradual change should be linked with cost reduction. Replacing the truck-mounting pivot, an automatic screw machine-made part, and the C clip with the purchased snap-in spring retainer was a sizable cost reduction.

THE HISTORY OF GREENBERG PUBLISHING COMPANY

A LOOK BACK AND A LOOK AHEAD — *Roland E. LaVoie*

Trains, it seems, have always been a part of Bruce Greenberg's life in one way or another. Bruce grew up in Collingswood, New Jersey, a small suburban town just outside Philadelphia. He lived only a few blocks from the tracks of the old Pennsylvania-Reading Seashore Lines. As a boy he was just old enough to remember little 0-6-0 steam switchers with slope-back tenders shunting coal cars back and forth at the local coal dealer, or perhaps the

In 1956 a Pennsylvania 0-6-0 switcher pauses at the Haddonfield, New Jersey station. The B6 0-6-0 switchers were catalogued by Lionel as 227, 228, 230, and 231. All Lionel versions were numbered "8976" under the cab windows. Photograph courtesy of Robert Long, National Railway Historical Society.

This is the front cover of the 1936 Lionel catalogue, which shows Lionel beginning its prewar swing to more realistic trains. What collector would not have been thrilled by the catalogue illustrations of the Pennsy Torpedo, Red Comet, Flying Yankee, and Hiawatha for the first time? This was one of the first Lionel catalogues reproduced by Bruce Greenberg.

big Pennsy K-4 Pacifics thundering through town on their way to the Atlantic City race track or the shore points, trailing a long string of tuscan P-70 passenger coaches in their smoky wakes.

Like most boys of his age, Bruce had toy trains as a favorite plaything. He recalls tinkering with them as a youngster, proudly announcing to his parents each new lighted Plasticville building gracing his basement layout. He replaced his tinplate layout with an HO setup when he was thirteen, but somehow these smaller trains lacked the intrinsic charm of the larger toy trains.

The demands of schooling and career development soon shunted all thoughts of trains aside — but they were not quite forgotten. In 1967, when Bruce was a graduate student of political science at the University of Michigan in Ann Arbor, he chanced to visit the home of Marvin Fry. While there, he saw a large collection of Standard Gauge trains of the 1920s and 1930s, with their interpretive designs, bright colors, and shiny brass and nickel trim. Those beautiful toy trains resurrected Bruce's buried memories of the trains of

his boyhood as nothing else could, and he soon found himself searching for these trains once again.

As Bruce started his collection, he found that the trains he sought were readily available; in fact, an "Old Toy Trains Wanted" advertisement in the newspaper produced more trains than Bruce could afford on a graduate student's somewhat penurious income. Consequently, Bruce became a trader, buying and selling trains to maintain his collection. He was a willing student and observer of variations, but at the time there were no systematic price guides available, and, aside from a few scattered catalogue reprints, the collector was truly "on his own." To an analytic student, the lack of research resources for these trains was an unacceptable state of affairs. However, by the time Bruce completed his graduate work in 1970, toy train documentation had become a little better. A few reproduction catalogues had been published, including the famous 1929 Lionel catalogue, and there were some early pre-1918 Lionel catalogue reproductions as well. Still, there was no systematic listing or evaluation of postwar Lionel, American Flyer S Gauge, or prewar Lionel.

Upon the completion of his graduate work, Bruce was appointed Assistant Professor of Political Science at Knox College in Galesburg, Illinois. In this position, he taught such subjects as voter behavior, legislative socialization, and methods of political analysis. A local train collector and friend, Reverend Robert Prendergast, the Chaplain of St. Mary's Hospital in Galesburg, had the good fortune to acquire some 1931 to 1936 Lionel catalogues from a local junk shop. He, too, was always seeking to unravel the history and chronology of toy trains. Upon this fortuitous acquisition he called Bruce, who, quite excited by the discovery, hurried to Bob's apartment on the top floor of the hospital. Bruce and Bob eagerly pored over these marvelous, long-lost documents, savoring the illustrations and information before them. Since they knew that many other collectors would like these catalogues as a collecting guide, they wanted to share their new-found knowledge somehow.

Bruce placed an advertisement in a collector publication, and, to his delight, the fifty copies of this press run rapidly disappeared.

That got Bruce to thinking about Knox College's print shop. This shop used a very inexpensive paper plate technology to print the fifty to one hundred copies a faculty member might need for a course syllabus or for examinations. Bruce made a trial duplication of one of the catalogues on the press. Although the quality could be described as modest at best, the press nevertheless reproduced the images of the rolling stock and, more importantly, reproduced the descriptive text sharply and clearly. Bruce thus recognized that this print shop could be a means of making catalogue reproductions available to others inexpensively, and so, with Bob's blessings (literal and figurative, presumably, given Bob's status as a man of the cloth), he had the catalogues reproduced on the college's AM 1250 press. Assembly of the pages was another step — and what better place than Bruce's dining room table, with the help of a few neighborhood children? Bruce placed an advertisement in a collector publication, and, to his delight, the fifty copies of this press run rapidly disappeared. With this modest entry into publishing in 1970, Greenberg Publishing Company began.

About six months later, another collector friend, Frank Herman, who lived about seventy-five miles away in Mason City, Illinois, called Bruce with exciting news. He had acquired the inventory of a Lionel Service Station with thousands of parts and, more importantly, the entire Lionel Service Manual. For several weeks, Bruce and Frank excitedly pored over this amazingly complete reference work. No toy company had ever issued a better service reference than did Lionel with its encyclopedic Service Manual. Bruce soon recognized that many operational problems he had faced with his own trains — a jammed milk car, a balky switch, or a faltering reversing unit — could be remedied with the aid

of the Service Manual. Bruce was sure that there would be a terrific market for a reproduction of this work.

Bruce arranged to borrow the complete Service Manual and began his largest publishing undertaking thus far — fifty copies of a 1,500-page book. The little college print shop was overwhelmed by the order, and, as is often the case in the printing trade, the production schedule fell far behind. Collating the manual with no mechanical devices was, as Bruce puts it, endless. Again, the work was done on the trusty dining room table. Bruce walked around that table so many times that he literally wore a path into the rug! Then, to finish the project, he used a small hand punch to put three-ring holes into twenty pages at a time for all fifty sets of 1,500 pages.

After resting his gnarled fingers for a while (and a total of 75,000 sheets of paper and numerous paper cuts), Bruce again advertised in the collector journals. He quickly sold all fifty copies — remarkable in view of the modest four-line size of the ad.

With this success behind him, Bruce began to explore a higher quality technology for his future printing projects. There was a sophisticated printing shop in Galesburg which did both black and white and four-color printing using plastic film negatives and metal plates. (The original prewar Lionel catalogues of the late 1930s were printed by just such a process.) However, the pre-press cost for a single black and white page printed in this way was about $10, a high cost which would have to be amortized by a larger print run. Given Bruce's small market of one hundred to two hundred potential buyers, the high-quality black and white method was not feasible. Thus, he stayed with the cruder paper plate technology, although he did so very reluctantly. It is well to remember that in 1971 the entire membership of the Train Collectors' Association was only about three thousand — less than one-fifth its 1988 membership. Bruce did not anticipate the larger markets of future years.

In late 1973 Bruce was offered a senior administrative position as an Assistant Provost of Antioch College. This represented a substantial promotion; consequently, Bruce and his family moved to Columbia, Maryland. This was no small undertaking, since Bruce and his wife, Linda, now had two young children, Paul and Leslie, to care for. After Bruce had established himself, he tried to find suppliers in the Maryland area for his growing publishing business, with the hope that he could produce a higher quality reproduction at a price commensurate with his small market. After an intensive search, Bruce found a firm with paper plate technology to do his Service Manual, but he still had no luck in finding a reasonably-priced metal plate technology. The Bendix Corporation had an in-house print facility to service its NASA contracts, and Bruce found that he could get good black and white reproductions of his catalogues done there. By this time Bruce felt that there was a market for 500 copies of a catalogue reproduction to be sold over a period of two to three years. Using Bendix, Bruce produced black and white catalogue reproductions with color covers for all the Lionel catalogues from 1922 to 1942 except for the 1929 catalogue. These were to sell at $6. After Bruce received the first batch of these catalogues, the 1923 to 1928 versions, another company put out a full-color reproduction of a Lionel catalogue for only $10.

Greenberg's Guide To

Lionel Train Values:

O and O-27, 1915-1942;
Standard Gauge, 1906-1940.

The first printing of the Lionel Prewar Guide was done with paper plate technology on uncoated paper. The cover of this book is shown. About 1,000 copies were printed.

Bruce was shocked by the low price of this competitive catalogue because he immediately saw that either the competitor had discovered an alternative color technology at a lower price or a much bigger market than Bruce had suspected. This was his first serious market challenge; to meet it, Bruce redoubled his efforts to find other printing technologies at lower costs.

Bruce soon learned about the two major cost components associated with color printing. One is the color separation process, which in 1974 was about $100 per page. The other component was the cost of the printing press' precise application of the four separate colors to paper. These initial print costs must be amortized over the print run; in other words, the more copies Bruce could run, the lower his per-unit costs would be. Therefore, even though Bruce had a large inventory of unsold black and white catalogue reproductions, he knew that he had to respond to his new competitor if he wanted to stay in the market. This was a very difficult and potentially expensive situation!

The response to Bruce's price reduction was immediate and dramatic.

After three months of investigation and phone contacts, including contacts with every color printer in Baltimore and Washington, as well as every color separation house in both cities, Bruce finally found a shop that would print full-color reproductions at a moderate price which would allow Bruce to meet a $10 retail price, assuming a total market size of 3,000 and a first-year market of 1,500. Bruce then contracted for the Lionel 1932-1934 and 1936-1941 catalogues

$4.95

GREENBERG'S PRICE GUIDE TO LIONEL TRAINS

O and O-27 Trains, 1915-1942;
Standard Gauge Trains, 1906-1940.

The second printing of the Lionel Prewar Guide was printed by a large book manufacturing press on enameled paper and featured, for the first time, both a full-color cover and color photographs inside.

in four-color versions and offered these at the extremely risky price of $6 each. He held his breath to see if his expectations were correct.

The response to Bruce's price reduction was immediate and dramatic. Huge order quantities came in, five hundred in the first two weeks alone. Bruce felt that the potential market would be as high as 1,500 buyers in the first year, which would certainly make the product economically feasible. But as the months went by, the initial deluge slowed to a trickle. Clearly, the market was only about 750 buyers. Bruce found himself with a terrific inventory of beautiful products, substantial printing bills, and really discouraging expectations.

By this time, Bruce had two competitors, and they too discovered that they had overestimated the market. This cleared the way for negotiations between Bruce and his competitors to market their products more economically. Eventually, Bruce bought the inventory of one of the competitors at a modest price and, more importantly, secured the negatives to the catalogues as well.

During these days, Bruce's main career as Assistant Provost at Antioch became less and less rewarding. He stayed with the college for a year but resigned in January 1975 because of his dissatisfaction with the college's administrative policies and his frustration with the resistance to his suggestions for changes that he felt should have been made. Typically, Bruce disliked constant argumentation with no resulting problem-solving. He decided to devote his full time to the publication business. Therefore, January 1, 1975, is the real birth date of Greenberg Publishing Company.

Since Bruce had exhaustively studied the paper plate technology in metropolitan Baltimore, he decided that if he owned his own paper plate camera, he could profitably capture the small-run market of two hundred to four hundred and, at the same time, achieve better quality control. He would also have more control over his delivery dates, since he had experienced real problems with subcontracted work. Since then, it has been Bruce's belief that the more in-house control, the better. This belief was to pay important dividends later during the formation of Bruce's informal Lionel research "network." This, he felt, would ensure that everyone contributing to his Lionel guides would be among the most competent train experts in the country.

The color catalogue saga had one last round to be played. Fundimensions, the General Mills subsidiary producing Lionel trains in those days, apparently believed that there was a much greater market for reproduction catalogues than anyone had believed. Therefore, the firm brought out two color reproductions of its own, a small sixteen-page version of the 1946 catalogue and a 1937 catalogue. These were sold at just $3.50 retail. Since Bruce's price for the 1937 catalogue was still $6, he had to meet this new competition. Consequently, he commissioned the printing of the more complete twenty-page 1946 catalogue and reduced the price of his 1937 catalogue to meet that of Fundimensions. A surge of orders resulted, but the result for Bruce was more red ink on the balance sheet. However, to Bruce this market strategy was necessary if he wanted to remain in the running.

This is clearly no way to run a business. With a commodity such as reproductions of catalogues, entry into the market is easy and market pressures force prices inevitably to the production price itself — or less! In addition, catalogues do not always square with the actual production of the factory, and they do not provide an assessment of current prices and values, a factor which many train collectors wanted but which did not exist. A new product was needed — a comprehensive production and values guide of some

GREENBERG'S PRICE GUIDE TO LIONEL TRAINS

O and O-27 Trains, 1945-1977

The cover of the first Postwar Guide to Lionel Trains featured a beautiful color photograph of the popular Pennsylvania GG-1. Since then, each edition has featured a color photograph of Lionel's finest toy trains.

GREENBERG'S GUIDE TO MARX TRAINS

by Eric Matzke

In 1975 the company published its first guide to Marx Trains written by Eric Matzke. The "MARX" logo on the cover obscured a large gun on a flatcar. The book's editor could not agree if the car was a Marx product or not. The book was issued in both paper- and hardback versions.

kind which would work like an encyclopedia of toy trains. Bruce saw that this was the direction to take. Such a product would be his own enterprise, not just a reproduction. The potential market was larger — much larger!

In 1975 Bruce began planning a series of collector guides that would feature a comprehensive list of production as well as current market values. The first of these was his guide to prewar Lionel trains, beginning with Standard Gauge production in 1906. Since Bruce already had an extensive archive of color and black and white catalogue illustrations, he used these materials to illustrate the book. These catalogue illustrations provided an historical record, which, for the most part, was clear and accurate, since Lionel had made significant investments in artwork and designs for these catalogues. In their day, the catalogues were the most important selling tool for Lionel in a highly competitive market. The second printing of the prewar guide used a beautiful reproduction of the 1937 catalogue cover as its cover.

More importantly, Bruce was able to enlist the support of a number of knowledgeable collectors in the Baltimore area to put the book together. This marked the beginnings of the collaborative editorial "network" which has persisted to this day. The Greenberg network has become truly nationwide; dedicated collectors have assisted in making these guides as accurate as possible. As a reward of sorts, Bruce has made sure that everyone who has made a contribution to the guides has been acknowledged, not only in the customary "thank you" section, but also in the entries themselves. Inclusion in this manner has been a great encouragement to collectors all over the country to send information for the next edition of each guide. One edition of the post-1970 volume even had an article contributed by a collector from Rio de Janeiro, Brazil! These expert collectors in the "network" also serve as a check on one another; many people are enlisted as "readers" to check the accuracy of each contribution. Very few errors can survive that kind of scrutiny! Each edition is more complete than its predecessor; in recent years, the guides have become more comprehensive than ever because of the inclusion of research articles on particular aspects of train collecting written by some of the most observant people in the hobby. Their pride of authorship shows more brilliantly with every edition.

In that same year, 1975, the much more demanding but ultimately rewarding work on *Greenberg's Guide to Lionel Trains, 1945-1977* was begun. By 1977 the late William Eddins had built one of the leading Lionel collections in America. His awesome collection had examples of nearly every postwar and Fundimensions piece and, in many cases, all the variations for each piece. The magnitude of the postwar project far exceeded Bruce's expectations; the sheer volume of pieces to be photographed was overwhelming even for Bruce's energy. Bruce felt strongly that each piece needed a description which would identify each of its major components, particularly trucks, couplers, body colors, and lettering styles. That kind of systematic analysis had never been done before. The impact of the analysis, if it were done properly, would be to recreate the history of a manufacturer and its product like no other before it. Such analysis laid the groundwork for the 1977 edition and all of its successors.

The most important feature of the systematic analysis Bruce had in mind was that it should be built upon directly observable data rather than supposition, no matter how logi-

This was the Oklahoma Road tower occupied by the Greenberg Publishing Company until late 1984. Although it may seem like an idyllic site for a publishing company devoted to toy trains, the space was barely adequate, and the electrical supply was hopelessly inadequate for the computerization Bruce needed in order to streamline operations.

cal. In other words, Bruce was proposing the use of the Scientific Method in the study of toy trains! Up to this point, collectors had noticed, for example, that some trucks had staple ends and some had bar ends, or that some worked by electromagnetic coils and some by mechanical plates, but they had not really dated these changes nor paid much attention to their significance in the manufacturing process. As Bruce studied Bill's collection, he noticed that if one described one difference between two similar cars, there would inevitably be other differences as well. From all this observation came a main thesis for the postwar guide: the Lionel Corporation was a well-organized manufacturing concern which made changes in a systematic way; these changes could, furthermore, be observed, described, and assigned significance.

The writing of this first Lionel postwar guide took an extraordinary amount of time, almost a man-year! The photography, which documented every piece in the collection, became extraordinarily expensive because of the thousands of items. Bruce thus found himself far over budget and in financial difficulties because of the magnitude of the project and his own limited resources. Based upon an earlier assessment of both the size of the product and his editorial cost, Bruce had seriously underpriced the product. However, the book established a new standard for the study of toy trains, and later editions would fully justify Bruce's effort. Upon release in October 1977, the first press run was rapidly sold.

In 1978 Linda Greenberg joined Bruce in developing and expanding the fledgling company's ability to work on multiple titles. Linda had been "unofficially" helping Bruce in the evenings and over the weekends, but because of the career demands of her position with Westinghouse Health Systems, she found that working both jobs was an impossible task. Since much of Linda's work at Westinghouse had involved administration, research, and writing, she looked forward to continuing these activities — but now her efforts would be devoted to the family firm.

Linda first edited several Lionel primers and then adopted the job of editing the first non-Lionel title, the *Greenberg's Guide to Marx Trains*. This book was one of the first to use the collegial approach to gathering and synthesizing data. Such a systematic analysis would prove to be useful as the guides continued to proliferate. It rapidly became evident to Linda that for the firm to thrive as it should, and to support the intensive research each title required, more readers and book buyers would have to be found. The way to do this efficiently was for Bruce and Linda to call upon the skills of train collectors. That is precisely what has happened, because several train collectors became editors and readers for the guides.

Today, one of Linda's main roles is the development of new titles in new areas, working with prospective authors to produce innovative and interesting books. One glance at a Greenberg catalogue will show how well Linda does her job. There are books either finished or in progress about such diverse topics as *Field Equipment of the Infantry*, LGB trains (both collecting and model railroading editions), Athearn and Varney HO trains, *Finishing Touches* for dollhouses, Marx toys, Aurora slot cars, and many, many others. Linda also oversees production of all of the Greenberg catalogues.

Since that first postwar edition, some other interested collectors have contributed their talents to subsequent editions. After the postwar guide was reissued in a new edition in 1979, Dr. Philip Catalano offered to edit the next edition for 1982. He went through the entire book, line by line, item by item, and made hundreds of changes, some very subtle, but others quite obvious. This careful reading by Dr. Catalano made the 1982 Third Edition the best postwar guide yet. He had dramatically improved the work.

Roland LaVoie was appointed editor of the postwar guide in 1983. This occurred due to Bruce Greenberg's encouragement. In 1980 Roland wrote a letter to Bruce about an unusual hopper car he had acquired. (All editions of the Greenberg guides encourage such letters by the enclosure of a form for that purpose.) Bruce wrote a long reply, and from those letters a lively correspondence developed. A year later, Roland was doing train demonstrations for Bruce's Philadelphia public train shows, and by 1983 a fine working relationship had ensued. This story has been repeated at least a dozen times with other train enthusiasts who have become Bruce's main editors and contributors.

In the eleven years since that 1977 postwar guide was published, Bruce Greenberg's efforts for the guides have ventured far afield. A large variety of books have been produced to provide the same kind of comprehensive coverage for American Flyer, Athearn, Ives, Kusan-AMT, LGB, Lionel HO, Marx, Märklin, and more! Many of the original books have been revised in new editions — always with "something more," like expanded color sections and analytical articles.

ON WITH THE SHOW

To examine another field of effort for the Greenberg Publishing Company, we must return in time to 1975, when Bruce attended several train meets in order to sell his publications. Bruce noted that many of these meets attracted a large crowd, but they were not run as well as they should be. Many were in dingy, overcrowded halls, and dealer tables were stacked so close that actual territorial fights broke out. The biggest of all, the TCA York Meets held twice a year in York, Pennsylvania, were restricted to TCA members. Bruce felt that there was a market for a train show where people could buy and sell trains and see them in operating layouts. He reasoned that if these public shows were well organized and operated, he could develop a steady following among train dealers. Thus was born Greenberg's Great Train, Dollhouse, and Toy Shows, which are now held along the entire eastern seaboard from Massachusetts to Florida.

In the train meets of 1975, typically a train collector would rent a small hall with fifty tables or so and advertise his event by giving out flyers at other shows. Large display advertisements in newspapers or national hobby magazines were unknown then. In December 1976 Bruce sponsored his first show at the Armory in Ellicott City, Maryland. He secured television coverage, spent money on large display advertisements, and sent press releases to the media. The show was an instant and popular success. Thousands of train enthusiasts came to the show, causing massive traffic jams! Within a year the Armory had been hopelessly outgrown, so in 1978 the show was moved to the large Towson Center at Towson State University. By 1980 Bruce was also offering train shows in Pittsburgh and Philadelphia. There

Thousands of train enthusiasts came to the show, causing massive traffic jams!

was a tremendous pent-up interest in trains that had not been met before. In fact, Bruce's sense of timing was just right. In the late 1970s and early 1980s, the country was swept by a boom of nostalgia for things Americana, and Bruce was just in time to capitalize upon it.

In 1984 Bruce decided to add a dollhouse and miniature component to the shows, and this addition (despite some initial skepticism from train people) has developed a loyal and steady following. In fact, the people attending the shows for the dollhouses and miniatures soon become captivated by the train segment, and vice-versa. This cross-pollination of hobbies has worked to everyone's benefit.

Initially, Bruce attended all the shows, working right alongside the crews in setting up and taking down the shows — a practice he still follows on occasion. However, he still has a growing company to administer, so now he depends upon a competent show crew in each location, as well as traveling show managers. A train show scheduled for a Saturday and Sunday actually begins the previous Wednesday with the loading of trucks and trailers; it ends the following Tuesday with the unloading process. Fortunately for Bruce, the show's first manager was Ralph Barger, a lifelong model railroader of considerable skills. With his wife Lois, who initiated the dollhouse and miniatures concept, Ralph, a retired Army colonel, traveled with the show across the northeast

This is the train show flyer for the Towson show of September 1978. The demolition derby and train races are not currently offered, but now there are many "hands-on" layouts at the shows, plus building and repair clinics, and numerous layouts from local clubs exhibited in all gauges. The shows are currently held in thirteen locations.

corridor. He played a critical role in the show's development by insisting upon organization and discipline in the administration of the shows. (Show crew members remember how exacting Ralph could be when loading a trailer — "OK, bring me the rectangular boxes with the dishware emblems!") Ralph retired — for a second time — in early 1984 to write a definitive study of North American passenger cars (the multivolume *A Century Of Pullman Cars*). Joe and Sharon Armacost then took over the show's administration. Sharon streamlined the registration process for dealers, while Joe instituted efficiencies in show operations, particularly the setting up and breaking down of layouts. In 1990 Brynn Robbins enthusiastically took Sharon's place. As the show schedule continued to expand in the busy winter months of 1989, additional staff were added for those weekends when Joe was already managing another show in a different location: Al and Liz Passman, Dave Randolph, Dwayne Lindsay, and Bill Dove.

In June 1987 the company moved down the block from the firehouse (7543 Main Street) in Sykesville to its new office building at 7566 Main Street. The new building has 9,000 square feet.

An adjunct to the show business is the recently-created series of Greenberg Auctions. These auctions were designed to provide train collectors with an efficient forum for selling their trains, whether they had a single piece or a large collection. The first auction took place in March 1988, followed by a second in October of the same year. A world record was set in March 1989, when Greenberg Auctions sold one of the few salesmen's samples of Lionel's "Boys' Set" for a whopping $23,000.

PUBLISHING EXPANDS

There is a kind of Murphy's Law associated with the growth of a company — the space required for a growing company expands in inverse proportion to the space available to house it. Although the steady growth of the Greenberg Publishing Company is no doubt a welcome event, it has also meant that there have been logistics problems in finding adequate work space for the staff. Bruce Greenberg has gone through headquarters in Columbia, Ellicott City, and three different sites in Sykesville, Maryland since 1978! One of the most picturesque sites was on Oklahoma Road in Sykesville, where Bruce rented two stories of a converted flour mill tower.

It was not too long before the Oklahoma Road site became too crowded and inefficient. Bruce had decided to computerize his word-processing and bookkeeping, to save both time and money — a move which has paid handsome dividends over the past five years. The Oklahoma Road site could never have handled such a conversion.

Just as it seemed that the tower was to burst at its seams, Francis Stem came to Bruce's rescue. Stem, a Greenberg show staffer, had been active with the Sykesville Fire Department for a long time. He told Bruce that the firehouse on Main Street was about to be sold, since the Sykesville Volunteer Fire Company was about to move to larger quarters. This older building was perfect for Bruce's efforts. Initially, the fire hall, 5,000 square feet on two floors, seemed very large. It enabled Bruce to store all his show layouts as well as his growing book inventory in the lower floor. He set up offices in the spacious upper floor for his growing computer setup. He even set up repair and construction facilities for the layouts and a photographic darkroom on the lower floor. But, in a short three years the building was filled to capacity with staff and inventory. Consequently, Tom Zissimos, the building manager, used his creative skills to make the 5,000 square feet seem even larger with the addition of shelving and raised storage platforms. Train collectors who run out of storage space for their treasures know how Bruce felt!

Just as the rebuilding process was concluding, Bruce learned that a large, local office building (almost 9,000 square feet) was to be auctioned. He attended the auction and in a very few minutes found himself the owner of much larger quarters. June, July, and August were a very busy time; renovating the new building and moving the business were major tasks. Although the new building has improved working conditions, there is still the challenge of staying ahead of the growth of staff and inventory.

This is one of the ideas that did not work as planned. In 1977 the time seemed right for a news magazine aimed at the growing army of tinplate train collectors. Unfortunately, it was somewhat ahead of its time, and it was discontinued after only three issues. Its functions have since been fulfilled by the articles found in the individual Greenberg Guides.

NEW LINES

The last few years have seen not only improvement in the popular series of collector guides, but also the introduction of a new series of *Greenberg's Model Railroading* books. These informative how-to books instruct novices and experienced modelers alike on the ins-and-outs of layout design, construction, wiring, and more. So far, model railroading books have been published for Lionel, LGB, Märklin HO, and Märklin Z.

Another new arena for Bruce's efforts is the field of prototype railroading. Bruce entered this market with publication of Ralph Barger's *A Century of Pullman Cars*, Volume I, which received very favorable response from rail historians. It was followed by the acclaimed second volume, *The Palace Cars*. Another reference, *Steam Locomotives of the Reading and P & R Railroads*, soon followed. With the publication of Volume II of the Pullman series and the fascinating *Royal Blue Line* (covering the Baltimore & Ohio Railroad's famous Washington-Philadelphia-New York route), Greenberg Publishing has firmly planted its feet in this dynamic portion of the hobby.

In addition to expansion in these new fields, Greenberg Publishing also plans to expand its offering of "walking tours." These books provide insights into small towns and show how present-day visitors to these towns can find remnants of the past. The first of these books, *Sykesville Past and Present*, describes the quaint town where the company is located. This book has been joined by books about Ellicott City, Maryland and Gatlinburg, Tennessee.

The last few years have also seen staff development. In each department of the Greenberg Publishing Company, people have become increasingly skillful and creative in carrying out department functions. The Public Relations Department sends out thousands of informational packages each year in support of the shows and regularly places advertisements in over one hundred newspapers and magazines. The Editorial Department produces twenty-five new books or book revisions per year, a task they can handle easily since the advent of the computer as a word processor. Several of Bruce's editors in the field have had computers made available to them on a lease basis, an arrangement which has been of benefit to all concerned. The Accounting Department keeps in close touch with over five hundred stores and five hundred vendors per year. The Photography Department shoots and processes over 1,000 rolls of film per year for all the publications. The Art Department does layout and makeup work for not only books, but also catalogues, press releases, and announcements of all kinds.

The brief span of fifteen years has seen the Greenberg Publishing Company progress from one man wearing a path in the rug around his dining room table to a modern, small, and thriving publishing firm with over forty-five employees, including a mix of part-time and full-time personnel.

THE FUTURE

In 1990 several publishing firms approached Greenberg with acquistion in mind. These firms wanted to incorporate the well-developed Greenberg toy train line with their more general line of publications. These offers came at a strategic time because Bruce and Linda were concerned whether Greenberg Publishing would be able to continue to expand and to offer the same benefits over the next decade.

As of January 1991 Greenberg Publishing was acquired by the Kalmbach Publishing Company. Kalmbach is the leading publisher of model railroad magazines and books in the United States. Most HO and H Gauge enthusiasts rely on their line of books and avidly read *Model Railroader* on a monthly basis. Together Kalmbach and Greenberg will publish books for every toy train and model railroad enthusiast.

The Greenberg staff will also benefit from the more sophisticated organization and support system that Kalmbach can provide. Greenberg, of course, brings to Kalmbach a line of books which are state of the art.

The challenge now is to continue doing what Greenberg does best — publish books on toy trains — and to continue to grow with Kalmbach Publishing Company.

INDEX

-C — indicates color photograph; ( ) — number in parentheses means number does not appear on car.